Lecture Notes in Computer Science 4715

Commenced Publication in 1973
Founding and Former Series Editors:
Gerhard Goos, Juris Hartmanis, and Jan van Lee

Jörg M. Haake   Sergio F. Ochoa
Alejandra Cechich (Eds.)

Groupware: Design, Implementation, and Use

13th International Workshop, CRIWG 2007
Bariloche, Argentina, September 16-20, 2007
Proceedings

 Springer

Volume Editors

Jörg M. Haake
FernUniversität in Hagen
Department of Mathematics and Computer Science
Universitätsstr. 1, 58084 Hagen, Germany
E-mail: joerg.haake@fernuni-hagen.de

Sergio F. Ochoa
Universidad de Chile
Department of Computer Science
Av. Blanco Encalada, 2120, Santiago, Chile
E-mail: sochoa@dcc.uchile.cl

Alejandra Cechich
Universidad Nacional del Comahue
Computing Sciences Department
Buenos Aires 1400, 8300 Neuquén, Argentina
E-mail: achechich@uncoma.edu.ar

Library of Congress Control Number: 2007934512

CR Subject Classification (1998): H.5.2, H.5.3, H.5, K.3.1, K.4.3, C.2.4

LNCS Sublibrary: SL 3 – Information Systems and Application, incl. Internet/Web and HCI

ISSN	0302-9743
ISBN-10	3-540-74811-3 Springer Berlin Heidelberg New York
ISBN-13	978-3-540-74811-3 Springer Berlin Heidelberg New York

Springer is a part of Springer Science+Business Media

springer.com

© Springer-Verlag Berlin Heidelberg 2007
Printed in Germany

Typesetting: Camera-ready by author, data conversion by Scientific Publishing Services, Chennai, India
Printed on acid-free paper   SPIN: 12120192   06/3180   5 4 3 2 1 0

Preface

This volume constitutes the proceedings of the 13th International Workshop on Groupware (CRIWG 2007). The conference was held in Spain (Medina del Campo) in 2006, Brazil (Porto de Galinhas) in 2005, Costa Rica (San Carlos) in 2004, France (Autrans) in 2003, Chile (La Serena) in 2002, Germany (Darmstadt) in 2001, Portugal (Madeira Island) in 2000, Mexico (Cancun) in 1999, Brazil (Buzios) in 1998, Spain (El Escorial) in 1997, Chile (Puerto Varas) in 1996, and Portugal (Lisbon) in 1995.

The CRIWG workshops have been motivated by advances in computer-supported cooperative work (CSCW), and by the need for CSCW to meet the challenges of new application areas. This workshop aims at providing a forum for academic researchers and professionals to exchange their experiences and their ideas about problems and solutions related to the design, development and use of groupware applications. Researchers report their ideas, models, designs and experiences to CRIWG submitting full-paper contributions to present achieved or mature works, and shorter papers to report work in progress.

CRIWG 2007 received 65 submissions from 15 different countries, 49 full papers and 16 work-in-progress papers. Each article was reviewed by at least three members of the Program Committee, using a double-blind reviewing process. Based on the reviewers' recommendations 27 papers were finally accepted: 17 full papers and 10 work-in-progress papers. These papers were grouped into six tracks: group awareness and social aspects, groupware design and development, computer-supported collaborative learning, groupware applications and studies, group negotiation and knowledge management, and groupware activities and evaluation. In addition, we are pleased to have had Jonathan Grudin from Microsoft Research, USA, as keynote speaker.

CRIWG 2007 would not have been possible without the work and support of a great number of people. First of all we want to thank the members of the Program Committee for their valuable reviews of the papers. We are grateful for the advice and support provided by the CRIWG Steering Committee. We extend a special acknowledgement to our sponsor organizations: Universidad Nacional del Comahue (Argentina), Universidad de Chile (Chile), FernUniversität in Hagen (Germany), Microsoft Research (USA) and Microsoft Chile (Chile), SADIO (Argentina).

Last, but certainly not least, we thank the attendees for their interest in CRIWG 2007. We hope they had an enriching experience at the conference.

Please get involved!

September 2007

Joerg M. Haake
Sergio F. Ochoa
Alejandra Cechich

Conference Organization

Program Committee Chairs

Joerg M. Haake, FernUniversität in Hagen, Germany
Sergio F. Ochoa, Universidad de Chile, Chile

Program Committee

Mark S. Ackerman, University of Michigan, USA
Rosa Alarcón, Pontificia Universidad Católica de Chile, Chile
Roberto Aldunate, University of Illinois at Urbana-Champaign, USA
Analía Amandi, UNICEN, Argentina
Richard Anderson, University of Washington, USA
Pedro Antunes, Universidade de Lisboa, Portugal
Jaco Appelman, Delft University of Technology, The Netherlands
Nelson Baloian, Universidad de Chile, Chile
Jean-Paul Barthés, Université de Technologie de Compiègne, France
Marina Bers, Tufts University, USA
Marcos Borges, Universidade Federal do Rio de Janeiro, Brazil
Patrick Brézillon, Laboratoire LIP6, Université Paris 6, France
Robert O. Briggs, University of Nebraska at Omaha, USA
Traci Carte, University of Oklahoma, USA
César Collazos, Universidad del Cauca, Colombia
Gert-Jan de Vreede, University of Nebraska at Omaha, USA
Atanasi Daradoumis, Open University of Catalonia, Spain
Bertrand David, Ecole Centrale de Lyon, France
Alanah Davis, University of Nebraska at Omaha, USA
Dominique Decouchant, LIG Laboratory, Grenoble, France
Alicia Díaz, Universidad Nacional de La Plata, Argentina
Yannis Dimitriadis, Universidad de Valladolid, Spain
Tom Erickson, IBM T. J. Watson Research Center, USA
Jesus Favela, CICESE, Mexico
Alejandro Fernández, Universidad Nacional de La Plata, Argentina
Christine Ferraris, Université de Savoie, France
Hugo Fuks, Pontifícia Universidade Católica do Rio de Janeiro, Brazil
Matt Germonprez, University of Wisconsin - Eau Claire, USA
Werner Geyer, IBM T.J. Watson Research Center, USA
Eduardo Gómez-Sánchez, Universidad de Valladolid, Spain
Víctor M. González, University of Manchester, UK
Tom Gross, Bauhaus University Weimar, Germany
Luis A. Guerrero, Universidad de Chile, Chile
Andreas Harrer, University of Duisburg-Essen, Germany

Ulrich Hoppe, University of Duisburg, Germany
Ned Kock, Texas A&M International University, USA
Gwendolyn Kolfschoten, Delft University of Technology, The Netherlands
Filippo Lanubile, University of Bari, Italy
Stephan Lukosch, FernUniversität in Hagen, Germany
Gloria Mark, University of California, Irvine, USA
Alejandra Martínez, Universidad de Valladolid, Spain
Sonia Mendoza, CINVESTAV-IPN, Mexico
Alberto Morán, UABC, Mexico
Bjørn Erik Munkvold, Agder University College, Norway
Leandro Navarro, Polytechnic University of Catalonia, Spain
Miguel Nussbaum, Pontificia Universidad Católica de Chile, Chile
Álvaro Ortigoza, Universidad Autónoma de Madrid, Spain
Yvan Peter, University of Lille 1, France
José A. Pino, Universidad de Chile, Chile
Steven Poltrock, Boeing, USA
Atul Prakash, University of Michigan, USA
Nuno Preguiça, Universidade Nova de Lisboa, Portugal
Alberto Raposo, Catholic University of Rio de Janeiro, Brazil
Christoph Rensing, Technische Universität Darmstadt, Germany
Flávia Santoro, Universidade Federal do Estado do Rio de Janeiro, Brazil
Choon Ling Sia, University of Hong Kong, Hong Kong
Guillermo Simari, Universidad Nacional del Sur, Argentina
Carla Simone, University of Milan, Italy
Till Schümmer, FernUniversität in Hagen, Germany
Ralf Steinmetz, Technische Universität Darmstadt, Germany
Julita Vassileva, University of Saskatchewan, Canada
Aurora Vizcaíno-Barceló, Universidad de Castilla-La Mancha, Spain
Juergen Vogel, European Media Laboratory GMBH, Germany
Jacques Wainer, State University of Campinas, Brazil
Martin Wessner, Ludwig Maximilian University of Munich, Germany
Volker Wulf, Fraunhofer FIT, Germany
Ilze Zigurs, University of Nebraska at Omaha, USA

Doctoral Colloquium Chairs

Pedro Antunes, Universidade de Lisboa, Portugal
Alejandro Fernández, Universidad Nacional de La Plata, Argentina

Organizing Committee Chair

Alejandra Cechich (Local Chair), Comahue National University, Argentina

Organizing Committee

Silvia Amaro, Comahue National University, Argentina
Gabriela Aranda, Comahue National University, Argentina
Agustina Buccella, Comahue National University, Argentina
Andrés Flores, Comahue National University, Argentina
Adriana Martín, Comahue National University, Argentina
Nadina Martínez, Comahue National University, Argentina
Andrés Neyem, Universidad de Chile, Chile

Table of Contents

Group Negotiation and Knowledge Management

Group Awareness and Social Aspects

Groupware Design and Development

Computer Supported Collaborative Learning (CSCL)

Groupware Applications and Studies

Groupware Activities and Evaluation

The Gap Between Small Group Theory and Group Support System Research

Joey F. George

College of Business
Florida State University
Tallahassee, FL 32306-1110 USA
+1-850-644-7449
jgeorge@cob.fsu.edu

Abstract. Small group research and the development of small group theory have flourished in recent years, yet most group support systems (GSS) research is conducted without regard to theories of small groups. Here we contrast the richness of small group theory with the theoretical poverty of most experimental group support systems research. We look first at the state of small group theory, contrasting it with the state of theory in GSS work, using 10 recently published GSS studies as examples. Looking to small group theory as the basis for GSS research would add a great deal to GSS work, the topic of the next section in the paper. Absent a reliance on small group theory, however, we propose an alternative approach: Drop the GSS term altogether and return to a term that better describes what GSS research has always been about, supporting meetings, as captured in the phrase Electronic Meeting Systems.

Keywords: Group support systems, small group theory, electronic meeting systems.

1 Introduction

The group support systems (GSS) we know today were first developed 25 years ago at leading universities ([8], [10]), and research dealing with such systems began almost as soon as the first prototypes were operational. As word spread, GSS research became extremely popular, especially in the late 1980s and early 1990s, and although not as popular now, research interest continues. However, despite literally hundreds of experimental studies [13], the research results have been confusing and disappointing.

At the same time, research about small groups has blossomed and spread throughout many disciplines, from management to education to sociology to communication. While some of this research has focused on the relationship between small group work and information technology, the bulk of it has been focused on other issues related to group development and group work [35]. With few exceptions, GSS experimental research has not profitably utilized and has in fact rarely referenced the small group literature. At one time, GSS research was of great interest to small

J.M. Haake, S.F. Ochoa, A. Cechich (Eds.): CRIWG 2007, LNCS 4715, pp. 1–14, 2007.

group researchers ([21], [31]), but those days have passed. Experimental GSS research has become increasing isolated from the social science world.

This paper argues that experimental GSS researchers should either take seriously the word "group" in the GSS term, and re-connect to the world of small group research, or they should drop the GSS term altogether in favor of an earlier label applied to these systems, Electronic Meeting Systems (EMS) [8]. To make this argument, we first contrast the theoretical richness of small group research with the theoretical poverty of experimental GSS research. Then we demonstrate how basing GSS research on small group theory could address both the quality of the research being conducted and improve the chances for meaningful findings built on a strong research foundation. Finally, we discuss abandoning the group connection altogether, suggesting that we bring back the 20-year old term of EMS, discarding the distracting and false GSS and GDSS terms, thereby strengthening past research with a tighter retrospective focus and improving new research through a similar focus on a clear simple theme. These three steps are the basis for the next sections of the paper, which then ends with a conclusion.

2 Small Group Theory

Theories of small group interaction are numerous, and as stated previously, come from many different academic traditions. Tracking down and describing all of these theories would be a huge effort and far beyond the scope of this paper. Fortunately, Poole and Hollingshead [35] have assembled a book about small group theory, and each chapter describes one of nine theoretical perspectives. Each perspective includes several different theories about small groups. Each of these perspectives from the Poole and Hollingshead book is briefly summarized below:

Functional perspective: Researchers who study groups from the functional perspective are interested in the factors that help distinguish one group from another on the basis of group performance. The central research issue is determining which group behaviors and activities predict good performance. An important assumption is that groups are goal-oriented. From a functional perspective, inputs include such things as task, group structure, group cohesiveness, and the environment. Outputs include the well-known constructs of efficiency, effectiveness, and satisfaction. Well-known theories included in this perspective include the functional theory of group decision making [19] and the external view of groups [1]. The functional perspective has produced more studies than any other perspective.

Psychodynamic perspective: A key focus of the psychodynamic perspective is the affective and emotional side of groups. This perspective assumes that groups are formed out of human instinct to bind together with others for survival, and hence group activities are driven by emotional dynamics, which remain a part of all social interactions. Studies in this tradition emphasize process and outcomes over inputs. As might be inferred, this perspective is influenced by Freud and further developed in the Bales' work on SYMLOG (Systematic Multilevel Observation of Groups) [4].

Social identity perspective: "Social identity is based on the attributes shared among members of particular social groups and categories....the social identity approach starts from the premise that the group is in the individual, rather than vice versa" ([2], p. 100). The idea is that individuals obtain a part of their individual identities from the social groups to which they belong, whether the groups are based on ethnic identity, organizational units, or being a member of a competitive team. While this research has focused primarily on relations between different social groups, it has also been used to study within-group dynamics. Social identity scholars studying small groups have investigated deindividuation, group cohesion, leadership, and decision making.

Conflict-power-status: This perspective starts with the assumption that there are inequalities in group member status, power, and resources. Group member inter-action, then, is explained in terms of group dynamics related to these and the group structures related to these dynamics. Important group processes studied in this perspective include conflict management, influence, consensus building, negotiation and distribution of resources. Important theories of conflict, power and status include social exchange theory [43] and power dependency theory [12].

Symbolic-interpretive perspective: This perspective is defined as "an approach concerned with understanding the nature, practices, and consequences of symbol usage within groups, as well as how groups and group processes are themselves products of symbolic activities" ([14], p. 186). Included in this perspective are structuration theory and its well-known variant of adaptive structuration theory (AST) [11] and bona fide group theory [36]. According to AST, group structures emerge through group member choice of processes and tools and are reinforced through subsequent process and tool use. Central to AST is the idea of appropriation, and whether the use of a tool or process is consistent with the purpose for which it was designed. Bona fide group theory has as its two main tenets the fluidity of group boundaries and the interdependence of group and context. Bona fide group theory also takes into account that group members belong to many groups simultaneously and that these multiple memberships shape their actions within and their views of the groups they belong to.

Feminist perspective: The feminist perspective typically starts with the idea that group structures and conditions are designed to favor men's views and perspectives over those of women. Differences in group dynamics and outcomes are traced to differences in male and female motivations, views, and life experiences. The most important input here is the gender composition of groups, and one of the more common issues is the elimination of domination in all groups.

Social network perspective: According to studies undertaken from this perspective, groups are not separate entities but rather are part of larger networks. A group's position in the larger social network affects its functioning and outcomes. From a social network point of view, a group is either a structural feature of a network, a subset of connected nodes emerging from the network, or an externally determined categorization of a bunch of people within a larger network. The focus is on the relationships among units rather than on the units themselves, and a core idea is that people's behavior is best predicted by the web of relationships in which they are embedded rather than their drives, attitudes or demographics [25].

Temporal perspective: The temporal perspective is of course about time and how groups change and develop over time. Within the larger perspective, time is viewed as a context, a resource, a mediator or a moderator of other processes. Process is emphasized over inputs and outputs. Many different theories come under the temporal perspective, including Tuckman's five stage development model of forming, storming, norming, performing and adjourning [44], Poole and Baldwin's decision development theory [34], and Gersick's punctuated equilibrium theory [17]. In the task groups that Gersick studied, group behavior was set by processes and themes adopted early in each group's first meeting and continued with little change until the group reached the mid-point of its time together. At exactly the mid-point, each group became acutely aware of the time they had left, looked to people external to the group for help, and dramatically changed direction in their work. Adaptive structuration theory [11] is also included as a temporal theory, given that the processes involved in structuration must necessarily take place over time, as structures emerge and are either rejected or reinforced.

Evolutionary perspective: Here the basic idea is that group structure and interaction reflect evolutionary forces that have shaped human behavior for centuries. The types of groups that people form and the norms that govern behavior in groups have developed throughout human history and are the result of natural selection processes.

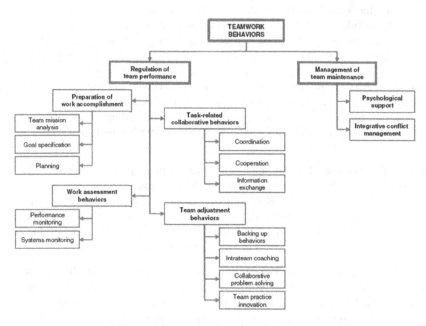

Fig. 1. Integrative Framework of Teamwork Behaviors (from [38])

While the authors in the Poole and Hollingshead [35] book have written their respective chapters to focus on one of the nine theoretical perspectives on small groups, another way to look at the richness of small group theory is to create a framework that crosses perspectives. Figure 1 illustrates such a framework, which represents an integration of teamwork behaviors [38]. This integrated framework is itself based on 29 separate frameworks that deal with team behaviors. As the figure shows, there are two main categories of team behaviors, those that deal with managing group performance and those that deal with group maintenance. Organizing these teamwork behaviors into this framework allows researchers and practitioners to focus on behaviors that allow team members to work effectively with each other and thus to enhance their performance.

Figure 2 illustrates how the content of a particular theoretical perspective can be represented to simplify and clarify the perspective. Chang, Duck and Bordia [6] developed a representation of the group development literature, so Figure 2 is based in the temporal perspective of small group theory. They identified over 100 group development theories that have been developed over the years and organized these theories into a three dimensional space with the following axes: content, population, and path dependency. Content refers to whether the development is specific to a particular type of development or more comprehensive, referring to all aspects of group development. Gersick's and Poole's work anchors the axis at the specific end, while Tuckman's work anchors the comprehensive end. Population refers to whether the development theory applies to particular types of groups or to all types of groups. Bales' work is an example of developmental theory that applies to only certain types of groups, while Tuckman's theories apply to all types of groups. Path dependency deals with whether there is a single developmental path, again, as is the case with Tuckman's work, or whether there are many different trajectories a group could follow over its lifetime or its task, as demonstrated by Poole's work. Looking across dimensions, then, non-sequential models of group development, such as those developed by Gersick and Poole, would be located in the *content specific-population*

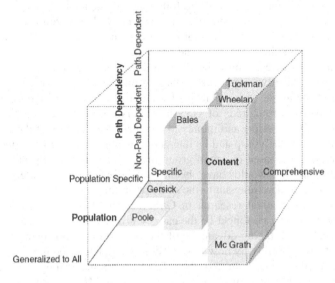

Fig. 2. Integration of Group Development Literature (from [6])

specific-non-path dependent corner of the definition space. Such frameworks can foster a better understanding of a complex set of related theories and help researchers choose the appropriate model for studying a particular situation.

3   Theoretical Basis for Past GSS Research

Despite the richness of theory dealing with small groups, the group support system (GSS) literature, especially that dealing with laboratory experiments, has been largely atheoretical, relying on models and frameworks or on nothing at all (cf. [7] and [15] for examples of typical early experimental GSS studies.)   Some researchers have suggested potentially fruitful theoretical bases for GSS work. Rao and Jarvenpaa [37] suggested three possible theoretical bases suitable for GSS work: Human information processing, minority influence, and communication theories. Nunamaker and colleagues [33] adapted Steiner's ideas [42] of process losses and gains as a basis for understanding how group process could be facilitated through GSS use. (It is interesting to note that Steiner's work is never referenced in [35].) DeSanctis and Poole [11] adapted Gidden's structuration theory [18] into adaptive structuration theory (AST) as a means to help explain how group structure emerged from GSS tool and process appropriation.

Despite these attempts at suggesting and developing theory for understanding the interaction of groups and technology in GSS, few researchers have paid heed. The result has been dozens of atheoretical GSS studies, which has yielded disappointing and confusing results. Meta-analyses have pointed out the limitations of what has been discovered in GSS research to date. Fjermestad & Hiltz [13] concluded from a meta-analysis of 200 experimental studies that the modal finding of research comparing GSS to unsupported face-to-face work has been "no difference." The results of these 200 studies point to the following: To generate a positive effect in a GSS experiment, use a level-2 system, with medium to large groups not made up of undergraduate students, with a facilitator and a planning task, and do not measure efficiency or satisfaction.   Dennis and Wixom [9], in another meta-analysis of experimental GSS studies, summarized the findings from the 61 articles they analyzed as follows: For a positive result, use a large group, meeting in a decision room to perform idea generation, with the help of a facilitator. Neither study conclusion is much of a payoff for hundreds of GSS laboratory-based studies, studies that took large amounts of time, effort and money to conduct. And neither of these summaries addresses the role of the group and its interaction with the technology. Had the larger research agenda been based on small group theory, one cannot help but believe that the research findings would have been more diverse, more interesting, more comprehensive, and more relevant to the study of groups.

While past experimental research in GSS may not have been guided by small group theory, such may no longer be the case. Current work may have broken out of the atheoretical mold, taking advantage of the blossoming work being done now in small group theory. Surely by now most GSS research has made the linkage to small group research being done in other fields. To check on this assumption, I did a quick review of the most recently published GSS work in the MIS literature. Confining the timeframe to 2006 and 2007, I searched for GSS articles in the following journals:

Information Systems Research (ISR), MIS Quarterly (MISQ), Communications of the ACM (CACM), Small Group Research (SGR), Group Decision and Negotiation (GDN), Decision Support Systems (DSS), and *Computers in Human Behavior (CHB).* The search turned up 10 papers. There were no GSS papers published in *MISQ* or *CACM* in this time period. *SGR* and *CHB* had the most published GSS papers, at three each. Of the 10 articles, seven were reports on GSS laboratory experiments (Table 1). Each of these experiments involved small groups coming together for a single short meeting (with the exception of Briggs, Reinig & de Vreede [5], where, while there was a single meeting, each meeting ran as long as one full day). The remaining three studies varied in their content: Kolfschoten, et al. [27] is a survey of facilitators; Lewis, et al. [29] is a global survey of GSS adoption; Klein, et al. [26] is a conceptual paper outlining a program of research.

Table 1. GSS laboratory studies published in 2006-07 in a select set of MIS journals

Author	Year	Source	GSS	Task	Meetings	Topic/Theory
Vathanophas & Liang	2007	*CHB*	Group Systems	Solve a murder mystery	One, no more than 2 hrs long	Information exchange but no grand theory
Huang & Li	2007	*CHB*	SAMM	Admissions & Foundation tasks	One, no more than 2.5 hrs long	Informational & normative influence but no grand theory
Mejias	2007	*SGR*	Group Systems	Idea generation & preference rating	One, no more than 1 hr long	AST; Steiner's process gains & losses
Schwarz & Schwarz	2007	*SGR*	Group Systems	Foundation task	One, no duration reported	Perceived Characteristics of Innovation; no grand theory
Limayem, Banerjee & Ma	2006	*DSS*	SAMM	Foundation task	One, no duration reported	AST; IV is decision guidance & appropriation is mediator
Heninger, Dennis & Hilman	2006	*ISR*	GSS simulator	Admissions task: Hidden profile	One faux meeting, no duration reported	Focus on dual-task interference, no grand theory
Briggs, Reinig & de Vreede	2006	*SGR*	Group Systems	Post-meeting questionnaire for real group facilitators	One, 3 hrs to 1 day in duration	Model of perceived goal attainment; no grand theory

Several things can be seen from an examination of the information in Table 1. These GSS laboratory experiments have several things in common. First, all seven involved groups that met only once, and most of the meetings were short. Only one study investigated meetings that were unscripted and lasted up to one full day. Second, most of the studies used the same GSS, GroupSystems, two used SAMM, and the seventh used a GSS simulator. The tasks used were also familiar to GSS researchers: Three used Watson's Foundation Task and two used a college admissions decision task. Fjermestad and Hiltz [13] found 73% of the studies analyzed had groups that met only once, the most common GSS used was GroupSystems, and 52% used a decision-making task like the Foundation Task. Another 31% used an intellective task, like the college admissions task.

These seven experimental studies, then, do not seem to vary much from the standard modal GSS study design as defined in 1999. The implication is that little progress has been made since 1999 in the way in which experimental GSS studies are being conducted. That alone is disappointing. Even more disappointing, however, from the perspective of this paper, is that five of the seven experimental studies are not based on grand theory. Grand theory is any theory which attempts an overall explanation of social life, history, or human experience [41]. The five studies that are largely atheoretical base their study designs on independent variables that are appealing to the authors but that are not part of a larger theoretical web of predefined constructs and relationships. These independent variables include information exchange [45]; informational and normative influence [22]; dual-task interference [20]; and goal attainment [5]. While the remaining study [40] did not rely on grand theory, it was based on the Perceived Characteristics of Innovation theory, a subset of a larger Theory of Innovation. In the two remaining papers ([30], [32]), the authors sought to use a grand theory, adaptive structuration theory (AST), as the basis for their work, However, both of these studies had groups meet only once, and AST provides little intellectual leverage in the context of a single meeting. AST is listed under Poole's and Hollingshead's temporal perspective on small group theory because of the importance of time in how the theory works. While group members may choose to use a GSS tool in a GSS supported meeting, but that is not the same as appropriation, which necessarily occurs over extended periods of time, as groups grow used to their task, the GSS, their work context, and each other, and appropriate tools and processes accordingly.

What can we conclude from this brief review of recently published GSS studies? To begin with, it appears that current study designs have not departed much from the common designs of GSS laboratory studies of the past. Second, it appears that the research being done remains largely atheoretical, despite the extensive base of small group theory in other academic fields. Ultimately, we have to ask ourselves: So what? What is GSS research missing through its disconnect with small group theory?

4 How Small Group Theory Can Improve GSS Research

Kurt Lewin once said "There is nothing so practical as a good theory" ([28], p. 169). Although such a statement may at first sound odd, a moment of reflection will show that it really makes a lot of sense. A theory is defined as "a statement of relations among concepts within a set of boundary assumptions and constraints. It is no more than a linguistic device used to organize a complex empirical world....The purpose of theoretical statements is twofold: to organize (parsimoniously) and to communicate (clearly)" ([3], p. 496). A theory then can be seen as a system of constructs and their interrelationships, developed to help explain some phenomenon. A theory becomes practical when it helps us devise research questions and then specific hypotheses that allow us to better understand whatever it is we are studying. Supported hypotheses are important, because they reinforce the view of the thing we are studying, as already defined in the theory. But unsupported hypotheses are just as important, if not more so, because these results make us reexamine the theory, in an effort to improve it and make it a better system of explanation. If enough hypotheses are not supported over time, then the theory itself becomes suspect and may eventually be falsified, discarded, and replaced with a theory that better reflects "reality."

From the perspective of a social scientist, a grand theory already includes the important constructs and relationships to be investigated. New constructs and new relationships can be added, but this occurs within the context of the already existing theoretical structure. A grand theory can serve as a map for research, showing what is known well, what is only partly understood, and what is not understood well at all. In this sense, a grand theory might best be thought of as an analog to early maps of the entire planet, where parts of the world were well-defined, other parts were only partially drawn in, based on limited explorations and extrapolations from what was known, and where still other parts were completely blank. A grand theory shows social scientists where the little understood and unknown areas are that will benefit most from additional study.

A grand theory is not only practical in the beginning of a study, however. The choice of a research question determines the choice of constructs and relationships to be investigated, the choice of constructs determines the variables to be used, and the choice of relationships drives the formulation of the hypotheses. Once data have been collected and hypotheses tested, a grand theory then allows researchers to *understand* what they have found by providing a context into which new results can be inserted and examined. To continue with the metaphor of the incomplete global maps, new results are comparable to refining the known coastline of South America or providing the first drawings of the coastline of Australia on these maps. The meaning of the new additions is clear in context, while the additions in isolation might not add up to much. The additions come from several different studies or explorations, all of which contribute to refining what is known and adding to what is not. All of these findings together add to the overall picture and can be understood as such, instead of being seen as individual findings of questionable origin that stand in isolation from each other. A global theory, then, provides the framework for study and the context for understanding what the results mean.

A grand theory of small groups would provide the map for GSS research that is missing now in the MIS discipline. Given that the term GSS starts with the word "group," it seems intuitive that the development and study of group support systems should take place in the context of a grand theory (or theories) of small groups. In fact, one could argue that much GSS work has occurred within the context of the functional group perspective, identified in the Poole and Hollingshead taxonomy of group theory, although the work is largely fragmented and stakes its claim to the functional perspective indirectly and implicitly if at all. Much GSS work has had a focus on inputs to the process and on the typical outcomes of effectiveness, efficiency and satisfaction. Groups are assumed to be goal-oriented and otherwise rational in their behavior, although this assumption is rarely made explicit. Actually mapping past GSS work into an explicit functional group framework would provide many of the benefits grand theory would provide, but lacking this, the work continues to be ad hoc and disjointed. Even if one concedes that functional group theory provides a partial theoretical foundation for GSS work, there are at least eight other theoretical perspectives (as we have seen) that could serve as grand theory.

Of those eight, some GSS research has been based on the temporal perspective, but this research has been limited, and there is much, much more which could be done. Fjermestad and Hiltz [13] found that only 51 of the 200 studies in their analysis were longitudinal, defined as groups meeting at least twice. Two meetings is of course a rather liberal definition of longitudinal. But even if that point is conceded, it is not at all clear that GSS studies, where groups meet more than once, draw from and return to the temporal theories of small group interaction. Most of these studies focus on the resolution by student groups of a series of small, structured tasks in a series of short structured meetings [16]. The groups do not act much like groups in the interim – they are groups only for the short meetings where they are brought together to work on their structured tasks. The emphasis seems to have been more on group performance, reflecting a functional group perspective, rather than on group development and change over time, although it is true that group cohesion is often one of the outcome variables studied. If there is a theoretical foundation at all, it tends to be AST, while other theories such as punctuated equilibrium theory and decision development theory are ignored. With each study using its own constructs and relationships, and with no larger perspective in which to place and compare findings, the result is a patchwork of hints and allegations where the overall meaning is unclear.

The remaining seven theoretical perspectives have rarely if ever been applied to GSS research. Some of the AST work falls into the symbolic interpretive perspective (as opposed to the temporal perspective), and a few studies have been done from the conflict-power-status view (cf. [39]), but no GSS studies that I am aware of have been conducted within the psychodynamic, social identity, feminist, social network or evolutionary perspectives. The main reason this is the case is most likely ignorance of these theoretical perspectives on the part of GSS researchers. There is, after all, only so much reading and investigation any scholar can do, and most of this study tends to be confined to one's own area. There is, however, a more overarching reason that helps explain not only why these perspectives are not used but also why small group theory from any perspective is underutilized in GSS research. And that reason is that GSS research is not really about groups at all. It is about meetings.

5 An Alternative: Focus on the Meeting and Forget the Group

It stands to reason that, if experimental GSS research were really about groups, the conceptual basis for this work would in fact have something to do with groups. But what is a group? A group is a social unit, made up of individuals, but is it more than the sum of the individual members. Groups, once created, exist as a separate entity from the individuals that comprise them, and they experience a dynamic life cycle, a life cycle that is again separate from and complementary to the lives of the group's members. A group is not a small number of undergraduates who have never previously seen each other and who have been brought together for an hour to work on an artificial problem using an unfamiliar technology. Yet, according to Fjermestad and Hiltz [13], the latter is what we have tended to study in our GSS experiments, not the former. The entity we study in the GSS lab has no continuity. It does not exist over time and experiences no dynamic life cycle. It lacks the very elements that make a group a distinct social unit. So maybe, then, it is not surprising that the experimental GSS literature lacks a conceptual basis in small group theory. Maybe we do not study groups at all. But what do we study? What do we call the ad hoc assembly of undergraduates who come together to brainstorm about the parking problem at their university? It is not a group – it is a meeting.

Twenty years ago, in our first major publication on the research we were then doing at the University of Arizona [8], we coined the term Electronic Meeting Systems (EMS) to describe the system developed there and the initial research we were doing that focused on that technology. The focus in our work was the technology and how it supported meetings, not on the people using the technology. After all, the system had been designed to support the activities common to meetings: Generating ideas, consolidating those ideas, and prioritizing them somehow. The system was not designed to support groups. Meetings are defined by constraints: Meeting times, durations, agendas, attendance lists, goals. Groups are defined by none of these things. Once a meeting of a group ends, the group continues. Groups can (and do) have meetings, but meetings do not need groups – meeting only require a bunch of individuals who will sit down together (literally or figuratively) at a particular point in time to work on some pre-defined problem. Yet, despite the superiority of the EMS label for the work we were doing at Arizona, and despite our missionary zeal to convince our colleagues of the appropriateness of the term, it did not stick. Instead we got GSS. And note that GSS started out as GDSS – group *decision* support systems.

How did this happen? At the time EMS first appeared on the scene in academia, in the early 1980s, the field of MIS was heavily involved in the development and testing of individual decision support systems (DSS). There was even an annual DSS conference that was well-attended and was considered somewhat prestigious. When EMS were first being developed, it seemed like a natural extension to add the word "group" before the DSS term. While a DSS is a system designed to support individual decision making, it seemed natural that a system designed for use by a number of individuals jointly should be also be called a support system, although it is not entirely clear why the term became GDSS instead of simply GSS. It is also difficult to pinpoint the first use of the GDSS term, but some searching shows that Huber used it in his 1984 *MIS Quarterly* paper [23]. In this article, he cites his own 1982 paper "Group Decision Support Systems as Aids in the Use of Structured Group Management Techniques," from the second DSS conference, so that could well be the first use of the GDSS term. Regardless, the term had become established by the time the seminal paper by DeSanctis and Gallupe was published [10]. The GDSS term became so entrenched that it later seemed natural to extend the DSS term again to cover systems designed for supporting decisions at the organizational level, giving us organizational DSS or ODSS. Fortunately, the *decision* part of GDSS was gradually dropped, as it became more obvious to researchers in the area that decisions were rarely made during the meetings where people used the systems. By 1993, when Jessup and Valacich published their influential edited volume of papers on the topic, the name they chose for the book was *Group Support Systems* [24]. However, the group part of the term continued. But just as the decision part of GDSS faded away, it now seems time for the group part of GDSS to be retired as well.

There is no shame in admitting that one studies meetings rather than groups. Such an admission may bring with it a fear that we are somehow giving up part of our standing as social scientists when we admit we study meetings and not groups. Studying meetings seems more practical than theoretical. This diminishing threatens to lessen our contact with and membership in mainstream social science. I would argue, however, that our claims to study groups are already tenuous, making our claims to the mantle of group researchers already suspect. Admitting that we are really interested in meetings, not groups, may actually result in us standing a little taller in they eyes of our colleagues who do study groups. If we agree that we are actually studying meetings and not groups, then we can focus on the conceptual basis for meetings, the work that takes place in them, and the ways in which information technology can support them. The conceptual basis for studying meetings is underdeveloped and will necessarily grow as we focus explicitly on meetings in our research. We can let these ideas guide our research about meetings and not be distracted by a need to seek out theory that deals with something – groups – that we are studying only indirectly and incompletely.

6 Conclusions

Fjermestad & Hiltz [13] end their paper with this thought: "If researchers learn the lessons summarized in this paper in terms of what is already known and what experimental procedures need to be followed … the next generation of experiments will be very rewarding." It is not clear that experimental GSS researchers learned the lessons summarized in their paper, and it is not clear how rewarding the last generation of experiments has been. However, if GSS studies are not as rewarding as they might have been, the only reason – or maybe even the main reason – is not because researchers did not learn the lessons Fjermestad and Hiltz taught. The main reason is that researchers continue to struggle with the problem of either trying to fit GSS work into a theoretical base that is not appropriate or abandoning theory altogether. It seems clear that theory is too practical a tool to abandon. What remains is to recognize the appropriate theoretical base for GSS work. While GSS work is tangentially related to small group theory, the more appropriate base for it is a theory of meetings.

References

1. Ancona, D.G., Caldwell, D.F.: Bridging the boundary: External activity and performance in organizational teams. Administrative Science Quarterly 37, 634–665 (1992)
2. Abrams, D., Hogg, M.A., Hinkle, S., Otten, S.: The social identity perspective in small groups. In: Poole, M.S, Hollingshead, A.B. (eds.) Theories of Small Groups, pp. 99–137. Sage Publications, Thousand Oaks, CA (2005)
3. Bacharach, S.B.: Organizational theories: Some criteria for evaluation. Academy of Management Review 14(4), 496–515 (1989)

4. Bales, B.F., Cohen, S.P.: SYMLOG: A System for Multiple Level Observation of Groups. Free Press, NYC (1979)

5. Briggs, R.O., Reinig, B.A., de Vreede, J.G.: Meeting Satisfaction for Technology-Supported Groups. Small Group Research 37(6), 585–611 (2006)

6. Chang, A., Duck, J., Bordia, P.: Understanding the Multidimensionality of Group Development. Small Group Research 37(4), 327–350 (2006)

7. Connolly, T., Jessup, L.M., Valacich, J.S.: Effects of anonymity and evaluative tone on idea generation in computer-mediated groups. Management Science 36, 689–703 (1990)

8. Dennis, A.R., George, J.F., Jessup, L.M., Nunamaker, Jr., J.F., Vogel, D.R.: Information Technology to Support Electronic Meetings. MIS Quarterly 12(4), 591–624 (1988)

9. Dennis, A.R., Wixom, B.H.: Investigating the moderators of the group support systems use with meta-analysis. Journal of MIS 18(3), 235–257 (2001-2002)

10. DeSanctis, G., Gallupe, R.B.: A foundation for the study of group decision support systems. Management Science 33(5), 589–609 (1987)

11. DeSanctis, G., Poole, M.S.: Capturing the complexity in advanced technology use: Adaptive structuration theory. Organization Science 5(2), 121–147 (1994)

12. Emerson, R.M.: Power-dependence relations. American Sociological Review 27, 31–41 (1962)

13. Fjermestad, J., Hiltz, S.R.: As assessment of group support systems experimental research: Methodology and results. Journal of MIS 15(3), 7–149 (1998-1999)

14. Frey, L., Sunwolf.: The symbolic-interpretive perspective on group life. In: Poole, M.S, Hollingshead, A.B. (eds.) Theories of Small Groups, pp. 185–239. Sage Publications, Thousand Oaks, CA (2005)

15. George, J.F., Easton, G.K., Nunamaker, Jr., J.F., Northcraft, G.B.: A Study of Collaborative Group Work With and Without Computer-Based Support. Information Systems Research 1(4), 394–415 (1990)

16. George, J.F., Jessup, L.M: Groups Over Time: What Are We Really Studying? International Journal of Human-Computer Studies 47(3), 497–511 (1997)

17. Gersick, C.J.: Time and transition in work teams: Toward a new model of group development. Academy of Management Journal 31(1), 9–41 (1988)

18. Giddens, A.: The constitution of society: Outline of the theory of structuration. California Press, Berkeley, CA (1984)

19. Gouran, D.S., Hirokawa, R.Y.: Functional theory and communication in decision making and problem-solving groups: An expanded view. In: Hirokawa, R.Y., Poole, M.S. (eds.) Communication & group decision making, 2nd edn., Sage Inc, Thousand Oaks, CA (1996)

20. Heninger, W.G., Dennis, A.R., Hilman, K.M.: Individual cognition and dual-task interference in group support systems. Information Systems Research 17(4), 415–424 (2006)

21. Hirokawa, R.Y., Poole, M.S. (eds.): Communication and group decision making, 2nd edn. Sage Publications, Thousand Oaks, CA (1996)

22. Huang, W., Li, D.: Opening up the black box in GSS research: explaining group decision outcome with group process. Computers in Human Behavior 23, 58–78 (2007)

23. Huber, G.: Issues in the design of group decision support systems. MIS Quarterly 8(3), 195–204 (1984)

24. Jessup, L.M., Valacich, J.S. (eds.): Group Support Systems: New Perspectives. Macmillan Publishing Company, NYC (1993)

25. Katz, N., Lazer, D., Arrow, H., Contractor, N.: The network perspective on small groups: Theory and research. In: Poole, M.S, Hollingshead, A.B. (eds.) Theories of Small Groups, pp. 277–312. Sage Publications, Thousand Oaks, CA (2005)

26. Klein, E.E., Tellefsen, T., Herskovitz, P.J.: The use of group support systems in focus groups: Information technology meets qualitative research. Computers in Human Behavior (2006)
27. Kolfschoten, G.L., den Hengst-Bruggeling, M., de Vreede, J.G.: Issues in the Design of Facilitated Collaboration Processes. Group Decision and Negotiation (2006)
28. Lewin, K.: Field theory in social science. In: Cartwright, D. (ed.) selected theoretical papers, Harper & Row, NYC (1951)
29. Lewis, L.F., Bajwa, D.S., Pervan, G., King, V.L.S., Munkvold, B.E.: A Cross-Regional Exploration of Barriers to the Adoption and Use of Electronic Meeting Systems. Group Decision and Negotiation (2007)
30. Limayem, M., Banerjee, P., Ma, L.: Impact of GDSS: Opening the black box. Decision Support Systems 42, 945–957 (2006)
31. McGrath, J.E., Hollingshead, A.B.: Groups Interacting with Technology. Sage Publications, Thousand Oaks, CA (1994)
32. Mejias, R.J.: The Interaction of Process Losses, Process Gains, and Meeting Satisfaction Within Technology-Supported Environments. Small Group Research 38(1), 156–194 (2007)
33. Nunamaker, Jr., J.F., Dennis, A.R., Valacich, J.S., Vogel, D.R., George, J.F.: Electronic Meeting Systems to Support Group Work: Theory and Practice at Arizona. Communications of the ACM 34(7), 40–61 (1991)
34. Poole, M.S., Baldwin, C.L.: Developmental processes in group decision making. In: Hirokawa, R.Y., Poole, M.S. (eds.) Communication & group decision making, 2nd edn., pp. 215--241. Sage Publications, Inc., Thousand Oaks, CA (1996)
35. Poole, M.S, Hollingshead, A.B.: Theories of Small Groups. Sage Publications, Thousand Oaks, CA (2005)
36. Putnam, L.L., Stohl, C.: Bona fide groups. In: Hirokawa, R.Y., Poole, M.S. (eds.) Communication & group decision making, 2nd edn., pp. 147--178. Sage, Thousand Oaks, CA (1996)
37. Rao, V.S., Jarvenpaa, S.L.: Computer support of groups: Theory-based models for GDSS research. Management Science 37(10), 1347–1362 (1991)
38. Rousseau, V., Aubé, C., Savoie, A.: Teamwork Behaviors: A Review and an Integration of Frameworks. Small Group Research 37(5), 540–570 (2006)
39. Sambamurthy, V., Poole, M.S.: The effects of variations in capabilities of GDSS designs on management of cognitive conflict in groups. Information Systems Research 3(3), 224–251 (1992)
40. Schwarz, A., Schwarz, C.: The Role of Latent Beliefs and Group Cohesion in Predicting Group Decision Support Systems Success. Small Group Research 38(1), 195–229 (2007)
41. Skinner, Q. (ed.): The Return of Grand Theory in the Human Sciences. Cambridge University Press, Cambridge, UK (2006)
42. Steiner, I.D.: Group process and productivity. Academic Press, NYC (1972)
43. Thibault, J.W., Kelly, H.H.: The Social Psychology of Groups. Wiley, NYC (1959)
44. Tuckman, B., Jensen, M.: Stages of small group development. Group and Organizational Studies 2, 419–427 (1977)
45. Vathanophas, V., Liang, S.Y.: Enhancing information sharing in group support systems (GSS). Computers in Human Behavior 23, 1675–1691 (2007)

Alternative Dispute Resolution Based on the Storytelling Technique

Pedro Antunes[1], Sara Relvas[1], and Marcos Borges[2]

[1] Department of Informatics of the Faculty of Sciences of the U. of Lisboa, Portugal
paa@di.fc.ul.pt
[2] Graduate Program in Informatics, NCE & IM, U. Federal do Rio de Janeiro, Brasil
mborges@nce.ufrj.br

Abstract. This paper describes a groupware prototype addressing the alternative resolution of legal conflicts. The groupware prototype integrates the storytelling and argumentation models with the legal process, accomplishing two major complementary objectives: eliciting spontaneous and informal explanations about the conflict, while contributing to the process with correct inferences and logic. The paper discusses in detail the integrated information model and provides a prototype implementation. These results were significantly enriched by a formative evaluation conducted by a dispute resolution professional. The contributions of this research to the state of the art are twofold: (1) the innovative integration of the storytelling and argumentation models; and (2) the support to self-help legal representation based on group technology.

1 Introduction

The major purpose of Alternative Dispute Resolution (ADR) is to resolve conflicts out of the court. ADR has been accepted by many companies seeking to resolve litigations in a more expedite and less expensive way, and many authorities trying to rationalize their legal systems.

ADR has also gained momentum with the popularity of e-commerce, considering that the world-wide market, new business opportunities and extended flexibility – as well as new threats, such as identity theft and lack of clear legal borders – brought by e-commerce should, at least, be accompanied with equally flexible mechanisms to resolve disputes. Online Dispute Resolution (ODR) is a kind of ADR providing fully-automated or assisted-automated mechanisms to resolve conflicts utilizing online technologies and in particular the Internet [1]. Examples are the Cybersettle, Settlementonline and Clicknsettle sites.

Electronic communication is one feature adopted by most ODR [2]. This feature is implemented in various ways, including email, chat and video conferencing. However, it is recognized that electronic communication introduces an impersonal factor reducing the effectiveness of ODR [3]. Very often, behind this problem, lie the difficulties participants have intervening in the most clear, convenient and efficient ways. This has been expressed in the research literature as worries about the quality of self representation from people who may not know in detail how to align their

J.M. Haake, S.F. Ochoa, A. Cechich (Eds.): CRIWG 2007, LNCS 4715, pp. 15–31, 2007.
© Springer-Verlag Berlin Heidelberg 2007

interventions with the requirements of the legal process, instead of relying on professional representation [4].

This research reports our efforts developing an ADR groupware prototype supporting self representation. The prototype relies upon the Issue Based Information System (IBIS) [5] argumentation model to facilitate the expression of arguments.

We nevertheless regard argumentation models – and IBIS in particular – as artefacts which are difficult to master, especially by untrained users [6]. In our perspective, some additional support is necessary to effectively integrate argumentation models in ADR/ODR technology.

To overcome this problem, we tested the applicability of the storytelling technique as a front-end for eliciting arguments in ADR. Storytelling is a narrative technique allowing to express complex information using a conceptual scheme that is well-known by the untrained user: telling stories [7]. Storytelling allows expressing unstructured and incomplete events using a narrative framework from where logical and temporal relationships may later emerge [8]. Storytelling is inherently a group activity, which has been found to improve knowledge recall, creating synergy and providing richer information about past events [9].

In this paper we argue that: (1) telling stories is a simple and adequate approach for expressing conflicting situations; (2) Storytelling may be combined with argumentation models with the purpose to derive arguments from stories; and (3) Storytelling and argumentation models may by combined with ADR.

Our prototype addresses the above assumptions. It allows gathering information about a dispute as a collection of stories. It also supports a mediator or arbitrator analyzing the story, deriving and organizing the facts relevant to the resolution process.

The paper is organized in the following way. We start with a review of the major concepts involved in the prototype: ADR/ODR, argumentation and storytelling. We propose a model integrating these concepts. We then address the model evaluation and finish the paper with a discussion of the obtained results and open issues.

2 Literature Review

ADR and ODR. ADR is an amicable and extrajudicial approach to reestablishing dialog among conflicting parties, sustaining healthy relationships, applying justice, and restoring social harmony whenever it has been damaged [10]. The major advantages of ADR rely on the possibility of resolving disputes based on the social and economic responsibilities and self-organization of the conflicting parties.

Although ADR is nowadays mostly focussed on resolving e-commerce disputes, its origins rest in family law, where it has been considered an absolute necessity [10]. Also, in many countries of the European Union, ADR is considered a mandatory preliminary procedure in labour law. These two fields of law, although very different, share one common defining characteristic of ADR: the interest in maintaining good communication and future relationships.

The ADR process helps two conflicting parties reaching an agreement with the assistance of one neutral third party. The ADR process falls into one of the following categories [11]: negotiation, mediation and arbitration. In negotiation, the third party is responsible for assisting communication. In meditation, the third party has no decision power but tries to convince the other parties to reach an agreement. In arbitration, the third party hears the arguments from the other parties, gathers evidence and reaches a decision, although such decision may not be legally enforced.

Within the European Union, arbitration is not considered an ADR process, as it is considered part of the traditional court system [10]. In Portugal, only mediation and arbitration are currently accepted as legal ADR processes. An ADR should provide the following guarantees [10]:

- Impartiality of the third party – The third party must not have any interest in the conflict, and may not represent of defend any one of the other parties.
- Transparency –The parties must have access to the necessary information during the whole ADR process.
- Effectiveness – The ADR should be accessible and cost efficient relative to the normal dispute resolution processes.
- Fairness – Both parties should be treated equally.
- Confidentiality – The information in the process should be confidential.

ODR provides the online technology necessary to efficiently implement the ADR process. This comprises simplified procedures for initiating, litigating and resolving disputes, and communication mechanisms necessary for self-help/unassisted participation [4]. Although the use of the Internet is not mandatory, ODR is in general considered an Internet-based service [3].

ODR is in general dependent on the different purposes of negotiation, mediation and arbitration [2]. The supplied services are differentiated according to these categories, and have most impact on the support to the third party. Considering negotiation, these services are focused on avoiding the human negotiator. In this context, litigants must assume bidding roles, while the ODR supports communication and optionally highlights potential satisfactory settlements. ODR support to mediation is mostly focused on the human mediator. This functionality is comparable to meeting facilitation [12], as it supports facilitative interventions aimed at maintaining communication, avoiding conflicting behaviors and clarifying issues. On the other hand, ODR support to arbitration is mostly centered on empowering the arbitrator's reasoning about the conflict, such as identifying facts or establishing causality through information models.

Lodder and Zeleznikow [13] analyzed various ODR systems and identified three critical success factors: (1) ODR should provide feedback on the likely outcomes of the dispute if the negotiation fails; (2) ODR should attempt to resolve conflicts using dialogue techniques; and (3) ODR should employ trade-off strategies to facilitate conflict resolution. Our goals are fundamentally aligned with the second critical factor, improving dialogue techniques with argumentation support.

Argumentation Support. Argumentation is a social activity aiming at producing correct inferences from given premises through thinking, speaking and writing [14]. Argumentation is founded on the persuasion of others about the strengths of one explanation of a conflicting situation. Argumentation provides logic structure to dialogue, mentioned above as one critical success factor. Argumentation also affords constructing rational-legal authority [15], which is fundamental to resolve conflicts.

Toulmin [16] proposed a model integrating these two facets of argumentations: rationality and persuasion. The model identifies six constructs: the *claim*; the *grounds* offered by who asserts the claim; the *warrant* implicitly linking the grounds to the claim; the additional justifications *backing* warrants; *qualifiers*, expressing the degree of force attached to the claim; and *rebuttals*, expressing the limitations of the argument. In the context of ADR/ODR, this model facilitates the expression of coherent arguments supporting the facts of the legal process.

IBIS [5] is another well-know argumentation model. It defines an argumentation system using three elements: *issue*, i.e. a conflict, misunderstanding or question; *position*, identifying a conflicting view over the issue; and *argument*, in support of or detriment of a position. The major advantage of IBIS in our context resides on the importance attributed to the issues, as they support the identification of conflicting views departing from a neutral situation: issues are neutral, only positions reveal the nature of conflicts. Contrasting the Toulmin's model with IBIS, we observe that IBIS is more adequate to dispute resolution, because it affords iterating the construction of arguments, including those that may not be accepted as facts, while the Toulmin's model is restricted to the final argumentation supporting the facts of the legal process.

A review of other argumentation models used in dispute resolution is given by Reed and Grasso [17]. These models have been used in ADR/ODR and Negotiation Support Systems (NSS), which are more broader in scope (see e.g. Yuan and Head [18]). Split-Up [19] is one ODR using the Toulmin's model. Zeno [20] and HERMES [21] are two ODR systems utilizing IBIS to organize arguments. gIBIS [22] is a NSS using the IBIS model and focused on visual representation. Research has shown that these models are useful for representing and summarizing argumentation [17]. However, several researchers have also pointed out that the adoption of these models is also problematic:

- They provide a narrow view of argument structure [17].
- They provide a coercive negotiation environment, in the sense that argument structures impose rules to the participants [23].
- Users find it difficult to participate in such a regulated way [20].
- Users classify and utilize the information structures in the wrong way [24].
- They pose inclusion problems, related with the need to master the technology and information structures [23].

We emphasize the perspective that argumentation models may restrict the interactions to formal structures not understandable and adhered by users. The consequence is that many of the benefits presented by argumentation models (e.g. logic structure, search capabilities) may be undermined. In fact, storytelling constitutes an information structuring technique more close to the participants' intentions and behaviors.

Storytelling. Telling stories is considered a simple and universal way to communicate and organize knowledge [25]. Humans are natural story tellers and unconsciously apply their inventiveness to convey their narrative intentions [26]. Stories evoke visual images and emotions, pulling the listener/reader into the scene [27]. Several studies show that information is more quickly remembered, persuasive and believable when presented as stories [27, 28]. In the context of ADR/ODR, storytelling could serve several purposes: (1) Offer a spontaneous, informal and stimulating way to convey past events related with the conflicting situation; (2) Trigger visual memories of past events; (3) Turn arguments more meaningful; (4) Strengthen understanding of the points made. Good stories, although having an informal nature, also present an underlying structure [27] which is well aligned with the purpose of ADR:

- Setting the scene – Time, place, players and context of the events.
- Build-up – The sequence of events leading to a troubling situation.
- Crisis or climax – The high point of the troubling situation.
- Learning – The retrospective inferences about what happened.
- Awareness – The understanding of what occurred after the troubling situation.

Groupware supports storytelling in various forms. Considering our focus on dispute resolution, we will especially address the support to knowledge recall, i.e. the reconstruction and articulation of past events through storytelling. The Group Storytelling technique utilizes storytelling performed by a group of people with the purpose to reconstruct events [9, 29]. The group context assumes an important role in this process because the complete knowledge of past events may be scattered among various persons and only the group allows fillings the gaps. Preliminary research results indicate that the Group Storytelling technique facilitates knowledge recall [9].

Although the links established here between storytelling and dispute resolution identify a compelling research line, we were unable to find any ADR or even ODR system supporting the storytelling technique. Storytelling has been conceptually associated to mediation and studied in the context of ADR, in what has been designated narrative mediation [30], thus stressing the important role of the mediator getting and reviewing alternative stories about a conflict. However, the focus is on the process, not the technology. Rainey discusses storytelling and ODR [31], but storytelling is again regarded a mediation process, which may be supported by a general-purpose ODR. Choi [32] points out that ODR, in an attempt to replicate face-to-face disputes, should support storytelling when the parties engage in such behavior, but also remarks there are new possibilities offered by virtual media that go beyond replicating face-to-face behavior.

In summary, there is evidence on the important role of storytelling in ADR/ODR, but technological support to storytelling in dispute resolution has not yet emerged. Our research aims to develop such support and combining it with the advantages offered by argumentation support.

3 Integration of Storytelling and Argumentation in ADR

Our goal is to develop groupware supporting dispute resolution. This preoccupation with technology naturally emphasizes the central role of the information model. In this section we will describe our model, integrating the generic objectives of ADR with argumentation and storytelling.

The context of this research was the Portuguese legal system, which does not consider negotiation within the scope of ADR [33]. Therefore, only mediation and arbitration are considered. Furthermore, we combine the mediation and arbitration perspectives into one single information model. The differences have natural impact on the final decision, which respectively belongs to the parties or the arbitrator. But in both cases the model facilitates the production of arguments and reasoning about those arguments, thus blending together the behaviors of the mediator and arbitrator.

Assuming an information systems perspective, the elements of the legal process have the structure illustrated in Figure 1 (the elements were drawn from the case 1 described in section 5). The elements are organized in dates, facts and evidences, where the facts necessarily have a date and follow a chronological order. Dates are central to the logic of the legal process. Facts are elements (events or documents) that should be supported with evidence, i.e. supporting documents.

Date	Fact	Evidence
02/01/06	Client phoned about the cancellation	Phone contact
01/04/06	Client was told to cancel by e-mail	E-mail
	Client was informed incorrectly	
	Client assumed the service cancelled	
02/04/06	Client cancelled the service by fax	Fax

Fig. 1. Elements of the legal process

In our model, the information associated with the legal process is produced by the third party without direct intervention from the other parties. The claimant and defendant are responsible for producing their own stories about the conflicting situation. Observe in Figure 2 how storytelling is organized. The claimant and defendant tell their own stories, each one designated *story-conflict*. A story-conflict is composed by a list of events organized according to the order of occurrence.

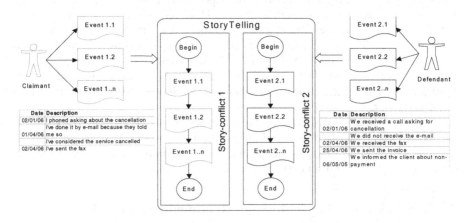

Fig. 2. Specification of story-conflicts by the claimant and defendant

We will now consider the integration of the IBIS argumentation model with storytelling. The adoption of IBIS is based on several arguments previously mentioned:

- IBIS departs from a neutral element to organize the argumentation process. Issues are neutral because they only identify what issue is in dispute, independently of the parties and their disagreements. We believe the opportunity to start from a neutral context facilitates the work from the third party and offers a positive environment for the argumentation process.

- IBIS integrates all arguments produced during the ADR process, including those that may not lead to facts. We believe this contributes to the impartiality, fairness and transparency of the ADR process.
- The IBIS process is inherently iterative and supports all parties working in parallel, sharing their positions and arguments.
- IBIS affords a hypertext visual representation.

The integration of IBIS and storytelling is done in the following way. The claimant and defendant create events in a story-conflict according to their temporal order. Each event is also a candidate issue, and for each candidate issue there is implicitly a position in favor from the person who specified the event. If there is a doubt or a disagreement with that event, e.g. because it conflicts with an event produced by the other party, the situation is explicitly expressed with an argument, and is implicitly associated with a position against. When there is a position against a candidate issue, it becomes an issue. The relationship between storytelling and argumentation is thus established by specifying arguments, which turn events into issues and automatically associate positions against the issues. According to the IBIS model, new arguments may be associated to previous arguments. In Figure 3 we illustrate how this argumentation process evolves through time.

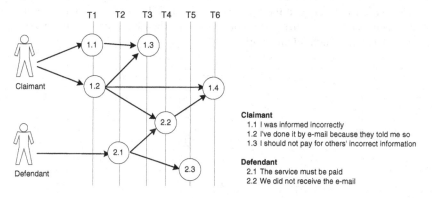

Fig. 3. Illustration of the argumentation process

Note that storytelling and argumentation may be intertwined. Also, we do not explicitly specify if the arguments are generated by the claimant and defendant without assistance from the third party, by any participant, or solely by the third party. We assume that these restrictions depend on many contextual variables, e.g. type of conduct from the third party or the capability of the claimant and defendant to construct their arguments. The proposed model is therefore independent from such contextual variables. We classify the arguments in the following categories:

- Initial arguments – Derived from positions against events in the story-conflict (e.g. 1.1, 1.2 and 2.1).
- Reinforcement arguments – Based on arguments previously expressed by a party, they persist or sustain a line of argumentation (e.g. 1.3).

- Composition arguments – Use any previous arguments to derive a new argument (e.g. 2.2 and 1.4).
- Decomposition arguments – They adopt part of a previous argument to define a new argument (e.g. 2.3).

Having established the links between storytelling (the story-conflicts) and argumentation (arguments and their implicit positions), we must now establish the links between the argumentation and the legal process. As mentioned previously, the third party is responsible for defining the legal process, an activity that is based on the evaluation of the available arguments. This is accomplished in two steps.

The first step concerns the definition of the *story-argument*, as shown in Figure 4. Recall that the claimant and defendant compose their story-conflicts by specifying events. Those events may then originate various types of arguments. Then, the third party selects which arguments are relevant to the legal process. The selected arguments set up then what is designated story-argument.

The fundamental purpose of the story-argument is twofold: (1) identify what arguments are elected to the legal process; and (2) define the logical sequence of the arguments. Note that although the arguments are related with events belonging to the story-conflicts, which have a temporal order, many times these arguments reflect conflicting views exactly about the timing of events. Consequently, we cannot specify any strict relationship between the order of events and the order of arguments in the story-argument. Only the third party, naturally with the help from the other participants, may determine such relationships.

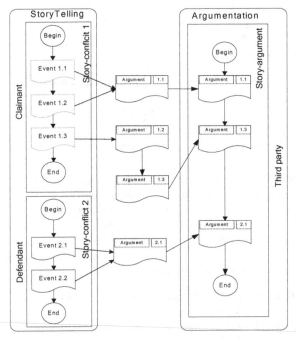

Fig. 4. Story-argument specification and its relationship with the story-conflicts

The second step in the construction of the legal process concerns the definition of what we designate the *story-legal*, illustrated in Figure 5. Through the definition of the story-argument, the third party determines what arguments seem to be relevant to the legal process. Then, it is time to deduce facts about the situation. The deduction of facts is accomplished in two steps. The first step concerns the definition of candidate facts. These are shown in the middle of Figure 5. Basically, a candidate fact identifies the arguments used in the deduction process, the date of occurrence and any evidence (external documentation) supporting the fact. The second step concerns selecting and organizing the facts in a temporal order, thus forming the story-legal.

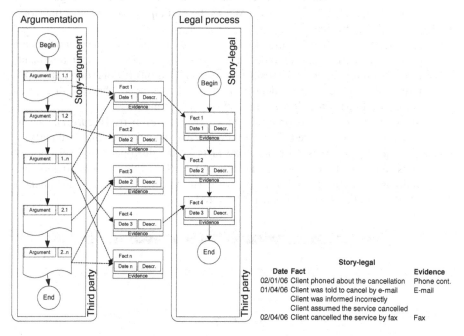

Fig. 5. Specification of the story-legal and its relationship with the story-argument

Finally, we would like to emphasize that the construction of these information elements is iterative and concurrent. The definition of the story-legal is not a logical consequence of the successive construction of the story-conflicts and story-argument. Instead, as the story-conflicts are being interactively constructed by the parties, and issues emerge, there is the responsibility of the third party electing arguments and deducing facts. Furthermore, since the story-conflicts, story-argument and story-legal are permanently available to all parties, all this information necessarily evolves with time: events and arguments may appear, disappear and be redefined; while arguments and facts are included and removed from the story-argument and story-legal.

4   Prototype

The model described in this paper was implemented in a software prototype. Our major concern developing the prototype was to validate the model, through the study of several ADR cases, rather than evaluating in detail any specific functionality or user-interface features. For legal reasons, it was not possible to evaluate the prototype in a real situation. The prototype was developed in Visual C# and uses a Web browser and an SQL database. The functionality is provided by several forms:

- Third party management – Supports defining personal data about the claimant and defendant, and the elements of the legal process, including process number, type of process (mediation or arbitration), starting and finishing dates.
- Story-conflict – Definition of the story-conflict by the claimant and defendant. The events in the story-conflict contain text and must have a date (Figure 6).
- Visualization of story-conflicts – Allows the participants to visualize the story-conflicts side-by-side.
- Argumentation – Specification of arguments by the parties. The arguments are either linked to events or other arguments. The classification of arguments (initial, reinforcement, composition or decomposition) is done implicitly. Different colours are used to identify the type of argument. There is no explicit use of positions, since they are implicit in the arguments.
- Story-argument – Selection of arguments by the third party (Figure 7). The arguments must be ordered. These arguments may be edited by the third party.
- Story-legal – Definition of candidate facts by the third party and selection of facts belonging to the story-legal (Figure 8). Each fact must have text and date, and can be accompanied with evidence (references to external documents). The facts in the story-legal must be ordered.

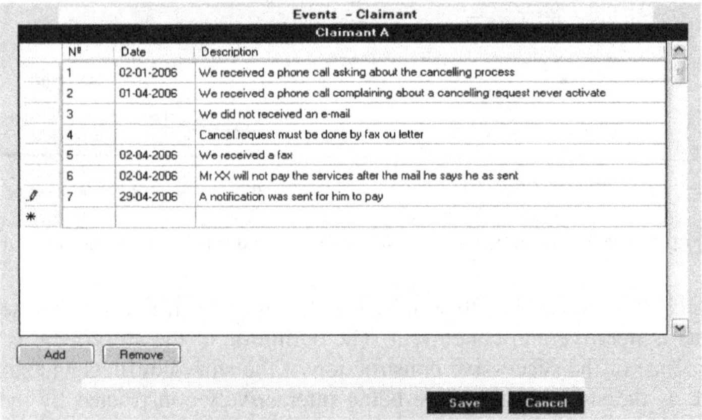

Fig. 6. Specification of a story-conflict by the claimant

Although our implementation is open to various types of strategies adopted by the third party, the following description illustrates the common prototype usage. After initialization by the third party, the claimant and defendant start writing their stories, introducing events and identifying when they occurred. Omissions and incorrectly specified events (e.g. arguments expressed as events) are expected. We also assume that at the beginning of the process the claimant and defendant will be focussed on their own stories.

Fig. 7. Specification of the story-argument by the third party

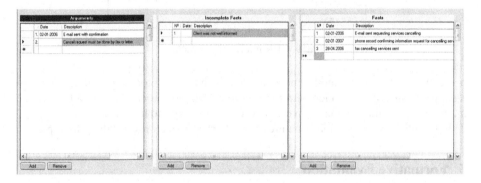

Fig. 8. Specification of incomplete facts and story-legal by the third party

After some time, the participants will start analyzing both stories. Whenever a conflicting view occurs, the participant may associate an argument with the conflicting event. During this period, the third party may edit the arguments generated by the claimant and defendant, seeking to clarify information and also to structure and elaborate arguments. New arguments may be drawn from previous arguments. The claimant and defendant may also come back to their stories, recalling new events and modifying or deleting events if necessary.

Meanwhile, the third party may start promoting arguments to the story-argument. This is a decision process that gives some indication to the parties about the direction where the legal process is leading, although this may still be influenced by the future actions taken by the parties.

Based on the available stories and consolidated list of arguments, the third party may then define incomplete facts. When, the stories and arguments appear to stabilize, the incomplete facts may be promoted to facts, thus defining a clear description of the conflicting situation. Finally, the parties may reach an agreement that no further information is relevant to the legal process.

Contrasting this functionality with the common ADR process, we would like to emphasize two positive issues. The first one is that the prototype has a strong focus on visually confronting the stories defined by the claimant and defendant, facilitating the

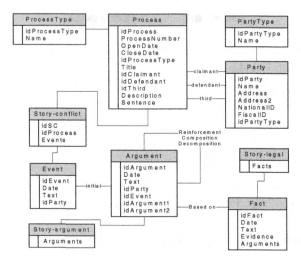

Fig. 9. ODR information structure

perception of conflicts. Another positive issue is that the prototype provides a mechanism to document and understand the reasoning behind the conflict, avoiding information losses while leading the participants from the story to the facts.

In Figure 9 we present the structure of the database developed for the prototype.

5   Formative Evaluation

Our model was subject to a formative evaluation, which was conducted side-by-side by one of the authors and a lawyer accredited as third party and experienced with ADR. In some way, the adopted approach resembles the pair-programming idea adopted by the agile software development movement [34]. The evaluation consisted of two major steps:

- Analysis and discussion of various ADR cases previously conducted by the lawyer. Two of them were selected as representative of mediation and arbitration processes. This was followed by a detailed deconstruction of the selected cases, with the identification of all their events and arguments.
- Reconstruction of the cases using the prototype. This was accomplished side-by-side, with the two participants playing the roles of claimant, defendant and third party, while defining the story-conflicts, story-argument and story-legal.

In both steps the comments and ideas discussed by the participants were documented for later analysis. In the spirit of formative evaluation, these comments and ideas were incorporated in the redesigned model presented in this paper. The selected ADR cases are briefly summarized below.

Case 1. This case concerned a complaint from a client over a service charged to him after he requested its cancellation. The client contacted the provider by telephone and was informed that he could request the cancellation by email. To his surprise, after several months, he found out that the service was not cancelled. Furthermore, he was informed that the email message was not received and thus the service was active and should be paid. After several other steps, which included a second request for cancellation sent by fax, the client was notified by a layer representing the company that a legal case would be initiated. The client decided to request an arbitration process, which was accepted by the other party.

Case 2. A client bought a new vehicle from a major car maker. Several times, during regular maintenance, she complained the car had a strange noise, which was undetected. Every time the vehicle was subject to maintenance, the issue was registered in the respective repair form. After the legal guarantee period, one component supporting the motor broke up and the car was immobilized. The maintenance company charged for the repair, but the client refused payment and submitted a complaint directly to the car maker. The client and maintenance company decided to submit the case to a mediation process.

Complete transcripts from the above cases were available during the evaluation, with proper authorization from the parties involved. Their use beyond the evaluation was denied and anonymity was also enforced. No contact with the claimant and defendant was established. The major outcomes from the formative evaluation were:

- Dates (of events) play a major role in the system. All events, arguments and facts are closely related with dates. Dates are fundamental to the logic and structure of the ADR process.
- The construction of the story-conflicts is mostly done individually, without immediate refutation from the other party. This allows initially eliciting the issues perceived as most important by each party, even though they may appear disorganized and incomplete. The analysis of the other party's story-conflict is done afterwards and allows consolidating the events in a more structured way.
- The creation of the story-conflicts was initially perceived as time consuming, considering that its value is only perceived later on, when building arguments.
- Regarding the creation of arguments, the separation between the argumentation process and the recollection of past events was positively regarded, giving more fluidity to the whole conflict resolution process.
- The creation of arguments was also perceived as time consuming.
- By insistence of the lawyer participating in the evaluation, the arguments were ordered according to the dates of the events they were related with, instead of the order of their creation. This person mentioned that the adopted order provided a more clear visual and mental organization of the case, and in fact lead to the definition of facts more early than expected.
- Facts were mostly created by cutting and pasting information contained in arguments, something that was very well regarded by the participants. It was observed that the way facts are constructed influenced the argumentation process, since arguments were defined with the purpose to become facts.
- The participants also perceived a strong relationship between facts and the events belonging to the story-conflicts, highlighting the requirement to make them visible during the creation of candidate facts and story-legal.

6 Discussion, Open Issues and Conclusions

The first issue we would like to discuss in more detail is related with validation. In this respect we should consider two important limitations in our research. In the one hand, the prototype was evaluated in artificial conditions; and, in the other hand, it involved one single stakeholder. We made attempts to experiment the prototype in real situations. However, this objective failed because the participants did not consent to participate and, in fact, there is no legal framework to support such an experiment, thus making its use in those conditions highly risky. One alternative that could have been considered would involve testing the prototype with real cases but false participants playing the roles of claimant and defendant. From our point of view, this could be beneficial to evaluate specific aspects of the prototype, e.g. the user interface, but not the information model. Since our intentions were doing a feasibility study centred on the model, we believe the adopted formative approach was more adequate.

Although one single stakeholder participated in the evaluation, she was highly experienced conducting mediation and arbitration processes. The deep knowledge of the alternative dispute resolution processes and the level of involvement in the definition of the information model gave us very insightful and invaluable information. These insights were codified in the solution described in this paper and provide good indications for future research. To cite Gray and Mandiwalla [35]: "we have reached the point where we need to expand what we can do with group support systems … to do so we need to invent, invent, invent rather than test, test, test what exists."

Although the formative evaluation was very insightful, we could not find concrete answers to several issues that remain open. Perhaps the most important one is related with argumentation and, more specifically, identifying who may produce and organize arguments. The model and prototype allow three distinct types of functionality: (1) only the claimant and defendant generate arguments; (2) every participant may generate arguments; and (3) only the third party produces arguments. We may identify several scenarios where some of these approaches could be more feasible or adequate than others. The third party participating in this research perceived the prototype as most beneficial to her own work, thus minimizing the roles attributed to the other parties, but we cannot generalize from this observation. More research is necessary to study which operation mode is most adequate to alternative dispute resolution.

Somewhat related with this issue are the difficulties users typically have interacting with argumentation models. We tried to reduce the impact of the argumentation model with two complementary approaches. The first one was avoiding using the model to control the participants' interactions, i.e. the model is used to organize information but not to define what the participants must do next. The second approach consisted in simplifying the use of issues and positions, considering that the former are inferred from events in the story-conflicts and the later are automatically derived by the system. Nevertheless, this issue is mostly related with usability and thus a different type of evaluation is necessary to come to conclusions about its effects.

We should also emphasize here that the proposed approach requires the participation of a human acting as third party. Unlike other approaches, which automate this role, mostly often because they are limited to exchanging information between the claimant and defendant, we rely on the human third party to accomplish a much more complex endeavour: organizing arguments, eliciting candidate facts and organizing the facts of the legal process. This focus on the third party naturally has advantages and disadvantages. One important disadvantage to consider is that the system may be more difficult to use in the ODR context. On the contrary, the human third party is beneficial in situations where the problem is very complex or delicate, e.g. family law. We should also note that we have not tested our prototype in the ODR context.

Besides all these open issues raised above, our research has come to some positive results that we would like to summarize. The first one to consider is the positive indication that storytelling and argumentation models may be integrated with the legal process in a groupware system. This unique combination facilitates arranging the legal process in two different levels. At the forefront, we find support to the elicitation of the events related with the conflicting situation in a simple way, which is adequate to the presumed non- legal/technical abilities of the claimant and defendant. At the backside, we find the support to the logical structure of the legal process, with facts and evidence, which is centred on the more legal/technical proficient third party. In this scenario, the argumentation model basically serves to intermediate the information flows between the two levels, and provides another very important functionality: support to self-help legal representation in the litigation process.

Further research will proceed in two different fronts: performing experiments in the ODR context, using the system through the Internet with different levels of intervention from the third party; and more formalized and detailed evaluation actions based on role playing real legal cases.

Acknowledgements. This work was partially supported by the Portuguese Foundation for Science and Technology, Project POSI/EIA/57038/2004.

References

1. Hammond, A.: How Do You Write "Yes"?: A Study on the Effectiveness of Online Dispute Resolution. Conflict Resolution Quarterly 20, 261–286 (2003)
2. Schultz, T., Kaufmann-Kohler, G., Bonnet, V.: Online Dispute Resolution: The State of the Art and the Issues. Université de Genéve, Genéve (2001)
3. Goodman, J.: The Pros and Cons of Online Dispute Resolution: An Assessment of Cybermediation Websites. Duke Law & Technology Review 4 (2003)
4. Tang, Z.: An Effective Dispute Resolution System for Electronic Consumer Contracts. Computer Law & Security Report 23, 42–52 (2007)
5. Kunz, W., Rittel, H.: Issues as Elements of Information Systems. Institute of Urban and Regional Development, University of California at Berkeley (1970)
6. Borges, M., Pino, J., Araujo, R.: Common Context for Decisions and Their Implementations. Group Decision and Negotiation 15, 221–242 (2006)
7. Decortis, F., Rizzo, A.: New Active Tools for Supporting Narrative Structures. Personal and Ubiquitous Computing 6, 416–429 (2002)
8. Appan, P., Sundaram, H., Birchfield, D.: Communicating Everyday Experiences. In: Proceedings of the 1st ACM Workshop on Story Representation, Mechanism and Context, pp. 17–24. ACM Press, New York, USA (2004)

9. Carminatti, N., Borges, M., Gomes, J.: Collective Knowledge Recall: Benefits and Drawbacks. In: Fukś, H., Lukosch, S., Salgado, A.C. (eds.) CRIWG 2005. LNCS, vol. 3706, pp. 216–231. Springer, Heidelberg (2005)
10. EU Opinion of the European Economic and Social Committee on the Green Paper on Alternative Resolution in Civil and Commercial Law. Official Journal of the European Union C85, 8–13 (2003)
11. Bonnet, V., Boudaoud, K., Gagnebin, G., Harms, J., Schultz, T.: Online Dispute Resolution Systems as Web Services. ICFAI Journal of Alternative Dispute Resolution 3 (2004)
12. Antunes, P., Ho, T.: The Design of a GDSS Meeting Preparation Tool. Group Decision and Negotiation 10, 5–25 (2001)
13. Lodder, A., Zeleznikow, J.: Developing an Online Dispute Resolution Environment: Dialogue Tools and Negotiation Support Systems in a Three-Step Model. Harvard Negotiation Law Review 10, 287–336 (2005)
14. Driver, R., Newton, P., Osborne, J.: Establishing the Norms of Scientific Argumentation in Classroom. Science Education 84, 287–312 (1998)
15. Weber, M.: Economy and Society. University of California Press, Berkeley (1978)
16. Toulmin, S.: The Uses of Argument. Cambridge University Press, Cambridge (1958)
17. Reed, C., Grasso, F.: Recent Advances in Computational Models of Natural Argument. International Journal of Intelligent Systems 22, 1–15 (2007)
18. Yuan, Y., Head, M.: The Effects of Multimedia Communication on Web-Based Negotiation. Group Decision and Negotiation 12, 89–109 (2003)
19. Stranieri, A., Zeleznikow, J., Gawler, M., Lewis, B.: A Hybrid-Neural Approach to the Automation of Legal Reasoning in the Discretionary Domain of Family Law in Australia. Artificial Intelligence and Law 7, 153–183 (1999)
20. Märker, O., Schmidt-Belz, B.: Online Mediation for Urban and Regional Planning. In: Märker, O., Schmidt-Belz, B. (eds.) Computer Science for Environmental Protection '00, Marburg (2000)
21. Karacapilidis, N., Papadias, D.: Computer Supported Argumentation and Collaboration Decision Making: The Hermes System. Information Systems 26, 259–277 (2001)
22. Conklin, J., Begeman, M.: Gibis: A Hypertext Tool for Exploratory Policy Discussion. ACM Transactions on Office Information Systems 6, 303–331 (1988)
23. Rehg, W., McBurney, P., Parsons, S.: Computer Decision-Support Systems for Public Argumentation: Assessing Deliberative Legitimacy. Artificial Intelligence & Society 19, 203–229 (2005)
24. Guerrero, L., Pino, J.: Preparing Decision Meetings at a Large Organization. In: IFIP WG 8.3 Open Conference on Decision Making and Decision Support in the Internet Age, Cork, Ireland, pp. 85–95 (2002)
25. Laurel, B.: Computers as Theatre. Addison-Wesley, Reading (1991)
26. Decortis, F., Rizzo, A.: New Active Tools for Supporting Narrative Structures. Personal and Ubiquitous Computing 6, 416–429 (2002)
27. Morgan, S., Dennehy, R.: The Power of Organizational Storytelling: A Management Development Perspective. Journal of Management Development 16, 494–501 (1997)
28. Denning, S.: The Leader's Guide to Storytelling. Jossey Bass (2005)
29. Santoro, F., Brezillon, P.: Group Storytelling Approach to Collect Contextualized Shared Knowledge. In: 16th International Workshop on Database and Expert Systems Applications (2005)
30. Winslade, J., Monk, G., Cotter, A.: A Narrative Approach to the Practice of Mediation. Negotiation Journal 14, 21–41 (2004)

31. Rainey, D.: Online Dispute Resolution: Some Context and a Report on Recent Developments. The Mayhew-Hite Report 4 (2005-2006)
32. Choi, D.: Online Dispute Resolution: Issues and Future Directions. In: Proceedings of the UNECE Forum on ODR 2003, Geneva, Switzerland (2003)
33. DR31/86: Voluntary Arbitration (in Portuguese). Official Journal of the Portuguese Republic, 31/86 (August 1986)
34. Lui, K., Chan, K.: Pair Programming Productivity: Novice-Novice Vs. Expert-Expert. International Journal of Human-Computer Studies 64, 915–925 (2006)
35. Gray, P., Mandiwalla, M.: New Directions for GDSS. Group Decision and Negotiation 8, 77–83 (1999)

Fostering Knowledge Exchange in Virtual Communities by Using Agents

Javier Portillo-Rodríguez, Aurora Vizcaíno, Juan Pablo Soto,
Mario Piattini, and Gabriela N. Aranda

Alarcos Research Group,
Information Systems and Technologies Department, UCLM-Soluziona Research and
Development Institute, University of Castilla – La Mancha, Spain
Paseo de la Universidad, 4-13071, Ciudad Real, Spain
javier.portillo@uclm.es, aurora.vizcaino@uclm.es,
jpsoto@proyectos.inf-cr.uclm.es, mario.piattini@uclm.es,
garanda@uncoma.edu.ar

Abstract. Nowadays, the increase in information and in sources from which to obtain knowledge have generated a large-scale development of knowledge sharing systems. However, these systems do not always live up to the expectations of the organisations that use them, as they do not take the fundamental social aspects necessary for the flow and sharing of knowledge between the members of a community into consideration. The objective of our work is to emulate the behaviour of communities of practice, where the confidence that exists between the members of these communities leads to an exchange of knowledge. We have, therefore, designed a three-level multi-agent architecture which takes into account both the way in which a community member behaves and the community to which that member belongs.

Keywords: Knowledge Management, Multi-agent Systems, Reputation, Trust.

1 Introduction: From Communities to Communities of Practice

Intellectual capital and knowledge management are currently growing since knowledge is a critical factor for an organization's competitive advantage [1]. This growth determines organizations' performance by studying how well they manage their most critical knowledge. One important instrument in knowledge management is communities [2], [3]. Although there is no generally accepted definition, a community can be defined as a group of socially interacting people who are mutually tied to one another and regularly meet at a common place [4]. The development of Internet and groupware technologies has led to a new kind of community - "virtual communities", where members may or may not meet one another face to face and may exchange words and ideas through the use of computers networks [5].

Our research is focused upon professionally-oriented comunities, which consists of company employees who communicate and share information in order to support their professional tasks. A special case of professionally-oriented communities are the

J.M. Haake, S.F. Ochoa, A. Cechich (Eds.): CRIWG 2007, LNCS 4715, pp. 32–39, 2007.

"Communities of Practice" (CoPs), defined by Wenger et al. [6] as groups of people who share a concern, a set of problems, or a passion about a topic, and who deepen their knowledge and expertise in this area by interacting on an ongoing basis.

The following section shows our proposal to support CoPs concepts by defining a Multi-Agent Architecture. In Section 3 we describe both a prototype with which to rate the architecture, and the manner in which the formulas to calculate reputation in virtual communities are defined. Finally, in Section 4 we compare our proposal with other related works.

2 Our Proposal: A Multi-agent Architecture to Support CoPs

In order to support concepts related to CoPs and Knowledge Management, we have designed a three level multi-agent architecture.

We have chosen the agent paradigm because it constitutes a natural metaphor for systems with purposeful interacting agents, and this abstraction is close to the human way of thinking about their own activities [7]. This foundation has led to an increasing interest in social aspects such as motivation, leadership, culture or trust [8]. Our research is related to the latter concept of "trust" since artificial agents can be made more robust, resilient and effective by providing them with trust reasoning capabilities.

The architecture is composed of Reactive, Deliberative and Social Levels and is mainly based on the concepts of trust and reputation. Trust can be defined as confidence in the ability and intention of a source of information to deliver correct information [9] and reputation as the amount of trust an agent has in a source of information, which is created through interactions with those information sources. It is important to take these concepts into account because if we wish to foster knowledge exchange in communities of practice we have to know that people in real life in general and in companies in particular, prefer to exchange knowledge with "trustworthy people" by which we mean people they trust. People with a consistently low reputation will eventually be isolated from the community since others will rarely accept their justifications or arguments and will limit their interactions with them. It is for this reason that we considered the Social Level to be an important contribution to the multi-agent architecture that we propose. The reactive and deliberative levels are considered by other authors as typical levels that a multi-agent system must have [10]. In the following paragraphs we shall describe each level of architecture in detail.

2.1 Reactive Architecture

This architecture was designed to the reactive level of the agent. The architecture must respond at the precise moment at which an event has been perceived. This architecture is formed of the following modules:

Agent's internal model: Because an agent represents a person in a community this model stores the user's features. Therefore, this module stores the following parts:

- The *interests*. This part is included in the internal model in order to make the process of distributing knowledge as fast as possible. That is, the agents are able to search for knowledge automatically, checking whether there is stored knowledge which matches its own interests. This behaviour fosters knowledge sharing and reduces the amount of work that employees have to do because they receive knowledge without having to make searches.
- The *user's profile*. This part describes the profile of the person on whose behalf the agent is acting. This module is composed of the users' preferences, expertise and position. The *Preferences* can be used to discover how the user prefers the agent to present the information to him/her. *Expertise* is the skill or knowledge of a person who knows a great deal about a specific thing. Since we are emulating virtual communities it is important to know the degree of expertise that each member of the community has in order to decide how trustworthy a piece of knowledge is, as people often trust in experts more than in novice employees. Another important piece of information considered in the user's profiles is that of *Position,* since employees often consider information that comes from a boss as being more reliable than that which comes from another employee in the same (or a lower) position as him/her [11]. Such different positions inevitably influence the way in which knowledge is acquired, diffused and eventually transformed within the local area. Because of this, in our research these factors will be calculated by taking into account a weight that can strengthen this factor to a greater or to a lesser degree.

Behaviour generator: This component is necessary for the development of this architecture since it has to select the agent's behaviour. This behaviour is defined on the basis of the agent's beliefs. Moreover, this component responds immediately to the perceptions received of the environment.

History: This component stores the agents' interactions with the environment.

Belief generation: This component is one of the most important in the cognitive model because it is in charge of creating and storing the agent's knowledge. Moreover, it defines the agent's beliefs.

Beliefs: The beliefs module is composed of three kinds of beliefs: inherited beliefs, lessons learned and interactions. Inherited beliefs are the organization's beliefs that the agent receives. For instance: an organizational diagram of the enterprise or the philosophy of the company or community. Lessons learned are the lessons that the agent obtains while it interacts with the environment. The information about interactions can be used to establish parameters in order to know what the agent can trust (agents or knowledge sources). This module is based on the agent's interests and goals, because each time a goal is realized, the lessons and experiences generated to attain that goal are introduced into the agent's beliefs as lessons learned.

2.2 Deliberative Architecture

This architecture was designed to the deliberative level of the agent (see Figure 1).

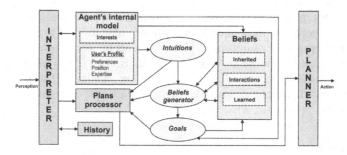

Fig. 1. Deliberative architecture

Its components are:

Agent's internal model: this module is the same as that which is described in the reactive architecture. It is composed of interests and of the user's profile.

Plans processor: This module is the most important in this architecture as it is in charge of evaluating beliefs and goals in order to determine which plans have to be included in the Planner to be executed.

Belief generator: As in the previous architecture, this component is in charge of creating, storing and retaining the agent's knowledge. In addition, it is also in charge of establishing the agent's beliefs. The belief creation process is a continuous process that is initiated at the moment at which the agent is created and which continues during its entire effective life.

Intuitions: Intuitions are hypothesis that have not been verified but which the agent believes to be true. According to [12] intuition has not yet been modeled by agent systems. In this work we have attempted to adapt this concept as we consider that people in real communities are influenced by their intuitions when they have to make a decision or believe in something. This concept is emulated by comparing the agents' profiles in order to obtain an initial value of intuition that can be used to form a belief about an agent.

History: This component stores the agents' interactions with the environment.

Goals: The goals are formed by using the agent's objectives. For instance, one of the goals of each member of a community of practice is knowledge exchange. The goals are defined in accordance with the community or group in which the agent interacts.

2.3 Social Architecture

This architecture is quite similar to the deliberative architecture.

The main differences are the *Social Model* and *Social Behaviour Processor*. The first one represents the actual state of the community, the community's interests, the members' identifiers and the goals that will be proposed by the agents in order to satisfy needs or interests related to its interactions with other agents. These goals should be coherent both with the agent's beliefs and with other agents' beliefs.

The *Social Behaviour Processor* processes the opinions and beliefs of the community's members. To do this, this module needs to manage the goals, intuitions and beliefs of the community in order to make a decision.

Both models represent the opinions and beliefs that the members of a community have about an agent, and their interaction with the community. The social focus that this architecture provides permits us to give the agents the social behaviour necessary for them to be able to emulate the work relationships in an organization. In addition, this layer permits the decentralization of decision making. That is, it provides methods by which to process or make decisions based on the opinions of the members of a community.

3 Prototype

In order to test our architecture we have developed a prototype system in which a community shares knowledge. The goal of this prototype is to allow software agents to help employees to discover the information that may be useful to them, thus decreasing the overload of information that employees often have and strengthening the use of knowledge bases in enterprises. In addition, we attempt to detect and thus avoid the situation of employees storing valueless information in the knowledge base.

To design this prototype we have designed a *User Agent* and a *Manager Agent*. The former is used to represent each person that may consult or introduce knowledge in a knowledge base or in a knowledge management system. Therefore, the *User Agent* can assume three types of behavior or roles similar to the tasks that a person may carry out in a knowledge base. The User Agent plays one role or another depending upon whether the person that it represents carries out one of the following actions:

- The person contributes new knowledge to the communities in which s/he is registered. In this case the User Agent plays the role of **Provider**.
- The person uses knowledge previously stored in the community. Then, the User Agent will be considered as a **Customer**.
- The person helps other users to achieve their goals, for instance by giving an evaluation of certain knowledge. In this case the role is that of a **Partner**. So, Figure 2 shows that in community 1 there are two User Agents playing the role of Partner, one User Agent playing the role of Consumer and another being a Provider.

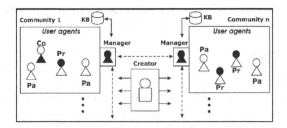

Fig. 2. Communities of agents

The second type of agent within a community is called the *Manager Agent* (represented in black in Figure 2) which must manage and control its community. In order to approach this, the agent carries out the following tasks:

- Registering an agent in its community.
- Registering the frequency of contribution of each agent.
- Registering the number of times that an agent gives feedback about other agents' knowledge.
- Registering the interactions between agents.

When a user wishes to join to a community in which no member knows anything about him/her, the reputation value assigned to the user in the new community is calculated on the basis of the reputation assigned from other communities where the user is or was a member. For instance, a User Agent called j, will ask each community manager where he/she was previously a member to consult each agent which knows him/her with the goal of calculating the average value of his/her reputation (R_j). This is calculated as:

$$R_j = \left(\sum_{i=1}^{n} R_{ij} \right)/n \qquad (1)$$

where n is the number agents who know j and R_{ij} is the value of j's reputation in the eyes of i. In the case of being known in several communities, the average of the values R_j will be calculated. Then, the User Agent j presents this reputation value (in a way similar to that in which a person presents his/her curriculum vitae when s/he wishes to join a company) to the Manager Agent of the community to which it is "applying". This mechanism is similar to the "word-of-mouth" propagation of information for a human [13]. We do realize that reputation is clearly a context-dependent quantity. For instance, one's reputation as a computer scientist should have no influence upon one's reputation as cook [14]. However, if we are trying to emulate the behavior of people working in communities of practice then we should emulate how some people's opinions influence others.

If any of the User Agents in the new community knows the person who wishes to join the community then his/her initial reputation value will be the average of the R_{ij} of agents who knows him/her.

R_{ij} is the value of reputation of j in the eyes of i. This value is computed as follows:

$$R_{ij} = w_e * E_j + w_p * P_j + w_i * I_j + \left(\sum_{j=1}^{n} QC_{ij} \right)/n \qquad (2)$$

where E_j is the value of expertise which is calculated according to the degree of experience that the person upon whose behalf the agent acts has in a domain.

P_j is the value assigned to a person's position. This position is defined in the agent's internal model of the reactive architecture described in Section 2.1.

I_j is the value assigned to intuition which is calculated by comparing each user's profile. For instance, users with similar profiles (preferences) could interact more times. Intuition is an important component both in the deliberative and in the social architecture because it helps agents to create their beliefs and behavior according to their own features.

In addition, previous experience should also be calculated. We suppose that when an agent A consults information from another agent B, the agent A should evaluate how useful this information was. This value is called QC_{ij} (Quality of j's Contribution according to the Agent i). To attain the average value of an agent's contribution, we calculate the sum of all the values assigned to these contributions by the Agent i, for instance n and we divide it by the number of evaluations (n).

Finally, w_e, w_p and w_i are weights with which the Reputation value can be adjusted to the needs of the organizations or communities. These weights represent different values depending on the category of each employee. For instance, if an enterprise considers that all its employees have the same category, then w_p=0. The same could occur when the organization does not take its employee's intuitions or expertise into account.

In this way, an agent can obtain a value related to the reputation of another agent and decide to what degree it is going to consider the importance of the information obtained from this agent. Formulas (1) and (2) are processed in the social and deliberative architecture respectively.

4 Related Work

This research can be compared with other proposals that use agents and trust in knowledge exchange. For instance, in [13], the authors propose a model that allows agents to decide which agents' opinions they trust more and propose a protocol based on recommendations. This model is based on a reputation or word-of-mouth mechanism. The main problem with this approach is that every agent must keep rather complex data structures which represent a kind of global knowledge about the whole network. In [15], the authors propose a framework for exchanging knowledge in a mobile environment. They use delegate agents to be spread out into the network of a mobile community and use trust information to serve as the virtual presence of a mobile user. Another interesting work is [14] where the authors describe a trust and reputation mechanism which allows peers to discover partners who meet their individual requirements through individual experience and by sharing experiences with other peers with similar preferences. This work is focused on peer-to-peer environments.

Barber and Kim present a multi-agent belief revision algorithm based on belief networks [9]. In their model the agent is able to evaluate incoming information, to generate a consistent knowledge base, and to avoid fraudulent information from unreliable or deceptive information sources or agents. In our case, the focus is very different since it is the receiver who evaluates the relevance of a piece of knowledge rather than the provider as in Barber and Kim's proposal.

Therefore, the main difference between our work and previous works is that we take into account factors that might influence the level of trust that a person has in a piece of knowledge and in a knowledge source. Moreover, we present a general and fairly simple formula to define the reputation concept. This formula can be adapted to different settings by modifying the value of the weights. This is an important difference from other works which are focused on particular domains.

Acknowledgements

This work is partially supported by the ENIGMAS (PIB-05-058), and MECENAS (PBI06-0024) project. It is also supported by the ESFINGE project (TIN2006-15175-C05-05) Ministerio de Educación y Ciencia (Dirección General de Investigación)/ Fondos Europeos de Desarrollo Regional (FEDER) in Spain.

References

1. Kautz, H.a.: Knowledge Mapping: A Technique for Identifying Knowledge Flows in SoftWare Organizations. EuroSPI (2004)
2. Gebert, H., Geib, M., Kolbe, L.M., Brenner.: Knowledge-enabled Customer Relationship Management - Integrating Customer Relationship Management and Knowledge Management Concepts. Journal of Knowledge Management 8(1) (2004)
3. Malhotra, Y.: Knowledge Management and Virtual Organizations. Book Crafters, Hershey (2000)
4. Hillery, G.A.: Definitions of Community: Areas of Agreement. Rural Sociology 20, 118–125 (1955)
5. Geib, M., Braun, C., Kolbe, L., Brenner, W.: Measuring the Utilization of Collaboration Technology for Knowledge Development and Exchange in Virtual Communities. In: Geib, M. (ed.) 37th Hawaii International Conference on System Sciences 2004 (HICSS-37), Big Island, Hawaii, IEEE Computer Society, Los Alamitos (2004)
6. Wenger, E., McDermott, R., Snyder, W.M.: Cultivating communities of practice: a guide to managing knowledge. H.B.S. Press, Boston (2002)
7. Wooldridge, M., Ciancarini, P.: Agent-Oriented Software Engineering: The State of the Art. In: Okamoto, E., Pieprzyk, J.P., Seberry, J. (eds.) ISW 2000. LNCS, vol. 1975, Springer, Heidelberg (2000)
8. Fuentes, R., Gómez-Sanz, J., Pavón, J.: A Social Framework for Multi-agent Systems Validation and Verification. In: Wang, S., Tanaka, K., Zhou, S., Ling, T.-W., Guan, J., Yang, D.-q., Grandi, F., Mangina, E.E., Song, I.-Y., Mayr, H.C. (eds.) ER Workshops 2004. LNCS, vol. 3289, pp. 458–469. Springer, Heidelberg (2004)
9. Barber, K., Kim, J.: Belief Revision Process Based on Trust: Simulation Experiments. In: 4th Workshop on Deception, Fraud and Trust in Agent Societies, Montreal Canada (2004)
10. Ushida, H., Hirayama, Y., Nakajima, H.: Emotion Model for Life like Agent and its Evaluation. In: Proceedings of the Fifteenth National Conference on Artificial Intelligence and Tenth Innovative Applications of Artificial Intelligence Conference (AAAI'98 / IAAI'98), Madison, Wisconsin, USA (1998)
11. Wasserman, S., Glaskiewics, J.: Advances in Social Networks Analysis. Sage Publications, Thousand Oaks (1994)
12. Mui, L., Halberstadt, A., Mohtashemi, M.: Notions of Reputation in Multi-Agents Systems: A Review. In: Alonso, E., Kudenko, D., Kazakov, D. (eds.) Adaptive Agents and Multi-Agent Systems. LNCS (LNAI), vol. 2636, pp. 280–287. Springer, Heidelberg (2003)
13. Abdul-Rahman, A., Hailes, S.: Supporting Trust in Virtual Communities. In: Abdul-Rahman, A., Hailes, S. (eds.) 33rd Hawaii International Conference on Systems Sciences (HICSS'00) (2000)
14. Wang, Y., Vassileva, J.: Trust and Reputation Model in Peer-to-Peer Networks. In: Proceedings of IEEE Conference on P2P Computing, IEEE Computer Society Press, Los Alamitos (2003)
15. Schulz, S., Herrmann, K., Kalcklosch, R., Schowotzer, T.: Trust-Based Agent -Mediated Knowledge Exchange for Ubiquitous Peer Networks. In: van Elst, L., Dignum, V., Abecker, A. (eds.) AMKM 2003. LNCS (LNAI), vol. 2926, pp. 89–106. Springer, Heidelberg (2004)

Leveraging Visual Tailoring and Synchronous Awareness in Web-Based Collaborative Systems

Mohamed Bourimi, Stephan Lukosch, and Falk Kühnel

FernUniversität in Hagen
Department for Mathematics and Computer Science
58084 Hagen, Germany
{mohamed.bourimi,stephan.lukosch,falk.kuehnel}@fernuni-hagen.de

Abstract. Web-based cooperative systems hardly use approved user interface concepts for the design of interactive systems and thereby aggravate the interaction of the users with the system and also with each other. In this article, we describe how the flexibility and usability of such systems can particularly be improved by supporting direct manipulation techniques for navigation as well as tailoring. The new functionality for tailoring and navigation is complemented by new forms of visualizing synchronous awareness information in web-based systems. We show this exemplarily by retrofitting the web-based collaborative system CURE. However, the necessary concepts can easily be transferred to other web-based systems.

1 Introduction

Web-based applications become more and more important and are used in different kinds of institutions and organizations. Google's initiative to make various applications, i.e. for communication, spreadsheets, and shared text editing, accessible by standard web browsers, represents a demonstrative proof of the importance of this observation. Google uses new standardized *Web 2.0* technologies such as *AJAX*, web services, or subscription services (like *RSS*) to overcome the drawbacks of existing web technologies and to implement more interactive and intelligent graphical user interfaces.

These technologies are often referred to as *Rich Internet Technologies (RITs)* and web applications using these technologies are often called *Rich Internet Applications (RIAs)* [1]. RIA solutions support visual direct manipulations [2] [3]. By using direct manipulation techniques, the number of necessary interaction steps for complex interaction scenarios can be considerably reduced. Today, many companies put a lot of effort in developing and establishing software standards in the area of the web-based applications [4]. This is an indicator for the future development of web-based applications, which still do not fully exploit their potential due to the limitations of the current HTTP standard [5].

An important category of web-based applications is represented by web-based collaborative systems, e.g. web-based learning platforms and environments. Such systems are characterized by complex scenarios supporting collaboration and

J.M. Haake, S.F. Ochoa, and A. Cechich (Eds.): CRIWG 2007, LNCS 4715, pp. 40–55, 2007.

cooperation in the respective domain. Often, this complexity is also reflected in the user interfaces. As result, the flexibility and usability of these user interfaces becomes even more important to optimally support the collaborating users. To achieve this flexibility, such systems often provide the end-users with tailoring functionalities and facilities.

To show the feasibility of our approach, we used the web-based collaborative system CURE [6]. CURE is used for collaborative work and learning. Typical collaborative learning scenarios are collaborative exercises, tutor-guided groups, virtual seminars, or virtual labs. When considering collaborative work typical use cases include group formation, group communication, document sharing, collaborative writing, collaborative task management etc. These scenarios have different requirements concerning the structure and functionality of the collaborative workspace. For that reason, CURE supports different tailoring levels, i.e. tailoring at the content, structural, and functional level [7]. The offered tailoring functionalities allow end-users to adapt the shared workspace to their needs.

Since 2003, CURE is successfully used in the above collaborative scenarios. However, our experiences show that end-users have problems in tailoring the shared workspace and that these problems stem from the usability of the web interface. Grudin's challenges for groupware developers [8] suggest that adding new functionality to an accepted application is more adequate than developing a new application. Compared to a completely new application, adding new functionality does not risk the acceptance of an application. Taking this into account, we decided to retrofit and extend CURE with support for visual tailoring and synchronous awareness while keeping the existing successful functionality.

In our opinion, tailoring as key design requirement for software systems [9] and for collaborative systems [10] [11] can benefit from the use of graphical manipulation possibilities. To support this adequately, a particularly intuitive form of the user interface is required as it can be achieved by supporting direct manipulation [3]. From our point of view, visual tailoring support in combination with synchronous awareness increases the end-users' productivity and motivates them to adapt the collaborative system to their needs as well as to support them efficiently. To validate this, we have extended CURE to support well-known user interface concepts which support visual tailoring by direct manipulation.

In the following, we first describe the essential concepts and features of the CURE system, before we analyze the requirements for a visual tailoring support in CURE by using a realistic scenario. Then, we will present our approach to meet these requirements and compare it to the current state of the art. We will conclude our paper with some first experiences and an outlook on future work directions.

2   CURE in a Nutshell

CURE [7] is a web-based collaboration space. It is based on the metaphor of virtual rooms, i.e. CURE uses the room as a representation of a virtual place for collaboration. Room metaphors [12] have been widely used to structure collaboration.

Figure 1 shows the abstractions that are offered by CURE. Users enter the collaborative learning environment via a virtual entry room named 'Hall'. Rooms can contain further sub-rooms, content in the form of so called pages, communication channels (e.g. chat, threaded mail) and users. The concept of virtual keys [13] is used to express the access rights a user holds for a certain room and the content of this room. Each key distinguishes three different classes of rights: key-rights defining what the user can do with the key, room-rights defining whether or not a user can enter a room or change the room structure, and interaction-rights specifying what the user can do in the room. Rooms with public keys are accessible by all registered users of the system.

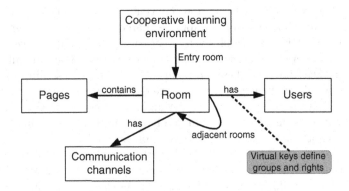

Fig. 1. CURE abstractions

When users enter a room, they can participate in collaborative activities and access the room's communication channels, i.e. by using the chat that is automatically established between all users in a room. They can also view the pages that are contained in the room. Users possessing suitable keys can freely edit the content of pages, with the changes being visible to all members in the room after uploading. Earlier versions of a page remain accessible to allow tracing of recent changes and support conflict resolution when multiple users have concurrently edited a page [14]. Pages may either be directly edited using a simple Wiki-like syntax, or they may contain binary documents, e.g. JPEG images, Microsoft Word documents etc. In particular, the syntax supports links to other pages, other rooms, external URLs or mail addresses. The server stores all artifacts to support collaborative access. Thus, when users leave the room, the content stays available, allowing them to come back later and continue their work on the room's pages. However, this implies that the CURE platform as such requires the user to be connected to the Internet to access content stored on the CURE server.

For user coordination, CURE supports various types of awareness information. A list of users with access to the room is available in the room's properties. Small images represent those users currently present in the room. If the chat is enabled in the room, users can directly start chatting to each other. Users can trace who has previously edited the current page. Finally, daily reports automatically posted to all users of a room include all changes made since the last report was sent.

3   Problem and Requirements Analysis

In this section, we will determine the requirements for effectively supporting end-users when tailoring their shared workspace. For that purpose, we will describe a realistic use case scenario in CURE. Additionally, we will refer to user feedback and log data which protocols the user activities over the last years when using CURE.

In the summer semester 2006, 120 students participated in cooperative exercises for the operating systems course. The cooperative exercises where held in CURE. From all participating students, 38 groups with 3 to 4 members were formed. Every group had its own sub-room beneath the global course room in CURE. To organize the different exercises, again one sub-room for each exercise was created in the group's room. Thereby, the teachers could prepare the exercises before releasing them with the help of different key configurations. The keys were timely restricted and controlled the interaction in the rooms, e.g. by limiting editing and communication rights until the submission date. Considering the necessary tailoring activities on the structural level, it is desirable to create rooms and add contents to these rooms in a efficient way. This requires a fast navigation between these rooms to avoid repeating intermediate steps, but currently the navigation and interaction in web-based systems is often difficult due to the used technologies [5]. The evaluation of the log data about the user activities in CURE showed that more than half of the user activities are read and navigation requests. Similar observations have been made in other systems such as BSCW [15]. Thus, if users are not adequately supported when navigating in their shared workspace, structuring these workspaces and adding content can become difficult and the following requirement has to be met:

R1: Support efficient navigation.

Since CURE is a Wiki system, content is mostly created by interlinking artifacts in the Wiki text. This presupposes that the entered links refer to rooms and pages which exist and are syntactically correct. CURE offers a link assistant for this purpose, but this assistant requires several interaction steps in case of incorrect inputs. Compared to the link specification, the configuration of the virtual keys for the room access rights is a similar use case in CURE. A web-based workflow guides users while allocating and assigning keys to other users. However, this workflow requires several interaction steps. With the help of direct manipulation techniques [2] [3] users could drag&drop a link to the desired position in the Wiki text or could execute artifact-dependent actions with the help of a context menu, e.g. creating, moving or deleting pages and rooms. Similarly, the configuration and assignment of virtual keys could be speed up. This leads to the following requirement:

R2: Support direct manipulation for user guidance and tailoring at the structural, functional, and content level.

During tailoring activities in web-based collaborative environments, end-users often miss a global overview about the shared workspace and the shared artifacts. In the case of CURE, this can be observed when users create new rooms. CURE informs users about the successful creation of the new room, but the log data shows that users still check on their own if the room creation was successful by accessing the room directory. By providing workspace and social awareness [16] [17], a user's perception of own activities and other users' activities can be improved and the interaction with the shared workspace becomes more efficient. Furthermore, direct manipulation can lead to an increased number of tailoring activities which might be conflicting. Again, group awareness can help to reduce the number of possible conflicts. Thus, the following requirement must be fulfilled:

R3: Support synchronous workspace and social awareness.

Studies have shown, that users permanently use only a subset of a system functionality in certain tasks [18]. While most systems make the whole functionality available in their user interface all the time, users often only want to see the artifacts on which they are currently working or those functionalities which they currently need. Thus, users want to have control about the user interface configuration, e.g. screen space, [19] [20] and the following requirement emerges:

R4: Allow users to adapt the user interface to fulfill their current requirements.

Users of web-based collaborative systems are often distributed geographically and work with different system configurations, i.e. different computers, operating systems etc. Frequently, users access web-based collaborative system from computers on which they are not allowed to install additional software. Therefore, the following requirement is to be fulfilled:

R5: Avoid the installation of additional client software and guarantee of the compatibility with standard web browsers without using proprietary technologies.

At the first glance, adding new functionality and enhanced interaction possibilities to existing systems seems attractive. However, adding new functionality often requires to add and modify a lot of source code. This often complicates the API and affords a redesign of the domain model [21]. Thus, an adequate approach which considers these implications and side effects of such an extension has to be used:

R6: Add the new functionalities and retrofit the collaborative system with minimal development costs.

4   Approach

Our requirements R1-R6 can be split into *functional requirements* (R1-R4) and *system requirements* (R5 and R6). In the following, we will first present how we met the functional requirements (R1-R4) by extending the CURE user interface with well-known and approved concepts which enable end-users to interact and tailor the shared workspace with the visual manipulations. After that we describe how our retrofitting approach and the resulting system architecture fulfill the system requirements (R5 and R6).

4.1   Efficient Navigation (R1)

To efficiently support the users' navigation, we integrated the room directory window as a permanent part of the CURE user interface (see Figure 2). This window contains a tree presentation of the artifacts (Figure 2 A) which the local user can access. Since CURE is a hierarchical system, the tree metaphor is particularly suitable for the representation of the rooms (nodes) and pages (leafs). This metaphor is well-known and successfully used in other collaborative systems like Dolphin [22] or BSCW [23]. Additionally, the room directory allows users to search for rooms and pages by means of the search function. By entering a search text in the search field (Figure 2 B) the user's room directory is filtered and shows only those entries matching the search text. The artifacts in the room directory as well as chat discussions can be opened in separate tabs (Figure 2 C and 2 D). Thereby, the access to often needed artifacts is improved and room-related or private chat discussion becomes possible. Consequently, the navigation in the system is efficiently supported, thereby fulfilling **R1**.

4.2   Support Direct Manipulation for Visual Tailoring (R2)

For tailoring, each artifact in the room tree offers a static context menu which provides various options, e.g. generating a link to a room, adding a sub-room, or adding a page (Figure 2 E). Obviously, the room tree presentation optimally supports visual tailoring by direct manipulation techniques. A generated link can be dragged and dropped directly to the right position of a Wiki page which is opened for editing in a separate tab. Rooms or pages can be moved directly into other rooms with the help of drag&drop manipulations. Dragging and dropping a room onto another room is the same as moving the room. The above examples show that the semantics of direct manipulations depend on the involved artifacts.

As another example for direct manipulation consider Figure 3. It shows how the key management is supported in CURE by using direct manipulation techniques. Assigning keys to individual users can be considered as tailoring at a

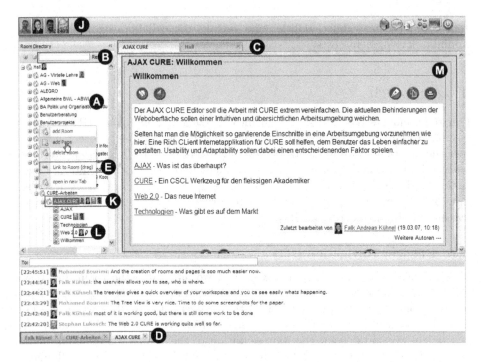

Fig. 2. Visual tailoring in CURE

structural and functional level. By direct manipulation, key assignments are more flexible than with the web-based workflow over several different pages. The room information window summarizes the properties of a room (Figure 3 F). The lower part of this window shows the current users of the room and their key configurations. An additional key manager window allows to find users with a search function (Figure 3 G). These users can be added to a list of selected users (Figure 3 H) which are assigned prepared key configurations (Figure 3 I). Furthermore, available keys and key configurations can be reused from the room information window by dragging and dropping them into the key manager window. The above examples show how well-known user interface concepts can support visual tailoring in web-based shared workspaces and how we fulfilled **R2**.

4.3 Synchronous Workspace and Social Awareness (R3)

To provide synchronous workspace and social awareness **R3**, we visualize different information in the user interface. The global presence indicator shows who else is currently working in CURE (Figure 2 J). If not all users can be visualized, the users are summarized in a user list which can be accessed by a special icon. In addition, the room tree shows which shared artifacts the other users are currently working on in the collaborative system (Figure 2 K). Since

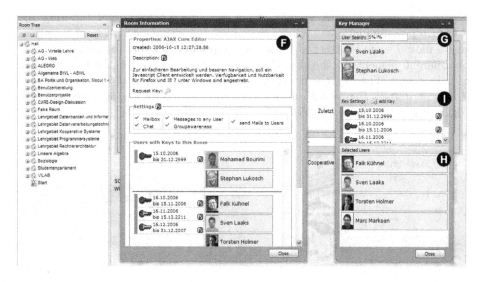

Fig. 3. Visual key management in CURE

a user can work on different artifacts simultaneously, a user's picture can appear next to several different rooms and pages at the same time. Furthermore, the presence indicator, i.e. a user's picture, sometimes reflects a specific action, e.g. a pen is shown next to the user's picture when the user is editing a page in CURE (Figure 2 L). We believe that such awareness information which were also already used in systems like Dolphin [22] helps to avoid potential conflicts.

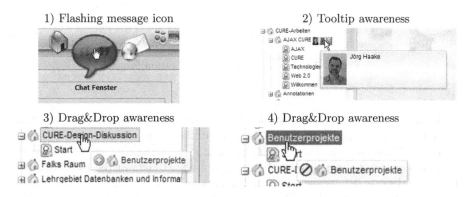

Fig. 4. Sample awareness indicators

Figure 4 shows further examples for synchronous awareness. In Figure 4.1, a message icon which is normally colored yellow flashes in red to inform the local user about incoming messages. Figure 4.2 shows artifact-related tooltips.

Figure 4.3 and 4.4 show specific awareness support for visual tailoring by drag&drop manipulations. In these examples, the visual element used to represent a moved room is attached to the mouse pointer. Moving the mouse pointer on different elements in the shared workspace triggers a proxy for the dragged visual element. Thereby, the proxy can indicate if the intended direct manipulation is permitted. Figure 4.3 shows the green plus icon for the positive case and Figure 4.4 shows the red forbidden icon.

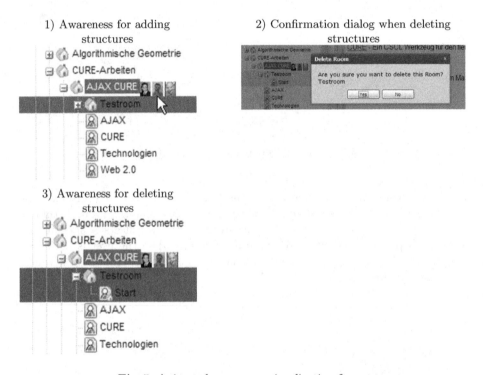

Fig. 5. Animated awareness visualization forms

As the shared workspace is subject of continuous parallel changes, the user must be informed in adequate manner about the changes performed by other users. Therefore, we integrated additional animated awareness widgets. These are visualized for each user viewing the manipulated artifacts in the room tree (cf. Figure 5). Figure 5.1 shows how added structures are highlighted in green in the room tree. The green color fades away continuously and disappears after some seconds. Before a room is deleted, a modal dialog is shown to the user performing the deletion, cf. Figure 5.2. In the background of the modal dialog, the structure that is about to be deleted is highlighted in yellow, until a confirmation or cancel button is clicked. Upon confirmation, the deleted room structure is highlighted in red which fades away after some seconds for all users, cf. Figure 5.3.

4.4   User Interface Adaptability (R4)

In order to allow users to adapt the user interface to their current needs, we added several configuration possibilities. Users can, e.g., adapt the screen space by hiding the room directory or the chat-based communication area. All windows can be resized. Furthermore, decoupling these windows from the border layout is possible, i.e. users can freely place the decoupled windows in their screen space. Many other useful settings, i.e. width and size of the different windows, collapsed or expanded items, coordinates of decoupled windows, opened pages in separate tabs etc., are stored after each session and restored when users return to the shared workspace. As this enables users to adapt their screen space and user interface to their needs, **R4** is fulfilled.

4.5   Retrofitting Approach and System Architecture (R5 and R6)

In the previous sections, we showed how we addressed the functional requirements (R1-R4) by extending the functionality of the user interface. These extensions are only possible with system support for refreshing, flashing, and animating specific parts of the user interface. For that purpose, the system has to support efficient and dynamic content generation mechanisms in order to avoid continuous and inefficient reloading of the user interface with each client request. To fulfil **R5** and thus avoid the installation of additional client software, we use a combination of AJAX technology and web services to update individual parts of the user interface and enable direct manipulation. The web services are used to process client requests at the server-side. We use AJAX to asynchronously send and receive XML data at the client-side. Additionally, we use AJAX-based libraries and frameworks for the user interface extensions at the client-side. These libraries and frameworks are widely accepted and supported by standard web browsers such that **R5** is fulfilled.

To support AJAX components at the client-side, we retrofitted CURE by using aspect-orientated programming (AOP). AOP empowers developers to modularize cross cutting concerns like authentication and logging into separate classes expressing those aspects [24]. This occurs with the help of mechanisms that permit intercepting and trapping events such as method calls at the application level. In AOP, the application execution flow can be modified for instance to execute additional or alternative code before, during or after as well as in place of method calls. Such points in the system are called joint points or point-cuts. Thereby, AOP allows to retrofit an application to support new functionality without changing the existing codebase. Compared to object-oriented or component-based approaches, AOP offers a higher grade of independency from the existing codebase and the result of an aspect-oriented retrofitting are separate (secondary) classes decoupled from the existing codebase.

Though retrofitting an existing collaborative system using AOP has a minimal impact on its codebase, several issues such as the application domain, composition of end-users' community, used technologies, developers' competencies have to be considered. To consider these issues, an analysis and design phase must take place. In our case, this design and analysis phase revealed the need to improve the usability of the user interface and to enhance communication and awareness functionalities. While adding new (secondary) functionality to existing ones is preferable than implementing a new system [8], we decided to use AJAX and a separate instant messaging system to accomplish this.

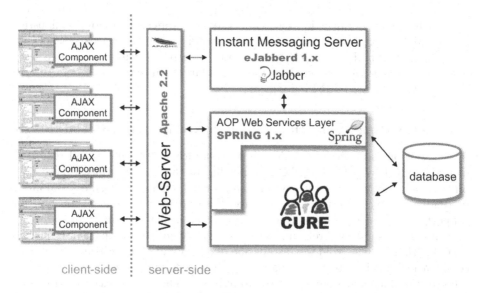

Fig. 6. System architecture of the retrofitted CURE system

Figure 6 shows the major components of the system architecture as a block diagram. The arrows indicate data transfer and the direction of the communication. Since the retrofitted CURE is still a web application, end-users can access it via their web browser. We used AOP in CURE to add a thin layer on top of the CURE codebase (cf. Figure 6). Thereby, the AOP layer handles the AJAX requests from the client. The AJAX components communicate with CURE via the web services in the AOP layer. For the integration of the AOP layer we used the Java-based Spring framework [25], as CURE is also implemented in Java. However, an aspect compiler could be used to generate binary code for web-based collaborative systems that are implemented using other programming languages.

The main task of the eJabberd instant messaging system [26] is to extend the communication and awareness functionality of CURE. In addition to global and private chat rooms, we create an eJabberd chat room that is hidden from the users for each CURE room. We use these hidden rooms to distribute update notifications for the AJAX components at the client-side. These notifications follow an XML schema which, e.g., indicates the manipulated artifact, the type (e.g. create, delete, update), timestamp and the originator of the manipulation etc. This information is processed by the AJAX components for actualizing the awareness information. Both, communication with eJabberd and the web services are offered via an Apache web server. We consider the AOP layer as thin layer, as adding it did not require to change the CURE domain model. Instead of changing the domain model, the AOP layer allows to access the model via clearly defined interfaces. Similarly, the integration of a separate eJabberd server can be done with minimal efforts. Thereby, we fulfil **R6**.

5 Related Work

User interface technology has advanced from command line interfaces to the established and approved use of direct manipulation or WIMP (windows, icons, menus and pointing) [2]. Existing web-based cooperative systems offer a wide variety of user interfaces. New technologies like AJAX or Flash are rarely used to improve graphical or visual support for cooperative tailoring.

The success of well-known and established Internet communities like *MySpace* [27] or *Yahoo!Groups* [28] is partially a result of their support for end-user tailoring. However, most of the web-based communities do still not support direct visual manipulations which is a pre-requisite for visual end-user tailoring.

So far, visual end-user tailoring has only been investigated on a groupware component-level [29] and we are not aware of a web-based cooperative system that fulfil the requirements R1 - R4. Applications like *Google Maps* [30], which e.g. allows to change the map view by direct manipulation, show the increasing importance of such manipulation techniques. However, most applications are designed for single users and not for collaborating users. Thus, they are not offering synchronous awareness support (R3).

Google Calendar [31] and *Google Docs* [32] are examples for web-based collaborative systems. They allow users to create and edit appointments, documents, and spreadsheets like in a normal desktop application without making use of standard web forms. *Apples .Mac* [33] and *Microsofts Live Mail* [34] try to recreate their own operating system based mail applications for the web. For that purpose, they support visual manipulations to edit and rearrange mails and folders. However, none of the mentioned applications supports synchronous awareness (R3) for enabling simultaneous manipulations in a shared workspace.

Proprietary browser extensions like *Netmite* [35] for Firefox or Peekko [36] try to create a group awareness by transforming the complete web to a meeting point. People visiting the same internet pages can see each other and get in contact via chat. Unfortunately, these extensions are strongly browser-dependent and need additional software (violating R5).

Finally, R6 strongly depends on the architecture of a collaborative system and is thus in the most cases difficult to verify. However, Cheng et al. [37] [21] introduced an aspect-oriented approach for retrofitting single-user applications to support collaboration. We applied and showed the feasibility of this approach in the context of collaborative applications to fulfil R6. Another approach for retrofitting collaborative system is based on components such as described by Gerosa et al. [38], Greenberg [39], Slagter and Biemans [40], and Won et al. [29]. The component-based approach requires an internal component-oriented architecture of the collaborative system. In most cases, e.g. in Gerosa et al. [38], this even implicates a re-factoring of the existing codebase before a component-based retrofitting can take place. This violates R6, as this often complicates the API and affords a redesign of the domain model.

Summarizing, none of the mentioned web-based collaborative systems fulfills our identified requirements. Our presented solution for support of visual tailoring in CURE is a vast improvement in comparison to those systems, since it allows the user to adapt CURE in a flexible way to his needs.

6   First Experiences

First experiences with the Web 2.0 user interface for CURE indicate that all our requirements are satisfied. Feedback from users with different background, i.e. expert as well as lay users from different departments at our university, indicates that the new interface improves the usability and is highly intuitive for navigating in and manipulating of the structural content.

By using AJAX components for the representation layer and a thin AOP layer to retrofit CURE, we reached a high degree of flexibility for developers as well as end-users. This enables us to support tailoring languages [11] at various levels and at the same time. As result, introducing different and simultaneous visual presentations and manipulation techniques at the presentation layer for an existing domain model becomes possible in a flexible way. For instance, the core CURE domain model does not support the key configurations. However, we added these to the presentation layer and integrated corresponding proxy classes in the AOP layer. When the corresponding proxy objects are modified, the changes are translated to calls to the core CURE domain model. Thereby, the old CURE user interface remains accessible all the time. This shows that our retrofitting approach represents a flexible possibility for migrating existing systems while keeping the old functionality.

Developers were satisfied with the retrofitting approach, since adding the new functionality had only little impact on the codebase of CURE and did not require expert knowledge of the CURE codebase. In our opinion, this shows that the aspect-oriented retrofitting allows to extend existing groupware with expert developers from other application domains, as these do not require expert knowledge about the retrofitted application anymore.

So far, we received almost only positive feedback and requests for additional functionality which implies a stronger usage of the existing system. Including standard user interface widgets allowed all users an easy transition to the new user interface, since most of the functionality was known from experience with standard single-user applications. From the added functionality, the room directory which allows to quickly navigate through the shared workspace and the possibility to adapt the screen space by temporarily hiding the room directory and chat-based communication area were especially appreciated.

Except from the positive feedback, we also received feedback that required additional improvements. Since it is now quite easy to delete rooms, users quickly requested the possibility to restore deleted rooms. Therefore, we introduced a designated trash room which contains deleted rooms for a specific period. Users with sufficient access rights in the deleted room are informed about the deletion and can restore the room within the given time period. For most of the users the supported drag&drop operations were quite intuitive. However, some users required additional explanations and therefore we will in future include small tutorial clips to explain the functionality.

7   Conclusions and Future Work

Feedback from users working with CURE and the analysis of the logged user activities have shown a great need for simplified methods of tailoring the shared workspace. The lack of usability led to less frequent usage of the system than actually required by the user.

In this article, we have presented how we extended CURE to leverage visual tailoring and synchronous awareness. We achieved this using new standardized Web 2.0 technologies. These technologies allowed us to add modern user interface functionality, like direct manipulation techniques, well-known concepts, such as the tree representation, and new forms of synchronous awareness to the CURE web client.

We envision that future web-based collaborative systems combine services of several different platforms to fulfill the current requirements of their users. Our aspect-oriented retrofitting approach has little impact on the codebase. It is based on the widely used and well-documented Java-based Spring framework [25]. This adds flexibility to integrate other established frameworks and the interoperability of CURE is increased due to the interface offered by the web services. Finally, this allows third-party developers to easily extend and re-use the functionality of CURE. Thus, our approach presents a first step to our vision of future web-based collaborative systems.

First experiences already show positive effects concerning user interaction and productivity. However, we plan to use and evaluate the new user interface of CURE in long-term collaborative activities such as lab courses or distributed research project. Hopefully, the results of such long-term evaluations and the additional user feedback will reveal new functional requirements. Due to our retrofitting approach, it will be simple for us to fulfill these requirements.

References

1. Jacobi, J., Fallows, J.: Pro JSF and AJAX: Building Rich Internet Components (Pro). Apress, Berkely, CA, USA (2006)
2. Maybury, M.T., Wahlster, W. (eds.): Readings in intelligent user interfaces. Morgan Kaufmann Publishers Inc., San Francisco (1998)
3. Shneiderman, B., Plaisant, C.: Designing the User Interface: Strategies for Effective Human-Computer Interaction, 4th edn. Pearson Addison Wesley (2004)
4. Ford, N.: Art of Java Web Development. Manning Publications Co. (2003)

5. Maurer, H.A.: Can WWW be successful? In: DS-8: Proceedings of the IFIP TC2/WG2.6 Eighth Working Conference on Database Semantics- Semantic Issues in Multimedia Systems, Deventer, The Netherlands, pp. 17–25. Kluwer, B.V, Dordrecht (1998)
6. Haake, J.M., Schümmer, T., Haake, A., Bourimi, M., Landgraf, B.: Supporting flexible collaborative distance learning in the cure platform. In: Proceedings of the Hawaii International Conference On System Sciences (HICSS-37), January 5-8, IEEE Computer Society Press, Los Alamitos (2004)
7. Haake, J.M., Schümmer, T., Haake, A., Bourimi, M., Landgraf, B.: Two-level tailoring support for cscl. In: Favela, J., Decouchant, D. (eds.) CRIWG 2003. LNCS, vol. 2806, pp. 74–82. Springer, Heidelberg (2003)
8. Grudin, J.: Groupware and social dynamics: eight challenges for developers. Communications of the ACM 37(1), 92–105 (1994)
9. Henderson, A.: Tailoring mechanisms in three research technologies. In: Workshop on Tailorable Groupware: Issues, Methods, and Architectures at the ACM Group'97 conference organized by Mørch, Anders; Stiemerling, Oliver; Wulf, Volker (1997)
10. Mørch, A., Stiemerling, O., Wulf, V.: Tailorable groupware: issues, methods, and architectures. SIGCHI Bull. 30(2), 40–42 (1998)
11. Wulf, V.: Let's see your search-tool! – collaborative use of tailored artifacts in groupware. In: Wulf, V. (ed.) GROUP '99: Proceedings of the international ACM SIGGROUP conference on Supporting group work, pp. 50–59. ACM Press, New York,NY, USA (1999)
12. Greenberg, S., Roseman, M.: Using a room metaphor to ease transitions in groupware. In: Ackermann, M., Pipek, V., Wulf, V. (eds.) Sharing Expertise: Beyond Knowledge Management, pp. 203–256. MIT Press, Cambridge,MA, USA (2003)
13. Haake, J.M., Haake, A., Schümmer, T., Bourimi, M., Landgraf, B.: End-user controlled group formation and access rights management in a shared workspace system. In: CSCW '04: Proceedings of the 2004 ACM conference on Computer supported cooperative work, Chicago, Illinois, USA, November 6-10, pp. 554–563. ACM Press, New York (2004)
14. Lukosch, S., Hellweg, M., Rasel, M.: CSCL, Anywhere and Anytime. In: Dimitriadis, Y.A., Zigurs, I., Gómez-Sánchez, E. (eds.) CRIWG 2006. LNCS, vol. 4154, pp. 326–340. Springer, Heidelberg (2006)
15. Appelt, W.: What groupware functionality do users really use? Analysis of the usage of the bscw system. In: Klöckner, K. (ed.) Ninth Euromicro Workshop on Parallel and Distributed Processing 2001, Mantova, Italy, pp. 337–343. IEEE Computer Society Press, Los Alamitos (2001)
16. Gross, T., Wirsam, W., Graether, W.: Awarenessmaps: visualizing awareness in shared workspaces. In: CHI '03: CHI '03 extended abstracts on Human factors in computing systems, pp. 784–785. ACM Press, New York, NY, USA (2003)
17. Gutwin, C.: Workspace Awareness in Real-Time Distributed Groupware. PhD thesis, The University of Calgary (1997)
18. McGrenere, J., Baecker, R.M., Booth, K.S.: An evaluation of a multiple interface design solution for bloated software. In: CHI '02: Proceedings of the SIGCHI conference on Human factors in computing systems, pp. 164–170. ACM Press, New York (2002)
19. Funke, D.J., Neal, J.G., Paul, R.D.: An approach to intelligent automated window management. International Journal of Man-Machine Studies 38(6), 949–983 (1993)
20. Kantorowitz, E., Sudarsky, O.: The adaptable user interface. Communications of the ACM 32(11), 1352–1358 (1989)

21. Cheng, L.T., Patterson, J., Rohall, S.L., Hupfer, S., Ross, S.: Weaving a social fabric into existing software. In: AOSD '05: Proceedings of the 4th international conference on Aspect-oriented software development, pp. 147–158. ACM Press, New York, USA, YK (2005)

22. Streitz, N.A., Geißler, J., Haake, J.M., Hol, J.: Dolphin: integrated meeting support across local and remote desktop environments and liveboards. In: CSCW '94: Proceedings of the 1994 ACM conference on Computer supported cooperative work, pp. 345–358. ACM Press, New York,NY, USA (1994)

23. Appelt, W., Mambrey, P.: Experiences with the BSCW shared workspace system as the backbone of a virtual learning environment for students. In: Proceedings of ED-MEDIA99 (1999)

24. Walls, C., Breidenbach, R.: Spring in Action. Manning Publications Co. (2005)

25. Spring Framework (June 2007), http://www.springframework.org/

26. EJabberd (June 2007), http://ejabberd.jabber.ru/

27. MySpace (June 2007), http://www.myspace.com/

28. Yahoo! Groups (June 2007), http://groups.yahoo.com/

29. Won, M., Maybury, M., Wulf, V.: Component-based approaches to tailorable systems. In: Lieberman, H., Paternó, F., Wulf, V. (eds.) End User Development, Springer-Verlag, pp. 127–153. Springer, Heidelberg (2006)

30. Google Maps (June 2007), http://maps.google.com

31. Google Calendar (June 2007), http://calendar.google.com

32. Google Docs. (June 2007), http://docs.google.com/

33. Apple.Mac. (June 2007), http://www.apple.com/dotmac/

34. Windows Live Ideas (June 2007), http://ideas.live.com/

35. Netmite (June 2007), http://www.netmite.com/

36. HomePage in Peeko Chat (June 2007), http://www.peekko.com

37. Cheng, L.T., Rohall, S.L., Patterson, J., Ross, S., Hupfer, S.: Retrofitting collaboration into UIs with aspects. In: CSCW '04: Proceedings of the 2004 ACM conference on Computer supported cooperative work. New York, NY, USA, pp. 25–28. ACM Press, New York (2004)

38. Gerosa, M.A., Pimentel, M.G., Fuks, H., de Lucena, C.J.P.: Development of groupware based on the 3C collaboration model and component technology. In: Dimitriadis, Y.A., Zigurs, I., Gómez-Sánchez, E. (eds.) CRIWG 2006. LNCS, vol. 4154, pp. 302–309. Springer, Heidelberg (2006)

39. Greenberg, S.: Toolkits and interface creativity. Multimedia Tools Applications 32(2), 139–159 (2007)

40. Slagter, R., Biemans, M.: Component groupware: A basis for tailorable solutions that can evolve with the supported task. In: ICSC Conference on Intelligent Systems and Application 2000 (2000)

Visualizing Shared-Knowledge Awareness in Collaborative Learning Processes

César A. Collazos[1], Luis A. Guerrero[2], Miguel A. Redondo[3], and Crescencio Bravo[3]

[1] IDIS Research Group, Systems Department, FIET, Universidad del Cauca, Colombia
ccollazo@unicauca.edu.co
[2] Department of Computer Science, Universidad de Chile, Chile
luguerre@dcc.uchile.cl
[3] Department of Information Systems and Technologies, School of Computer Engineering,
Universidad de Castilla-La Mancha, España
Miguel.Redondo@uclm.es, Crescencio.Bravo@uclm.es

Abstract. SKA (Shared-Knowledge Awareness) refers to the perception about the shared knowledge students have while working in a collaborative learning context. If we understand the shared comprehension of the problem to be solved as a key part of any collaborative learning activity, SKA will be an indispensable aspect to take into account when designing CSCL systems. In this paper, we propose some design guidelines that can help in the process of graphical user interface design for CSCL tools. We have evaluated some CSCL tools according to the proposed design guidelines depicting how these recommendations materialize in the graphical user interface of some CSCL tools.

1 Introduction

In a previous work, Collazos et al. have defined a new type of awareness for groupware systems called Shared-Knowledge Awareness or SKA [5]. SKA corresponds to the perception about the shared knowledge students have in a collaborative learning scenario. In this paper, we are going to present some mechanisms to visualize this kind of awareness in a Computer-Supported Collaborative Learning (CSCL) scenario. In CSCL scenarios, collaborative learning is effective if people succeed in building and maintaining a shared understanding of the problem [8]. For this reason, the shared understanding should be represented and promoted. We are recently working in trying to capture this shared understanding into an awareness mechanism. One of our hypothesis states that this shared understanding could be promoted if people are aware of its current performance during the collaborative activity, i.e., the individual accountability [21] is clear for each member in the context of the group work.

Information visualization that corresponds to the process of analyzing and transforming non-spatial data into an effective visual form is believed to improve our interaction with huge volumes of data [4, 22]. One central point of any successful

J.M. Haake, S.F. Ochoa, and A. Cechich (Eds.): CRIWG 2007, LNCS 4715, pp. 56–71, 2007.

visualization mechanism is the exploration possibility of visual perception principles. These kinds of visualizations could help an increasingly diverse and potentially non-technical community to gain overviews about general patterns and trends and to discover hidden –semantic semantic– structures. Besides, complex visualizations of different viewpoints of thousands of data objects can greatly benefit from storytelling [10]. One of our goals in this work is the use of techniques such as visual perception, story telling, and artistic aspects of visualization design, to visualize the shared-knowledge awareness. This paper describes a set of recommendations we propose in order to provide SKA visualization mechanisms in a CSCL application and shows how these recommendations materialize in the graphical user interface of some CSCL tools.

The paper is organized as follows. Section 2 describes the principal idea of SKA. Section 3 describes some design guidelines based on some questions that are necessary to ask in order to determine the presence/absence of SKA. Section 4 depicts some software tools we have evaluated according to the proposed design guidelines. In Section 5 we discuss some of the benefits of the model proposed and finally some conclusions and further work are described in Section 6.

2   Shared-Knowledge Awareness

SKA is consciousness on the shared knowledge of a group of students that carry out a collaborative learning activity. The shared knowledge is composed of the understanding of several aspects of the collaborative work, including coordination of the activities, communication of the group strategy, monitoring of the process, and the shared comprehension of the problem [5].

In a collaborative situation, every group member has his/her own individual knowledge of the problem to be solved. Part of this individual knowledge is shared by the group. However, in order to improve the collaboration process among group members, it is necessary to define mechanisms to support discussions and so, to acquire a consensus about the shared understanding of the problem. Thus, a good strategy is to enlarge the shared knowledge, because as Dillenbourg mentions, it contributes to an effective collaborative learning process [8].

In order to create this shared knowledge it is necessary to wonder how one may become aware of one's own knowledge and how the actions people do affect the knowledge of the other members within the group. We need mechanisms for self-controlling and self-monitoring the learning process. If a student is aware of his/her own knowledge and his/her teammate's knowledge, he/she can make well-founded strategic decisions. These strategic decisions are meta-cognitive decisions when they are explicit and they are communicated to the team members in order to reason on past or future actions. Such reasoning is precisely required by the negotiation involved when the learners wish to agree on decisions [7]. According to Borges and Pino, awareness mechanisms become crucial for group interactions [1]. If people are aware of what is happening around them through social, task, workspace, conceptual and shared knowledge, it is possible to promote interactions among the members of the group. According to Dillenbourg, this increment in the members' interactions could trigger learning mechanisms [8]. Every member of the group should have awareness of what the others are doing and where they are. They should also receive information about any new viewpoint concerning problem solving (e.g., if one of the participants makes a mistake). There will be a sustained communication among participants in order to share a study of the problem and to interchange solution strategies. Therefore, communicated persons are helping to make strategic decisions and change the participants' knowledge about the problem.

When a member of the group expresses his/her opinion in relation to the shared (and public) knowledge, this will be an attempt to synchronize his/her own understanding with the group-accepted version and make the disagreements clear if there are any. Depending on the outcome of this process, there may be further interactions and negotiations until a new meaning or shared understanding is fully accepted by the group. The key aspects of co-construction of knowledge, meaning, and understanding lie on this process interaction among individuals as well as on their shared and individual cognition [15].

3 The Proposed Model

In order to be aware of the shared knowledge in a collaborative activity we propose a set of questions. For constructing this shared knowledge it is necessary to wonder how one may become aware of one's own knowledge and, how the actions people do affect the knowledge of the other members within the group. It is self-control and self-monitoring of the learning process. We propose per every question a set of SKA design guidelines. These guidelines will be denoted by $Q_{i,j}$, where i denotes the number of the question and j denotes the specific design guideline for that question. Each of the questions we have proposed are based on some of the Gutwin's elements of knowledge contained within a "who, what and where" category of questions asked about workspace events in the present [11].

Question 1: What are the other members of the group doing to complete the task?
In a collaborative activity, every member of the group has a predefined task. Two levels of accountability must be structured into collaborative activities. The group must be accountable for achieving its goals and each member must be accountable for contributing his or her share of the work. Individual accountability exists when the performance of each individual is assessed and the results are given back to the group and the individual in order to ascertain who needs more assistance, support, and encouragement in learning. The purpose of collaborative learning groups is to make each member a stronger individual in his or her own right. Students learn together so that they subsequently can gain greater individual competency [13]. Thus, we propose the following design guidelines:

- Explicit sensor of task advance ($Q_{1,1}$): to include a mechanism that permits members or the group to know the task evolution.

- Explicit sensor of others' collaboration performance ($Q_{1,2}$): to include a mechanism that allows visualizing contributions the group members have made in order to complete the task in an appropriate way. There are mechanisms developed for providing information about the level of participation in a work group. Collaborative work requires people to participate in other member's activities. It is not desirable that any members perform their tasks with little or no concern about what is going on. Therefore, some level of watching is encouraged. For instance, during a group discussion the coordinator and facilitators receive information about the level of participation of the group members and the evolution in the discussion of ideas. The *participameter* and the *contributionmeter* are examples of such artefacts [1].

Question 2: Are the tasks done by others helping to solve the problem?

In order to be effective in a collaborative activity it is not only important to execute the task but the other members of the group execute their task in an improved way. Thus, it is important for people to do the task according to some criteria that allow the achievement of the proposed goals. The following design guideline is considered:

- Explicit sensor of others' collaboration performance ($Q_{2,1}$).

Question 3: What do other members know about the topic? What do other members need to know about the topic?

There are important cognitive activities and interpersonal dynamics that can only occur when students promote each other's learning. This includes orally explaining of how to solve problems, teaching one's knowledge to others, checking for understanding, discussing concepts being learned, and connecting present with past learning. Each of those activities can be structured into group task directions and procedures. Doing these tasks help to ensure that collaborative learning groups have both an academic support system (every student has someone who is committed to helping him or her to learn) and a personal support system (every student has someone who is committed to him or her as a person) [13]. Mechanisms as conceptual maps or storytelling can be used to support these aspects. It is widely accepted that concept maps can help students to effectively externalize their knowledge in a domain, and evoke and support meta-cognitive activities [16]. Conceptual mapping has been one of the most referenced in the literature [24]. Moreover, the use of concept maps seems to be useful in supporting knowledge management, which is a very important concern in societies rapidly expanding their knowledge resources. This question includes the following design guidelines:

- Explicit sensor of task advance ($Q_{3,1}$)
- Representation of received information ($Q_{3,2}$)
- Mechanism for classifying received information ($Q_{3,3}$)
- Others' user profiles (only if the profile defines part of the topic, i.e., if the profile denotes specific characteristics of the task executed by the group member) ($Q_{3,4}$)

Question 4: How can I help other students to complete the task?

In a collaborative activity, it is assumed that each of the group members is self-interested. That is, each member has his/her own preferences and desires about how the world should be better. We could represent a member's preferences by means of utility functions which assign an indicator to every outcome, showing how good the outcome is for each member. If each member obtains the best utility then the whole collaborative activity would obtain the best utility. Each member can share information relevant to sub-problems and tasks for helping to increase the member's utilities. This information may be shared proactively (one member shares information because he/she believes the other will be interested in it) or reactively (one member shares information in response to a request). This question is related to the following design guidelines:

- Representation of the received information ($Q_{4,1}$)
- Mechanism for classifying the received information ($Q_{4,2}$)
- Others' user profiles (only if the profile defines part of the topic or includes user's expertise) ($Q_{4,3}$)

Question 5: What did other members of the group learn from me?

Positive interdependence is successfully structured when group members perceive they are linked with each other in a way that one cannot succeed unless everyone succeeds. Group goals and tasks, therefore, must be designed and communicated to students in ways that make them believe they sink or swim together. When positive interdependences are solidly structured, it highlights that (a) each group member's efforts are required and indispensable for group success and (b) each group member has a unique contribution to make to the joint effort because of his or her resources and/or role and task responsibilities. This creates a commitment to the success of group members as well as one's own and it is the heart of collaborative learning. If there are no positive interdependences, there is no collaboration [13]. In that way, it is important to do the task in a better way, and to teach other members of the group the performed activity. For this question, we propose:

- Explicit sensor of self-collaboration performance ($Q_{5,1}$)
- Representation of the information received ($Q_{5,2}$)
- Mechanism for classifying the information sent ($Q_{5,3}$)

Question 6: Where are the other members of the group?

In a collaborative activity it is very important to know where the group members are (unless they were working face-to-face) in order to assign a new task or to communicate in a better way. Accordingly, we consider:

- Mechanism to highlight others' last contribution ($Q_{6,1}$)
- Mechanism to restart the actual state of the task (only asynchronous CSCL interfaces) ($Q_{6,2}$)

4 Experimented Tools

In this section, we describe some software tools based on collaborative activities we have designed including mechanism to provide SKA among group members. The design guidelines explained in the previous section are taken into account in order to develop the software tools we have experimented.

4.1 TeamQuest

This game is a labyrinth with obstacles [6]. The players of a team must reach a goal by satisfying sub-goals in each of the game stages. Each player is identified with a role image and name. The screen has three well-defined areas: game, communication and information (Fig. 1). The game area has four quadrants (each one assigned to a player who has the *doer* role; the other players are collaborators for that quadrant). In

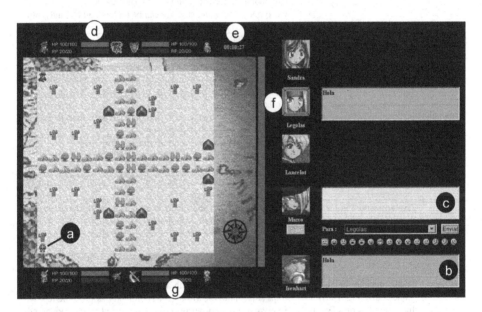

Fig. 1. TeamQuest user interface. This is the main interface of the designed software tool which incorporates the Shared-Knowledge Awareness mechanisms.

a quadrant, the *doer* must move an avatar from the initial position to the *cave* that allows entering the next quadrant. In the way, the *doer* must circumvent all obstacles and traps in the map (which are not visible to all players). Moreover, the *doer* must pick an item useful to reach the final destination. The user interface has many elements showing awareness: the *doer*'s icon, score bars, items that were picked up in each quadrant, etc. (see Fig. 1). Table 1 depicts the design elements of SKA that appear in this software tool.

Table 1. Shared-Knowledge Awareness mechanisms present in the game

Aspect	Design Element	Comments
$Q_{1,1}$	Avatar position in the game board (Fig. 1-a)	Collaborator: is the coordinator moving the avatar by skipping my traps?
$Q_{1,2}$	Dialogues boxes to receive messages (Fig. 1-c)	*Doer*: are the other members of the team sending me their traps? Collaborator: is the *doer* asking me something? Everyone: are the others' messages helping me to understand the game strategy?
$Q_{2,1}$	Group energy (Fig. 1-d)	Collaborator: after ending every player's turn, is the group energy better or not?
$Q_{3,1}$	Group energy (Fig. 1-d)	*Doer*: after ending my turn, does the group score increment or decrement?
$Q_{3,2}$	Dialogue boxes to receive messages (Fig. 1-c)	*Doer*: needs information about others' traps adjacent to the current avatar Collaborator: needs to know coordinator questions Everybody: the game strategy can be understood by analyzing the received information
$Q_{3,3}$	Dialogue boxes to receive messages (Fig. 1-c)	Separate dialogue boxes for each player (each participant identified with a different avatar)
$Q_{3,4}$	Avatar position in the game board (Fig. 1-a,f)	Every quadrant in the board is associated with the avatar of the participant that coordinates it. Therefore the avatar position defines the current profile of the other players (*Doer* or Collaborator) Collaborator: knowing who is the current *doer* helps to focalize answering his/her questions
$Q_{4,1}$	Dialogue boxes to receive messages (Fig. 1-c)	*Doer*: he/she has to read others' traps to skip them Collaborator: he/she has to read coordinator's questions to help him/her
$Q_{4,2}$	Dialogue boxes to receive messages (Fig. 1-c)	Separate dialogue boxes for each player (each participant is identified with an avatar)
$Q_{4,3}$	Avatar position in the game board (Fig. 1-a,f)	Every quadrant in the board is associated with the avatar of the participant that coordinates it. Therefore the avatar position defines the current profile of the other players (*Doer* or Collaborator) Collaborator: knowing who is the current coordinator helps to focalize answering his/her questions
$Q_{5,1}$	Avatar position in the game board (Fig. 1-a,f) Individual energy (Fig. 1-g)	Collaborator: after sending a message to the *doer* with his/her traps adjacent to the avatar, the coordinator skipped them. Everyone: my self-performance is reflected in the individual energy
$Q_{5,2}$	Dialogue boxes to receive messages (Fig. 1-c)	Everyone: observing others' questions and Comments can help him/her to perceive his/her performance
$Q_{5,3}$	Does not apply	This element is not present in the tool
$Q_{6,1}$	Dialogue boxes to receive messages (Fig. 1-c) Group energy (Fig. 1-d)	Everyone: others' messages are listed chronologically, therefore it is possible to see the last contributions of other players Collaborator: after seeing the mouse changing from one quadrant to another, the last contribution of the coordinator is reflected in the increasing or decreasing of the group energy
$Q_{6,2}$	Does not apply	This element is not present in the tool

4.2 DomoSim-TPC

DomoSim-TPC is a CSCL system for the learning of domotical design of models that should satisfy a specification. This system incorporates tools for organization, authoring, model building and simulation, communication and coordination, and assessment [17]. The learning activities consist of two phases: (a) *Collaborative Planning of Design*, and (b) *Detailed Design and Simulation*. The first phase is a reflexive task supported by asynchronous tools [19]. The second phase is an interactive task supported by synchronous tools [2]. In this study, we focus on the tools supporting the tasks of the first phase. DomoSimTPC has a specific workspace for the Collaborative Planning of Design. In this workspace, there are tools for individual planning of design (individual elaboration), argumentative discussion about the design strategies (collaboration) and organization of results (or artefacts).

The tool for individual planning of design is called PlanEdit [19]. A plan is specified as a partially ordered set of generic actions for the construction of a model. PlanEdit allows the learner to interactively define design strategies represented by mean of design plans and adapts to the strategy that the learner follows. Fig. 2 shows the user interface of PlanEdit. This is structured in separates areas: the problem formulation, the list of tasks to carry out to solve each sub-problem (a problem can be organized in sub-problems), the icon bars representing design actions (or domain operators), the sequence of design actions already planned, the current action under construction and a set of buttons dedicated to support several general functions.

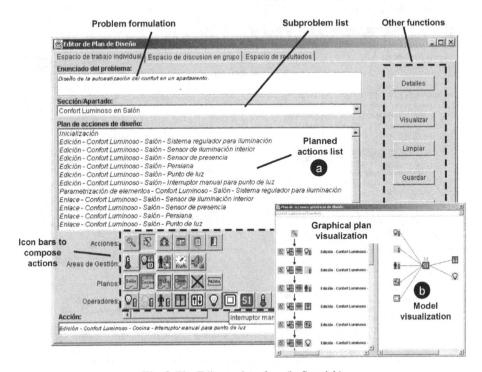

Fig. 2. PlanEdit user interface (in Spanish)

When a student has built a design plan, he/she has to present it to the rest of the group members arguing and justifying his/her design decisions. This is supported by the tool for argumentative discussion about the design strategies [18]. This tool structures the communication by means of a model inspired in the Conversation Based on Topics [20]; it hierarchically represents the evolution of the knowledge constructed in group and uses expert knowledge to guide the process. The objective of this guidance is to lead the group towards a solution in agreement. Fig. 3 shows the user interface of the argumentation tool. In the centre the hierarchical structure is located in the form of a reversed tree used to organize the contributions and to represent the evolution of the knowledge. This structure is called *Scheme of the Discussion and Argumentation Process* (SDAP). On the right, several interaction buttons are presented. The content of the selected contribution can be visualized with the corresponding button. This visualization depends on the kind of contribution. Mainly, they can be design plans or text messages.

In order to give a process-independent support to the organization, presentation and access to the final solution (or artefacts) elaborated and agreed by the group a *Table of Contents* is used. This table shows the epigraphs corresponding to the sub-problems in which the proposed problem was organized. These epigraphs are represented using two different icons. The first one (a *cross*) indicates that the problem does not have a solution in agreement yet and, therefore, it does not have a result associated. The second one (a *tick*) is used when the epigraph has already a solution in agreement.

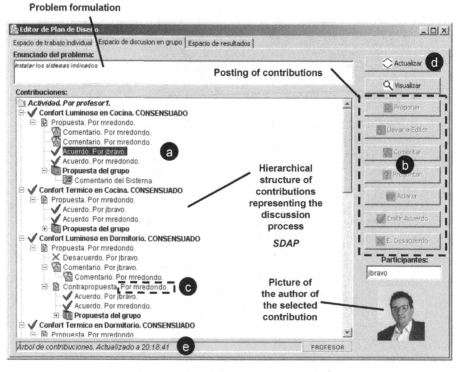

Fig. 3. User interface of the discussion and argumentation tool of PlanEdit (in Spanish)

Table 2. Shared-Knowledge Awareness mechanisms present in DomoSim-TPC

Aspect	Design Element	Comments
$Q_{1,1}$	Schema of the Discussion and Argumentation Process (SDAP) (Fig. 3-a)	The SDAP is a board (reversed tree) which is always displaying the task evolution. That is, this displays the posted contributions and their relations.
$Q_{1,2}$	Panel containing the list of planned design actions (Fig. 2-a)	The plan can also be graphically displayed (Fig. 2-b) in order to facilitate the interpretation of the model and to decide if it is finished.
$Q_{2,1}$	SDAP (Fig. 3-a) and the panel containing buttons which are used to post contributions (Fig. 2-b).	When a user proposes a model, other users can post critics and comments, and suggest improvements. All the users can visualize what the others propose, although restrictions can be established.
$Q_{3,1}$	SDAP (Fig. 3-b) and Table of Contents.	While the discussion process is carried out every user can observe what the rest of members have done (posted) and everyone can post new contributions. In the Table of Contents finished sub-problems and the constructed artefacts (plans) can be observed and reviewed.
$Q_{3,2}$	SDAP (Fig. 3-b)	The posted information is always represented, organized and structured in the SDAP. When new information is posted, it is necessary to relate it to another previous one contained in the SDAP.
$Q_{3,3}$	SDAP (Fig. 3-b and Fig. 3-c)	Labels are associated to the contributions indicating who has been the author of each one (Fig. 3-c).
$Q_{3,4}$	SDAP (Fig. 3-b)	The information posted by each user is visible and accessible to the rest of users from the SDAP. However, in the definition of the learning activity, restrictions can be established.
$Q_{4,1}$	SDAP (Fig. 3-b)	The posted information is always represented, organized and structured in the SDAP. When new information is posted, it is necessary to relate it to a previous one contained in the SDAP.
$Q_{4,2}$	SDAP (Fig. 3-b)	Labels are associated to the contributions indicating who has been the author of each one (Fig. 3-c).
$Q_{4,3}$	SDAP (Fig. 3-b)	The posted information is always represented, organized and structured in the SDAP. When new information is posted, it is necessary to relate it to a previous one contained in the SDAP.
$Q_{5,1}$	SDAP (Fig. 3-b)	Every contribution containing a design model can be moved to the individual workspace (Fig. 3-a) to be analyzed.
$Q_{5,2}$	SDAP (Fig. 3-b)	Everyone: observing others' questions and comments can help him/her to perceive his/her performance
$Q_{5,3}$	SDAP (Fig. 3-b)	Posted information as well as received information is represented in the SDAP.
$Q_{6,1}$	SDAP (Fig. 3-b)	The contributions are organized in a hierarchical structure in the form of a reversed tree. The leaves of the tree are the last posted contributions, but it is not possible to know when they were posted.
$Q_{6,2}$	Button *Actualizar* (Update) of the panel in the discussion tool (Fig. 3-d). Indicator of when the last update was carried out (Fig. 3-e). Mechanism of automatic and periodic update	The tool automatically and periodically updates the information and shows when it was the last update. Also, the user can request an update at any time.

The results of the Table of Contents serve as a starting point for the following phase of Detailed Design and Simulation in group. This phase is outside the scope of this work. Table 2 depicts the design elements of SKA that appear in the tools supporting Collaborative Planning of Design in the DomoSim-TPC system.

4.3 COLLECE

COLLECE (COLLaborative Edition, Compilation and Execution of programs) [3] allows distributed programmers to edit a program or code fragment, to compile it and to run it collaboratively. The system provides a shared workspace that supports an explicit collaboration protocol: first, the students create a program using a shared text editor; then, they are able to compile the program, receiving a list of compilation errors; finally, they can execute the program provided a compiled program is available. To support such protocol, the main user interface of the system includes four main areas (Fig. 4): the edition area at the top (Fig. 4-a), the console in the middle (Fig. 4-b), the chat at the bottom (Fig. 4-c), and the session panel on the right (Fig. 4-d). The console shows both the compilation errors and the execution outcome. In addition, a system function allows the users to consult the compilation statistics, so that the students are aware of their more frequently made mistakes (Fig. 4-e).

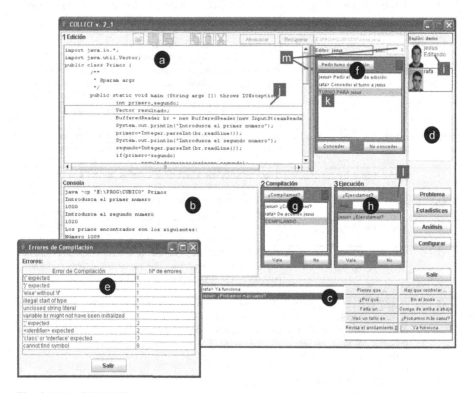

Fig. 4. Main COLLECE user interface which incorporates the Shared-Knowledge Awareness mechanisms (in Spanish)

Communication and coordination tools are available in the workspace for use when required. Communication is materialized by means of a structured chat, i.e. a chat with sentence openers (Fig. 4-c). Coordination processes are modeled with a simple protocol of actions extracted from language. In order to regulate the editor floor control, we identified the acts *Request the edition turn, Give* and *Don't give*. With these acts, a student can request the edition turn and his/her fellow students can express his/her agreement or disagreement (Fig. 4-f). When all the users in the group agree, the assignment is made. Similar acts are used for coordinating when to compile (Fig. 4-g) and when to execute the program (Fig. 4-h). These coordination tools support multiple proposals, that is to say, proposals coming from more than one user, and, as a result, lists are required to contain the historical proposals, enabling a user to select the proposal to which he/she wants to respond from such lists.

Besides this support, awareness support is available so that the users can easily perceive and gain knowledge of the interaction carried out by other people in the shared space [11]. The COLLECE awareness is materialized by means of a number of elements: session panel (Fig. 4-d); user's state (*editing, compiling* or *executing*) (Fig. 4-i); tele-pointers (Fig. 4-j); lists of interactions (Fig. 4-k); semaphores (Fig. 4-l); beeps, when actions occur; and other mechanisms (Fig. 4-m). Table 2 shows the design elements of SKA that are present in COLLECE. The COLLECE components most related to each design element are shown.

Table 3. Shared-Knowledge Awareness mechanisms present in COLLECE

Aspect	Design Element	Comments
$Q_{1,1}$	Edition area indicator (Fig. 4-m) Console (Fig. 4-b)	The edition area indicator shows the task advance indirectly, since it shows the edition position (the hypothesis is that the higher the position is, the longer the program and the more advanced the task are). The console showing the compilation errors also represents the task advance: the number of errors reduces as the task advances.
$Q_{1,2}$	Chat (Fig. 4-c) Lists of interactions (Fig. 4-k) Semaphores (Fig. 4-l)	The chat includes the users' performance at communication level. The different lists of interactions show the users participation textually; specifically, visual semaphores highlight active behaviours requesting agreements for carrying out shared tasks.
$Q_{2,1}$	Shared editor (Fig.4-a) Execution console (Fig. 4-b) Data input for execution	The program created with the shared editor means a solution to a problem. This program is manipulated, in coordinated turns, by the students. Thus, they help each other in solving the problem. The execution console is a shared space where the program is validated as a solution. The area for data input –this is not shown in the example of Fig. 3– contributes to the understanding of that validation.
$Q_{3,1}$	Compilation errors (Fig. 4-e) Shared editor (Fig. 4-a) Execution console (Fig. 4-b)	At level of task advance sensor, the compilation errors represent knowledge that students need to manage. On the same way, the program in the editor and the execution feedback involve a cognitive level that allows the students to validate the knowledge they have applied in solving the problem.
$Q_{3,2}$	Shared editor (Fig.4-a) Structured chat (Fig. 4-c) Lists of interactions (Fig. 4-k)	A number of components represent in different ways the information received involving knowledge about the topic: the programming instructions in the editor, the textual messages about the programming tasks in the chat, etc.

$Q_{3,3}$	Lists of interactions (Fig. 4-k) Semaphores (Fig. 4-l) Structured chat (Fig. 4-c)	Information about the coordination processes is organized in the lists of interactions. Semaphores help in identifying the open coordination processes. On the other hand, the chat classifies discussion information, especially because the chat structures the conversation by means of the sentence openers.
$Q_{3,4}$	Edition area indicator (Fig. 4-m)	The program line in which the editor user is working represents specific program instructions and algorithm fragments of his/her property (since he/she writes them), from which a user profile would be generated.
$Q_{4,1}$	Structured chat (Fig. 4-c) Lists of interactions (Fig. 4-k)	At communication level, the chat manages information students interchange to solve the problem; at coordination level, the lists of interactions collect coordination actions for leading the tasks
$Q_{4,2}$	Lists of interactions (Fig. 4-k), Structured chat (Fig. 4-c)	Both the lists of interactions and the chat classify the users' actions since they include the user's name.
$Q_{4,3}$	User's state (Fig. 4-i)	The user's state represents the task the leader is carrying out. This is the way that user employs to complete the global task under the others' supervision.
$Q_{5,1}$	Shared editor (Fig. 4-a) Structured chat (Fig. 4-c) Lists of interactions (Fig. 4-k)	The link between the edition and the communication, which allows discussing while editing the program code, promotes positive interdependence. Additionally, the lists of interactions mean sensors of collaborative performance.
$Q_{5,2}$	Shared editor (Fig. 4-a) Structured chat (Fig.4-c) Lists of interactions (Fig. 4-k)	The shared editor shows pieces of information (sequences of instructions) representing learning fragments. Again, the chat and the lists of interactions provide a textual representation of the discussion and coordination processes.
$Q_{5,3}$	Shared editor (Fig.4-a) Tele-pointer (Fig. 4-j) Structured chat (Fig. 4-c) Lists of interactions (Fig. 4-k)	The users' names in the different components and the tele-pointer colour are used to identify the information sent concerning learning.
$Q_{6,1}$	Shared editor (Fig. 4-a) Tele-pointer (Fig. 4-j) Edition area indicator (Fig. 4-m) Structured chat (Fig. 4-c) Lists of interactions (Fig. 4-k) Data input for execution	The COLLECE support for awareness provides rich information about where the last contribution took place.
$Q_{6,2}$	Does not apply	This element is not present in the tool.

5 Discussion

Effective collaboration requires students to engage in task-related, meta-cognitive, and socio-communicative activities. Most CSCL environments support only task-related and meta-cognitive activities. However, few CSCL environments attempt to support socio-communicative activities. One way to support socio-communicative activities may be through visualization of the social aspects of collaboration [9]. Visualization uses software tools and different representations to guide argumentative knowledge construction. Interfaces with different representational aids such as graphs, matrices or texts were found, which have different effects on CSCL [23]. Software tools may visualize the argumentation of learners [14]. For instance, diagrammatic representations visualize how arguments are related to each other and thus facilitate and guide the learners' awareness of the argumentative discourse [12].

In the model we have presented, we include some mechanisms to visualize what the group members are doing in order to determine if what one member is doing is in the correct way to reach the final goal. This information needs to be assimilated by the entire group in order to provide a better collaboration. One of our hypothesis states that this shared understanding could be promoted if people are aware of their current performance during the collaborative activity. The guidelines discussed previously permit group members to know what the other group members know about a certain topic for determining what information change should be tracked and displayed to participants, and what perspectives of viewing this information are relevant to the end user. All the design guidelines we have proposed are explained in the context of the designed software tools.

In a CSCL scenario, these kinds of changes will provide information to the students about the possible learning people have achieved. It is expected that these new tools will provide the students with useful awareness information. This awareness information may trigger explicit communication between students, which facilitates coordination of collaborative activities. This, in turn, may facilitate group processes and lead to better group products and better evaluations of group processes by the students. It is also expected that these new tools will help the teacher to better guide the students' group processes. In spite that the software tools analyzed correspond to different domains and functioning ways (synchronous and asynchronous), we have observed that these guidelines are taken into account. DomoSim-TPC has an asynchronous style and uses a complex structure (inverted tree) to represent the shared knowledge in a structured manner. In this representation, we have observed that is necessary to include some references about the exact time when participants are doing some modifications ($Q_{6,1}$). The other software tools are synchronous and fundamentally use text boxes to show and share messages, as the mechanism to contribute the shared knowledge construction, and some indicators to express that the user has the responsibility to do something (semaphores) and the quality of the task (*Group Score*). The same situation occurs in COLLECE through the cursor position in the edition text area. This last software tool has many elements to express awareness not only about the knowledge but also about the actions and interactions the group members are doing. Some of these elements (for example, the control panel that receives information about who is working every time) still do not have correspondence with the guidelines proposed previously. These aspects suggest us to include more elements in further work.

6 Conclusions and Further Work

Shared-Knowledge Awareness and the respective visualization elements can be used in many group work contexts. For instance, many modern organizations can be seen as network organizations. Participants of these network organizations are individuals as well as other organizations, which collaborate in distributed teams. In some knowledge-intensive domains, such as service engineering, consulting, communities of practice, etc., project teams are composed by participants from different disciplines and organizations that unite their special competencies to match project necessities. Problems occur when participants try to establish a shared knowledge repository and knowledge management mechanisms. A striking point here is the missing awareness of the team members, which leads to the ignorance of the competencies the organization has. One way to improve transparency over the activities of the organization is having SKA mechanisms to be integrated into groupware systems that are mainly used for collaboration needs. The main idea presented in this paper is the use of awareness visualization systems as part of the knowledge management tools, which permit visualizing the shared knowledge to every member of the group in order to help him/her to complete the task in a more effective way.

Of course, in CSCL environments the Shared-Knowledge Awareness is crucial. The group members need to build and maintain a shared comprehension of both the problem and the required tasks. Visualization mechanisms for this kind of awareness will help the group to work in a more efficient manner. Systematic methods for utilization of these mechanisms and the visualization elements are necessary. These methods can help the engineer to design and build new tools supporting learning and group work.

Acknowledgements

This work was partially funded by Spanish Ministry of Science and Tech., CICYT Project ADACO (TIN 2004-08000-C03-03), Colciencias (Colombia) Proj. N° 4128-14-18008 & 030-2005, and Fondecyt (Chile) grant N° 1040952 and 11060467.

References

[1] Borges, M., Pino, J.: Awareness mechanisms for coordination in asynchronous CSCW. In: Proceedings of WITS'99, Charlotte, North Carolina, pp. 69–74 (1999)

[2] Bravo, C., Redondo, M.A., Ortega, M., Verdejo, F.: Collaborative Distributed Environments for Learning Design Tasks by Means of Modelling and Simulation. Journal of Network and Computer Applications 29(4), 321–342 (2006)

[3] Bravo, C., Duque, R., Gallardo, J., García, J., García, P.: A Groupware System for Distributed Collaborative Programming: Usability Issues and Lessons Learned. In: Proceedings of International Workshop on Tool Support and Requirements Management in Distributed Projects (REMIDI'07) (2007) (in press)

[4] Card, S., Mackinlay, J., Shneiderman, B. (eds.): Readings in Information Visualization: Using Vision to Think. Morgan Kaufmann, San Francisco (1999)

[5] Collazos, C., Guerrero, L.A., Pino, J., Ochoa, S.: Introducing Knowledge-Shared Awareness. In: Proceedings of IASTED International Conference: Information and Knowledge Sharing (IKS 2002), St. Thomas, Virgin Islands, USA, pp. 13–18 (2002)

[6] Collazos, C., Guerrero, L.A., Pino, J., Ochoa, S.: Evaluating Collaborative Learning Processes. In: Haake, J.M., Pino, J.A. (eds.) CRIWG 2002. LNCS, vol. 2440, pp. 203–221. Springer, Heidelberg (2002)

[7] Dillenbourg, P., Self, J.: Designing human-computer collaborative learning. In: O'Malley, C.C (ed.) Computer Supported Collaborative Learning, Springer, Heidelberg (1995)

[8] Dillenbourg, P.: Some technical implications of the distributed cognition approach on the design of interactive learning environments. Journal of Artificial Intelligence in Education 7(2), 161–180 (1996)

[9] Erkens, G.: Dynamics of coordination in collaboration. In: van der linden, J., Renshaw, P. (eds.) Dialogic learning: Shifting perspectives to learning, instruction, and teaching, pp. 191–216. Kluwer Academic Publishers, Dordrecht (2004)

[10] Gershon, N., Ward, P.: What Storytelling Can Do for Information Visualization. Communications of the ACM 44(8) (2001)

[11] Gutwin, C.: Workspace Awareness in Real-Time Groupware Environments. Ph.D. thesis, Department of Computer Science, University of Calgary, Canada (1997)

[12] Hoppe, H.U., Gaßner, K., Mühlenbrock, M., Tewissen, F.: Distributed visual language environments for cooperation and learning. Journal Group Decision and Negotiation 9(3), 205–220 (2000)

[13] Johnson, D.W., Johnson, R.T., Holubec, E.J.: Cooperation in the Classroom, 6th edn. Interaction Book Company (1993)

[14] Kirschner, P., Buckingham Shum, S.J., Carr, C.S.: Visualizing argumentation. In: oftware tools for collaborative and educational sense making, Kluwer Academic Publishers, Dordrecht (2003)

[15] Lally, V.: Analyzing teaching and learning interactions in a networked collaborative learning environment: issues and work in progress. In: Procc. Of Euro CSCL'01 (2001)

[16] Novak, J.D.: Concept mapping: A useful tool for science education. Journal of Research in Science Teaching 27(10), 937–949 (1990)

[17] Redondo, M.A., Bravo, C.: DomoSim-TPC: Collaborative Problem Solving to Support the Learning of Domotical Design. Journal Computer Applications in Engineering Education 4(1), 9–19 (2006)

[18] Redondo, M.A., Bravo, C., Ortega, M.: Contextualized Argumentative Discussion for Design Learning in Group. In: Navarro, R., Lorés, J. (eds.) HCI related papers of Interacción 2004, pp. 317–328. Springer, Heidelberg (2006)

[19] Redondo, M.A., Bravo, C., Ortega, M., Verdejo, F.: Providing adaptation and guidance for design learning by problem solving. The DomoSim-TPC approach. Computers and Education 48(4), 642–657 (2007)

[20] Savery, J., Duffy, T.: Problem based learning: An instructional model and its constructivist framework. In: Wilson, B. (ed.) Constructivist learning environments: Case studies in instructional design, pp. 135–148. Prentice Hall, Englewwod Cliffs (1996)

[21] Slavin, R.: Using Student Team Learning. Center for Social Organization of Schools, Johns Hopkins University (1980)

[22] Spence, B.: Information Visualization. Addison-Wesley, Reading (2001)

[23] Suthers, D.D., Hundhausen, C.D.: Learning by constructing collaborative representations: An empirical comparison of three alternatives. In: Dillenbourg, P., Eurelings, A., Hakkarainen, K. (eds.) European perspectives on computer-supported collaborative learning, University of Maastricht, pp. 577–592 (2001)

[24] Wong, M.: The concept map: A tool for learning science concepts and understanding cognitive processes of preservice teachers – A Case Study. University of Malaysia Sarawak, Malaysia (1997)

An Improved Design and a Case Study of a Social Visualization Encouraging Participation in Online Communities

Julita Vassileva[1,*] and Lingling Sun[2]

[1] Computer Science Department, University of Saskatchewan, Canada
[2] Solutions AB TELUS Business Transformation, Edmonton, Canada
jiv@cs.usask.ca, gloriasun@hotmail.com

Abstract. The paper describes a further development of the design of a motivational visualization encouraging participation in an online community. The new design overcomes shortcomings in previous designs, by using more attractive appearance of the graphic elements in the visualization, by giving up the largely unused in the previous design user customization options. The visualization integrates more information in one view, and uses an improved user clustering approach for representing graphically their different levels of contribution. A case study of the new design with a group of 32 students taking a class on Ethics and Computer Science is presented. The results show that the visualization had a significantly effect participation and with respect to two activities (logging into the community and rating resources).

Keywords: participation, online communities, social visualization, evaluation.

1 Introduction

Social visualization approaches using different metaphors have been proposed to stimulate the activation of social norms in groupware and online communities [5, 8]. We proposed [2, 7] a motivational visualization aimed at encouraging participation in an online sharing community. Grounded on the theories of social conformity [1] and social comparison [6], this approach was evaluated in an online community, supporting undergraduate computer science students in a class of Ethics and IT. The experimental results and the user feedback [7] showed that the motivational visualization effectively increased the students' awareness of their community and encouraged social comparison. As a result the contributions of shared resources in the community increased significantly, and participants gave more comments and ratings.

We found that user-customizable views were hardly needed, since most users checked only the default view which displayed users ranked according to the number of resources they shared in the community and didn't explore the other views which showed ranking according to status, login frequency, or number of downloaded

---

* Correspondence authors.

J.M. Haake, S.F. Ochoa, and A. Cechich (Eds.): CRIWG 2007, LNCS 4715, pp. 72–86, 2007.

resources. This supports Erickson's first guideline [4] for design of community visualization.

From a technical point of view, a major issue in the design of the visualization is the algorithm used to classify users into four contribution levels based. Ideally, the algorithm should find a significant difference between the marginal cases on both sides of a boundary between two clusters. More specifically, if the list of nodes is sorted by the original contributions, there could be the case that the last node at the top level only shares one or two files more than the first node at the second level, which may share 10 more files than the second node at this level. A better algorithm should find reasonable gaps between contributions of users to classify these users into different levels. A compromise between desired sizes and sharper boundaries would be a direction to explore in the future.

We observed that as the quantity of contributions increased, their quality somewhat deteriorated. Several users found ways to game the system and exaggerate their nodes in order to gain higher status and visibility. A possible reason for this behavior was that the visualization showed only the quantity of the articles shared by each user regardless of the quality i.e. the visualization did not encourage comparison among the users with respect to the quality of their contributions. Motivating social comparison in the quality of the contributions, comments, and ratings was set as an important future direction of research. Motivating active users to continue their contributions or even increase them was another problem. We concluded that the visualization had to take into account both the quality and quantity of user contributions.

The paper describes a new version of the visualization which takes into account the requirements derived from the previous designs. It provides a minimal user interaction – it requires only the user to select a topic (an area of interest), instead of selecting both a topic and a sorting criterion. By default, the topic is set to the one discussed in the current week of the class, according to the course curriculum, so if the user wants to see the current view of the community, he/she doesn't need to select anything. The semantics of the different sorting criteria used in the previous version are represented into one picture with more complexity and dimensions, which generate visually more attractive and consistent view of the community. The visualization applies a better algorithm to smooth the classification of users into different levels of contributions. The visualization has been redesigned as a web-based application, supported by Apache Tomcat web server v4.0 and mySQL database server.

2 Design

The new design of the visualization had a new, more complex visual language, more attractive stars, a new clustering algorithm. The visualization uses again the nigh-sky metaphor. However, we use a more complex visual language. Unlike the previous design which used just two dimensions: the size (four possible sizes) and color (yellow filled circle or black empty one), in the current design we use four dimensions: size, colour, level of brightness and shade.

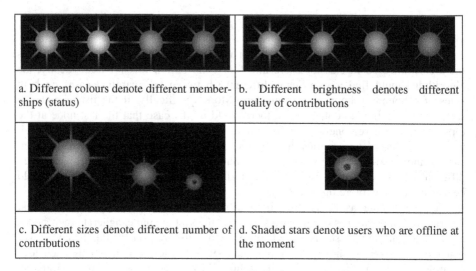

a. Different colours denote different memberships (status)	b. Different brightness denotes different quality of contributions
c. Different sizes denote different number of contributions	d. Shaded stars denote users who are offline at the moment

Fig. 1. The four dimensions of the graphical language

Each star also has a particular color and a certain level of brightness of that color. The color of a star indicates the membership level of the represented user (Fig.1a). The membership (status) is a combined measure of the user's participation which depends on the number and quality of the user's contributions (new links and ratings). A yellow star represents a user who holds Gold membership, a white star represents a user who has a Silver membership, a red star, a Bronze membership, and a Green star, the lowest "plastic" level of the membership (the initial membership level for everyone when s/he first starts to use the system).

Each star has a certain level of color density, which visually appears as the brightness to represent the reputation level of a user (Fig. 1b). There are also four levels of reputation. Brighter stars represent users with higher levels of reputation.

The size of a star indicates the number of links shared by the represented user (Fig.1c). There are four possible levels of contribution: the users who contribute the most links are at Level 1, and the users who contribute no links – at Level 4.

If the center of a star is covered a by a black shade, this indicates that the represented user is currently offline, otherwise, s/he is online (Fig. 1d). In this design, "a user is offline" means that the user has not been active in the past ten minutes in the Comtella community. A user may have a combination of any contribution level, membership level, reputation level, and be either online or offline.

The arrangement of the stars in representing the users in the visualization is fixed (see Fig. 2), while in the previous design it was a result of dynamic sorting according to the criterion chosen by the user. In this way the user can easily locate him/her self as s/he gets familiar with using the system. Each user can create his/her alias, under which s/he is known in the community. The users can see their alias name and the aliases of their peers by moving the mouse on top of a star.

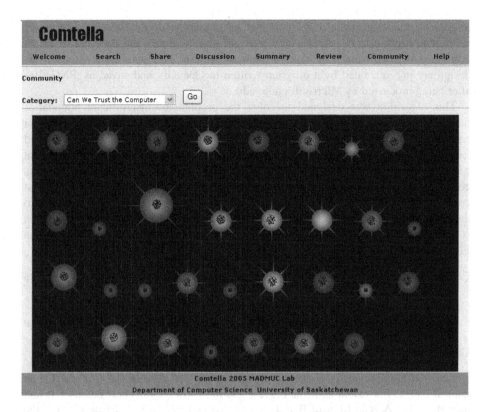

Fig. 2. A screen shot showing the new design of the visualization

Our hypothesis was that this design will continue to motivate users when they have already become good contributors, which was one of the problems in the previous design. It is almost impossible for a user to achieve the highest levels in all criteria, e.g. having the first contribution level, gold membership, and highest reputation. In this way, there will always be a way of improvement for the user, or a factor that motivates a user to contribute. As Fig. 2 shows the largest star does not necessarily have to be a gold member or the brightest star. This is because the size of a star is solely determined by the number of contributions (shared URLs) by the represented user, while the membership is calculated based on other criteria (the quality of these contributions, as well as by the number and quality of ratings given by the user for the contributions of other users). Some users may feel satisfaction from becoming the brightest small green star, by contributing only a few but highly rated papers.

The images used to represent users in this visualization design are cartoon versions of stars on a black background. In this design we gave up the idea of generating the stars on user request for the goal to having more realistic/beautiful stars. However, unlike the very first design of the Comtella visualization [2, 7], we did not use JPEG images of real stars since they could not be manipulated consistently in terms of colors and brightness to achieve the variety of sizes, colours and different levels of brightness that we wanted to have in the new version. The pictures we used in this design are pre-generated by a program written in OpenGL, and saved as .PNG files after being processed by Microsoft photo editor.

This algorithm was designed to solve the problem of insignificant boundaries between two consecutive clusters of users when classifying these users into different contribution levels. This problem was obvious in the previous design and created feelings of unfairness in the students who were close to the margins of different contribution classes. With the old algorithm, the first contribution level should always contain the top three users, and according to the contributions for topic 1 (i.e. the first column in Fig. 3), for example, some of the zero-contributors will be classified into the first contribution level, while the rest will be classified into the other levels, which is obviously not fair. The new algorithm prevents this unfairness. It is illustrated in Fig. 3, and works as follows:

Case 1: Sort in a list (L) the users in descending order of their contributions for a given topic.

Case 2: Set everyone who shares nothing with a contribution level = 4.

Case 3: If everyone shares something, but they all share the number of files i.e. make the same contribution, set their contribution level = 3.

Case 4: Else:

Find the biggest gap in contributions among the top 20% of the users in L and mark it gap_1. For example, if the biggest gap in this range falls between user A and user B, where A is in front of B in L (i.e. A shares more than B), then gap_1 = the index of A in L. Set users before gap_1 with a contribution level = 1.

Find gap_2 which is the biggest gap after gap_1 among the top 50% of the users in L, and set contribution level = 2 to all the users after gap_1 but before gap_2.

Find gap_3, the biggest gap among the rest of the users, and set everyone between gap_2 and gap_3 with a contribution level = 3, and those after gap_3 with a contribution level = 4. However, if there are some users who have not contributed anything, then gap_3 will be the index in L of the last non-zero contributor.

The brightness level is computed using the average reputation of the user's shared URLs (referred to as "paper-reputation" in the following context) defined in [3]. If the highest paper-reputation of all the users, either online or offline, is H then everyone whose paper-reputation is H will have the brightest star (i.e. the highest reputation level). If a user's paper-reputation is less than H, for example r, then another value R is computed as $R = r/H$. If $R > 0.9$ with an allowable margin of 0.05 (i.e. $R > 0.85$) then this user will also have the brightest star; otherwise, if $R > 0.55$ then this user will have a second brightest star (i.e. reputation level 2); otherwise, if $R > 0.35$ then this user will have a dark star (i.e. reputation level 3); and if $R <= 0.35$ then this user will have the darkest star (i.e. lowest reputation level), which makes it almost fade into the background.

topic 1	topic 2	topic 3	topic 4	topic 5	topic 6	topic 7	topic 8	topic 9	topic 10	overall
3	5	14	14	24	28	23	15	20	20	124
0	5	8	10	19	28	15	15	13	10	111
0	4	7	10	16	21	11	10	11	8	102
0	2	6	9	12	15	10	10	8	6	77
0	1	5	9	10	12	8	10	7	6	69
0	1	5	7	8	11	7	6	7	6	58
0	1	5	7	6	11	6	6	6	6	49
0	1	5	7	6	11	6	6	6	6	48
0	0	5	6	6	11	6	6	6	5	47
0	0	5	6	6	9	5	5	5	5	45
0	0	5	6	6	9	5	5	5	5	43
0	0	4	6	5	7	5	5	5	4	40
0	0	4	5	5	6	5	5	5	4	39
0	0	4	5	5	6	5	4	4	3	38
0	0	4	4	5	6	4	4	4	3	35
0	0	4	4	4	5	4	4	4	3	34
0	0	4	4	4	5	4	3	4	3	34
0	0	3	4	4	5	4	3	4	2	33
0	0	3	4	4	4	3	3	3	2	32
0	0	3	4	3	4	3	3	3	2	29
0	0	3	3	3	4	2	2	2	0	28
0	0	3	3	3	3	2	2	2	0	25
0	0	2	2	3	3	1	0	2	0	18
0	0	1	2	3	3	0	0	0	0	15
0	0	1	2	2	2	0	0	0	0	13
0	0	0	1	2	2	0	0	0	0	11
0	0	0	0	0	0	0	0	0	0	4
0	0	0	0	0	0	0	0	0	0	3
0	0	0	0	0	0	0	0	0	0	3
0	0	0	0	0	0	0	0	0	0	0

Fig. 3. An example output of the classification algorithm

3   Case Study

This design of the visualization was evaluated in a case study with a group of 32 forth-year computer science students taking CMPT 408, a class on Ethics in Computer Science, offered by the Department of Computer Science from January 17 to April 8, 2005, a total of 12 weeks. The first 10 weeks were dedicated to the experiment and the last two weeks were for the online questionnaire survey. The list of categories for sharing URLs corresponds to the topics discussed in the class. Each topic was discussed in one week following the class curriculum, except for "Computer Crime and Security" in the middle of the term which was discussed for two weeks with the reading-week break in between, so this topic ran over weeks 4, 5, and 6.

The experimental subjects were divided randomly into two groups of equal size, 16 students in each group, and the experiment duration was split into two equal parts as well, 5 weeks in each part (see Fig. 4). The midnight on Sunday February 20, 2005 was the "switching point" — at this point the two groups were switched so that

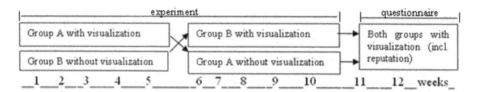

Fig. 4. Experiment Time Schedule

Group A, who had access to the visualization during the first five weeks, was not able to use the visualization any more, and Group B, who was not able to use the visualization in the first five weeks, gained access to the visualization. The reason for switching the two groups in this way was to reduce as much as possible the ordering effects and the effect of novelty. However, the novelty effect could not be entirely eliminated. In the case of this experiment, it was stronger on Group A than it was on Group B because Group A was the first group who had access to the visualization, so for them both the system and the visualization were new. The subjects in Group A had no knowledge about the visualization when they were exposed to it, but the subjects in Group B had at least heard about the visualization from their colleagues, with whom they shared classes, and worked on the class project. So the visualization was not as new to Group B as it was to Group A.

The hypothesis was that the visualization would motivate the subjects to contribute more papers and ratings and to participate more actively in the Comtella online community by logging in more frequently and reading more papers.

The quantitative results about the participation of the two groups are shown in Fig. 5. The dark dashed line in each chart represents the performance of the Group A and the lighter solid line represents the performance of Group B with respect to each activity. The X-axis shows the time duration of the experiment in terms of weeks, starting at Week 1 and ending at Week 10. The Y-axis shows the number of times subjects logged in to the Comtella system. Each data point represents the total number of activities of a given type for all students in the corresponding group and week. The groups were switched at midnight on the last day of Week 5 i.e. the beginning of Week 6. Weeks 4, 5 and 6 were dedicated to the same topic and the students, shared most of their URLs on this topic in Week 4 and almost nothing in weeks 5 and 6. Moreover, Week 5 was the reading-week break. This explains the big drop in Week 5 in each of the figures 5a-d.

Figure 5a represents the total number of logins made by the subjects each group on a weekly basis and Figure 5b represents the number of ratings given by subjects in each group on a weekly basis. Giving ratings is a major type of activity in the Comtella community. It takes effort to read and evaluate the material, and the rating constitutes a valuable contribution to the community since reasonable ratings will guide users to find good articles. Another important type of contribution is sharing papers (URLs). Figure 5c compares the number of URLs shared by the subjects of Group A with the number of URLs shared by the subjects of Group B on a weekly basis. Figure 5d represents how many times subjects from each group read a paper shared by others in the community (as a read we count just opening the URL of the paper).

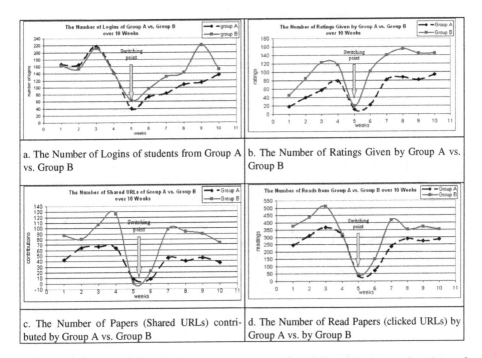

a. The Number of Logins of students from Group A vs. Group B

b. The Number of Ratings Given by Group A vs. Group B

c. The Number of Papers (Shared URLs) contributed by Group A vs. Group B

d. The Number of Read Papers (clicked URLs) by Group A vs. by Group B

Fig. 5. The different types of participation by the students in Group A compared to those of Group B

It is clear from Fig. 5 that there is a difference between the participation of Group A and Group B. Group B participated more actively than Group A in all activities. Since the experimental subjects were assigned randomly into groups, it happened so that one group contained more active members than the other. In this case, we need to adapt our hypothesis to correspond to this unintended bias. The modified hypothesis, that takes into account the fact that one of the groups (B) is more active is based on the original hypothesis: that the visualization would motivate both groups to participate more. This means that it is expected that the difference between the participation levels of the two groups would be smaller when the less active group has access to the visualization and the more active group does not have access to the visualization (which is the case during the first period of the experiment, before the switch). On the contrary, the difference between the participation levels of the two groups would be larger when the more active group has access to the visualization and the less active group does not have access to the visualization (the case during the second period of the experiment). Figure 6 illustrates the effect of the growing difference between the participation level (we will call it "performance" for brevity) of the two groups in the two periods of the experiment according to the modified hypothesis.

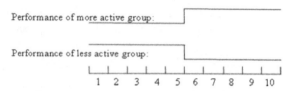

Fig. 6. Modified Experimental Hypothesis

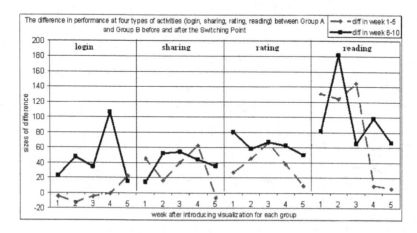

Fig. 7. Differences between the contributions of the two groups in the four activities

Fig. 7 shows the differences between the contributions made by Group A – Group B for each week and for each type of activity. The X-axis is divided into four sections, each representing the difference in the performances in a particular type of activity (login, sharing URLs, rating URLs, or reading). Each section along the X-axis contains five segments, from 1 to 5, each segment representing a pair of weeks (Week 1 paired with Week 6 as marked by 1, Week 2 paired with Week 7 as marked by 2, Week 3 paired with Week 8 as marked by 3, Week 4 paired with Week 9 as marked by 4, and Week 5 paired with Week 10 as marked by 5). Thus, each point on the darker solid line is comparable to the point on the lighter dashed line. For example, the first point on the solid line represents the first week when Group B had access to the visualization and Group A did not, and the first point on the dashed line represents the first week when Group A had access to the visualization and Group B did not, and so on for the rest of the points. The solid line is mostly above the dashed line which indicates that most of the times the difference in the performances of the two groups after the switching point is bigger than it is before the switching point. This seems to confirm the modified hypothesis.

We performed two tests for statistical significance on the differences in each activity: t-test and the Wilcoxon's Matched-Pairs Signed-Rank Test. We found a significant difference in the performances of the two groups regarding the *login* and the *rating* activities. According to both the t-test and the Wilcoxon's test, the significance for logins is greater than 95%: the significance for rating is 97.5% according to the t-test, and 95% according to the Wilcoxon's test. However, the results for sharing and reading activities are weak. The t-test shows the probability of the difference in sharing activity being random is 29%, and the probability of the difference in reading activity being random is 33%.

The visualization had stronger motivational effect on Group B, the active group, than it had on Group A, the less active group. The reason why the active group was motivated more effectively is not clear. One possible explanation is that if a group is generally more active then the students in this group probably care more about their contribution levels and care if other users see them as good users or freeloaders.

The users provided qualitative feedback in the last two weeks of the term by filling in a questionnaire for which they received a bonus participation mark of 2% towards their final grade. A summary of the user answers to each question related to the visualization are presented below.

1. Please rank the following reasons for which you used the visualization (1: most important; 5: least important):

	1	2	3	4	5
appears interesting	15%	20%	30%	20%	15%
find articles	10%	0%	20%	20%	50%
compare contributions	30%	35%	15%	5%	15%
check who contributed what	5%	20%	5%	35%	35%
find top contributors	15%	25%	30%	10%	20%

2. Please rank the following (from -2: "very poor" to +2: very good):

	-2	-1	0	1	2
overall	9%	0%	23%	59%	9%
support tool for the class cmpt408	9%	4%	13%	35%	39%
usability	11%	21%	21%	42%	5%
reliability (crashes etc.)	10%	19%	14%	43%	14%
visualization attractive	10%	5%	35%	30%	20%
visualization useful	10%	5%	35%	40%	10%
visualization intuitive	10%	15%	35%	25%	15%
visualization effective	25%	15%	40%	20%	0%
quality of shared links	20%	0%	25%	45%	10%
fairness	10%	0%	10%	65%	15%

Half of the subjects ranked "visualization attractiveness" as positive compared with the first design where only 34% of the subjects ranked this criterion positively and only 18% thought the first design "appeared interesting". 40% of the subjects thought the visualization was intuitive and 20% thought it was effective; however, the first design gave a slightly better result on the intuitiveness (48% positive ranking) than the final design. These numbers indicate that this version of the visualization is more successful in general compared with the first version.

3. What would be your reaction if you saw yourself as one of the smallest stars (regardless of its color and brightness) in the visualization?

a. Take immediate action: share more links to make your star larger (20%)
b. Think that you should probably share more links, but later (45%)
c. Feel unhappy but do nothing (0%)
d. Feel that the system is unfair, so it doesn't make sense to contribute (0%)
e. Do not care, so will do nothing (20%)
f. Other - please specify: (15%)

The data indicates that 65% of the users were motivated to contribute more if they saw their stars were not big enough in the visualization.

4. If you saw yourself as one of the largest stars (regardless of its color and brightness), would you:

a. Feel proud of your status and try to contribute even more. (40%)
b. Feel proud, but also in some sense "exploited", stop bringing more links. (10%)
c. Feel worried, you may be raising the bar too high and the others may hate you or you may be perceived as "overachiever" by the others. (10%)
d. Feel nothing, since it is not important for me. (35%)
f. Other - please specify: (5%)

Most (55%) of the users were not motivated to contribute more once their stars are big enough in the visualization, and there is some discouraging factor as option b indicates.

5. Please rank the following factors according to how strongly they motivated you to contribute (1: strongest; 6: weakest):

	1	2	3	4	5	6
community visualization	8%	19%	19%	11%	8%	35%
earn higher membership	22%	19%	18%	15%	15%	11%
earn higher marks	43%	21%	4%	14%	11%	7%
bringing good papers	23%	12%	35%	11%	11%	8%
being best user	11%	28%	14%	18%	11%	18%
having best papers	11%	25%	18%	18%	18%	10%

The results show that a significant source of motivation is the social comparison, stimulated by the visualization. Forty-six (46%) of the subjects ranked the community visualization as strong motivator (1 to 3), 53% - being the best user, 54% - bringing the best papers, 59% - the status. Yet, there were other, stronger motivators - the expectation of receiving good marks was ranked as a strong motivator by 68% (these students are obviously extrinsically motivated), and bringing good papers was ranked as strong motivators (1 to 3) by 69% - students who seem to be intrinsically motivated.

6. Did you find the final visualization represents fairly your overall level of contribution in the class?

a. Yes (60%)
b. No (25%)
c. If No, why?

The justification given by the students who selected "b" above was based mainly on the dichotomy between quantity vs. quality of contribution. They thought there should be more emphasis given on the quality of the shared materials. 15% of the subjects were not sure about the overall fairness, and from the given justifications, we found this uncertainty was caused by unfamiliarity with the system.

4 Discussion

Comparing with the feedback from the case study of the previous design of the motivational community visualization [7], these results show that users generally preferred the new design and found it more attractive. The feedback from the case study shows that a higher percentage of users (compared with the case study of the previous design) used the visualization to check who contributes how much and who the top contributors are. The new design of the visualization effectively motivated user contributions in each of the two groups A and B under the test condition. The experimental results confirm the hypothesis that the visualization helps shrinking the difference in the performances of the two groups when the less active group had access to the visualization and the more active group did not, and the visualization amplifies the difference in the performances of the two groups when the more active group had access to the visualization and the less active group had no access to the visualization. The motivational effect is more obvious on the active group than it is on the inactive group. The t-test and the Wilcoxon's Matched-Pairs Single Rank Sum test show that the difference in the performances of the two groups before and after the switching point is significant for login and rating activities but not for sharing and reading activities. To conclude on each specific type of activity separately, the experiment needs to be run for a longer period of time, or we need to double the size of the experimental subjects so that we could run the experiment with two groups, one group with the visualization and the other group without, in parallel. Due to the limited class duration (12-13 weeks) the first option is not feasible, but increasing the number of subjects or running experiments in the same class under the same conditions for two consecutive years could be a direction of research.

The users generally found the new visualization design useful and interesting. The effect of the community visualization on motivating contributions and more active participation was shown in both case studies, but the significance of the effect is different depending on what is visualized, how it is visualized (i.e. what graphical representation is used), if it is easy enough for users to read and understand the visual representation (i.e. how intuitive the pictures are), and so on. The results indicate that the visualization is more effective on people who are naturally competitive and care about others' opinions and views on themselves. For people who are not competitive, sociable, or do not care about others' opinions on themselves, the visualization is not an effective motivator, since it was designed to facilitate social comparison. Competition is a form of upward social comparison in which one compares and tries to "fit in" with the elite, top-performing sub-group [8].

One important conclusion is that the simpler the visualization is, the more predictable the effect is. As it was observed in the case study with the first design, users usually do not select any sorting criterion and rely on the default view, i.e. sorted by original contributions, so the node representing each user was only different in size. The nodes remained the same in color and there was no difference in brightness; even if users selected another sorting criterion, the visualization still visualized only one (the selected) criterion at a time. Therefore, the first design was one-dimensional visualization with the dimension determined by user's selection of the sorting criteria, which most of the times was "by original contribution" (the default view). The users related the size of their star with the number of their original contributions and this representation provided a clear direction for social comparison and improvement. That is why the first design was more effective in motivating original contributions, as the experimental results from the first study showed.

In comparison, the second design appears to be less effective than the first design in motivating user contributions in terms of original contributions (new shared papers / URLs). However, the second design was good in motivating diverse contributions, which is probably more desirable than one-dimensional contributions (just in one activity, sharing new papers). A complex visualization showing several dimensions at a time (e.g. size representing contribution level, color representing membership level, and brightness representing reputation level) is interpreted differently by users. Users can focus on different dimensions to compete, rather than one particular area of competition such as the number of contributions, so the motivational effect is dispersed to a variety of activities. If a longer time was available for the experiment and more data for analysis, perhaps we would have seen a significant effect of the visualization on other user activities, i.e. sharing papers, and reading papers.

One clear conclusion for the designer is that when there is a clear goal about which type of contributions or participation is needed for the community, the visualization should represent just the user performance according to this type of participation or contribution. During the lifetime of an online community, different needs arise and different activities should be encouraged at different times [3] and so the default community view should be adapted to represent the activity that has to be encouraged at the moment.

5 Conclusions and Future Directions

Most visualizations discussed in the literature have been created with the purpose of informing the users about activities in the online community, since they allow a quick grasp of complex information. To our best knowledge, there are no other visualizations specifically targeted at motivating user participation in the online communities.

This paper proposed a new, improved design of the motivational community visualization targeted on encouraging participations in an experimental sharing community. The whole experience of developing this prototype visualization tells that it is not straightforward to create a motivational visualization. Apart from the great amount of information that needs to be represented, it has to be easy to operate, intuitive, attractive, and powerful enough to represent different semantics.

There are other interesting directions for further research, including the following:

1. Dynamic adaptation of particular dimensions (e.g. different sorting criteria) that are visualized depending on what is needed mostly in the community (e.g. need more shared files, need better quality shared files, or need more people to rate or comment on the shared files).

2. If decided to present more than one dimension (e.g. size, color, brightness) in the design, it would be better to experiment on one dimension at a time, instead of testing all the dimensions at the same time. The experience from the two major experiments described in this thesis indicates that one-dimensional visualization is easier to be predicted and controlled because of less noise.

3. Exploring the impact on user participation of incorporating more semantics through new dimensions of the star metaphor that haven't been used so far: such as the distance between stars based on, for example, the similarity in taste or ratings given by users.

4. Representing likeness between users, e.g. who reads whose contributions most often, who rates whose contributions most often, who normally rates whose contributions high and rates whose contributions low etc.

5. Investigating the effects of different graphical representations of an online community. The proposed prototype of the visualization in this paper chose a specific metaphor, a staring sky, but there are alternatives, from simple representations such as dots, circles, beehives, tables with numbers, charts, graphs, to complex metaphors such as cities, gardens, or combinations of any of the above. Which particular representation works best depends on the purpose of the visualization and the online community that it serves (e.g. the age of the members, their attitudes to computers, etc.) Investigating the effect of different metaphors for presenting community information is worthwhile.

6. Creating a more advanced graphical representation, e.g. allowing the navigation in the cosmos, like in a 3-D game. For example, in the second design of the proposed prototype of the visualization interface, it might be possible to group users with similar interests into subgroups and visualize it by a galaxy, clicking on which will cause the expansion of this galaxy and displaying the inside view of this galaxy; or clicking on a star will navigate users to the group of friends of this star (based on what criterion to define a user is a friend of another user could be an interesting research topic), etc.

Acknowledgement. This work is supported by the NSERC Discovery Grant Program.

References

1. Asch, S.E.: Effects of Group Pressure upon the Modification and Distortion of Judgments. Groups, Leadership, and Men, 177–190 (1951)
2. Bretzke, H., Vassileva, J.: Motivating Cooperation in Peer to Peer Networks. In: Brusilovsky, P., Corbett, A.T., de Rosis, F. (eds.) UM 2003. LNCS, vol. 2702, pp. 218–227. Springer, Heidelberg (2003)
3. Cheng, R., Vassileva, J.: Design and Evaluation of an Adaptive Incentive Mechanism for Sustained Educational Online Communities. User Modeling and User-Adapted Interaction, special issue on User Modeling Supporting Collaboration and Online Communities 16(2/3), 321–348 (2006)
4. Erickson, T.: Designing Visualizations of Social Activity: Six Claims. In: ACM CHI'2003 Proceedings, Ft. Lauderdale Florida, USA (April 5-10, 2003)
5. Erickson, T., Kellogg, W.A.: Social Translucence: Using Minimalist Visualizations of Social Activity to Support Collective Interaction. In: Hook, K., Benyon, D., Munroe, A. (eds.) Designing Information Spaces: The Social Navigation Approach, pp. 17–41. Springer, London (2003)
6. Festinger, L.: A Theory of Social Comparison Processes. Human Relations 7, 117–140 (1954)
7. Sun, L., Vassileva, J.: Social Visualization Encouraging Participation in Online Communities. In: Dimitriadis, Y.A., Zigurs, I., Gómez-Sánchez, E. (eds.) CRIWG 2006. LNCS, vol. 4154, pp. 349–363. Springer, Heidelberg (2006)
8. Garcia, S., Tor, A.: Rankings and Competition: Social Comparison in the Sha-dow of Standards. In: Social Science Research Network Library (2005), available at, http://papers.ssrn.com/sol3/papers.cfm?abstract_id=880505#PaperDownload

Social Theatres: A Web-Based Regulated Social Interaction Environment

Hugo Paredes[1] and F. Mário Martins[2]

[1] Universidade de Trás-os-Montes e Alto Douro, Departamento de Engenharias,
Quinta dos Prados, 5000 Vila Real, Portugal
hparedes@utad.pt
[2] Universidade do Minho, Departamento de Informática,
Campus de Gualtar, 4710 Braga, Portugal
fmm@di.uminho.pt

Abstract. The growth of the Internet and its associated technologies did open space for a new type of human interaction: virtual, social interaction environments.The introduction of regulated interaction in these virtual interaction spaces may be a solution towards their organization and inherent increased credibility. In this paper we propose a model for interaction regulation and control for virtual, social interaction spaces, called Social Theatres. A multi-layer software architecture was developed to support this web-based interaction model, allowing easy construction of such social interaction spaces and adaptation to users' devices. This paper discusses the advantages of regulated interaction, addresses the Social Theatre metaphor and presents the software architecture for the implementation of these regulated social interaction spaces.

Keywords: Software architecture, interaction regulation, rules, roles, interaction workflow, Social Theatres, Social Spaces.

1 Introduction

In recent years an exponential growth of virtual communities covering different areas from education to industry may be found in the Internet, using several different technologies and interaction resources. These users' centric environments lead new research problems concerning virtual social interaction [1,2]. One of the main identified problems concerning virtual interaction is the lack of regulation.

A clarification of the possible interactions allowed at each moment, related to each well identified functional type of user, could contribute to their better integration and understanding of a given interaction environment, as well as give them a better focus on their goals. This explicit interaction organization is called interaction regulation. Regulation of interaction does not necessarily mean loss of freedom, because the subjects and the contents of the interaction activities remain free.

This paper proposes the Social Theatre model (metaphor) as a basis for the development of regulated virtual social interaction environments. Generically,

J.M. Haake, S.F. Ochoa, and A. Cechich (Eds.): CRIWG 2007, LNCS 4715, pp. 87–94, 2007.
© Springer-Verlag Berlin Heidelberg 2007

the concept of Social Theatre (ST) expands the theatrical interaction model to daily activities of social interaction in virtual interaction environments. The focus on ST aims to capitalize from their well known and easy to understand interaction model. There are roles, interaction workflow and rules, which are the foundations of the proposed virtual interaction model. The interaction model is implemented by the ST's supporting architecture, which, among other features, regulates the virtual interaction, adapts to the user's interaction capabilities and technology and may also adapt the virtual interaction environment at runtime.

The paper is organized as follows: Section 2 presents the major concerns of virtual interaction environments and related work. Section 3 introduces the ST model, namely its three key concepts: roles, rules and interaction workflow. Section 4 presents the systems architecture that was developed to support the ST. Section 5 presents a simple case study: a paper presentation Social Space. Section 6 discusses the work to be done at implementation level.

2   Virtual Interaction Environments

Virtual interaction environments are cyberspaces where people can interact with each other without meeting in the real world. In these environments people usually use other identities, and are free to strongly express their thoughts, ideas and feelings. According to Preece [3] the development and success of such environments is constrained by its usability and sociability. Usability focuses on the way users interact to perform their tasks. Sociability is concerned with planning and developing social policies which regulate the users' behavior and interaction in the environment. Virtual interaction environments also reflect the evolutionary behavior of humans, by being adaptive and dynamic according to users' needs and expectations.

Usability and sociability concerns in virtual interaction environments have been implicit and explicitly addressed in many research projects, such as that of Winograd and Flores [4] embodying the speach act within a Computer Supported Collaborative Work (CSCW) tool; the method for groupware task analysis proposed by van der Veer, Welie and Thorborg [5]; and Ferraris and Martels [1] groupware regulation model.

In the next section, we present the Social Theatre model, which proposes another technological approach to usability and sociability concerns within virtual communities, taking into consideration the evolutive nature of these environments.

3   Social Theatres (ST)

A Theatre is a space where actors play a story through their activities, which aim to present a situation and provoke (feelings on) the audience. Generically, in a theatre the actions of an actor are predictable because they follow a script which defines the roles and the actions to be performed. An actor may perform many roles within the play, but must always follow the script.

The Social Theatre concept (ST) is based on the application of the theatres interaction model to everyday situations within interactive virtual environments. A ST may therefore be defined as a meta-environment for virtual interaction, which may be instantiated into different interaction scenarios (spaces) where real social interaction contexts are virtually reproduced. These spaces are called Social Spaces (SSP) and are ruled by interaction scripts, each person/user plays a certain role or roles by executing the set of actions that, according to the regulation of the space, he/she is allowed to.

As a virtual interaction environment, STs also reveal usability and adaptation concerns besides the regulated interaction model. As far as usability characteristics are concerned, STs promote users' participation, allowing multiple types of user interfaces adaptable or even adaptive to the users' hardware and software capabilities. STs manage adaptation supporting the ability to dynamically create and adapt SSPs allowing the users to modify or rebuild the environment's social policies to suit specific requirements, during an interaction session, as well as, in the creation of new SSPs that fit their needs.

SSP's definition is based on three fundamental concepts: Roles, Interaction Workflow and Rules.

3.1 Roles

Roles define the part played by users within SSPs. Clearly defining the role played by users of a virtual interaction environment allows them to know, from the start, what their behaviour is expected to be like and which actions are allowed at each moment. Roles are more than simple tags. They define the interaction entities of the SSP. Roles have properties that define behaviour and some attribution conditions.

User-role associations are defined in the SSP's context as an Actor. Actors are the entities capable of interacting in the SSP. This association is performed when the user is admitted into the SSP, according to the role attribution conditions. During the interaction, depending on the roles' properties, the association user-role may change, allowing the user to play sub-roles defined within the active main role.

3.2 Interaction Workflow

In each SSP only a set of well defined actions are executable by defined actors. The interaction workflow guarantees the organization and coordination of the SSP's actions, which in turn assures the accomplishment of the interaction goals. Furthermore, the interaction workflow clarifies the flow of the interaction to the actor, as the script in the theatre metaphor.

The SSP interaction workflow is defined by (1) a set of actions and/or inner interaction workflows, (2) a set of transitions and (3) an optional set of workflow data. Actions define the interaction tasks that can be performed by actors. An interaction task can be a simple user data input/output, or the execution of a service operation as, for example, sending a message to a whiteboard (consider that there is a whiteboard service, with a send-message operation). A transition is a relation between actions, guarded by a condition. Transitions defined by an interaction workflow may follow the patterns defined in [6].

3.3   Rules

Rules are the protocols defined by the SSP in order to guarantee the virtual interaction regulation. Generically, a rule is a logical expression that combines information about the SSP's structure and state. Rules are applied to the actions of the interaction workflow, as well as to SSP's services, fitting out protocols for its coordination. There are two categories of rules: (1) functional/interaction rules, which are applied to the interaction workflow of the SSP; and (2) operational/coordination rules which define the protocols for the coordination of the SSP.

Besides the interaction regulation and SSP's coordination support, rules should be adaptable at runtime, to fulfil user's needs. Modification of rules may lead to potential conflicts that must be predicted in order to preserve the overall SSP's consistency. To solve rule conflicts, a priority level is assigned to each rule. However, rules that are crucial to the normal operation of SSP cannot be changed. These rules are called SSP laws.

4   Software Architecture

In section 2 the theoretical model of regulated social interaction environments was presented. In order to validate the presented model, a software architecture [7] to support the implementation of ST was defined and built.

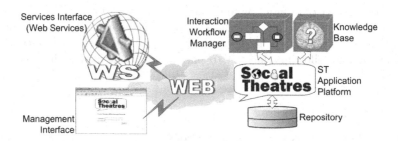

Fig. 1. Physical view of the Architecture

The main goal of the software architecture that supports the implementation of a ST is to create an infra-structure to implement the presented regulated social interaction environments, that is able to guarantee that: (1) the virtual interaction environments are regulated by interaction rules, which are adaptable at runtime, (2) the creation of a new SSP in the ST can be done in a simple way, describing the interaction workflow, the roles and the rules of that space; and finally (3) that the system has the ability to adapt the interaction contents to the characteristics of the users interaction device, as well as to provide accessible contents according to the profile of the user.

From a physical perspective (Fig. 1) the architecture provides two standard interfaces: a Web interface for management purposes and a Web Services API that provides a core of services for the development of client oriented applications. The application core of the architecture is delegated in four servers: ST application platform, knowledge base, repository and interaction workflow manager. ST application platform server hosts the logical application layer that implements the ST model.

From a logical perspective, the ST application platform lays on a vertical layer (Metadata layer), which provides the runtime creation of the necessary components to the horizontal functional layers (Adaptation and Interaction layer) Fig. 2. This architectural design allows the dynamic creation and modification of the SSP.

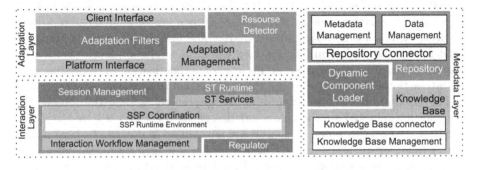

Fig. 2. Logical view of the ST application platform

The metadata layer is the platforms logical core kernel and has three main purposes: ST data and metadata management associated with runtime objects and components; creation of dynamic SSP's objects and components and management of the knowledge database.

The Repository functional block implements data management. This functional block includes a connector to a XML Database Management System where data representations of ST objects are stored as XML documents. This data representation is used to describe ST's objects as users, and SSP's components as roles, rules and interaction workflow. Metadata and data manager components are used to validate the data manipulation request. The interface of the Repository functional block is assured by the Repository Connector component.

The Dynamic component loader is responsible for the runtime creation of SSP components and objects from the respective metadata and data stored in the repository. This functional blocks operating basis is the transformation of XML Schemas and XML documents into classes and instances respectively [8].

The Knowledge Base functional block is a key component in user interaction regulation, since it stores and manages all the knowledge about the SSPs and their instances in the ST. It includes three components that guarantee the knowledge management, its integrity and an access interface.

The main goal of the interaction layer is the creation and management of the SSP's runtime interaction. In addition, it provides services to improve the users experience in the ST environment.

The SSP Coordination and Runtime functional block is the key component of this layer and is responsible for the instantiation and lifecycle management of the SSP. In order to perform these tasks, SSP Coordination and Runtime functional block operation depends on the Dynamic Component Loader in order to create the functional elements of the SSP (rules, roles and interaction workflow).

SSP Workflow manages the interaction workflow of the SSP, determining which action follows according to the SSP interaction workflow definition. The Regulator activity relies on the Knowledge Base, which is inferred in order to validate the execution of the actions in each state of the SSP lifecycle.

SSP interaction is also supported by the ST Services and the Session Management. ST Services provide SSPs actors with a set of common interaction services, such as a whiteboard, object sharing and history. The Session Management functional block is mainly required when the admission service is used to provide information about the user, his level of authentication in the system and his interaction resources, retrieving this information from the adaptation layer.

The adaptation layer is responsible for guaranteeing that the interaction contents are adapted to the characteristics of the devices used by the users and that the contents sent by the users are normalized in order to be used inside the ST's supporting architecture. The adaptation management block controls filters' activity and selection. It receives information about the client's resources, acquired by the resource detector block, and selects the most appropriate filter to apply.

5   Case Study

In this section we present a case study that was used for validating the architecture which presents its interaction and regulation mechanisms. We selected a common and well known social interaction scenario to be represented as a SSP: a paper presentation in a conference.

The SSP creation process starts with its definition, identifying and describing its roles, rules and interaction workflow. In a paper presentation, there usually are three kinds of participants: the author of the paper (paperAuthor), the session chair (sessionChair) and the audience (audience). Roles sessionChair and paperAuthor are unique, mandatory and must be assigned on the SSP's instantiation (creation). As far as interaction actions are concerned, we consider two different phases in the environment interaction: the paper presentation and the questions session. The identified actions were organized in the interaction workflow presented in Fig. 3. The operating rules defined for the SSP do not

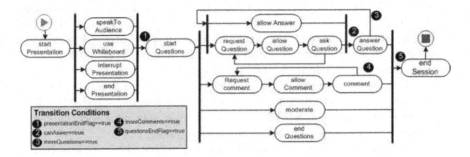

Fig. 3. Paper Presentation SSP Interaction Workflow Diagram

allow the execution of any service in the first phase of the SSP interaction work-flow(paper presentation) except the operation `consult` of services *whiteboard* and *chatting*. It is also defined that the default behavior for operating rules is *accept*. Interaction roles define which actor can perform each action, as for ex-ample, actions *speakToAudience*, *useWhiteboard* and *answerQuestion* are only performed by the actor `paperAuthor` (FR1).

Once the metadata of the SSP is defined, it is possible to request the creation of a SSP instance and evaluate the SSP runtime lifecycle. In order to have a successful instantiation of SSP Paper Presentation it is necessary to identify the users that perform the roles `paperAuthor` and `sessionChair`.

The created SSP instance has its interaction workflow initialized and enabled to perform the action *startPresentation*. After the execution of the action *start-Presentation* the user performing the role `paperAuthor` is able to present his work, requesting the execution of actions *speakToAudiance* and *useWhiteboard* (FR1) until the *endPresentation* action is executed. Generically, in order to exe-cute an action the ST processes the request and adapts the contents provided by the actor. The request is routed to the SSP, that retrieves session information and requests the validation execution to the regulator. A response is inferred based on the SSP's knowledge. If successful, the request is then routed to the interaction workflow to be executed. The result is stored in the knowledge base and returned to the actor, after the adaptation of response contents.

The SSP runtime lifecycle ends when the action *endSession* is executed. At this time the information about the SSP is registered into the history database of the ST, using the history service of the SSP. When this process is concluded, the resources allocated to this SSP instance are released.

6   Discussion and Future Work

In this paper we propose a possible solution to regulate virtual interaction in virtual interaction environments. Our goal is to create an integrated environment which defines a common model of interaction for all the interaction virtual spaces that may be created from the model, just like a class-instance relationship.

We use the theatre metaphor to retrieve the theatrical interaction model, which defines roles that are played by actors (users) in the interaction environment regulated by interaction rules. The main purpose of the hosted virtual environment is to represent everyday situations of social life, and since it uses the theatrical interaction model we named it ST.

The ST supporting architecture implements the virtual interaction regulation model and is intended to be generic and adaptive. Every definable SSP will have a well defined interaction workflow, a set of roles and rules according to the foundations of our proposed virtual interaction model.

The presented architecture has a dynamic core that supports the dynamics of the SSP. This allows easy runtime adaptation of the SSP to fulfill user needs and expectations. In addition, it can virtually support any kind of interaction device configuration.

We presented a case study for a concrete SSP, the paper presentation in a conference, to explain how the architecture works.

Further work on rule validation, cross dependency and overall consistency and adaptation is still being done, mainly driven directly by experiences with real users.

References

1. Ferraris, C., Martel, C.: Regulation in groupware: The example of a collaborative drawing tool for young children. In: CRIWG '00: Proceedings of the 6th International Workshop on Groupware, Washington, DC, USA, p. 119. IEEE Computer Society Press, Los Alamitos (2000)
2. Churchill, E.F., Snowdon, D.N., Munro, A.J. (eds.): Collaborative Virtual Environments: Digital Places and Spaces for Interaction. Springer, Heidelberg (2001)
3. Preece, J.: Online Communities: Designing Usability and Supporting Socialbilty. John Wiley & Sons, Inc., Chichester (2000)
4. Flores, F., Graves, M., Hartfield, B., Winograd, T.: Computer systems and the design of organizational interaction. ACM Trans. Inf. Syst. 6, 153–172 (1988)
5. van der Veer, G., van Welie, M.: Groupware task analysis. In: Tutorial Notes for the CHI99 workshop Task Analysis Meets Prototyping: Towards seamless UI Development (1999)
6. van der Aalst, W.M.P., ter Hofstede, A.H.M., Kiepuszewski, B., Barros, A.P.: Workflow patterns. Distributed and Parallel Databases 14, 5–51 (2003)
7. Garlan, D., Shaw, M.: An introduction to software architecture, Carnegie Mellon University, Pittsburgh, PA, USA. Technical report, School of Computer Science (1994)
8. McLaughlin, B.: Java & XML Data Binding. O'Reilly (2002)

The Collaboration Engineering Approach for Designing Collaboration Processes

Gwendolyn L. Kolfschoten[1], and Gert-Jan de Vreede[1,2]

[1] Delft University of Technology, Faculty of Technology, Policy and Management, Department of System Engineering, Jaffalaan 5, 2628BX, Delft, The Netherlands
G.L.Kolfschoten@tudelft.nl
[2] University of Nebraska at Omaha, Department of Information Systems & Quantitative Analysis, Institute for Collaboration Science, 1110 South 67th street, Omaha, NE 68182-0116
USA
Gdevreede@mail.unomaha.edu

Abstract. Collaboration Engineering is an approach to design and deploy collaboration processes that can be executed by practitioners for high value recurring tasks. A collaboration engineer designs collaboration processes and transfers them to practitioners in an organization. Through the recurring nature of the task, combined with lower investment in training, the approach is more likely to be successful in organizations because it is easier to adopt and sustain collaboration support in this way. In order to be successful, collaboration engineers need to develop collaboration process designs that have many more functions and requirements than traditional process agenda's of facilitators. This paper describes a step-by-step approach for the design of such collaboration processes. The approach was evaluated in a number of iterations. The evaluation results provide support for the usefulness of the approach.

Keywords: Collaboration Engineering, ThinkLets, Design approach, Design patterns.

1 Introduction

Facilitation and technology support for collaboration such as Group Support Systems (GSS) can improve the efficiency and effectiveness of collaboration in organizations [1]. However, research on GSS and facilitation has indicated that it is difficult to implement sustained collaboration support in organizations for a number of reasons [2, 3]: First, a support facility for collaboration often does not support a core business process. Second, it therefore often has uncertain revenue. Finally, it requires an extensive set of skills and competences that are difficult to develop and transfer. To address these challenges, the Collaboration Engineering approach is developed. Collaboration Engineering is an approach to design and deploy high value recurring collaborative work practices that can be executed by practitioners by themselves without ongoing support from professionals [4-6]. The Collaboration Engineering

J.M. Haake, S.F. Ochoa, and A. Cechich (Eds.): CRIWG 2007, LNCS 4715, pp. 95–110, 2007.

approach prescribes that a collaboration engineer designs an efficacious, acceptable, reusable, transferable and predictable collaboration process [7], which is then transferred to a practitioner, a domain expert in the organization. After this transition, which requires a (short) training [8], the practitioner can facilitate the collaboration process, without the support of a professional facilitator, and without having to learn extensive facilitation skills [3, 9]. Due to the absence of extensive facilitation skills and experience, the design created by the collaboration engineer should be of higher quality and should be more robust. Therefore the challenge of Collaboration Engineering research is to increase our understanding of the design and transition of collaboration processes. This paper aims to increase the understanding of the Collaboration Engineering design process.

Collaboration Engineering researchers are developing guidelines to the design process that foster high quality collaboration processes. These guidelines assembled in the Collaboration Engineering approach are organized according to the "ways framework" from [10] that enables a structured description of any design approach or methodology according to its Way of Thinking, Way of Working, Way of Modeling, and Way of Control. The Way of Thinking encompasses a set of theories about collaboration quality aspects such as productivity [11], participant satisfaction [12], technology transition [3, 13], commitment [14], and other phenomena that indicate quality aspects of collaboration processes and the use of collaboration support. The Way of Control concerns methods to measure these quality aspects and thus control the quality of a collaboration process around these aspects [15]. The Way of Modeling addresses the design artifacts that are developed, i.e. the representation and documentation of the collaboration process and its constituent building blocks [16-19]. Finally, the Way of Working provides the design strategies and steps required to design and transfer a collaboration process that allows practitioners to guide groups executing their collaborative tasks.

This paper focuses on the Way of Working in Collaboration Engineering, and specifically on the design of a collaboration process. The design of a collaboration process is described in literature as a critical success factor, see e.g. [20-23]. This paper reports on efforts to formalize such an approach based on existing design approaches and best practices from the Collaboration Engineering field. Such a design approach will:

- Provide design support for (novice) collaboration engineers.
- Increase our insight in the critical steps of the design of collaboration processes.
- Provide a basis for the creation of design support tools.
- Provide a basis for the training of collaboration engineers.

The remainder of this paper will first describe the basis of the approach, which is grounded in a variety of problem solving and design methods. Next we will describe the design approach in detail. Last, we will describe the results of an iterative evaluation of the approach, followed with conclusions and suggestions for further research.

2 Background

A process often used for design (creativity) or problem solving exists generally of several steps that include [24-31]: identification of the issue, analysis, finding (and evaluating) alternatives, choice and implementation. These steps can be used as a basis for the Collaboration Engineering design approach, but some adjustments are required to make it suitable for the design of a transferable collaboration processes that can be instantiated for different instances of the task. The Implementation step will be outside of the scope of this paper, as is identification of the issue, which we consider a step that precedes design as described by [32].

In Collaboration Engineering, we use design patterns to support the design process called thinkLets [3, 16, 19]. Design patterns are descriptions of known, reusable solutions to recurring problems. The concept of patterns is old, but became popular through the work of Alexander and the gang of four [33, 34]. ThinkLets, are named, scripted, reusable, and transferable collaborative activities that give rise to specific known variations of the general patterns of collaboration among people working together toward a goal [4]. ThinkLets offer the building blocks for collaboration process design.

The creation of the design approach for Collaboration Engineering was based on a number of previous studies in this research area. First, we used a survey among facilitators to identify the activities they performed when designing a collaboration process and the information they needed in that effort [35]. Furthermore we used the thinkLet concept [16, 17, 19] and knowledge about successful combinations of thinkLets [36]. Next, we performed a series of in depth interviews with facilitators to determine the considerations they made when choosing among thinkLets [37, 38]. Finally, we executed a research project on the transition of collaboration processes for which we developed a template for a thinkLet script and a training approach [8, 18]. The insights from these studies informed the approach to design thinkLets-based collaboration processes, which can be transferred as collaborative work practices to practitioners.

3 Design Approach

With the use of thinkLets the design approach alters slightly. While in a regular design process time is spend on finding and evaluating alternatives, in Collaboration Engineering we use a library of thinkLets. Hence, the key design activity becomes 'choice'. Between analysis and the thinkLet choice we need to decompose the task into steps of activities that can be performed with thinkLets. After these iterative steps, the agenda can be built and the design can be validated. Documentation of the process design for transition is a process that occurs parallel to each of the steps above. An overall representation of the Collaboration Engineering design approach is depicted in figure 1, each step in the approach will be described in more detail.

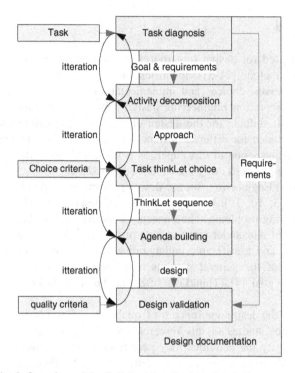

Fig. 1. Overview of the Collaboration Engineering design approach

As in software engineering, it is clear that these steps are usually not executed sequentially, but may be iterative and incremental in nature [39, 40]. Insights and choices in every step can affect past and future steps and choices [41]. Furthermore, the documentation of the collaboration process prescription will take place on a continuous basis during the design process.

3.1 Task Diagnosis

Design is an evolving process that starts with the initial conversation with stakeholders involved in the Collaboration Engineering process in which the collaboration engineer determines, adjusts and negotiates about the requirements and constraints on the collaboration process with respect to the task, the stakeholders involved the resources available and the practitioners. The following information should be documented in a problem description:

Task analysis: Goal, deliverables, and objectives
The practitioner will have to gain commitment from the group with respect to the goal, objectives and deliverables that are determined by the collaboration engineer, and thus these should be established very carefully. The goal and deliverable can be tangible, or can be experiences such as awareness and shared understanding.

Stakeholder analysis: Group, stakes, roles and needs

Many collaboration processes have to be used with a variety of groups. However, information on aspects such as group size, age, sex, culture, education background, and organization level can help the collaboration engineer to customize the process design, for instance by adjusting the tone of the script (formal/ informal) or to select appropriate tools to support different group sizes. Additionally a stakeholder analysis to consider the team history, and to determine for each stakeholder their individual stakes, their expectations, their expertise, motivation and whether they are willing to commit to the process and result is required. A collaboration process design should accommodate stakes as much as possible to increase commitment of resources (knowledge and effort) and to foster acceptance of the process and results. It is also possible to assign and document different roles to different stakeholders.

Resource analysis: time, knowledge, effort and physical resources

The collaboration process design must make optimal use of the available resources. In discussion with the organization a time frame, resources, technology and budget need to be determined. The timeframe of a collaboration process design may not always be very flexible, but it might be possible to create a "light version" of the process in which some steps are removed to fit a shorter time-frame. Depending on the reliable availability of resources, a process can be designed in which specific resources are indicated or in which requirements to the resources are specified as capabilities.

Practitioner analysis: skills, experience, personality, domain expertise

The practitioner analysis can be done based on two scenarios: Either the selection of practitioners is already determined and the design should be adjusted to these practitioners or the practitioner profile, or the collaboration engineer is asked to create a profile that is used to select practitioners. Practitioners are domain experts.

The above considerations can be used as a checklist to analyze or negotiate the requirements and constraints to the collaboration process design. In this analysis it is important to determine whether constraints and requirements are fixed or dynamic. In case of dynamic requirements or constraints the collaboration engineer should provide guidelines for instantiation.

3.2 Task Decomposition

When the goal and requirements are sufficiently clear, the basic collaboration process needs to be determined. To do this the collaboration engineer needs to further analyze and decompose the task into activities. A first step is to determine if the organization has already a pre-defined way of executing the task. If the traditional practice is functional and results can be improved by making it collaborative then it can be used as a starting point. If no process is followed in the organization, then standards in the literature might provide a starting point for the activity decomposition. If the process is first of its kind, then a completely new process for the task should be defined. To define a process from scratch the deliverables need to be determined, based on which activities to create the deliverables are elicited. These activities should be named and sequenced to derive a rudimental process and deliverable description. The next step is to further decompose this process into smaller steps. For this purpose there are two approaches: process decomposition and result decomposition. Both can be used in combination, but we will explain each separately.

Process decomposition

Process decomposition is guided by the patterns of collaboration. Patterns of collaboration characterize a group activity as the members move from an initial state to a next state [9]. The activities of the rudimental collaboration process can be directly matched to a pattern of collaboration, or be further decomposed into constituent sub activities that can then be matched. The patterns of collaboration are [4, 14]:

- *Generate:* Move from having fewer to having more concepts in the pool of concepts shared by the group
- *Reduce:* Move from having many concepts to a focus on fewer concepts that the group deems worthy of further attention
- *Clarify:* Move from having less to having more shared understanding of concepts and of the words and phrases used to express them.
- *Organize:* Move from less to more understanding of the relationships among concepts the group is considering
- *Evaluate:* Move from less to more understanding of the relative value of the concepts under consideration
- *Build consensus:* Move from having fewer to having more group members who are willing to commit to a proposal.

Result decomposition

Results decomposition consists of a further analysis of the deliverables and requirements to come up with the elementary activities to create the results. Decomposition of results should lead to a level of activities where deliverables of each activity cannot be usefully decomposed any more. Decomposition depends on the requirements defined in the first phase, task diagnosis, such as time, project embedding, cognitive load, technology available, practitioner skills and task requirements. The following classification of results of collaborative work can be used as a basis for results decomposition:

- *Input:* There are four types of input that we could distinguish; *creative* input such as ideas and solutions, *informative* input such as facts and experiences, *visionary* input such are future requirements, visions, scenario's and trends and *reflective* input such as comments, preferences and opinions.
- *Structure:* We distinguish several types of structure: a *cluster* of related concepts, a *ranking* of concepts based on some criterion, a *model* in which more complex relations can be indicated and a *sequence* in which the timely relationship of concepts is indicated.
- *Focus:* Results in this category include a *selection* where only a few concepts are chosen by the group, a *summary* in which concepts with similar meaning are integrated without removing unique input, a *scope* in which the boundaries for a

collection of constructs are formulated, and a *direction* in which concepts that fit a specific cause of action are taken into account.

- **Shared understanding:** We distinguish several types of shared understanding. First, *shared knowledge*, followed by, shared meaning about the knowledge in the group. Next is *mutual learning*: people might learn from each other and advance both their own knowledge and the group knowledge. Last, *mutual differences* and disagreements can be revealed to gain understanding on different types of conflicts.

- **Commitment:** One type of commitment is a *decision*, which can be made based on majority or on more sophisticated and inclusive decision making rules. Another option is to simply get *support* for a plan or proposal. Yet another type of commitment is an *agreement*, for instance to spend an amount of resources or to create a specific deliverable. A last type of commitment is a *consensus*, in which all critical stakeholders commit to the proposal [42].

- **Empathy:** Empathy results are: *respect* for other stakeholders, *shared stakes* when people accommodate the stakes of others among their own, *consideration*, taking those stakes into account, and a *team bond* in which mutual goals are pursued.

3.3 ThinkLet Choice

After decomposition, the activities can be matched with thinkLets. This match is again made based on criteria and guidelines. After choosing thinkLets, the collaboration engineer can also modify and instantiate them. When choosing among thinkLets there are four key tradeoffs to consider [38], see figure 2.

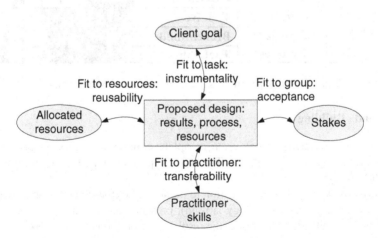

Fig. 2. Trade-offs in the choice among facilitation techniques

The choice of a thinkLet is a complex task. Many factors influence the fit of the thinkLet to each of the dimensions. Taking all factors into account and comparing them to the characteristics of the thinkLets is difficult. To support this task we developed two supporting maps. One offers a classification of thinkLets based on results or patterns of collaboration. The other offers insight in the value of thinkLet combinations when output of one thinkLet is used as input for the next thinkLet. In the choice map, the thinkLets displayed vertically follow the thinkLets displayed horizontally, e.g. the square that is marked with x indicates the combination FreeBrainstorm followed by OnePage. The color of each square indicates whether the combination is excellent (green), possible but tricky (orange), or impossible (red).

Pattern: Generate	Result: Input	ThinkLet combination: Good=* Tricky =^ Impossible =■	FreeBrainstorm	OnePage	Comparative	LeafHopper	DealersChoice	PlusMinus	TopFive	BranchBuilder	TheLobbyist
FreeBrainstorm	FreeBrainstorm										
OnePage	OnePage										
Comparative	Comparative										
LeafHopper	LeafHopper										
DealersChoice	DealersChoice										
PlusMinus	PlusMinus										
TopFive	TopFive	**Starting point?**	*	*	*	*	*	■	■	*	■
BranchBuilder	BranchBuilder	**FreeBrainstorm**	■	x	*	^	■	^	■	^	*
TheLobbyist	TheLobbyist	**OnePage**			^	^	^	*	■	*	*
DimSum	DimSum	**Comparative**				^	^	^	■	^	*
PointCounterP.	PointCounterP.	**LeafHopper**					*	*	*	^	*
	StrawPoll	**DealersChoice**					*	*	*	^	^
	MultiCriteria	**PlusMinus**					^	^	^	^	*
	CheckMark	**TopFive**						^	^	^	*
	StakeHolderPoll	**BranchBuilder**						^		^	*
	BucketVote	**TheLobbyist**									

Fig. 3. Result & pattern classification and Choice Map example

3.4 Agenda Building

A sequence of thinkLets is not yet a complete collaboration process prescription. Some additional steps are required. The most important steps besides the thinkLets are the following:

Introduction, ice breaker, introduction to the technology used and a small warm-up exercise (when complex technology is used), presentations to introduce the focus of the collaboration effort, or to present the results from previous steps, breaks, decisions in which the practitioner should choose a path in the process based on certain criteria for the output, Wrap up of the workshop, and evaluation of the process, e.g. through a questionnaire.

The agenda should specify all relevant information for each thinkLet, relevant for validation. A format for the agenda is displayed below.

Activity	Description	Question/ Assignment	Deliverable	ThinkLet & Pattern	Time
1					
2					
Etc...					

Fig. 4. Agenda format

The first column is to identify and number the activities. Note that breaks, presentations and other activities should also be included in the process prescription. The second column describes the task. An example of an activity is "categorize ideas" or "brainstorm requirements". The next column is reserved for the specific questions or assignments to the group. The next column describes the deliverable: a specification of the expected output or a more general output like "ranking of the results", or "categorization of the ideas". The fifth column indicates the thinkLet and pattern it aims to evoke. The last column lists the estimated time needed for each activity.

Based on the information in the agenda, the flow of the collaboration process can be graphically represented using a Facilitation Process Model (FPM) [9] is used. A FPM focuses attention on the logic of the flow of the process from activity to activity. An FPM uses four symbols to document the process flow (see figure 5 for an example).

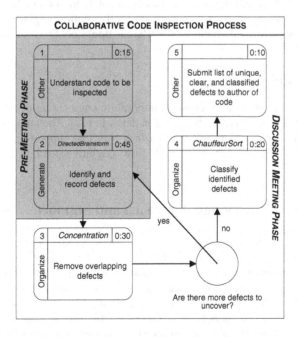

Fig. 5. Example of a Facilitation Process Model (based on Vreede et al. 2005)

Each activity is represented as a rounded rectangle that has three fields. The top left field gives the activity number, corresponding with the agenda. The top center field gives the thinkLet name. The top right field lists the time required for the activity. The largest field contains a description of what the team is supposed to do in the activity. Finally, the field on the left names the primary pattern of collaboration to be created in the activity. Decision points in the process flow are represented as circles and the decision outcomes are indicated along the flow arrows.

3.5 Design Validation

The agenda includes all information required to validate the collaboration process design. There are four ways to validate:

- *Pilot testing:* This is simply a small scale implementation of the collaboration process which might allow the team members to assess the quality of the process.
- *Walk-through:* A final assessment of the collaboration process can be done by walking through the activities in the process with the practitioners and the client or a few of the participants.
- *Act it out (Simulate):* A simulation can be done using role-playing by the collaboration engineer himself. By simulating the design, the collaboration engineer tries to answer the questions he poses in the design himself, and considers if those answers can be used in the next activity.
- *Expert Evaluation:* As each facilitator or collaboration engineer has his own style, each will have different solutions for a collaboration challenge. Discussing the design with colleagues will help the collaboration engineer to find better solutions for difficult activities and different thinkLets or methods for a certain challenge.

3.6 Documentation

To document a collaboration process a collaboration engineering design template has been developed. The template is described in detail in [18]. The template is created to offer the practitioner complete information in a way that supports both training and execution of the design with sufficiently low cognitive load to enable efficient learning [8].

4 Evaluation of the Design Approach and Support

To evaluate the design approach we created a design booklet: a step-by-step manual illustrating each step in the design approach both conceptually and with specific examples. We then let groups of students use the booklet in combination with a set of thinkLets to design collaboration processes based on a case description as part of a course on facilitation. Based on the feedback from the students we enhanced the design approach and its supporting techniques.. In this section we describe the evaluation process and the key outcomes. The approach as described in section 3 represents the final iteration of the approach based on the evaluation results.

4.1 Method

The design booklet describing the Collaboration Engineering approach contained the following information:

- An introduction to explain how to use the booklet.
- A description of the characteristics of a high quality design.
- A step-by-step explanation of the design approach with a running example for each step.
- A list of design guidelines and best practices.

To evaluate the Collaboration Engineering design approach we let 26 students at the University of Nebraska at Omaha, and Delft University of Technology in the Netherlands design a collaboration process based on a case description. The group was a mix of graduate and undergraduate students that participated in a course on Facilitation, GSS and Collaboration Engineering. The students received a booklet with the design approach and a set of thinkLet descriptions. The case was based on a real project description of a GSS session run in the Netherlands by professional facilitators. Names of the organizations involved were changed. The students were graded for this assignment. The students had to design a collaboration process according to the case description. The students only had to create a description and decomposition of the collaboration process, build the agenda, and create the facilitation process model. The students filled out a questionnaire after completing their assignment. Their questionnaires were collected after grades had been posted.

To evaluate the design approach, we used the following metrics to measure whether the different elements of the design support booklet were helpful in designing a collaboration process:

- (1) Actual use of the design booklet.
- (2) Usefulness of the design booklet.
- (3) The design booklet is saving time.
- (4) The design booklet is easy to use.
- (5) The design booklet is understandable.
- (6) The design booklet helps to improve the design.
- (7) The design booklet needs of improvement.

We also asked the students to reflect on their efforts for the design task and we asked them to specify what could be improved to support them better in the design assignment. Finally, we asked the students for tips for improvement, using questionnaires and informal evaluation sessions and interviews. Based on these insights we revised the booklet several times. The evaluation of version 1 revealed various suggestions for improvement. Based on this feedback, the next version of the design booklet provided a running example, as this was a need indicated by many students. Furthermore we added an introduction on how to use the booklet, describing the purpose of each element, and extended and updated the descriptions of the approach and documentation requirements. Finally, we added an explanation of the criteria for high quality design. Feedback on this version informed the third iteration of the booklet. In this version, we further updated the design approach explaining its iterative nature and integrating the high level and low level decomposition to one step. Furthermore, we added a preliminary checklist for the analysis. The explanation of the choice among thinkLets and the tradeoffs involved were elaborated in this version as well.

In the fourth version, the explanations each element of the design approach were fine-tuned. We also extended the checklist for analysis, explained the quality trade-offs for the choice among thinkLets, and explained how choice and decomposition can affect each other. Finally, we added the classifications and the choice map.

The fourth version of the booklet was evaluated in a case study with graduate students and faculty members of the Manchester Business School. 16 people participated in a two day workshop. Some participants where novices to facilitation, others were experienced facilitators but used different approaches (mostly based on decision theories). In the first day they experienced and got familiar with approximately 10 thinkLets in a GSS setting. On the second day the participants were first introduced to the design approach and the supporting materials. Then they had two hours to work on a case-based collaboration process design. Not all participants were able to finish the process design, but most managed to create a sequence of thinkLets that they would use to support the group. After the design exercise, the participants filled out a questionnaire to collect their perceptions on the design approach as presented in the booklet.

4.2 Results

Tables 1 present the results of the questionnaire among participants for the final version of the design support booklet (the numbers in the first column correspond with the questions below). Two questionnaires were excluded because they were not entirely filled out, so n=14 for all questions. For all tables, the scale is 1-5: (1) strongly disagree, (2) disagree, (3) neutral, (4) agree, and (5) strongly agree. μ= mean, st= standard deviation

Table 1. Design approach & support evaluation

construct	design approach		quality criteria		guidelines		agenda		FPM		choice map		classi-fication	
	μ	st	μ	st	μ	st	μ	st	μ	st	μ	st	μ	st
1	3.6	1.1	3.1	1.1	2.8	1.3	3.8	0.9	3.4	1.1	3.4	1.3	3.1	1.1
2	4.0	0.6	3.8	0.4	3.6	0.7	4.0	0.4	3.9	0.5	4.1	0.7	3.9	0.5
3	3.9	0.6	3.4	0.8	3.2	0.7	3.8	0.6	3.6	0.8	3.6	0.8	3.4	0.6
4	3.9	0.5	3.2	0.6	3.3	0.7	3.7	0.7	3.9	0.5	3.6	0.8	3.6	0.6
5	4.1	0.5	3.4	0.9	3.5	0.5	3.6	0.7	3.9	0.7	3.9	0.6	3.7	0.5
6	3.4	0.5	3.5	0.7	3.3	0.7	3.9	0.5	3.6	0.9	3.4	0.7	3.6	0.6
7	2.5	0.7	3.1	0.8	2.7	0.8	2.7	0.9	2.9	0.9	2.7	1.0	2.7	0.6

- (1) Actual use of the design booklet.
- (2) Usefulness of the design booklet.
- (3) The design booklet is saving time.
- (4) The design booklet is easy to use.
- (5) The design booklet is understandable.
- (6) The design booklet helps to improve the design.
- (7) The design booklet needs of improvement.

Since the participants had only two hours to perform the design exercise, the use of the supporting materials is somewhat limited, and had a high standard deviation. This is consistent with the fact that some of the participants were able to create a process design within the two hours while others did not manage to do so. However, since we presented the information and explained it in an example we feel that the results on usefulness, time saving, ease of use, understandability and supportiveness are representative. Each of these factors scored slightly to fairly positive. The design approach, agenda format and the choice map were considered most useful, followed by the classification and facilitation process model. The design guidelines and quality criteria scored lower on usefulness and also on time saving. This is not surprising as these aspects are mostly used for validation and further iterations of the design.

Further, it was stated that the design guidelines were considered useful only for users that already know a set of thinkLets by heart. The suggestions for improvement included the following: for the design approach, more examples were considered useful; for the quality criteria the participants requested more explanation and more examples about the tradeoffs and the specific tradeoffs that emerge when choosing among thinkLets. Some participants also suggested that the guidelines should be clustered, for instance to the patterns of collaboration. The choice map and classification were found to be rather complex, yet at the same time useful. The agenda format and facilitation process model were considered overlapping. However, while the agenda was considered more useful, the facilitation process model was more easy to use and more understandable. The agenda format and the classification of the thinkLets were considered most supportive. The design guidelines and choice map were considered least supportive. All supporting elements scored low on the need for improvement.

5   Conclusions

Based on the experiences with 40 users, we conclude that the Collaboration Engineering design approach, as described in the booklet, offers useful and effective support, especially for novice process designers. However, it takes a considerable amount of time to digest and use the information and supporting materials. Some elements are considered rather complex. We feel that it will be very hard to further improve the current approach on 'paper'. The minor improvements suggested regarding the final version of the booklet will only increase the amount of information without adding new insights and support. To better support collaboration process design efforts, we feel it is critical to create a computer based expert tool.

In this paper we presented the Collaboration Engineering design approach and design support to help the collaboration engineer in designing a collaboration process that is efficacious to its goal and acceptable for the stakeholders involved. To support efficaciousness we offered selection guidance on individual thinkLets and thinkLet combinations. We also provided guidance how the collaboration engineer should analyze the group and stakeholders involved in order to increase acceptance of the designed process. The acceptance of the collaboration process design is further facilitated by the nature of thinkLets: Since thinkLets are 'best practices' [16, 19], they have been accepted by groups in many situations. The reason for this is that many thinkLets are based on principles such as equity and democracy. For example, in many generate thinkLets every participant gets equal opportunity to contribute and in most evaluation thinkLets a democratic voting method is used.

Future efforts to improve the Collaboration Engineering design approach will focus on:

- Documenting thinkLets with the explicit notion of alternatives, and their impact on the quality of the collaboration process design.
- Using design guidelines as a basis for the validation of the collaboration process design, e.g. a check on staying within the time frame allocated for the meeting and having sufficient thinkLets with discussion elements can be checked automatically when the appropriate information is recorded in a database.
- Automating the generation of design documentation.

A next step in our research will therefore be the creation of a Computer Aided Collaboration Engineering tool which supports the collaboration engineer in selecting, sequencing and instantiating thinkLets to design a collaboration process according to the approach. Such a tool should increase the efficiency and quality of the design effort, while containing or further decreasing the cognitive effort involved.

References

1. Fjermestad, J., Hiltz, S.R.: A Descriptive Evaluation of Group Support Systems Case and Field Studies. Journal of Management Information Systems 17, 115–159 (2001)
2. Agres, A., de Vreede, G.J., Briggs, R.O.: A Tale of Two Cities: Case Studies of GSS Transition in Two Organizations. Group Decision and Negotiation 14, 256–266 (2005)
3. Briggs, R.O., de Vreede, G.J., Nunamaker, Jr., J.F.: Collaboration Engineering with ThinkLets to Pursue Sustained Success with Group Support Systems. Journal of Management Information Systems 19, 31–63 (2003)
4. Briggs, R.O., Kolfschoten, G.L., de Vreede, G.J., Dean, D.L.: Defining Key Concepts for Collaboration Engineering. In: AMCIS, AIS, Acapulco, Mexico, vol. 12 (2006)
5. Koneri, P.G., de Vreede, G.J., Dean, D.L., Fruhling, A.L., Wolcott, P.: The Design and Field Evaluation of a Repeatable Collaborative Software Code Inspection Process. In: Fukś, H., Lukosch, S., Salgado, A.C. (eds.) CRIWG 2005. LNCS, vol. 3706, pp. 325–340. Springer, Heidelberg (2005)

6. Tarmizi, H., Payne, M., Noteboom, C., Zhang, C., Steinhauser, L., de Vreede, G.J., Zigurs, I.: Technical and Environmental Challenges of Collaboration Engineering in Distributed Environments. In: Fukś, H., Lukosch, S., Salgado, A.C. (eds.) CRIWG 2005. LNCS, vol. 3706, pp. 38–53. Springer, Heidelberg (2005)

7. Kolfschoten, G.L., de Vreede, G.J., Briggs, R.O., Sol, H.G.: Collaboration Engineerability. In: Kersten, G.E., Rios, J. (eds.) GDN conference, Concordia University, Mt Tremblant (2007)

8. Kolfschoten, G.L., Pietron, L., de Vreede, G.J.: A training approach for the transition of repeatable collaboration processes to practitioners. In: Seifert, S., Weinhardt, C. (eds.) International Conference on GDN, Universitatsverlag Karlsruhe, Karlsruhe (2006)

9. de Vreede, G.J., Briggs, R.O.: Collaboration Engineering: Designing Repeatable Processes for High-Value Collaborative Tasks. In: HICSS, IEEE Press, Waikoloa (2005)

10. Seligmann, P.S., Wijers, G.M., Sol, H.G.: Analyzing the Structure of IS Methodologies. In: Proceedings of the 1st Dutch Conference on Information Systems, Amersfoort, The Netherlands (1989)

11. Briggs, R.O.: The Focus Theory of Team Productivity and its Application to Development and Testing of Electronic Group Support Systems, Tucson (1994)

12. Briggs, R.O., Qureshi, S., Reinig, B.: Satisfaction Attainment Theory as a Model for Value Creation. In: HICSS, IEEE Press, Waikoloa (2004)

13. Briggs, R.O., Adkins, M., Mittleman, D.D., Kruse, J., Miller, S., Nunamaker, Jr., J.F.: A Technology Transition Model Derived from Qualitative Field Investigation of GSS use aboard the U.S.S. Coronado. Journal of Management Information Systems 15, 151–196 (1999)

14. Briggs, R.O., Kolfschoten, G.L., de Vreede, G.J.: Toward a Theoretical Model of Consensus Building. In: AMCIS, AIS press, Omaha (2005)

15. den Hengst, M., Dean Kolfschoten, G.L., Chakrapani, A.: Assessing the Quality of Collaborative Processes. In: HICSS, IEEE press, Waikoloa (2006)

16. Kolfschoten, G.L., Briggs, R.O., de Vreede, G.J., Jacobs, P.H.M., Appelman, J.H.: Conceptual Foundation of the ThinkLet Concept for Collaboration Engineering. International Journal of Human Computer Science 64, 611–621 (2006)

17. Kolfschoten, G.L., van Houten, S.P.A.: Predictable Patterns in Group Settings through the use of Rule Based Facilitation Interventions. In: Kersten, G.E., Rios, J. (eds.) GDN conference, Concordia University, Mt Tremblant (2007)

18. Kolfschoten, G.L., van der Hulst, S.: Collaboration Process Design Transition to Practitioners: Requirements from a Cognitive Load Perspective. In: Seifert, S., Weinhardt, C. (eds.) GDN conference, Universtatsverlag Karlsruhe, Karlsruhe (2006)

19. de Vreede, G.J., Briggs, R.O., Kolfschoten, G.L.: ThinkLets: A Pattern Language for Facilitated and Practitioner-Guided Collaboration Processes. International Journal of Computer Applications in Technology 25, 140–154 (2006)

20. Hayne, S.C.: The Facilitator's Perspective on Meetings and Implications for Group Support Systems Design. DataBase 30, 72–91 (1999)

21. Clawson, V.K., Bostrom, R.P.: The Importance of Facilitator Role Behaviors in Different Face to Face Group Support Systems Environments. In: HICSS, pp. 181–190. IEEE Press, Los Alamitos (1995)

22. Nunamaker, Jr., J.F., Briggs, R.O., Mittleman, D.D., Vogel, D., Balthazard, P.A.: Lessons from a Dozen Years of Group Support Systems Research: A Discussion of Lab and Field Findings. Journal of Management Information Systems 13, 163–207 (1997)

23. Antunes, P., Ho, T., Carriço, L.: A GDSS Agenda Builder for Inexperienced Facilitators. In: Ackermann, F., de Vreede, G.J. (eds.) 10th Euro GDSS Workshop, Copenhagen, Denmark. Delft University of Technology, pp. 1–15 (1999)
24. Simon, H.A.: The New Science of Management Decision. Prentice Hall, New York (1960)
25. Mitroff, I.I., Betz, F., Pondly, L.R., Sagasty, F.: On Managing Science in the Systems Age: Two Schemas for the Study of Science as a Whole Systems Phenomenon. TIMS Interfaces 4, 46–58 (1974)
26. Drucker, P.F.: The Effective Executive, London (1967)
27. Brady, R.H.: Computers in Top-Level Decision Making, pp. 67–76. Harvard Business Revie (1967)
28. Ackoff, R.L.: The Art of Problem Solving. John Wiley & Sons, Chichester (1978)
29. Couger, J.D.: Creative Problem Solving And Opportunity Finding. Danvers, Mass: Boyd And Fraser (1995)
30. Checkland, P.B.: Systems Thinking, Systems Practice. John Wiley & Sons, Chichester (1981)
31. Simon, H.A.: The Structure of Ill Structured Problems. Artificial Intelligence 4, 181–201 (1973)
32. Dean, D.L., Deokar, A., Ter Bush, R.: Making the Collaboration Engineering Investment Decision. In: HICSS, IEEE Press, Kauai (2006)
33. Alexander, C., Ishikawa, S., Silverstein, M., Jacobson, M., Fiksdahl-King, I., Angel, S.: A Pattern Language, Towns, Buildings, Construction. Oxford University Press, New York (1977)
34. Gamma, E., Helm, R., Johnson, R., Vlissides, J.: Elements of Reusable Object-Oriented Software. Addison-Wesley Publishing Company, Reading (1995)
35. Kolfschoten, G.L., den Hengst, M., de Vreede, G.J.: Issues in the Design of Facilitated Collaboration Processes. In: Group Decision and Negotiation (in press)
36. Kolfschoten, G.L., Appelman, J.H., Briggs, R.O., de Vreede, G.J.: Recurring Patterns of Facilitation Interventions in GSS Sessions. In: HICSS, IEEE Press, Waikoloa (2004)
37. Kolfschoten, G.L., Rouwette, E.: Choice Criteria for Facilitaition Techniques. In: Briggs, R.O., Nunamaker, Jr., J.F. (eds.) First HICSS Symposium on Case and Field Studies of Collaboration, Kauai (2006)
38. Kolfschoten, G.L., Rouwette, E.: Choice Criteria for Facilitation Techniques: A Preliminary Classification. In: Seifert, S., Weinhardt, C. (eds.) GDN conference, Universtatsverlag Karlsruhe, Karlsruhe (2006)
39. Boehm, B.W.: Software Engineering Economics. Prentice-Hall, New-York (1981)
40. Schach, S.R.: An Introduction to Object-Oriented Systems Analysis and Design with UML and the Unified Process. McGraw-Hill, New York (2004)
41. Lehman, M.M.: Uncertainty in Computer Applications and its Control trought the Engineering of Software. Journal of Software Maintenance 1, 3–28 (1989)
42. Briggs, R.O., Kolfschoten, G.L., de Vreede, G.J.: Instrumentality Theory of Consensus. In: Briggs, R.O., Nunamaker, Jr., J.F. (eds.) First HICSS Symposium on Case and Field Studies of Collaboration, Kauai (2006)

A Proposal of Integration of the GUI Development of Groupware Applications into the Software Development Process

A.I. Molina[1], W.J. Giraldo[2], M.A. Redondo[1], and M. Ortega[1]

[1] Department of Information Technologies and Systems,
College of Computer Science and Engineering,
Castilla – La Mancha University,
Paseo de la Universidad, 4. 13071 – Ciudad Real. Spain
{AnaIsabel.Molina,Miguel.Redondo,Manuel.Ortega}@uclm.es
[2] Systems and Computer Engineering, University of Quindío, Quindío, Colombia
wjgiraldo@uniquindio.edu.co

Abstract. In the last years the production of systems supporting work-in-group has been high. However, the design and development of this kind of systems is difficult, especially due to the multidisciplinarity involved and technical complexity (concurrence, distribution, data sharing, user interface, etc.). We propose a design and development process of the user interface in this kind of applications. This process is based on the use of several models for representing collaborative and interactive issues. In this process several techniques and notations are used. In this paper we introduce our methodological approach and describe how it is integrated into the Software Engineering Process.

Keywords: GUI development, Software Engineering, Groupware design, interaction design, model based design, Methodological framework.

1   Introduction

The development of applications to electronically support the realization of activities in group work is a difficult task due, among other reasons, to the multiple disciplines that converge in the process of their design. The difficulty comes from problems that can be located in the following three dimensions: social nature, distributed systems and software engineering. Those problems are related with issues such as the support of cooperative and collaborative behaviour modeling, the use of shared spaces and communication technology. However, those issues become fundamental requirements to consider during the development of this kind of applications. The design of the interaction and the User Interface (UI) are specially affected by these issues.

Model-based design is an extended technique in the UI development process. Reviewing the Software Engineering (SE) and Human-Computer Interaction (HCI) literature we can observe the existence of some notations proposed for conceptual modeling of group work issues, although these notations are too far from the most

J.M. Haake, S.F. Ochoa, and A. Cechich (Eds.): CRIWG 2007, LNCS 4715, pp. 111–126, 2007.
© Springer-Verlag Berlin Heidelberg 2007

extended software development processes. According to their approaches, the proposals can be classified in the following categories:

1. User-centered notations, to realize a *task* analysis and modeling and based on techniques such as decomposition tasks (*tasks/subtasks*), specification of tasks flow (*order*), modeling of the *objects* associated to the tasks or *information passing*. Some examples are GOMS [1], HTA [2], CTT [3].
2. Group-centered notations, which explicitly approach the *interaction* between users who use a distributed application to carry out *activities jointly*. Some exampleas are CTT [3], the GTA framework [4], CUA notation [5].
3. Process-centered notations, for modeling the *processes* that take place inside the organization, which is considered as a work flow with coordination necessities. In these models the aspects specified are relative to the user behavior, data flow and transformation, and interaction among agents (humans or computers). APM [6], Proclets [7] are examples of this kind of notations.

The techniques of notations derived from the existing conceptual modeling proposals have some deficiencies related to the following aspects [8]:

1. Theoretical and computational models that allow specifying *computer-supported group activities* appropriately.
2. Notations that allow modeling the existing difference between *cooperative* and *collaborative tasks* according to Dillenbourg's remarks [9][1]. There are differences between cooperation and collaboration which must be considered. These differences affect the division of tasks, the roles participation in the tasks and the obtained product as a result in a joint activity.
3. Notations that *approach jointly* interactive and group work issues.

These problems bring to light the lack of a methodological framework, which supports the design interaction layer of collaborative tools. This situation makes us raise the hypothesis of defining a notation to express in a differentiated way collaborative and cooperative tasks. This notation must make its characterization evident based on the task division (which affects the task model), the participation of the different roles in these (which affects the task and user models) and the product obtained as a result of the joint activity (which affects the data and domain models). This notation will be used for completing a methodological framework for designing work group systems.

In this article the methodological proposal CIAM (*Collaborative Interactive Applications Methodology*) is presented. CIAM [13, 14] is based on the use of specific notations, for the design of interactive workgroup applications. This methodology intends to connect high-level requirements models with low-level interaction models with the aim of deriving the final UI more directly. In this paper

---

[1] We consider the definition presented by Dillenbourg: "Cooperation and collaboration do not differ in terms of whether or not the task is distributed, but by virtue of the way in which it is divided; in cooperation the task is split into independent subtasks; in collaboration cognitive processes may be divided into intertwined layers. In cooperation, coordination is only required when assembling partial results, while collaboration is a coordinated, synchronous activity that is the result of a continued attempt to construct and maintain a shared conception of a problem".

we relate CIAM and the Unified Software Development Process. Other authors have pointed ideas on the connection of the interaction design and the software development processes [10-12]. Nevertheless, these proposals are very general and they do not consider the modeling of work-in-group issues. In section 1 the CIAM methodological approach is shown, enumerating its several stages, and the aspects that are specified in each. Section 2 explains the integration of this methodological proposal into the Software Development Process. Finally the conclusions extracted from this work are presented.

2   CIAM: A Methodological Approach for User Interface Development of Collaborative Applications

In this section we present the stages in our methodological approach, named *CIAM* (*Collaborative Interactive Applications Methodology*). Our proposal implies adopting different viewpoints for creating models of this kind of systems. The first stages undertake a group-centered modeling, going on in subsequent stages to a process-centered modeling (cooperative, collaborative or coordination process), approaching, as we go deeper into the abstraction level, a more user-centered modeling, in which interactive tasks are modeled, that is, a dialog between an individual user and the application. Two first modeling approaches describe the context in which the interactive model is created, and serve as starting point for the last one. In this way, collaborative issues (groups, process) and interactive (individual) modeling problems are tackled jointly. These framework acts as a guide for designers to create conceptual specifications (models) of the main issues that define the presentation layer in CSCW systems. Specified information in each stage serves as a basis for modeling in the following stage. This information is extended, related or specified in a more detailed way in the next stage in the process.

The stages in or methodological proposal (see figure 1) and their objective are enumerated as follows.

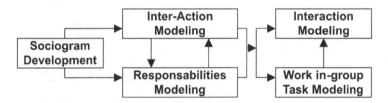

Fig. 1. CIAM methodological proposal stages

While reviewing approaches that deal with the modeling and development of user interfaces supporting collaborative tasks, we have detected that there is not a proposal that links interactive and collaborative characteristics. Unlike the rest of studied proposals, CIAM made a clear *distinction* between the interaction in the group (called *inter-action*), and the individual interaction that occurs between a user and the tool he/she uses. Besides, unlike other approaches which only tackle the individual and/or cooperative modeling, our proposal tackle the modeling of *purely collaborative aspects*.

This methodological framework is supported by a coherent *set of notations* for designing interactive and collaborative tools. This notation is called CIAN (*Collaborative Interactive Applications Notation*) [13]. This notation is a simplification of another notation for *workflow* modeling, called APM (*Action Port Model*), proposed by Carlsen [6]. This notation has been enriched to support a differentiated modeling of cooperative and collaborative tasks, while it has been simplified in some aspects (to characterize a task just a task identification, the roles involved and the objects manipulated are included). In CIAM several specification techniques are used. In Table 1 we summarize the specification techniques used in the several stages of our methodological approach, the notation used and the product obtained in each.

Table 1. Stages in the CIAM proposal and specification techniques

CIAM Methodology Stage	Specification Technique	Representation Type	Result obtained
Sociogram Development	Sociogram	Graphic	Organizational Structure Specification (roles, agents, software agents, etc)
Responsibilities Modeling	Responsibilities Model	Textual	Detailed Specification of the responsibilities of each role
Inter-Action Modeling	Participation Table	Textual	Relationshops between the main tasks and roles of the system
	Inter-Action Model	Graphic	Work Structure and workflow to be performed by the organization
Work in-group Tasks Modeling	Access Control Matrix	Textual	Relationships between data objects (or attributes) and roles at level of work in-grop task
	Table of Operation Permissions on the Shared Context	Textual	Relationships between operations and roles at level of work in-grop task
Cooperative Tasks Modeling	Responsibilities Decomposition Graph	Graphic	Responsibilities Distribution in a cooperative task Specification
Collaborative Tasks Modeling	Shared Context Specification (class diagram in standard UML notation)	Graphic	Specification of the Shared Context in a collaborative task, the division in visualization areas and the finalization policy
Interaction Modeling	Interactive Tasks Decomposition Tree (CTT notation enriched with icons for specifying visualization areas in collaborative tasks)	Graphic	Interaction Modeling at individual responsibility level; interaction with the shared context in collaborative tasks

2.1 Sociogram Development

In this stage a diagram, called *sociogram*, is created. This diagram allows representing the organization structure, as well as the relationships between its members.

Organization Members are in one of these categories: *roles, actors, software agents*; or groupings of the previous ones, giving rise to *groups*, that is, groups of actors with homogeneous responsibilities, or *work teams*, consisting of several roles. The elements in these diagrams might be interconnected by means of three kinds of basic relationships:

- *Inheritance* relationship. Responsibilities can be inherited, whenever a certain *precondition* occurs (which can be added to the model).
- *Performance* relationship. It allows relating *actors* and *roles*. This relationship can be annotated by *cardinality* (the number of actors that can play a certain role in the organization).

Association relationship. This kind of relationship allows associating roles to each other, indicating that there are situations in which these roles cooperate or collaborate to carry out a joint task.

Figure 2 shows the visual aspect that a *sociogram*[2] represented in CIAN notation presents. We will not go deeply into the description of the diagram on figure 3 because it is not the main objective of this paper. A detailed description of the CIAN notation and examples of its application can be found in [14].

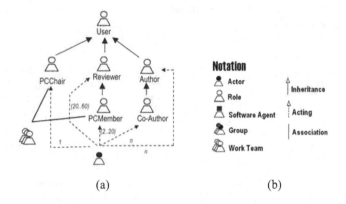

(a)   (b)

Fig. 2. An example of *sociogram* (a) represented in CIAN Notation (b)

2.2 Inter-action Modeling

In this stage, the main tasks (or processes), which define the work-in-group developed in the organization previously defined, are described. For each process, the roles involved, the data manipulated and the product generated (indicating the modes for accessing the object, this is, reading, writing or creation), are specified. Each task must be classified in one of the following categories: *cooperative task, collaborative task* and *individual task* (figure 3.b). The process will be interconnected by means of

---

[2] We have modeled a standard congress management system (CMS), this problem has been a common example in HCI literature.

several kinds of relationships that can be interpreted as dependencies: *temporal dependencies* (order relationship), *data dependencies* (when processes need data manipulated by previous processes) and *notification dependency* (it is necessary that a certain event occurs so that the work flow continues). In addition to these types of relationships between processes, it is necessary to consider dependencies of an individual nature, that is, the iteration of a certain task or the maintenance of a certain condition during its execution. In this case the following types of conditions are distinguished: *completion condition* (ending conditions for iterative execution), *period condition* (it indicates temporal events for tasks completion) or *execution condition* (conditions indicating optional execution). In this stage two descriptive techniques are used that will be presented subsequently in detail (they are the *Participation Table* and the *Inter-Action model*). Figure 3 shows an example of *inter-action* model in CIAN notation. It consists of six tasks of high level of abstraction. Two of them are of individual execution (those labeled with numbers 1 and 3), and other two of them are of a cooperative nature, with a clear division in subtasks that will be indicated in later stages of refinement (those labeled as 4 and 5). Finally, there are two tasks of a collaborative nature (labeled as 2 and 6). We can see how in these two last types we must specify the roles involved in its execution, whereas in the individual tasks only a role must appear. For all the tasks the objects manipulated are indicated, preceded by the corresponding access modifiers. In this case the work flow is sequential (the temporal operator used is >>).

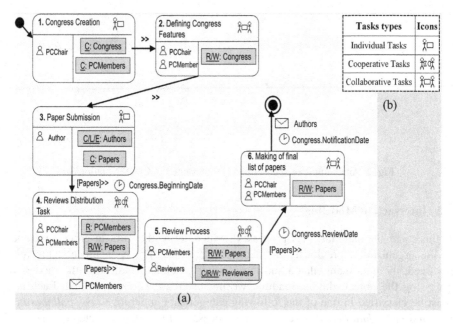

Fig. 3. An example of *an inter-action model* in CIAN notation (a). Types of tasks handled by notations used in the methodology stages (b).

As an example we can see that the execution of the task of *Paper Submission* (task 3) concludes when the deadline for submitting papers is reached, being necessary to transfer these papers ([]>>) to the following task (*Reviews Distribution Task*). This task (number 4) is of a cooperative nature, being both the *PCChair* and the *PCMembers* involved in its execution. It is necessary to indicate that the objects that are manipulated during the execution of a task (in this case, the objects *PCMembers* and *Papers*) must be created in some of the previous stages of the process. Checking this circumstance allows validating the coherence of the model created. Once the execution of the task has concluded, the decisions taken should be notified to *PCMembers*. For executing the following task (*Revision Process*), it is necessary to use the papers as they have been used after the execution of the previous tasks. There are not only a *temporal dependence* (>>) among the tasks but also a *data dependence* among them.

2.3 Responsibilities Modeling

Once group work has been specified at high level by means of the Inter-Action Model, attention is paid to the individual perspective of each organizational member, that is, their roles. Using the information specified in the previous stage, the responsibilities of each role are extended, adding individual responsibilities that are not developed in group. These responsibilities imply carrying out tasks/actions that handle objects. Therefore, for each task the object manipulated has to be specified, as well as the pre-requirements that allow their correct execution (that is, the tasks/actions need to have been completed and the data created before a given task/action begins). The information detailed in this stage is supplementary to the one in the previous stage, being necessary for both models to be coherent (for example, when the present task needs to have some data created, a previous task should have already created them). In figure 4 we can see an example of the responsibilities model.

Responsibility	Task Type	Object in Domain Model	Pre-requirement	
			Task	Data
Congress Creation	웃□	C: Congress	INI	
Defining Congress Features	 웃□웃	R/W: Congress	Congress Creation	Congress
Reviews Distribution Task	 웃 ♂	R/W: Papers	Paper Submission	Papers
Making the final list of papers	 웃□♂	R/W: Papers	Review Process	Papers

Fig. 4. An example of the *responsibilities model* in CIAN notation

2.4 Work-in-Group Tasks Modeling

In this stage the group tasks identified in the previous stage are described in a more detailed way. There are two different kinds of tasks, which must be modeled in a differentiated way (figure 5):

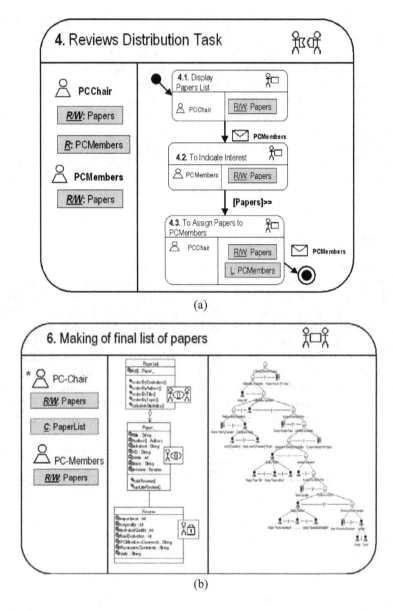

Fig. 5. Modeling of a cooperative (a) and a collaborative (b) task in CIAN notation

-   *Cooperative Tasks* are specified by means of the so-called *responsibilities decomposition graph*, in which subtasks make up the group task, so that in a lower abstraction level only an *individual task* must appear. When specifying the data manipulated by a certain task, we can handle several levels (Object Collection/Objects/Attributes). Thus, *different instances* of the same object or objects collection can be manipulated, or *different pieces* of the same information that compose an object (even manipulation at attribute level). This situation involves situations of *concurrence of tasks*. Also, different versions from the same object can be handled. This situation implies the existence of a temporal (non-concurrent) relation between the different tasks involved in the process of cooperative work.

- *Collaborative Tasks* modeling includes specification of the roles involved, as well as the data model objects manipulated by the work team (that is, the *shared context* specification). Shared context is defined as the set of *objects* that are visible to the users set, as well as the *actions* that can be executed on them. Once the objects that make up the *shared context* have been decided, it is necessary to fragment this information in three different parts: the objects and/or attributes manipulated in the *collaborative visualization area*, the ones which appear in the *individual visualization area* and the ones that make up the *exclusive edition segment* (a subset in the data model that is accessed in an exclusive way for only one application user at the same time).

2.5 Interaction Modeling

In the last stage interactive issues of the application are modeled. In this stage the designer is centered on specifying the dialog that can take place among the users (individual users) and the applications (user interface) that mediate in the collaborative process defined. An *interaction model* for each individual task detected in the diverse stages of the gradual refinement process is created. To model the interaction, a notation exists broadly diffused in the community of the Computer Human-Interaction. This language is CTT [3, 15]. Using CTT we can reach high levels of detail in the interaction model. This facilitates the obtaining of the final design of the user interfaces. CTT is oriented to cooperative tasks that are specified by means of a cooperative model that relates individual tasks. However, CTT cannot be used to model collaborative tasks and shared context. We propose using this notation to model the interactive aspects of the collaborative tasks. In addition, in the particular case of collaborative tasks and using the models that we have constructed in previous stages, the CTT tree that models the interaction can be generated directly. For this, the definition of the shared context and the information relative to visualization and lock issues are used. Our methodological approach includes the way of obtaining this model from the shared context modeling. However, its explication exceeds the scope of the present paper.

3 Integration of CIAM in the Software Development Process

A *software development process* is a method to organize the activities related to the creation, presentation and maintenance of the software systems [16]. The approach of the fields of the HCI (Human-Computer Interaction) and the SE (Software Engineering) are taking a great importance and attention in the last years [11, 12, 17].

On the one hand, the SE begins to consider *usability* like a quality attribute that must be measured and promoted [18]. On the other hand, if the proposed techniques in HCI want to gain solidity within the field of the SE they should clearly indicate how to integrate their techniques and activities within the process of software development. The integration of approaches of model-based design and development with UML notation was the object of discussion in several workshops where the participants agreed that it is conceptually possible to relate main concepts of HCI to the classic ones in SE [19]. The tasks models are useful in several stages of the development of interactive applications: in the requirements analysis, in the design of the UI, in the usability evaluation process, as a documentation technique, etc. Figure 6 shows our proposal of integration of the software development process and the model-based UI development process (MBUID).

Like other proposals our integration process includes two parallel development paths, related to each other. One of them (the ES path) approaches the development of the processing and persistent storage layers in the context of a development that follows a three-tier architecture [20]. The presentation layer, forgotten by other ES proposals, uses the information extracted from the conventional requirements analysis stage (mainly from the use cases and the glossary of terms definition). To these requirements it is necessary to add those that have direct relation with the process of development of the presentation layer, this is, the usability requirements, users analysis and platform information (for which we are going to design the UI). This last feature will allow the development of plastic UIs.

As for the information obtained in the requirements analysis stage (ES path), it is necessary to point out that the use cases provide information of interest for the development of the task models. The use cases identify the tasks, at the upper abstraction level, that must be performed by the users, the system and their interaction. In [10] a way of obtainig a preliminary structure of the task model that satisfies the requirements indicated in a case uses diagram is explained. The mapping between the use cases and the task models can be based on the following basic transformations [21]:

- The use cases represent the highest levels of abstraction in the hierarchical task models.
- The "uses" relations can be interpreted as temporal order expressions (in particular a sequence connection).
- The "extends" relations indicate optional behaviors. This situation can also be specified in a task model.

The UI design stage is based on the creation of the so-called *Interaction Model*. This can be composed, as well, by other models. We consider as basic the task model of the application in which certain temporal information (precedence and coordination information) is represented. This information can be enriched through using information related with the domain (that is extracted from the models of the ES process). In particular the domain model can be represented by means of the *classes diagram* of the application. The rest of models (of *dialogue* and *presentation*) will be generated during the MBUID process from the previous diagrams [22].

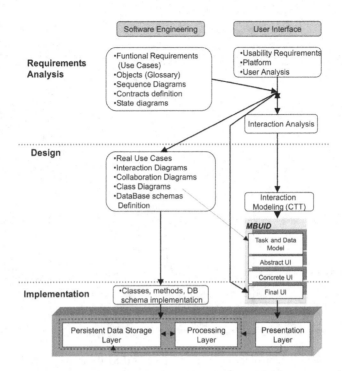

Fig. 6. Scheme of integration of the development process (ES) and the model-based UI development process (UI)

The stage that we have labeled as MBUID indicates that it is possible to apply any method and MBUID environment existing in the literatute, whenever they start from a modeling of the interactive tasks. Most of MBUID processes start from data and interative task models and allow obtaining several representations of the final UI (the abstract UI, the concrete UI and the Final UI). The mapping process (well-known as the *"mapping problem"* [11]), consists in going from an abstract representation of the system interaction requirements (the task model) to a concrete representation (dependent on the final platform and on the widgets supplied by the toolkit used for developing the UI). Several systems have attempted to automatically generate user interfaces in a model-based environment (UIDE [23], Mecano [24], Trident [25]). The idea of these systems was to try to automate the interface generation process from a task model as much as possible.

Next we are going to present our integration scheme including our methodological proposal. In Figure 7 we can see the resulting process.

A new work path is added that is parallel to the two previous ones and related to them. The requirements analysis of this new branch of development is based on an ethnographic analysis [26]. This is the most extended requirements gathering technique for the development of CSCW systems. The data obtained in this stage is gathered to the analysis information of the other two ways considered, so that the system requirements are complete and can be used as starting point of the three development ways.

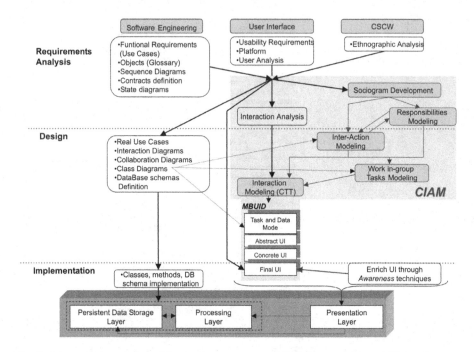

Fig. 7. Scheme of integration of the development process (ES), the model-based UI development process (UI) and the CIAM proposal (CSCW)

In order to integrate the CIAM proposal in the overall scheme it is necessary to clarify the stages that can be considered of analysis or of design. In general the definition of the concepts of analysis and design, as well as its distinction is not very clear, being the passage from one to another one diffuse. Both concepts can be considered different stages in a same line of work. Figure 8 represents this idea.

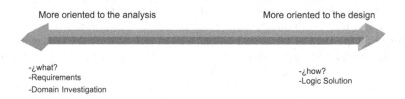

Fig. 8. Distinction between analysis and design tasks

Once we have clarified this distinction, we consider the *Sociogram Development* and the *Responsibilities Modeling* stages as analysis stages. This last stage can be considered, in fact, as a responsibilities analysis task, that is, of identification of the tasks entrusted to the different roles of the system. The way in which these responsibilites are carried out is specified by means of the *Inter-Action Model*. In this model the sequence, coordination and dependencies between tasks carried out by the several members of the workteam are detailed.

As much for the creation of the sociogram as for the identification of responsibilities, the use of the information contained in the use cases and the glossary of terms is very helpful. Therefore, the data collected in each of these three ways in the analysis process serves as input to the stage of design of the functional (ES), interaction (UI) and collaboration (CSCW) issues.

The information contained in the *Classes Diagram* of the application allows the improvement of the modeling of the interactive issues as well as of the most advanced stages of the CIAM proposal. The detailed design of the domain model of the application is used in the *Work-in-group Tasks Modeling* stage. In particular the specification of the collaborative tasks includes the *shared context* modeling (*objects* that are visible to the users, as well as the *actions* that can be executed on them). Therefore, this information must be defined at this level of detail before starting the detailed specification of the work-in-group tasks. Besides, the recent proposals of MBUID processes consider of interest to joint the interactive tasks modeling and the domain model for obtaining the several models that specify the UI of an application. The domain definition serves, therefore, as input to most of the development processes, and even to the automatic generation of UIs.

The *Interaction Modeling* stage includes interaction models associated to the individual tasks as well as to work-in-group ones, which will serve as starting point to MBUID processes. Unlike the modeling of cooperative applications supported by the CTT notation (in which a cooperative model and an individual model for each role are created), CIAM allows obtaining interaction models associated to individual and work-in-group tasks (or responsibilities). The connection between these interaction models is specified by the *Inter-Action Model*.

In the design stage, the development of the the functionality of the system and the design of the UI that support this functionality are carried out in parallel way. At implementation level, the final UI can be enriched by means of the incorporation of *awareness* techniques. In future works we propose to consider the information specified in the first stages (roles, tasks, access modifiers, tasks types, etc.) for enriching the interaction model and consider these issues in the selection of awareness widgets.

As a summary, we can say that the integration process of our methodological proposal for the design and specification of the presentation layer in groupware systems with the lifecycle of software development has the following main features:

- The process model shown shows the *interrelationships* that exists between the three areas of parallel development (the ES, the design and development of the UI and the design and modeling of CSCW systems).
- It is a development process that follows the *architecture of separation in three-tiers*, so much supported in the field of ES.
- In the overall process there are certain *dependencies,* between the several stages and development paths, that must be respected. Thus, for example the following ones occur:
    - The UI design is based on the domain layer. Therefore, it is necessary that this stage occur later, at least, than the stage of ES requirements analysis.
    - If we want to include a MBUID process that guides, if possible, the semiautomatic obtaining of the final UI we need a more detailed knowledge of

the manipulated objects, that is, the classes diagram of the application need to be defined.

- Also the classes diagram serves as starting point to the work in-group tasks modeling, since it is necessary to know the classes diagram of the system for defining the shared context when specifying the collaborative tasks.
- The model considers three parallel paths with dependencies among them. These paths have in common several activities of requirements analysis and the final integration (an activity included in the implementation stage) of the component created for each of the three layers of the software system.
- At level of the design of the presentation layer it allows the inclusion of development processes of the UI based on conceptual models (MBUID).

4 Conclusions

In this paper we have shown our proposal of integration of the interaction design into the Unified Development Process. In particular, we focus on the integration of a methodological approach for Model Based User Interface Development of Collaborative Applications. We have introduced our methodological approach to deal with the conceptual design of applications for supporting work in group, called CIAM. This approach is organized in several stages in which conceptual models are created using the CIAN notation.

We have located the stages of CIAM into the main stages in the Software Development Process. The organizational modeling (organizational structure and responsibilities) is considered as a requirements analysis technique. The interaction modeling and the collaboration modeling are used in the first phases of the design and are integrated with habitual model-based processes of UI design. In the implementation stage we obtain a final UI that contemplate functional requirements and requirements of interaction and collaboration.

Now, we are working in the formal and detailed description of the mapping between the models supported in the CIAM proposal and the UML models supported in the Software Development Process. We are also evaluating the acceptance of the CIAN notation by some groups of students and HCI experts. At the moment, the results are promising. Next, we will work for the integration of this proposal with a Usability Engineering process and its relationship with Model Driven Architecture approach.

Acknowledgments. This work has been supported by the Castilla – La Mancha University and the Junta de Comunidades de Castilla – La Mancha in the project GAMTest (PCI-05-005).

References

1. Card, S., Moran, T., Newell, A.: The Psycology of Human-Computer Interaction. Hillsdale (1983)
2. Annett, J., Duncan, K.D.: Task Analysis and Training Design. Occupational Psychology 41, 211–221 (1967)

3. Paternò, F.: ConcurTaskTrees: An Engineered Notation for Task Models. In: Diaper, D., Stanton, N.A. (eds.) The Handbook Of Task Analysis For HCI, LEA, Mahwah, NJ, pp. 483–501 (2004a)
4. van Welie, M., van der Vee, G.C.: Groupware Task Analysis. In: Hollnagel, E. (ed.) Handbook Of Cognitive Task Design, LEA., NJ, pp. 447–476 (2003)
5. Pinelle, D., Gutwin, C., Greenberg, S.: Task Analysis for Groupware Usability Evaluation: Modeling Shared-Workspace Tasks with the Mechanics of Collaboration. ACM Transactions on Computer-Human Interacion 10(4), 281–311 (2003)
6. Carlsen, S.: Action Port Model: A Mixed Paradigm Conceptual Workflow Modeling Language. in 3rd IFCIS International Conference on Cooperative Information Systems (1998)
7. van der Aalst, W.M.P., et al.: Proclets: a framework for lightweight interacting workflow processes. Journal of Cooperative Information Systems 10(4), 443–482 (2001)
8. Molina, A.I., Redondo, M.A., Ortega, M.: Analyzing and modelling user task in DomoSim-TPC system for adapting to mobile devices. In: Navarro, R., Lorés, J. (eds.) HCI related papers of Interacción 2004, pp. 221–241. Springer, Heidelberg (2005a)
9. Dillenbourg, P., et al.: The Evolution of Research on Collaborative Learning. In: Reimann, P., Spada, H. (eds.) Vol. Learning in humans and machines. Towards an interdisciplinary learning science, London, pp. 189–211 (1995)
10. Paternò, F.: Towards a UML for Interactive Systems. In: 8th International Conference on Engineering for Human-Computer Interaction. Lectures Notes Computer Science (2001b)
11. Granollers, T.: MPIu+a. Una metodología que integra la Ingeniería del Software, la Interacción Persona-Ordenador y la Accesibilidad en el contexto de equipos de desarrollo multidisciplinares. In: Workshop Tendiendo Puentes entre la Interacción Persona-Ordenador (IPO) y la Ingeniería del Software (IS), Madrid (2005)
12. Ferré, X., Moreno, A.M.: Integración de la IPO en el Proceso de Desarrollo de la Ingeniería del Software: Propuestas Existentes y Temas a Resolver. In: V Congreso Interacción Persona-Ordenador (Interacción 2004), Lleida, España (2004)
13. Molina, A.I., Redondo, M.A., Ortega, M.: A conceptual and methodological framework for modeling interactive groupware applications. In: Dimitriadis, Y.A., Zigurs, I., Gómez-Sánchez, E. (eds.) CRIWG 2006. LNCS, vol. 4154, Springer, Heidelberg (2006)
14. Molina, A.I., Redondo, M.A., Ortega, M., CIAM: A methodology for groupware user interface development. Journal of Universal Computer Science (2007)
15. Paternò, F., Mancini, C., Meniconi,: ConcurTaskTree: A diagrammatic notation for specifying task models. In: IFIP TC 13 International Conference on Human-Computer Interaction Interact'97, Kluwer Academic Publishers, Sydney (1997)
16. Larman, C.: UML y Patrones. Introducción al análisis y diseño orientado a objetos. Prentice-Hall, Englewood Cliffs (2002)
17. Soares, K., Furtado, E.: RUPi - A Unified Process that Integrates Human-Computer Interaction and Software Engineering. In: Workshop Bridging the Gap Between Software-Engineering and Human-Computer Interaction at ICSE'03.OR (2003)
18. Ferré, X.: Integration of Usability Techniques into the Software Development Process. In: Workshop Bridging the Gaps Between Software Engineering and Human-Computer Interaction, ICSE-2003, Portland (OR), USA (2003)
19. Artim, J., et al.: Incorporating work, process and task analysis into industrial object-oriented systems development. SIGCHI Bulletin 30(4) (1998)
20. Schulte, R.: Three-Tier Computing Architectures and Beyond. Published Report Note R-401-134. Gartner Group (1995)

21. Lu, S., Paris, C., Vander Linden, K.: Towards the automatic generation of task models from object oriented diagrams. In: Chatty, S., Dewan, P. (eds.) Engineering for Human-Computer Interaction, Kluwer academic publishers, Boston (1999)
22. Luyten, K., et al.: Derivation of a Dialog Model from a Task Model by Activity Chain Extraction. In: Jorge, J.A., Jardim Nunes, N., Falcão e Cunha, J. (eds.) DSV-IS 2003. LNCS, vol. 2844, Springer, Heidelberg (2003)
23. Foley, J., et al.: UIDE-An Intelligent User Interface Design Environment. Intelligent User Interfaces, 339–384 (1991)
24. Puerta, A.R.: The MECANO Project: Comprehensive and Integrated Support for Model-Based Interface Development. In: CADUI96: Computer-Aided Design of User In-terfaces, Numur, Belgium (1996)
25. Vanderdonckt, J.M., Bodart, F.: Encapsulating Knowledge for Intelligent Automatic Interaction Objects Selection. In: InterCHI'93, ACM Press, New York (1993)
26. Schwartzman, H.: Ethnography in Organizations. Qualitative Research Methods Series, vol. 27. Sage, Newbury Park CA (1993)

Coordinating Multi-task Environments Through the Methodology of Relations Graph

Adailton A. Cruz[1], Léo P. Magalhães[2], Alberto B. Raposo[3], Rafael S. Mendes[2],
and Dennis G. Pelluzi[2]

[1] Federal University of Dourados, Brazil
[2] Department of Computer Engineering and Industrial Automation, School of Electrical and
Computer Engineering, State University of Campinas, Brazil
[3] Computer Science Department, Pontifical Catholic University of Rio de Janeiro, Brazil
adacruz@terra.com.br,
{leopini, rafael, pelluzi}@dca.fee.unicamp.br,
abraposo@tecgraf.puc-rio.br

Abstract. This paper presents Relations Graph – GR a methodology to automate the generation of coordination mechanisms in computational environments. GR explores encapsulation and compacting capabilities of Colored Petri Nets to generate temporal coordination mechanisms, although the use of the GR methodology does not depend on the knowledge of PN formalism. GR supports alternative temporal behaviors and alternative activities changing the temporal relations among activities in processing time. An algorithm to identify and model coordination mechanisms linear to the number of activities and its application to an illustrative collaborative authoring environment will be presented.

Keywords: Coordination, Petri nets, temporal behaviors modeling.

1 Introduction

Activities represent well-defined fragments within the general functioning of a process and involve in our context interdependency relations. A collaborative system may be viewed as a group of processes that are defined by a group of logically related activities. The execution of activities in collaborative environments may present conflicting requirements and interests that must be anticipated and solved in order to reach the desired goals. The effort aiming to foresee and solve the conflicts derived from dependencies among activities is defined as coordination [8] and it establishes the mechanisms that guarantee the (temporal, spatial, causal, etc.) behaviors defined by these interdependencies.

Our approach deals with dependencies considering both activities that are directly related and those indirectly related, facilitating the work of designers, which otherwise should identify and verify all the relationships – direct and indirect – for consistency.

Providing a solution for this issue is the motivation for this new methodology that enables the analytical and graphical representation of interdependency relations

J.M. Haake, S.F. Ochoa, and A. Cechich (Eds.): CRIWG 2007, LNCS 4715, pp. 127–142, 2007.

among activities in a computational environment. This methodology then generates coordination mechanisms that also model the global behavior, i.e., mechanisms that ensure the execution of all the interdependencies defined for the group of activities.

This way, the GR (Relation Graph) methodology considers the global and the local aspects of a coordination problem. The global approach is responsible for coordinating the necessary conditions to authorize the beginning of an activity. The local approach coordinates the execution of two authorized activities, complying with the kind of relation defined for them. Furthermore, this methodology does not restrict the quantity of relations in which an activity may be involved.

The coordination mechanisms are generated by an algorithm of complexity $O(n)$, n being the number of activities. This algorithm automates the identification and modeling of temporal restrictions among activities resulting in a coordination mechanism with the following characteristics:

1. Adherence to restrictions: the execution of an activity never violates any temporal restriction.
2. Behavior selection: it is possible to select different behaviors (activity interdependencies) for the same subset of activities.
3. Activity selection: it is possible to define whether a subset of activities will be executed or not.

The GR methodology does not gear a specific application. Its goal is to obtain coordination mechanisms considering the concepts of activity and interdependency.

Section 2 presents a discussion about coordination in computational environments. Section 3 introduces the GR methodology. Section 4 presents a case study. Conclusions are presented in Section 5.

2 Overview

The issue of activity coordination in collaborative environments has been the subject of varied scientific research [4], [6], [8], [10], [13] and has attracted the interest of experts in search for tools that help to coordinate computational environments.

This section briefly presents situations to illustrate the need for coordination models to couple with local and global aspects of computational environments.

A set of coordination mechanisms to manage temporal dependencies and resource dependencies among the participants of a collaborative environment was presented in [12]. For each participant, a Petri Net is designed, modeling the participant's activities and the dependencies among them. Then, possible dependencies among different participants are defined, concluding the first abstraction level, called by the author *workflow level*. Once the workflow level has been designed, the system's model is obtained automatically; in a second abstraction level, called *coordination level*, the activities, represented by transitions, are expanded according to a predefined model. The coordination mechanisms that correspond to the dependencies are added (they are also predefined), and the model of the collaborative system is obtained.

The separation between activities and dependencies, and the use of predefined coordination mechanisms provide the advantage of automatically generating the system's model based on the workflow level. The designer can focus only on specifying the system at the workflow level. The coordination mechanisms presented by [12] to temporal dependencies allow relating the activities two-by-two, thus ensuring the observance of temporal restrictions derived from this dependency. A global analysis and a verification of temporal inconsistencies (temporal behaviors that cannot be executed) must be made by the system designer.

In workflow applications, the cooperation among the different actors (human, computer, organization, etc.) in charge of executing the activities that define the processes must be promoted. A powerful coordination component is required by the dependency relation the activities usually present [1]. Dealing with possible conflicts among activities becomes more complex when the workflow involves multiple organizations [12]. An activity-based model using high-level Petri Nets (colored, temporized and hierarchical) to model both the workflow and the workflow's coordination system is proposed in [15]. Some of the difficulties found in the coordination and development of multi-organizational workflows are exposed in [16], which introduced a tool based on analysis techniques for Petri Nets to inspect multi-organizational workflows. The processes are specified in an XML-based language that is subsequently transformed into a specific Petri Net to verify if the workflow is correct.

In a multi-agent environment, the execution of tasks might affect or be affected by other tasks, which characterizes a dependency relationship among them. If the tasks refer to different agents, then the relationships among them represent a nature here called *non-local dependency*. This configuration restricts the agent's ability to select adequate actions, because the agent is not aware of restrictions derived from non-local dependencies [3], which motivates the use of coordination mechanisms for this purpose. Methodologies based on high-level Petri Nets, particularly colored ones, used in the problem of coordinating the behaviors of agents, have been presented by [9] and [17].

The dependency class (causal, resource, simultaneity, prerequisite, producer-consumer, etc.) among activities varies according to the context of the problem to be modeled, but a common denominator among these classes seems to be the time factor. Thus, temporal models are essential to express dependencies among activities in order to support applications in different research fields [18], [19].

The following section introduces a new methodology to model coordination mechanisms. The concept of coordination will be further developed, because apart from (identification/association) specification, a linear-cost algorithm will be introduced for the automatic generation of coordination mechanisms based on the specification of temporal behaviors.

3 Methodology

The GR methodology consists in generating coordination mechanisms based on the temporal behaviors specified for the activities executed in the environment. These behaviors correspond to temporal dependency relations among the activities.

Three abstraction levels are defined (Fig. 1a). The *specification level* establishes a temporal order among the activities through an expression. At the *coordination level*, the coordination mechanism is built after modeling all dependencies among the activities described in the previous level. At the *execution level*, a program called *coordinator* will implement the coordination mechanism obtained in the coordination level. This coordinator interacts with the set of activities, obeying the specification made at the specification level.

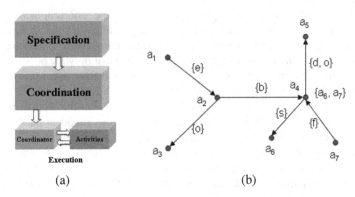

Fig. 1. (a) Abstraction levels. (b) Graph of temporal behaviors of an application

At the more abstract level temporal behaviors are specified by an activity-based model; it has as essential element non-null intervals. These intervals contain the activities executed in the system, which on their turn may establish relationships among themselves through temporal primitives [7], [19]. The set of temporal primitives introduced by [2] was adopted as the possible temporal relationships among activities.

Table 1 presents seven temporal primitives relations between two activities **a** and **b**, occurring in time intervals $x = [a_i, a_f)$ and $y = [b_i, b_f)$, with a_i and a_f, b_i and b_f being the beginning and the end of **a** and **b**, respectively, and the relations according to the temporal primitives of the set $D = \{e, s, d, f, o, m, b\}$,

Table 1. Temporal primitive relations between activities **a** and **b**

e(**a**, **b**): equal	↔	$a_i = b_i$ and $a_f = b_f$ - **a** is executed in the same time interval as **b**.
s(**a**, **b**): start	↔	$a_i = b_i$ and $a_f < b_f$ - **a** and **b** begin together, but **a** ends before **b**.
d(**a**, **b**): during	↔	$a_i > b_i$ and $a_f < b_f$ - **a** begins after **b** and ends before **b**.
f(**a**, **b**): finish	↔	$a_i > b_i$ and $a_f = b_f$ - **a** begins after **b**, but **a** and **b** end together.
o(**a**, **b**): overlap	↔	$a_i < b_i$ and $b_i < a_f$ and $a_f < b_f$ - **a** begins before **b**, which begins before **a** is over. **a** ends before **b**.
m(**a**, **b**): meet	↔	$a_f = b_i$ - **b** is executed immediately after the end of **a**.
b(**a**, **b**): before	↔	$a_f < b_i$ - **a** must be executed before **b**.

In the GR model, temporal behaviors are represented by a labeled oriented graph whose vertices correspond to system activities and edges correspond to the dependency relations among them. Fig. 1b illustrates a hypothetical example with 7 activities. The direction of the edges indicates the order in which the activities are related, and their labels state the type of dependency among them. For example, the label of edge a_2,a_4 – {b} – specifies that activity a_2 must be executed before activity a_4. The label in edge a_4,a_5 specifies alternative dependency relations, which means that any one of the alternatives may take place each time these activities are activated by the application. The selection of one relation instead of the other is made in execution time, according to environment requirements.

Still at specification level, alternative activities can be anticipated; for instance, the label of activity a_4 indicates that one of the activities a_6 or a_7 must be selected to be related with a_4. This selection occurs each time activity a_4 is activated through events fired by the application, and any of the activities in its label can be selected.

The specification of a system S is stated by an expression E(A,R,F), an oriented and labeled[1] graph, with an acyclic subjacent[2] graph, where:

- A is a set of vertices representing the activities,
- $R \subset A \times A$ is a set of edges representing the relations,
- F is a function $F : R \rightarrow \wp(D)$ where $\wp(D)$ is the set of D parts, called edge (relation) labeling function – D={e, s, d, f, o, m, b}, and
- G is a function $G : A \rightarrow \wp(A)$ where $\wp(A)$ is the set of A parts, called vertex (activity) labeling function, which satisfies the following properties:

1. If $b \in G(a)$, then the edge defined by a and b belongs to R;
2. If $b \in G(a)$, then $a \notin G(b)$;
3. If $b \in G(a)$, then $\exists c \in G(a) \mid c \neq b$.

Applying the above definitions to the example in Fig. 1b, the following qualified expression (E, G)[3] is obtained:

$A=\{a_1, a_2, a_3, a_4, a_5, a_6, a_7\}$;
$R=\{(a_1,a_2), (a_2,a_3), (a_2,a_4), (a_4,a_6), (a_7,a_4), (a_4,a_5)\}$;

The edge labeling function F is given by $F(a_1,a_2)=\{e\}$, $F(a_2,a_3)=\{o\}$, $F(a_2,a_4)=\{b\}$, $F(a_4,a_6)=\{s\}$, $F(a_7,a_4)=\{f\}$, and $F(a_4,a_5)=\{d, o\}$, and the vertex labeling function G is given by:

$G(a_4)=\{a_6,a_7\}$ and $G(a_1)= G(a_2)= G(a_3)= G(a_5)= G(a_6)= G(a_7)=\varnothing$

Once the temporal ordering among the activities is known, construction of the co-ordination mechanism begins. This process corresponds to modeling the temporal constraints derived from the dependency relations among the activities.

3.1 Abstract Levels and Coordination Mechanisms

Fig. 2a shows the diagram – a colored Petri Net – of an activity a at coordination level.

---

[1] A graph is called node-(or edge-) labeled when to each vertex (or edge) there is an associated set, called label [14]. In this text, we consider node- and edge-labeled graphs, which we call simply labeled graphs.
[2] The subjacent graph is the one obtained from the oriented graph by removing the directions of the edges [14].
[3] A qualified expression is a pair (E,G) where E is an expression E(A,R,F) and G is the function defined above.

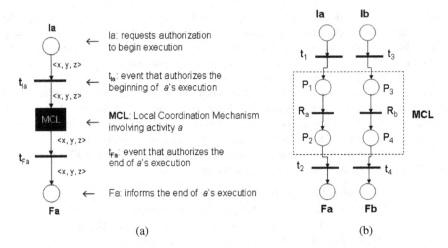

Fig. 2. (a) Diagram of an activity at coordination level. (b) Colored Petri Net of r(a,b).

The beginning of activity **a** is authorized by the event generated by firing transition t_{Ia}; firing transition t_{Fa} generates the end of execution of activity **a**. The MCL - Local Coordination Mechanism - commands the beginning of **a** and waits for the end of **a**'s execution. The ordered triple **<x , y , z>** represents the colored token so that $(y,z) \in R$ and $x \in F(y,z)$, where **R** is the set of edges of an expression and **F** is the edge labeling function.

The diagram in Fig. 2b details the MCL for the relation between activities **a** and **b**; activity **a** is related to activity **b** through relation $r \in D - r(a,b)$. Firing transition t_1 (t_3) corresponds to the event that authorizes the beginning of execution of activity **a** (**b**), while firing transition t_2 (t_4) corresponds to the event that authorizes the end of

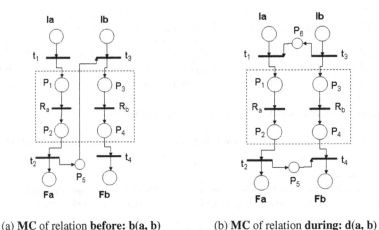

(a) **MC** of relation **before: b(a, b)**   (b) **MC** of relation **during: d(a, b)**

Fig. 3. Examples of basic MCs

execution of activity **a** (**b**). The time spent in the execution of an activity is represented using the concept of transition with token reservation [11]. In this type of transition, the firing takes place in two moments. Firstly the tokens are removed from the input place when the transition is active; secondly the tokens are sent to the output place after a given time span.

Fig. 3 illustrates the relations before(a,b), or b(a,b), and during(a,b), or d(a,b), derived from Fig. 2b.

The GR methodology also allows the specification of alternative temporal behaviors and the anticipation of alternative activities.

Fig. 4 shows the case in which alternative temporal relations must be anticipated, at specification level, between the activity pairs that define such behaviors. The selection of one behavior instead of another is made in execution time, according to environment requirements. This mechanism, called basic MC – Coordination Mechanism – models all relations anticipated for activities **a** and **b** and allows only one of them to be selected at a time.

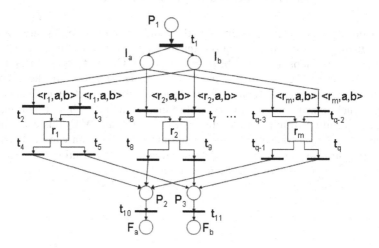

Fig. 4. Basic MC for alternative behaviors – relations

Fig. 5 presents the basic mechanism that allows the anticipation of alternative activities in the specification of a temporal behavior. The alternative activities that take part in a given behavior are selected at execution time. This basic MC allows the selection of any one of the activities to be related with activity **a**. Such selection is made according to the token color at places Ia and Ib_i (i={1, 2, ... m}).

Following, the construction of coordination mechanisms of an expression with more than one dependency relation will be derived from the basics MCs. The construction procedure is based on the connection of pairs of coordination mechanisms (MC_1, MC_2) with a common activity, i.e. the same activity modeled both in MC_1 and in MC_2. Figs. 6 (a) and (b) illustrate the mechanisms corresponding to *before* and *during* relations, respectively, **b** being the common activity.

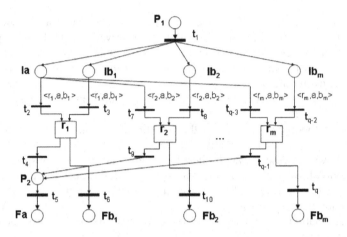

Fig. 5. Basic MC for alternative behaviors – activities

Transitions t_2 and t_5 (t_4 and t_7) in Figs. 6 (a) and 6 (b), respectively, are associated to the beginning (end) of **b**'s execution. Input arcs to these transitions correspond to the temporal restrictions involving **b**; firing t_2 (t_4) in MC_1 and t_5 (t_7) in MC_2 indicates that all temporal restrictions involving **b** were satisfied, resulting in the events that authorize the beginning (end) of their execution in the respective mechanisms. To keep the synchronization condition regarding the beginning of **b**'s execution, in the mechanism resulting from the connection between MC_1 and MC_2 this event must be generated by a single transition. This synchronization condition can be satisfied by merging transitions t_2 and t_5 (t_4 and t_7), generating a single transition that receives all temporal restrictions involving the beginning (end) of **b**. Fig. 6 (c) illustrates the **MC** resulting from the connection operation between MC_1 and MC_2.

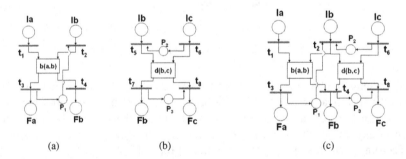

(a)   (b)   (c)

Fig. 6. (a) MC_1: relation *before* **b(a,b)**; (b) MC_2: relation *during* **d(b,c)**; (c) MC resulting from the connection operation between MC_1 and MC_2

The **merging** of two transitions t' and t" is executed by transferring to one of them all the input and output arcs of the other.

The extension of basic MCs for alternative behaviors consists in inserting a feature, here called connection feature. Fig. 7 presents the basic MC for alternative dependency relations with the connection feature for activity **a**. This extension, identi-fied by traced arcs, splits the transitions (see definition below) t_2, t_6, $\cdots$, t_{q-3} from Fig. 5 into the transitions t_2' and t_2'', t_6' and t_6'', $\cdots$, t_{q-3}' and t_{q-3}'' in Fig. 7, respectively, and adds places P_4 and P_5 and transition t_N. The temporal restrictions derived from relations r_1, r_2, $\cdots$, r_m that must be imposed on activity **a** correspond to the input arcs of transitions t_2', t_6', $\cdots$, t_{q-3}' (Fig. 7). These restrictions are not represented here be-cause relations r_1, r_2 $\cdots$, r_m are generic.

Splitting transition t into transitions t' and t" consists in attributing all input arcs of t to t' and all output arcs of t to t".

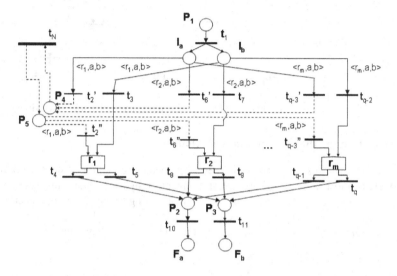

Fig. 7. Basic MC with connection features for alternative relations

The extension of the coordination mechanism from one dependency to two or more dependencies can be reached performing connections between MCs as follows.

Considering Fig. 7, to perform the connection operation between the basic MC for alternative dependency relations and another MC, a **merge** must be made between transition t_N and a transition from the other MC that generates the authorization event to begin activity **a**, as well as a merge between transition t_{10} and a transition from the other MC that generates the authorization event to end activity **a**, considering **a** as the common activity to these mechanisms.

The extension of basic MCs for alternative activities is completely analogous to that of basic MCs for alternative relations. Fig. 8 presents this basic MC with the con-nection feature to activity **a**. The temporal restrictions derived from relations r_1, r_2, $\cdots$, r_m that must be imposed on activity **a** correspond to the input arcs of transitions t_2', t_7' $\cdots$, t_{q-3}'. Firing one of the transitions indicates that the temporal restrictions derived from one of the alternative relations was fulfilled, which allows transition t_2'' whose firing generates the authorization event to begin execution of activity **a**.

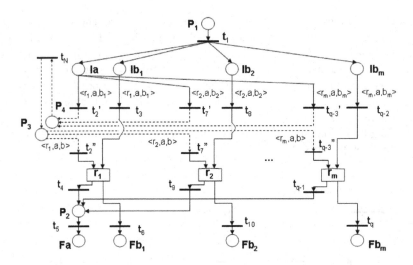

Fig. 8. Basic MC with connection features for alternative behaviors – activities

3.2 Algorithm for the Coordination Mechanism

Now that the basic mechanisms have been introduced, we can construct the coordination mechanism of an expression through connection operations among them. A possible approach is to build the mechanisms corresponding to each edge and each vertex of the relation graph according to their labels and then make the connections according to the graph's adjacencies. The steps of the algorithm are listed below.

```
Given an expression ε⁴
Obtain Partition of A: P(A) = {I₀, I₁, …, I_u}
For k ← 1 step 1 until (number of elements of P(A)) do
   Step 1. Select set I_k of activities a_i;
   Step 2. Identify and model the list of direct re-
strictions for each a_i-star, a_i ∈ I_k;
   Step 3. Connect the MC of a_i-stars, a_i ∈ I_k with the
proper MC of a_j-stars, a_j ∈ I_{k-1};
End for
If center I_u from ε has two activities a_p and a_q
   then connect MCa_p with MCa_q;
End algorithm
```

In step 1 of the algorithm, the selection of set I_k of the current iteration is made based on the definition of sub expressions of ε and the partition of set **A**. Although the identification process can be initiated by any set of activities, it is interesting to define an activity selection order. This provides advantages to the identification process of global conditions, because the fact that an activity a_i is a leaf (an activity with only

---

[4] ε denotes the expressions **E(A, R, F)** and **(E, G)**.

one dependency relation $\partial(a_i)^5 = 1$) or is internal (an activity with more than one dependency relation $\partial(a_i) > 1$) can be known beforehand and used to simplify the modeling process.

To determine this order, given an expression ε, a partition of activity set A is obtained, denoted by $P(A)$. The subsets that determine $P(A)$ are established through a sequence of expressions $\{\varepsilon_i\}$, $i = 0,1,2,...,u$, obtained from the original expression ε, according to the formation rule in Table 2.

Table 2. Formation Rule

ε_i	**Formation Rule**
ε_0	is the original expression ε;
ε_1	Expression derived from ε_0, eliminating the activities with degree 1 from ε_0;
ε_2	Expression derived from ε_1, eliminating the activities with degree 1 from ε_1;
$\vdots$	$\vdots$
ε_u	Expression derived from ε_{u-1}, eliminating the activities with degree 1 from ε_{u-1}.

Sequence $\{\varepsilon_i\}$ has maximum size $u+1$, smaller than or equal to half the number of activities n involved in an expression ε, i.e. $u \leq n/2 - 1$. The largest value of u occurs in linear expressions.

A partition P of activity set A of an expression ε is given by $P(A) = \{I_0, I_1,...,I_u\}$, where $u \leq n/2 - 1$, n being the number of activities and

$$I_0 = \{a_i \in \varepsilon_0 \mid \partial(a_i) = 1\}$$
$$I_1 = \{a_i \in \varepsilon_1 \mid \partial(a_i) = 1\}$$
$$I_2 = \{a_i \in \varepsilon_2 \mid \partial(a_i) = 1\}$$
$$\vdots$$
$$I_u = \{a_i \in \varepsilon_u \mid \partial(a_i) = 1\}$$

The purpose of sequence $\{\varepsilon_i\}$ is to formalize the partition criterion for A. In fact, it is neither necessary nor convenient to effectively create $\{\varepsilon_i\}$. Computing a list containing the degree of all activities is sufficient. Thus, I_0 is determined by selecting the a_i activities in the list such that $\partial(a_i) = 1$. To determine I_1, the list must be updated. For each activity a_i from I_0 : i) remove a_i from the list; ii) subtract one unit from the degree of activity a_j related to a_i. Then I_1 is determined by all a_j activities, $j \neq i$ such that $\partial(a_j) = 1$. This procedure ends with a list that has only one or two activities, i.e. the center of the expression, which corresponds to set I_u.

Once the partition criterion has been established, without losing generality an outside-in selection order is determined, i.e. from external activities (set I_1) towards internal ones (I_2, I_3,..., I_u). An advantage of this selection order is to begin by I_1 rather

---

[5] $\partial(a_i)$ denotes activity degree, i.e., the number of activities a_j ($j \neq i$) related to a_i.

than by I_0. I_0's temporal restrictions can be determined when I_1's activities are processed.

Step 2 of the algorithm determines for each a_i the list of direct restrictions. This requires knowing the activity set a_j related to it.

An a_i-star is a sub-expression determined by a_i, by the activity set a_j related to a_i and by its respective relations.

Analyzing an a_i-star means determining the set of direct restrictions activity a_i must satisfy, called a_i's direct restriction list. To do this, consider A and B as two sets of temporal restrictions and the following conventions:

1. **A .and. B** is the set formed by all temporal restrictions of A and B, read as A conjunction B;
2. **A .or. B** is the set formed by all temporal restrictions of exclusively A or B, read as A disjunction B.

The direct restrictions of the a_i-star are the temporal restrictions derived from all relations involving a_i and formed by the conjunction of C_1, C_2 and C_3, where:

C_1 is the conjunction of the restriction sets derived from the relations between a_i and the a_j activities that satisfy the following properties:

1. $a_j \notin G(ai)$;
2. the label of the edge defined by a_i and a_j is unitary (has one primitive).

C_2 is the disjunction of the restriction sets derived from the relations between a_i and the a_j activities such that:

1. $a_j \in G(a_i)$.

C_3 is the conjunction of C_{ij}'s where each C_{ij} is the disjunction of the restriction sets derived from the relations of the edge's label, defined by a_i and a_j provided that a_j satisfies the following properties:

1. $a_j \notin G(a_i)$;
2. the label of the edge defined by a_i and a_j is not unitary.

Illustrating the algorithm using the example in Fig. 1b, we have:

1. Considering the expression presented in Fig. 1b: a_1, a_3, a_5, a_6, a_7 are degree 1 activities.
2. Following the outside-in order, first the basic MCs must be built for the labels of edges (a_1, a_2) and (a_2, a_3), and the connection operation between these two basic MCs must be executed.
3. Then the basic MC for edge (a_4, a_5) and the basic MC for the label of activity a_4 are built, and the connection operation between these two basic MCs is executed.
4. To determine the next basic MCs to be built, degree 1 activities are removed from the graph; the resulting graph will display new degree 1 activities.
5. Basic MCs must be built for these edges involving degree 1 activities, and connection operations must be executed according to the graph's adjacencies.

In the next section the GR methodology will be explored in a case study.

4 Case Study

In this section, we present a case approaching the use of the methodology presented in the previous section. The case study illustrates a situation involving a collaborative authoring environment.

The authoring tool allows an author to write and/or to review a paper's section. In this example, there are three authors (A, B and C). Each author writes one section. The section 2 is reviewed by author A and the section 3 is reviewed by either author B or author A. The temporal dependencies between the activities are showed in Fig. 9.

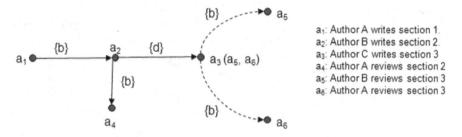

a_1: Author A writes section 1.
a_2: Author B writes section 2.
a_3: Author C writes section 3
a_4: Author A reviews section 2
a_5: Author B reviews section 3
a_6: Author A reviews section 3

Fig. 9. Relation graph of the case study

The relation graph showed in Fig. 9 is formally specified in the expression $E(A, R, F)$ and in functions G, provided as follows.

$A = \{a_1, a_2, a_3, a_4, a_5, a_6\}$
$R = \{(a_1, a_2), (a_2, a_4), (a_2, a_3), (a_3, a_5), (a_3, a_6)\}$
$F(a_1, a_2) = \{b\}, F(a_2, a_4) = \{b\}, F(a_2, a_3) = \{d\}, F(a_3, a_5) = \{b\}, F(a_3, a_6) = \{b\}$
$G(a_3) = \{a_5, a_6\}$, others $G(a_i) = \varnothing$.

Now we construct the coordination mechanism using the algorithm described in section 3. The partition P of activity set A of the expression E is given by $P(A) = \{I_0, I_1\}$, where $I_0 = \{a_1, a_4, a_5, a_6\}$ and $I_1 = \{a_2, a_3\}$. According to the algorithm, we begin the construction of the coordination mechanism selecting the activities of set I_1.

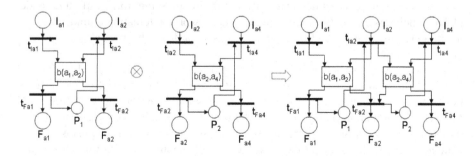

Fig. 10. Connecting MC of relations $b(a_1, a_2)$ and $b(a_2, a_4)$

Fig. 10 illustrates the connection of MC of relations (a_1, a_2) and (a_2, a_4), which share a common activity (a_2), through merging the transitions t_{Ia2} and t_{Fa2}.

The same operation is done with the a_3 activity's relations. Finally, we connect the MC of relation (a_2, a_3) with the MC of activities a_2 and a_3. Fig. 11 presents the final coordination mechanism.

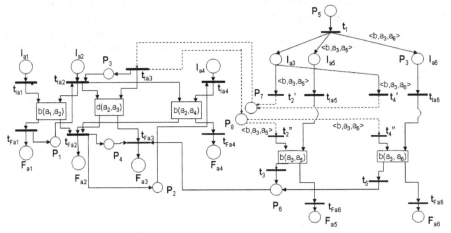

Fig. 11. Final Coordination Mechanism

The selection of relation (a_3, a_5) or (a_3, a_6) is done putting the appropriate token in the place P_5. If the token is $<b, a_3, a_5>$ then the relation (a_3, a_5) will be selected. On the other hand, if the token is $<b, a_3, a_6>$ then the relation (a_3, a_6) will be selected.

5 Conclusion

This work has presented a methodology to describe and coordinate interdependencies among a set of activities performed in a computer environment. An algorithm was also presented to automate the generation of a Coordination Mechanism (MC) free from temporal inconsistencies, with a time linear to the number of activities.

The GR methodology allows automating the generation process of coordination mechanisms by means of modeling tools and of the algorithm to identify and model global conditions. Apart from reducing designers' work, automation eliminates errors in the determination of such conditions and standardizes the process of modeling global conditions.

The coordination policy adopted in GR explores the advantages of both global and local coordination. At the local level, the MCL explores the concept of modularization, which allows modifying local mechanisms without interfering with the global MC. This coordination policy enhances the use of the methodology presented herein in collaborative environments, because generating coordination mechanisms that operate at the global level and at the local level simultaneously is one of the difficulties found in the coordination of collaborative activities [5].

Inserting one coordination level allowed a distinction between task coordination and how this task is performed. The GR methodology does not determine how the task is carried out, but what must be done and when. Another advantage of the abstraction-level approach is to make the use of the GR methodology independent from previous knowledge of the formalism used to model the MCs (in this case, Petri Nets).

References

1. Agostini, A., De Michelis, G.: A Light Workflow Management System Using Simple Process Models. Computer Supported Cooperative Work 9, 335–363 (2000)
2. Allen, J.F.: Towards a General Theory of Action and Time. Artificial Intelligence 23, 123–154 (1984)
3. Chen, W., Decker, K.S.: Coordination Mechanisms for Dependency Relationships among Multiple Agents. In: Alonso, E., Kudenko, D., Kazakov, D. (eds.) Adaptive Agents and Multi-Agent Systems. LNCS (LNAI), vol. 2636, pp. 172–173. Springer, Heidelberg (2003)
4. Crowston, K.: A Taxonomy of Organizational Dependencies and Coordination Mechanisms. In: Malone, T.W., Crowston, K., Herman, G. (eds.) Organizing Business Knowledge, pp. 85–108. MIT Press, Cambridge (2003)
5. Cruz, A.J.A., Raposo, A.B., Magalhães, L.P.: Coordination in Collaborative Environments - A Global Approach. In: de Janeiro, R. (ed.) Proceedings of the 7th International Conference on Computer Supported Cooperative Work in Design – CSCWD, Brazil, pp. 25–30 (2002)
6. Dellarocas, C.N.: A Coordination Perspective on Software Architecture: Towards a Design Handbook for Integrating Software Components. PhD Thesis, Dept. of Electrical Engineering and Computer Science, MIT (1996)
7. Presti, S.L., Bert, D., Duda, A.: TAO: Temporal Algebraic Operators for Modeling Multimedia Presentations. Journal of Network and Computer Applications 25, 319–342 (2002)
8. Malone, T.W., Crowston, K.K.: The Interdisciplinary Study of Coordination. ACM Computing Surveys 26(1), 87–119 (1994)
9. Moldt, D., Wienberg, F.: Multi-Agent-Systems base on Colored Petri Nets. In: Proceedings of the 18th International Conference on Application and Theory of Petri Nets,Toulouse, France, June 23-27, pp. 82–101 (1997)
10. Prasad, S.K., Balasooriya, J.: Fundamental Capabilities of Web Coordination Bonds: Modeling Petri Nets and Expressing Workflow and Communication Patterns over Web Services. In: Proceedings of the 38th Hawaii International Conference on System Sciences, Big Island, Hawaii, Jan. 5-8, pp. 12–19. IEEE Computer Society Press, Los Alamitos (2005)
11. Ramamoorthy, C.V., Ho, G.S.: Performance evaluation of asynchronous concurrent systems using Petri Nets. IEEE Transactions in Software Engineering 6(5), 440–449 (1980)
12. Raposo, A.B., Magalhães, L.P., Ricarte, I.L.M.: Petri Nets Based Coordination Mechanisms for Multi-Workflow Environments. International Journal of Computer Systems Science & Engineering, Special Issue on Flexible Workflow Technology Driving the Networked Economy 15(5), 315–326 (2000)
13. Schmidt, K., Simone, C.: Coordination Mechanisms: Towards a conceptual foundation of CSCW systems design. Computer Supported Cooperative Work: The Journal of Collaborative Computing 5(2-3), 155–200 (1996)

14. Szwarcfiter, J.L.: Grafos e algoritmos computacionais (Graphs and Computational Algorithms). Editora Campus, 2nd edn., Rio de Janeiro, Brazil (1986)
15. van der Aalst, W.M.P., van Hee, K.M., Houben, G.J.: Modeling and analyzing workflow using a Petri-net based approach. In: Proceedings of the 2nd Workshop on Computer-Supported Cooperative Work, Petri nets and related formalisms, pp. 31–50 (1994)
16. Verbeek, H.M.W., van der Aalst, W.M.P., Kumar, A.: XRL/Woflan: Verification and Extensibility of an XML/Petri-Net-Based Language for Inter-Organizational Workflows. Information Technology and Management 5(1-2), 65–110 (2004)
17. Weyns, D., Holvoet, T.: A Colored Petri Net for Multi-Agent Application. In: Proceedings of Modeling Objects, Components and Agents (MOCA'02), Aarhus, Denmark, pp. 121–140 (2002)
18. Yoon, K., Berra, P.B.: Interactive Temporal Model for Interactive Multimedia Documents. In: Proceedings of the International Workshop on Multimedia Database Management Systems (IW- MMDBMS), pp. 136–144 (1998)
19. Zaidi, A.K.: On temporal Logic Programming Using Petri Nets. IEEE Transactions on Systems, Man, and Cybernetics – Parte A: Systems and Humans 29(3), 245–254 (1999)

Fostering Groupware Tailorability Through Separation of Concerns

Diego Torres, Alejandro Fernandez[*], Gustavo Rossi, and Silvia Gordillo

Lifia – Facultad de Informática
Universidad Nacional de La Plata – Argentina
[*] Also at Universidad Nacional de Luján – Argentina
{Name.Lastname}@lifia.info.unlp.edu.ar

Abstract. Groupware must deal with a myriad of concerns. Some of them are typical of "conventional" software while others are idiosyncratic of CSCW applications (e.g., awareness). We claim that separating concerns fosters tailorability. While existing approaches for groupware design deal with the basic problem of separation of concerns (e.g., using well-known object-oriented techniques), they do not address the problems triggered by crosscutting concerns –i.e., when the realization of the same concern is scattered along multiple components, or when different concerns are "tangled" in the same component. This paper presents a concern-oriented approach to requirement specification of groupware, characterizing the situations in which crosscutting exists. It follows the Theme approach for identification and design of crosscutting concerns, uses AOP to eliminate tangling and scattering, and proposes a concern centric approach to groupware tailorability.

1 Introduction

Groupware provides support for communication, coordination and collaboration to a group of users that strive to achieve a common goal or complete a group task. For this reason, groupware must deal with a myriad of concerns. Some of them are typical of "conventional" software, while others are idiosyncratic of CSCW applications. The only way to deal with these concerns is to be able to correctly identify and modularize them and to understand the relationships and trade-offs among them. Furthermore, it is necessary to inspect the relationships between the design artifacts that realize those concerns, being able to separate them to maximize maintainability and reuse, and to make them easier to understand.

While existing approaches for tailorability deal with the basic problem of separation of concerns (e.g., using well-known object-oriented techniques), they do not address the problems triggered by crosscutting concerns –i.e., when the realization of the same concern is scattered along multiple components, or when different concerns are "tangled" in the same component (e.g., a class or a method). For example, awareness behavior such as providing information about the actions of other users in a shared editing session is usually "tangled" with base editing functionality and it is scattered among all modules that implements editing actions.

J.M. Haake, S.F. Ochoa, and A. Cechich (Eds.): CRIWG 2007, LNCS 4715, pp. 143–156, 2007.

The Early Aspects community [5] has proposed mechanisms to deal with the identification, representation, and composition of aspects at the requirements specification level (see for example [4] and [16]).

This paper shows how to apply these techniques to improve the design of Groupware, thus enabling up-front identification of concern interdependencies. Information about concern interdependencies is used during the design stage to separate concerns and foster tailorability. The contributions of this paper are threefold: (i) offer a concern-oriented approach to requirement specification of groupware, characterizing the situations in which crosscutting exists; (ii) provide architecture and design advice for the separation and composition of crosscutting concerns; (iii) propose a concern centric approach to groupware tailorability. By using a step by step approach in a well-known example, we show how different concerns can be incrementally and modularly integrated into a system when new requirements (corresponding to groupware concerns) arise.

The paper is organized as follows: Section 2 uses the example of a shared whiteboard to show how groupware can be specified in terms of separated concerns. Section 3 discusses how modularization in terms of separated concerns fosters tailorability. Section 4 discusses the limitations of traditional design techniques to support tailoring in terms of groupware concerns. Section 5 follows the Theme approach [4] to separate groupware concerns in aspects that are later composed using AspectJ (www.aspectj.org). Section 6 discusses some related work in the field. Closing, Section 6 presents conclusions and outlook.

2 Concerns in Groupware. A Practical Example

IEEE [10] defines concern as "those interests which pertain to the system's development, its operation or any other aspect that are critical or otherwise important to one or more stakeholders". Focusing on requirements, a concern implies any coherent set of functional or non-functional requirements (e.g., all requirements referring to a particular theme or behavioral application feature).

Let us analyze a shared whiteboard application. Users can create whiteboard documents and add text, pictures and freehand drawings to the documents. Changes are immediately propagated to all connected users working on the document. The shared whiteboard supports collaboration by allowing users to simultaneously work on the same document. Coordination is implicitly supported via the provision of awareness information regarding focus, activities, data changes, and presence.

The shared whiteboard can be seen as supporting requirements in several (crosscutting) concerns. These concerns are summarized in the subsections that follow. Detailed requirements are provided later in the paper.

2.1 The Base Shared Whiteboard

As the first concern, let us consider the set of requirements which are essential to the most basic task namely, creating and modifying whiteboard documents. That is, basically, the functionality of a single user whiteboard, e.g., select tools, add figures, etc. We will call this concern the *Electronic Whiteboard* concern *(EW)*.

A key requirement for the implementation of a shared whiteboard is to allow users at various distributed workstations to synchronously work on whiteboard documents (to browse and eventually change them). The *Data Synchronization concern* (DS) – that is how we will call this concern – documents requirements of concurrency, change propagation, and consistency, e.g., it should be possible to modify objects simultaneously from several stations.

Access to whiteboard documents must be guarded. Therefore, some form of access control must be implemented. It coarsely consists of requirements for registration of new users and authentication at log-in. We refer to this concern as the *Access Control* concern (AC).

2.2 Awareness Concerns

By composing the concerns presented so far, we have a fully functional, minimalist, shared electronic whiteboard. Distributed users can synchronously browse and modify whiteboard documents. However, effective collaboration requires awareness of other users' activities and intentions.

There are various scenarios where knowing the focus of other users is important. In a large whiteboard document, knowing the part of the document that is visible to other users helps to assess the likelihood of conflicting changes. If a user is looking at a different portion of the document, it is likely that his changes will not conflict with those of another user. But if a user wants to discuss some aspects of the document with a colleague (e.g., over IP phone), he needs to make sure that his window and that of his colleague show the same portion of document (or, at least, he needs to know what the other user's window shows). Requirements dealing with tracking and communicating users' focus fall into the *Focus Awareness* concern (FA).

Synchronous collaboration depends on users being simultaneously "on-line". Such rendezvous situations can be arranged in advance or can occur serendipitously. In any case, knowing that other users are "in-the-system" is valuable. The *Presence Awareness* concern (PA) clusters the requirements that deal with capturing and communicating the "on-line" state of users.

Focus awareness and presence awareness inform us if other users are present and where they are. To have a better idea of what is going on, we need to know *what* they are doing. Are they editing text? Are they moving pictures? Are they lurking? Requirements in the *Activity Awareness* concern (AA) deal with the detection and/or inference of user activities and with informing other users about these activities.

Users need information about the changes that occur in the documents they are working on, to complete the picture that enables them to contribute to the group "in context". The requirements which refer to detecting and communicating changes in a whiteboard document belong to the *Change Awareness* concern (CA).

2.3 Summary: Overview of Groupware Concerns

The previous sub-sections showed how requirements can be grouped in separated concerns. Two groups of concerns were presented: those concerns that, when composed, will result in a base collaborative whiteboard, and the set of awareness concerns.

Figure 1 provides an overview of other important concerns in a shared electronic whiteboard. Though the list is not exhaustive it should give the reader an idea of how requirements in a groupware application can be grouped to form concerns and how concerns may be grouped in higher level ones –being each column in the figure a higher level concern.

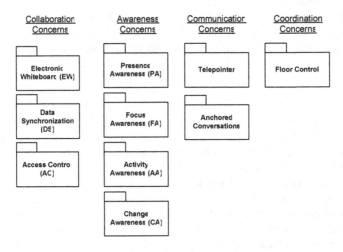

Fig. 1. Concerns of a Shared Electronic Whiteboard

In the previous example we have followed the Theme approach [4] to identify concerns. In fact, each of the elements in the above figure represents a theme. Finer decomposition could still be achieved; for example, the Electronic Whiteboard concern could be further decomposed. However, for the purpose of this paper (that is, to identify and isolate reusable, groupware concerns) only coarse granularity themes are of interest.

3   Tailoring in Terms of Concerns

The right choice of groupware specific functionality to be included in an application is a matter of exploration and tailoring [11, 17]. For example, different work settings (i.e., group configuration, culture, task, process, tools, and context) require different awareness configurations. Moreover, the right configuration evolves as the settings change (and they do change). In consequence many of the concerns presented in Figure 1 could be considered optional. They need to be included in a system, only if the context of use proves them useful. We refer to the possibility of changing the behavior of a groupware system by dynamically adding or removing support for a particular concern as "tailoring by integration of concerns".

Assume for example that we choose to integrate change awareness in our application. The specification of the Change Awareness concern can still leave room for tailoring with a finer granularity. For example, it may include the requirement that the notifications' lifetimes can be configured as a user preference. We call this kind of tailoring "tailoring by customization of concerns". These types of tailoring (by integration and by customization of concerns) are a specialization of the forms of tailoring originally identified by Anders Mørch [15].

Separating concerns to support concern-centric tailorability implies designing and developing the functionality corresponding to each concern as an independent software module while keeping coupling between modules to a minimum.

Separation of concerns has a positive impact in groupware tailorability. However, existing approaches to tailorable groupware do not support the kind of tailoring we have described. The strategy followed by most existing approaches to tailoring is to propose a one-fits-all technology (to allow customization, integration and/or extension) and to define tailoring in terms of such technology. Although the proposed technologies empower tailoring with relation to some concerns, they hinder tailoring with relations to others, crosscutting concerns. The early aspects community refers to this problem as "the tyranny of the dominant decomposition" [21]. We leave the discussion of why some renowned approaches to tailorable groupware fail to support tailoring in the presence of crosscutting concerns to Section 7.

4   Limitations in Traditional Forms of Separation of Concerns

Software designers understand that reducing coupling between software components fosters reuse, and improves understandability and maintainability. To reduce coupling, designers apply some well-known design strategies such as object oriented design, design patterns, and layered architectures. One may argue that such strategies should be enough to reduce tangling and scattering between the components that implement groupware concerns, thus simplifying tailoring in terms of concerns. In this section we argue that traditional techniques, for example those used to implement the data distribution concern (DS) presented in section 2.1, are not enough to achieve modularity.

To illustrate our point we next present in detail the Electronic Whiteboard concern (EW) –the base concern-, and the Data Distribution concern (DS) –the crosscutting concern-.

Electronic Whiteboard Concern
Let us review a minimalist specification of an electronic whiteboard. The electronic whiteboard works on whiteboard documents. The following requirements define the Electronic Whiteboard concern. The list of requirements is not exhaustive, although enough detail has been included to show dependencies between concerns.

> **R-EW1.** Documents can be created.
> **R-EW2.** Documents can be destroyed.
> **R-EW3.** Available documents can be listed.
> **R-EW4.** Documents can be edited.
> **R-EW5.** The user can use the text tool to create and place a text object in the whiteboard document.
> **R-EW6.** The user can use the selection tool to select objects in the document, move them around, and delete them.

In a similar fashion the user can select other tools to add other objects (e.g., freehand drawing tool). The requirements for other object creation tools are intentionally left out of the specification.

Data Synchronization Concern

To turn the single user whiteboard specified by the EW concern into a shared whiteboard we introduce the Data Synchronization concern consisting of the following requirements

R-DS1. It should be possible to access and modify the application's data objects simultaneously from several stations.

R-DS2. Changes in any of the application's data objects must be immediately visible in all stations

R-DS3. Removing one of the application objects should only be possible if the object is not being used at any station

There is a strong dependency between these three concerns and those in the EW. It should be possible to browse the list of existing documents, simultaneously from several stations (that is R-DS1 expressed in relation to R-EW4). It should be possible to open a document in the whiteboard window simultaneously from several stations (R-DS1 in relation to R-EW5). When new documents are created or destroyed, this must be immediately made visible to all stations (R-DS2 in relation to R-EW1 and R-EW2). Documents can be destroyed only if they are not being used at any station (R-DS3 in relation to R-EW2).

The previous analysis shows that several requirements in the data synchronization concern bear a relationship with one or several requirements in the electronic whiteboard concern. Both concerns are tightly coupled through "stamp coupling", as the components that implement them will need access to the same data structures, for example the properties of objects representing the document and its elements. Moreover, there is also "control coupling", since data synchronization operations in the component that implements the DS concern are controlled by changes in the component that implements the EW concern. It is well known that coupling hinders maintainability, understandability, and tailoring.

Synchronous object replication frameworks have already been used to free the groupware developer from the technical details of object replication and to reduce coupling (e.g., Coast [19], and DreamObjects [13]). Such frameworks introduce an object replication and synchronization layer that separates the DS concern form the groupware application concern.

In a layered architecture coupling occurs in only one direction, that is, the services provided by lower layers impact the design of layers built on top of them. This separation allows tailoring by customization and continuous improvement of the lower layers, as long as the contracts signed with the upper layer are honored. The price for using such frameworks is paid by application developers. They must commit to a particular application design mandated by the framework. Although they do not write data synchronization code (what is to say, there is no data synchronization code scattered across the application code), significant changes in the framework design may still demand changes in applications build on top of the framework.

For further discussion of why traditional techniques are not enough to separate crosscutting concerns, we point the reader to [4].

5 Separating Groupware Concerns with Aspects

Aspect Oriented Programming [12] is seen by many as the natural approach to tackle separation of crosscutting concerns during design and implementation. There is few documented experience of the application of AOP in the development of groupware (see for example, [18]). We next introduce the results of our research in this direction. Two groupware concerns are covered; access control (AC) and Activity Awareness (AA).

Access Control Concern
As the next incremental step in the design of the shared electronic whiteboard we integrate the access control concern. The requirements for the access control concern are the following:

> **R-AC1.** The user should be authenticated before any shared data is accessed. Authentication is required only once per session through a log-in window.
>
> **R-AC2.** The "log-in" window allows registering new users and setting the access password.

Requirement R-AC1 affects all requirements in the electronic whiteboard concern that deal with accessing shared data. That is, authentication should occur before documents are listed, created, or opened (e.g., R-EW2, R-EW5)

Integrating the access control concern requires the introduction of some form of database and operations to record and retrieve user information. It is increasingly common to find that this database and associated operations are shared among several applications that require authentication. This is commonly known as single sign-on (i.e., use the same username and password for several apps, and authenticate only once for each session). Authentication defines a highly cohesive set of data and operations that could beneficially be encapsulated and separated in an independent module. However, the authentication module and the operations in the main applications would be coupled through control coupling, as authentication affects the execution of those operations. Moreover, modules and applications that need to use the authentication database are coupled to each other through stamp coupling, as they access and modify the authentication database.

Implementing authentication as an independent service, following the principles of service oriented architectures [6], could be a good approach to separate authentication in an independent module without the damaging impact of coupling. The service operations are called by the applications when they need to authenticate. Separating authentication as a service reduces the impact of stamp coupling and enables continuous improvement and tailoring by customization of the authentication service. However, this approach has a drawback. The code that calls the operations published by the authentication service is scattered in all operations that access shared data, in all applications.

To overcome the drawback of scattered authentication code, the authentication server component (implementing the AC concern) is integrated with the whiteboard component using Aspect Oriented techniques.

Figure 2 provides a code snippet for the implementation of the AccessControl aspect. The aspect acts as the glue between the base program (the electronic whiteboard) and the authentication service. The authentication glue aspect has two parts, the pointcut and the advice. The pointcut intercepts all methods annotated with the @resctrictedArea Java annotation. These are all methods that are identified as a first access to a shared artifact (i.e., populateDocumentList(), and openDocument() methods of the whiteboard implementation). That means that the aspect's advice will be automatically executed before any of these methods. The aspect's advice checks that the user has already authenticated and, if not, it opens the login window and calls an authentication operation on the authentication server. If authentication succeeds, the intercepted method continues, otherwise, execution is interrupted.

```
public aspect AccesControlAspect {

        // Pointcut "accessPoints" applies to all methods
        //annotated with @RestrictedArea
        pointcut accessPoints() : @annotation(RestrictedArea);

        //Advice for the accessPoints pointcut throws an exception
        // if access has not been granted to the user
        void around():accessPoints(){
                if (Gatekeeper.getInstance().isAccessGranted()) {
                        proceed();
                } else {
                        throw new AccessDeniedRuntimeException();
                }
        }
}
```

Fig. 2. Access control aspect

Figure 3 shows the resulting architecture after introducing the authentication server and the aspect that glues the electronic whiteboard to the authentication server. For the electronic whiteboard component, the integration of authentication is transparent.

Authentication is a classical example of the use of AOP in almost every domain. We next show how to deal with more specific groupware concerns.

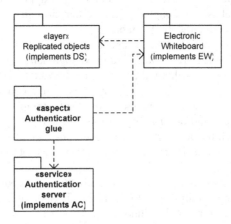

Fig. 3. Overview of the architecture after introducing access control

So far we have defined a shared electronic whiteboard that allows collaboration via synchronous creation and editing of whiteboard documents. It also ensures that only authenticated users have access to shared data. To help users contribute in context, we will add awareness information. Next, we integrate the activity awareness concern.

Activity awareness (AA)
Tight collaboration requires being aware of the activities of other users. A module that implements the activity awareness concern covers the following requirements:

R-AA1. Provide awareness of the tool selected by each user/station.
R-AA2. If a user/station has no tool selected or selects a tool with a read-only semantic, mark the user/station as lurking
R-AA3. Deselect the selected tool after 2 minutes of the last modification (necessary for R-AA2 to be effective)
R-AA4. After 5 minutes of input inactivity, mark the station/ user as idle

Let us observe the relationships and dependencies among these requirements and those of the electronic whiteboard concern and discuss the alternatives for separation of concerns. R-AA1 and R-AA2 must be provided on all requirements that deal with tool selection, in this case R-EW5 and R-EW6. Every time a tool is selected, its semantics need to the determined and the activity awareness information needs to be updated. A modular implementation regarding this relation can be cleanly achieved through aspect composition if the whiteboard concern has clear defined points where tool selection can be detected (e.g., it has been implemented following the command design pattern [8]).

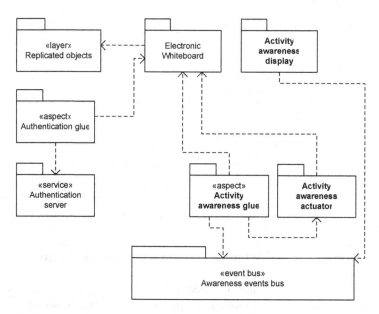

Fig. 4. Overview of the architecture after introducing activity awareness

Requirement R-AA4 implies the need of detecting user input and therefore affects the whiteboard concern (and any other concern with a user interface window). How complex is to detect input activity (e.g., mouse and keyboard) depends on the choice of programming language and on implementation decisions in the user interface components. Knowing that this dependency exists helps designers and programmers to choose a design alternative with foresight.

Activity awareness can be added to the architecture following the same pattern used for Focus awareness. An aspect (the activity awareness glue component in architecture depicted in Figure 4) intercepts methods in the electronic whiteboard and infers activity events. These events are published via the event bus. The activity awareness display is notified of activity events and updates its views. Figure 5 presents part of the AspectJ implementation of the Activity Awareness (glue) aspect.

The activity awareness concern detects and publishes user activity. Additionally, to provide R-AA3 (deselect the selected tool after two minutes of inactivity), when a tool selection is detected, a countdown timer is reset. When the timer elapses, the tool selection is changed to "no-tool". To implement this autonomous behavior a new component is included: the actuator. The actuator receives input form the aspect. When necessary, the actuator calls operations on objects of the electronic whiteboard (e.g., to set the selected tool to "no-tool"). The actuator obtains references to those objects (or proxies for those objects [8]) in notifications made by its aspect.

Figure 4 provides an overview of the resulting architecture. The components implementing the activity awareness concerns are marked with bold face.

```
pointcut readToolSelected(): call(@ActivityAwarenessAction * *(..))&&
    @args(ReadTool);

pointcut writeToolSelected():call(@ActivityAwarenessAction * *(..)) &&
    @args(WriteTool);

pointcut selectedTool(Tool tool): call(@ActivityAwarenessAction * *(..))
&& @args(tool);

after(Tool tool):selectedTool(tool){
    this.getActivityClient().publishActionSetted(tool.name());}

after(): readToolSelected() {
    this.setActivityState(Lurking.getInstance());
    user = ContextManager.getInstance().getActivityClient();
    user.startStateTimers();}

after(): writeToolSelected() {
    this.setActivityState(Writing.getInstance());}
```

Fig. 5. Pointcuts and advices for the ActivityAwareness aspect

6 Adapting Groupware Concerns to Other Applications

Section 5 shows how AOP can be used to separate groupware concerns during implementation. Each of the identified groupware concerns can be implemented as a separate package. We applied the approach in the construction of a collaborative electronic whiteboard. However, our goal is to specify and implement groupware concerns in a manner that makes it possible to reuse them in other applications. For example, they could be weaved into a collaborative UML editor.

The aspect's pointcut descriptor is the binding between the base application (the editor) and the implementation of the groupware concern. Briefly stated, the pointcut of an aspect indicates where in the execution of the application, the aspects's advice should be executed. It also indicates how parameters are passed from the application to the aspect. Source code in Figure 6 specifies an aspect called "writeToolSelected" that triggers its advice whenever the method selectTool() in class Whiteboard executes and its argument is an instance of class TextTool. Although that is the most common technique to specify aspects, aspects specified this way suffer the *pointcut fragility* problem. That is, changes in the base application (e.g., changes in class names) render the aspect useless. Moreover, regarding or goal of building reusable implementations, aspects making explicit reference to classes and methods in the Whiteboard application cannot be weaved into other applications.

```
pointcut writeToolSelected(): call(Whiteboard.selectTool(TextTool tool))
         && @args(tool);

after(): writeToolSelected()
         {this.setActivityStateToWritting();}
```

Fig. 6. Simple aspect specified in terms of specific classes and methods

If we look closely at the aspect, we realize that its intent it to execute its advice whenever a tool is selected and such tool can be characterized as a write mode tool. In fact, that is the declarative approach followed in the aspects shown in section 5. To decouple aspects from the specific classes and method of the base application, we use a recent AspectJ and Java facility called annotations. Figure 7 shows a variation of the pointcut, now stated in terms of annotations. It relies on the assumption that the Java code of the base application has been annotated. For example, it assumes that the selectTool() method of class Whiteboard has been annotated with the @Activity Change annotation.

```
pointcut writeToolSelected():call(@ActivityChange * *(..)) &&
     @args(WriteTool);
```

Fig. 7. Advice specified in terms of annotations

Designers of reusable implementations of groupware concerns cannot expect application developers to include annotations in their code. Doing so would tie base code implementations to the reusable groupware concerns. Annotating the base application's code is the responsibility of the developer composing the base application and all required groupware concerns. Annotations are introduced in the already compiled base application via annotation injection (another modern AspectJ facility). To do so, the developer needs knowledge of the source code of the base application. Figure 8 presents the AspectJ code that injects some of the annotations needed by the ActivityAwareness concern. The first declaration annotates the class TextTool as a @WriteTool.

```
/*
 * Annotate class LineTool as a @WriteTool (inject the annotation)
 */
declare @type:TextTool :@WriteTool;

/*
 * Annotate class ZoomTool as a @ReadTool (inject the annotatoin)
 */
declare @type: ZoomTool+:@ReadTool;

/*
 * Annotate the method selectTool() as an @ActivityChange
 */
declare @method:public void *.selectTool(Tool):@ ActivityChange;
```

Fig. 8. Injection of annotations

To implement a groupware concern, developers think of a model for a family of the base groupware application, for example, collaborative editors. Such model includes artifacts (e.g., tools) and events (e.g., change of activity). The aspects that glue the concern to the application are defined in terms of those events and artifacts. Annotations mark the points in a given base application (e.g., UML editor) where artifacts lie and events occur. A file declaring injections of annotations constitutes a mapping between the model thought by the groupware concern implementor, and the model actually present in the implementation of the base application.

7 Related Work

In [14] the idea of radical tailorability as an approach to match cooperative work tools to their contexts of use is introduced. Radically tailorable systems allow end users to create a wide range of different groupware applications by progressively modifying a working system. His approach, instantiated in a system called OVAL, is based on four key building blocks. Structured objects represent domain elements such as people, tasks, messages and meetings. User customizable views display collections of objects and can be used to edit individual object's properties. Rule based agents automatically perform tasks on behalf of users without requiring human intervention. Links represent relationships among objects. Radical tailoring is done by defining new types of objects, adding fields to existing object types, selecting and configuring views, creating agents and rules, and inserting new links. This approach to tailorability is reminiscent of computer programming generally, and object based, rule-based programming specifically. It is rare to find much flexibility in a system that does not manifest itself as some kind of programming. Although his approach is powerful as it offers fine granularity tailoring, it suffers from the problematic tyranny of the dominant decomposition (as object oriented design does).

Slagter [20] proposes a design methodology for groupware based on the principle of composing generic groupware services. A groupware application provides a Groupware Service (GS). The groupware service is composed of several Groupware Service Modules (GSM). End users can select and compose GSMs in a GS to obtain the desired behavior. In a finer granularity, GSM consist of Groupware Service Module Elements that represent elementary units of externally observable, groupware behavior (e.g., starting a conference). The key criteria behind the success of this approach to enable end-user tailoring is that users can find and learn about module elements (i.e., understand the groupware behavior associated with a GSME) and use them to describe and prescribe groupware. The tyranny of dominant decomposition is also present in Slagter's approach. Concerns such as awareness are not separated artifacts (e.g., components) but functionality that crosscuts several GS.

In [2] the authors have explored the applications of aspect oriented programming (AOP) in the domain of groupware. While our goal is to specify groupware as a combination of separated concerns and later use AOP as one possible mechanism for artifact separation and composition, their goal is to extend single user applications with groupware functionality using AOP.

8 Conclusions and Outlook

We presented a concern centric approach to groupware tailorability. Our approach includes tailoring by integration of concerns and tailoring by customization concerns. A concern centric form of tailoring is possible because groupware concerns are separated during design and implementation using aspect oriented programming practices.

Separation of concerns during design is critical to manage complexity, increase readability, and foster evolution and composition of groupware systems. We have provided an example of how requirements can be grouped to map separated concerns. Our motivation for separating concerns during design is to enable separation of the artifacts that implements such concerns. We claim that conceiving groupware as the composition of separated concerns provides a better alternative for groupware tailorability than existing, component based approaches, who suffer from the problem of the dominant decomposition.

The focus of our work has been mainly on the separation of concerns at the business logic level. As future work we plan to identify, study and separate (if possible) graphical user interface concerns. As of today, each groupware concern that is weaved onto a base application has its own GUI.

References

1. Buschmann, F., Meunier, R., Rohnert, H., Sommerlad, P., Stal, M.: Pattern-Oriented Software Architecture - A System of Patterns. Wiley and Sons, Chichester (1996)
2. Cheng, L., Patterson, J., Rohall, S.L., Hupfer, S., Ross, S.: Weaving a social fabric into existing software. In: Proceedings of the 4th international Conference on Aspect-Oriented Software Development AOSD '05, Chicago, Illinois, March 14 - 18, 2005, pp. 147–158. ACM Press, New York, NY (2005)
3. Chung, L., Nixon, B., Yu, E., Mylopoulos, J.: Non-Functional Requirements in Software Engineering. Kluwer Academic Publishers, Dordrecht (2000)

4. Clarke, S., Baniassad, E.: Aspect-Oriented Analysis and Design. The Theme Approach. A-Wesley, Object Technology Series (2005) ISBN: 0-321-24674-8
5. Early Aspects Home: Last accessed (May 2006), www.early_aspects.net
6. Erl, T.: Service-Oriented Architecture (SOA). Concepts, Technology, and Design. Prentice Hall, Englewood Cliffs (2005)
7. Filman, R., Elrad, T., Clarke, S., Aksit, M. (eds.): Aspect-Oriented Software Development. Addison-Wesley, Reading (2004)
8. Gamma, E., Helm, R., Johnson, R., Vlissides, J.: Design Patterns: Elements of Reusable Object-Oriented Software. Addison-Wesley, Reading (1995)
9. Gutwin, C., Greenberg, S.: Support for Group Awareness in Real-time Desktop Conferences. In: Proceedings of The Second New Zealand Computer Science Research Students' Conference, Hamilton, New Zealand (1995)
10. IEEE: IEEE Recommended Practice for Architectural Description of Software-Intensive Systems. IEEE Std.1471- 2000 (Approved 21 September 2000)
11. Johnson-Lenz, P., Johnson-Lenz, T.: Rhythms, Boundaries, and Containers: Creative Dynamics of Asynchronous Group Life. The International Journal of Man Machine Studies 34, 395–417 (1991)
12. Kiczales, G., Lamping, J., Mendhekar, A., Maeda, C., Lopes, C., Loingtier, J.-M., Irwin, J.: Aspect-oriented programming. In: Aksit, M., Matsuoka, S. (eds.) ECOOP 1997. LNCS, vol. 1241, pp. 220–242. Springer, Heidelberg (1997)
13. Lukosch, S., Unger, C.: Flexible Synchronization of Shared Groupware Objects. ACM SIGGROUP Bulletin 20(3), 14–17 (1999)
14. Malone, T.W., Lai, K.-Y., Fry, C.: Experiments with oval: A radically tailorable tool for cooperative work. In: Turner, J., Kraut, R. (eds.) Proceedings of the ACM CSCW'92. Conference on Computer Supported Cooperative Work, Toronto, Canada (New York), pp. 289–297. ACM Press, New York (1992)
15. Anders, M.: Three Levels of End-user Tailoring: Customization, Integration, and Extension. In: Proceedings of the 3 rd Decennial Conference: Computer in Context: Joining Forces in Design, Aarhus (1995)
16. Moreira, A., Rashid, A., Araújo, J.: Multi-Dimensional Separation of Concerns in Requirements Engineering in Proceedings of the 13th IEEE International Requirements Engineering Conference (RE 2005), Paris, France, August 2005. IEEE Computer Society Press, Los Alamitos (2005)
17. Wanda, J.: Orlikowski, Improvising Organizational Transformation over Time: A Situated Change Perspective. Information Systems Research 7(1), 63–92 (1996)
18. Pinto, M., Amor, M., Fuentes, L., Troya, J.M.: Collaborative Virtual Environment Development: An Aspect-Oriented Approach. In: Proceedings of the 21st international Conference on Distributed Computing Systems ICDCSW, April 16 - 19, 2001, p. 97. IEEE Computer Society, Washington, DC (2001)
19. Schuckmann, C., Kirchner, L., Schümmer, J., Haake, J.M.: Designing Object-Oriented synchronous groupware with COAST. In: Proceedings of the ACM 1996 Conference on Computer Supported Cooperative Work (CSCW'96), Boston Mass, November 16-20, pp. 30–38. ACM Press, New York (1996)
20. Slagter, R.: Dynamic groupware services - modular design of tailorable groupware, Ph.D. thesis, University of Twente (2004)
21. Tarr, P., Ossher, H., Harrison, W., Sutton, Jr., S.M.: N Degrees of Separation: Multi-Dimensional Separation of Concerns. In: Proceedings of the International Conference on Software Engineering (ICSE 21) (May 1999)

An Approach to the Model-Based Design of Groupware Multi-user Interfaces

María Luisa Rodríguez, José Luis Garrido, María V. Hurtado, and Manuel Noguera

Departamento de Lenguajes y Sistemas Informáticos, Universidad de Granada
E.T.S.I.I.T., c/Periodista Daniel Saucedo Aranda s/n, 18071 Granada, Spain
{mlra,jgarrido,mhurtado,mnoguera}@ugr.es

Abstract. The rapid development of technology allows organizations to operate on interactive environments in which work is organized and assigned to groups of people cooperating in order to reach their purposes. In groupware applications, the user interface is essential because it must support the process of sharing information and group work appropriately. Thereby, the user interface design requires the understanding of the tasks that a group must accomplish in the system and the different users' characteristics, as well as to address technological issues. The use of models, at different abstraction levels, should be taken into account in order to tackle the complexity while designing groupware interfaces. This paper proposes an approach to the model-based design of multi-user interfaces for groupware applications.

Keywords: Groupware applications, model-based development, multi-user interfaces, group awareness.

1 Introduction

The natural complexity of CSCW systems demands great efforts in specifications and development [1]. The development of groupware applications is more difficult than that of single-user applications given that social protocols and group activities must be considered in order to obtain a successful design.

The user interface of these systems must support that, within the group, tasks are to be accomplished in a cooperative manner. This is not only an execution problem but also a design concern. In addition, the graphic user interface is a crucial aspect of groupware applications usability since it allows the improvement of communication, collaboration and coordination among users interacting with the system. Therefore, new approaches should be applied to guide the whole development process.

During the user interface development, the design based on models is one of the most used technologies [11, 12]. The aim is to define models which allow designers to create and analyze software systems from a semantics-oriented level rather than to begin immediately with the implementation. Particularly, a model is called declarative because it does not contain codes but expressive descriptions. Some of the most referenced declarative models in the literature are the information, user, task, presentation, implementation, application, etc. models.

J.M. Haake, S.F. Ochoa, and A. Cechich (Eds.): CRIWG 2007, LNCS 4715, pp. 157–164, 2007.
© Springer-Verlag Berlin Heidelberg 2007

There exist different proposals for the development of user interfaces in the Human –Computer Interaction field [3, 10]. None of them consider most of relevant concepts in the cooperative systems, although proposals that integrate interactive aspect into cooperative systems have been developed [2, 9]. AMENITIES [4] is a methodology which allows addressing the analysis and design of CSCW systems systematically and which facilitates subsequent software development. It allows the realization of a conceptual model of cooperative systems and focuses on the group concept. It covers significant aspects of both group behaviour (dynamism, synchronization, etc.) and structure (organization, laws, etc.). The resulting specification contains relevant information (cooperative tasks, domain elements, person-computer and person-person dialogues, etc.) to the creation of the user interface. However, it does not include any mechanism to guide the user interface design.

This research work aims to analyse and propose a model-based approach to the design of multi-user interfaces for groupware applications. The focus of the paper is on the definition and use of some relevant models, which provide relevant information for the design of multi-user interfaces on the basis of design guidelines.

The remainder of this paper is organized as follows. Section 2 presents the approach to the design of multi-user interfaces for groupware applications. Section 3 introduces a support platform for the implementation of groupware interfaces. In Section 4 an example of application of the approach described is shown. Finally, conclusions and future work are given in Section 5.

2   Approach to the Development of Multi-user Interfaces for Groupware Applications

This section presents a new approach in order to address the design of user interfaces for groupware applications, according to the general schema shown in Figure 1. The first subsection describes the main foundations of this proposal, i.e., the specific models that define a cooperative system. The next subsection establishes connections between system models and those used to create user interfaces. The last subsection introduces a general description of the design process.

2.1   Foundations

The starting point of the approach proposed in this paper are the models used in the AMENITIES methodology. In this methodology, the description of a cooperative system is composed of two sets of models [6]:

1. Models used in techniques for the capture and description of requirements. The requirements elicitation process is mainly accomplished by means of the application, mainly, of ethnography and use case techniques.
2. Cooperative model: It is a conceptual model that describes the basic structure and behaviour of the complete cooperative system. This model is built hierarchically on the basis of other models, each one focused on providing a different view of the system. A structured method is proposed in order to build the cooperative model systematically. This method consists of the following stages: Specification of the organization, role definition, task definition and specification of interaction protocols.

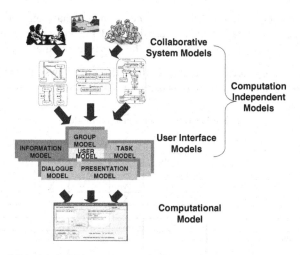

Fig. 1. Models involved in the process of creation multi-user interfaces

All previous models provide relevant information to define a set of user interface models to embrace the intrinsic characteristics of this kind of systems. The focus of these models is on the integration of individual and cooperative aspects of the interaction.

2.2   Models for the Multi-user Interface Design

We propose an approach to designing multi-user interfaces for groupware applications on the basis of the following specific models and the particular concepts encompassed by them:

1. Information Model: It defines the information domain of the application, i.e., information objects managed by the application and actions that use these information objects.
2. User Model: It describes the characteristics of the desired end user of the application to be developed, i.e., individual tasks associated to each role and capabilities acquired by actors and interrogated by laws.
3. Group Model: It describes the group of end users of the application to be developed, i.e., since cooperative work is to be carried out by a group of user, this model permits to describe cooperative tasks associated to each role and the context and environment for each user.
4. Task Model: It defines all the tasks that end users perform using the software? application to be developed, i.e., types of tasks, roles associated to tasks, information objects required by tasks, temporal-ordering between tasks, number of times in which each task is accomplished and number of actors involved in a task.
5. Dialog Model: It describes the syntactic structure of human-computer interaction, i.e., actions on the interactive system and interaction protocols.

6. Presentation model: It determines the components that can appear on an end user's display, their layout characteristics, and the visual dependencies among them, i.e., components to be included in the interface and their relationships.

Table 1 depicts connections between the different views of the AMENITIES cooperative models and specific models useful in the creation of multi-user interfaces.

Table 1. Connections between models

AMENITIES MODELS	MODELS FOR MULTI-USER INTERFACE					
	Information	User	Group	Task	Dialog	Presentation
Applied Ethnography	X	X	X	X	X	X
Use Cases		X		X		X
Specification of the Organization		X	X	X		X
Role Definition	X	X	X	X		X
Task Definition	X	X	X	X	X	X
Specification of Interaction Protocols			X	X	X	X

2.3 Design Process

The objective of design process is to derive specific computation models of special interest in the building of multi-user interfaces. Relationships between the models described above allow us to identify the main elements involved in the design process of the interactive system (see Table 1). In turn, these elements and their relationships will be mapped onto elements of a computation model. Thus, this last step consists of creating a concrete interface from standard and specific components for groupware applications. The platform of multi-user widgets used will be introduced in the following section.

3   Supports for the Creation of Groupware Interfaces

Groupware interfaces should allow a group to accomplish cooperative work in a simple and natural manner. Hence, they should support the interaction between user and system, in the case of performing individual and cooperative work using artefacts, and between members of a same group who are working together in a non-structured, cooperative task. Furthermore, the system must provide mechanisms to fulfil the group awareness requirements. These requirements stress the need of providing suitable support for the creation of interfaces for groupware applications. Accordingly, it has been developed a multi-user widget platform accessible through an API [8] that aims to facilitate the development of groupware interfaces. The platform, based on the proposal presented in [5], consists of a functional and semantic extension to standard components (buttons, menus, text fields, etc.) and specific components for groupware applications (telepointers, list of online actors, chat, etc.). Moreover, the components can be replicated; their implementation assures a global consistent state in case of simultaneous interaction of several users. Table 2 depicts the current set of components available in the platform. The platform also includes a module to manage metainformation dynamically. Similar toolkit can be found in [7].

Table 2. Components implemented in the platform

Name	Functionality	Semantic properties	Comments
DIList	Selection, addition and subtraction of elements	Hide/read/write	Replicated/ local
DIComboBox	Opening and closing of the list.	Hide/read/write	Replicated
DIButton	Press and releasing the button	Hide/read/write	Replicated
DIToggleButton	Press and releasing the button	Hide/read/write	Replicated
DICheckBox	Tick and untick of the checkbox	Hide/read/write	Replicated
DITextField	Inserting and removing of text	Hide/read/write	Replicated
DITree	Opening and closing for the tree levels.	Read/write	Replicated
DJMenu	Show the user's ID who is interacting	Hide/read/write	Replicated
DIChat	Chat for online users	Hide/read/write	Distributed
DIRoleChange	Show current role and enable to change to others	Read/write	Replicated
DICurrentRole	Only show active roles	Read/write	Replicated
DIOnlineUserList	Online Users	Read/write	Replicated
DIUserListRolePlayed	Online Users and the role played for each one	Read/write	Replicated
DIUserListSameRole	Online users playing the same role	Read/write	Replicated
Telepointer	Pointer movements of another user	Read/write	Local (write)/ Replicated (read)

4   Case Study

In order to apply the proposal, we consider a case study based on a help system for the decision of risky operations by financial institutions. We describe a business process to grant a mortgage which a client has applied for in a branch office. The first step in a business process to grant a mortgage consists of realizing a feasibility study and making a report with all the information. The case study includes three organizations: branch, valuation office and notary office. The Branch organization has three roles: Bank Manager, Head of Risk and Teller.

We have focused on describing some relevant aspects to support group work. The Table 3 shows the connections between the models for the case study, which will be described in detail along this case study.

Table 3. Mapping between the models for the case study

COOPERATIVE MODEL	MODELS FOR USER INTERFACE						COMPUTATIONAL MODEL
	Information	User	Group	Task	Dialog	Presentation	
Organization diagram							
Role Change		X	X	X		X	DIRoleChange Precondition
Task diagram							
Cooperative task			X	X	X	X	DIUserListRolePlayed DIUserListSameRole DICurrentRole
Interaction protocols							
Type				X	X	X	DIChat Video conference
Shared-workspace				X	X	X	Telepointer Shared-text box

Following the organization diagram, defined in the organization specification stage, some members may dynamically change the roles they play as a result of various circumstances. One example of these requirements is that the organization imposes laws such as *[Absent(bankManager)]*, i.e. the actor playing the *headOfRisk* role can become the *bankManager* if the bank manager is absent. These requirements described in the cooperative model are translated into this example (see Table 3 above) using the component *DIRoleChange* of the Figure 2. The component *DIChangeRole* allows that the user presses the *Change* button to change roles. As a consequence, the user interface adapts to the new situation, showing the new *bankManager* role (2) and the new *Give Approval* task (3).

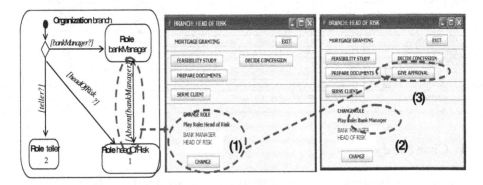

Fig. 2. Mapping of additive transaction to the multi-user interface

In the task definition stage, each previously specified task is subdivided into related subactivities and actions required to achieve the objective. In this case COMO-UML task diagrams are used to define individual/group tasks. Figure 3 defines *mortgageGranting* task. Each subactivity/action includes the specification of the responsible roles needed to accomplish it. For example, the subactivity *decide-Concession* is realized by the *bankManager* and *headOfRisk* roles. In order to implement this restriction of the cooperative model, the user interface of each partici-pating role has to contain the necessary information about the context of work of this task (see Table 3 above). This collaboration requirement will be satisfied with the replicated components developed, *DIUserListRolePlayed* (1), *DIUserListSameRole* (2) and *DICurrentRole* (3).

In the last stage the interaction protocols between participants must be identified and described. The identification of such protocols is extremely helpful since they identify system requirements such as the type of communication required and the type of communication channel for supporting collaboration. In particular, the subactivity *decideConcession* specifies two communication requirements to accomplish it: that a shared workspace exists *(shared-workspace)* and that each participant can see the others (which corresponds to a *face-to-face* interaction) (see Table 3). In Figure 3 we can observe the user interface of the subactivity *decideConcession*, which presents a shared workspace (the *Debt Report*) and a *DIChat* component (4) to implement the interaction between the actor playing the *bankManager* role and the actor playing the *headOfRisk* role. Besides, we observe a *Telepointer* component (5) on debt report corresponding to the action of the actor playing the *bankManager* role at that moment.

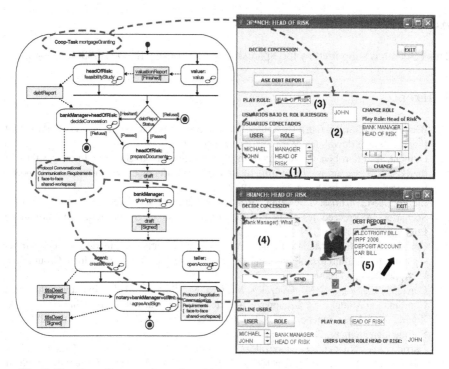

Fig. 3. Mapping of cooperative task and interaction protocols to groupware components

5   Conclusions

A primary goal of CSCW systems is to allow people to work together productively and naturally. These systems need to provide user interfaces that support group work appropriately. In this paper, we have presented a proposal for the design of multi-user interfaces for groupware applications. These interfaces are obtained from the specification of the cooperative system through a transformation process applied to a set of models. This proposal allows design multi-user interfaces systematically. The add-on value of the approach is that multi-user interface adapts its structure and behaviour to the different system preferences and requirements. Furthermore, we have presented a platform to facilitate the development of groupware multi-user interfaces. This platform provides a set of replicated components that can be used in the creation process of multi-user interfaces. In particular, an extension to single-user components and new groupware specific components has been developed.

Future research will be focused on completing the formal specification of the system and to build a CASE tool in order to support the system modelling and the subsequent semi-automatic generation of the interfaces. Finally, we plan to integrate the design process proposed in this paper into an MDA-based development process for groupware applications [6].

Acknowledgements

This research is supported by the Spanish MCYT project TIN2004-08000-C03-02.

References

1. Beaudouin-Lafon, M. (ed.): Computer Supported Cooperative Work, Université Paris.Sud, France. John Wiley&Sons, West Sussex, England (1999)
2. Dumont, A., Pietrobon, C.: A Method for Specification of Collaborative Interfaces through the Use of Scenarios. In: Fifth International Conference on Computer Supported Cooperative Work in Design, pp. 15–19 (2001)
3. Elkoutbi, M., Khriss, I., Keller, R.K.: Generating User Interface Prototypes from Scenarios. In: Proceedings of the Fourth IEEE International Symposium on Requirements Engineering, pp. 1–25 (1999)
4. Garrido, J.L., Gea, M., Rodríguez, M.L.: Requirements enginnering in cooperative systems, In: Requirements Enginnering for Sociotechnical Systems, Idea Group, Inc., USA, pp. 226–244 (2005)
5. Garrido, J.L., Noguera, M., González, M., Gea, M., Hurtado, M.V.: Leveraging the Linda Coordination Model for a Groupware Architecture Implementation. In: Dimitriadis, Y.A., Zigurs, I., Gómez-Sánchez, E. (eds.) CRIWG 2006. LNCS, vol. 4154, pp. 286–301. Springer, Heidelberg (2006)
6. Garrido, J.L., Noguera, M., González, M., Hurtado, M.V., Rodríguez, M.L.: Definition and use of Computacional Independent Models in an MDA-based groupware development process. Science of Computer Programming 66(1), 25–43 (2007)
7. Hill, J., Gutwin, C.: Awareness Support in a Groupware Widget Toolkit. In: Proceeding of the 2003 International ACM SIGGROUP Conference on Supporting Group Work, pp. 258–267. ACM Press, New York (2003)
8. Ibánez Santórum, J.A.: Diseño e implementación de una plataforma para el desarrollo de sistemas groupware. In: Proyecto fin de carrera. Dpto. Lenguajes y Sistemas Informáticos, Universidad de Granada (2006)
9. López Nores, M., et al.: Formal specification applied to multiuser distributed services: Experiences in collaborative t-learning. The Journal of Systems and Software 79(8), 1141–1155 (2006)
10. Pinheiro da Silva, P., Paton, N.W.: UMLi: The Unified Modeling Language for Interactive Applications. In: Evans, A., Kent, S., Selic, B. (eds.) UML 2000. LNCS, vol. 1939, pp. 117–132. Springer, Heidelberg (2000)
11. Schlungbaum, E.: Model-based User Interface Software Tools Current state of declarative models. Research Report, Georgia Institute of Technology, Graphics, Visualizations & Usability Center, GIT-GVU-96-30 (1996)
12. Traetteberg, H.: Model-based User Interface Design. Phd thesis. Department of Computer and Information Sciences. Norwegian University of Science and Technology (2002)

Computer Aided Pattern-Based Collaboration Process Design: A Computer Aided Collaboration Engineering Tool

Gwendolyn L. Kolfschoten[1], Gert-Jan de Vreede[1,2], and Robert O. Briggs[1,3]

[1] Delft University of Technology, Faculty of Technology, Policy and Management, Department of System Engineering, Jaffalaan 5, 2628BX, Delft, the Netherlands
G.L.Kolfschoten@tudelft.nl
[2] University of Nebraska at Omaha, Department of Information Systems & Quantitative Analysis, Institute for Collaboration Science, 1110 South 67th street, Omaha, NE 68182-0116 USA
Gdevreede@mail.unomaha.edu
[3] University of Nebraska at Omaha, Department of Business administration, Institute for Collaboration Science, Roskens Hall Room 512B, Omaha, NE 68182 USA
rbriggs@mail.unomaha.edu

Abstract. As many business processes are collaborative in nature, process leaders or process managers play a pivotal role designing collaboration processes for organization. To support the design task of creating a new collaborative business process, best practices or design patterns can be used as building blocks. For such purposes, a library of design patterns and guidelines would be useful, not only to capture the best practices for different activities in the process in a database, but to also offer the users of this database support in selecting and combining such patterns, and in creating the process design. This paper describes the requirements for a tool for pattern based collaboration process design, specifically for design efforts following the Collaboration Engineering approach.

Keywords: Collaboration process design, Collaboration Engineering, thinkLets, Design patterns, Pattern language.

1 Introduction

With collaboration and team work becoming the organizational norm to innovate and create value (see e.g. Evans and Wolf 2005; Nunamaker et al. 2001; Munkvold and Zigurs 2005), new business processes predominantly involve collaborative work practices. To change a collaborative work practice, participants need to be trained or require facilitation support (Briggs et al. 2003). The transition of new collaborative work practices is a complex task because a new work practice needs to be accepted and adopted by its users. A key requirement is the users' willingness to change. Briggs describes a Value Frequency Model to explain the behavioral intention (willingness) to change a work practice [1]. In this model, the willingness to change is

J.M. Haake, S.F. Ochoa, and A. Cechich (Eds.): CRIWG 2007, LNCS 4715, pp. 165–172, 2007.

caused by an individual judgment of the value of change and the expected frequency in which this added value is experienced. Therefore, in order to transfer a new collaborative work practice, this needs to be designed in a way that offers its users a recurring added value.

The design of a new collaboration process poses several, sometimes conflicting, requirements: It needs to offer the prescription of an instrumental, predictable and transferable collaborative work practice. Design patterns are re-usable solutions to address frequently occurring problems [2], they can be used to support design, combined in a pattern language. A pattern language offers a designer or community of designers a library of best practices for a specific domain and product that can be used and combined to create solutions to problems in the organization. The design pattern concept was adopted in various domains, including software engineering [3-5], workflow management [6], e-learning [7], Project management [8], and Collaboration Engineering [9, 10].

While a pattern language offers support in documenting and sharing best practices in process design and process support, it does not directly offer support on how to use these best practices. To support this Computer Aided Software Engineering (CASE) tools can be used. The IEEE standard for the adoption of CASE tools describes three gains from the use of CASE tools: increased design productivity, improvements in the quality of the software produced and improved consistency and uniformity of the design approach [11]. In this paper we propose requirements for a Computer Aided Process Engineering (CAPE) tool. We will derive our requirements based on the example of Collaboration Engineering, an approach to the design and deployment of repeatable collaboration processes. The challenges in Collaboration Engineering will pose several additional requirements to the resulting collaboration process design, and thus to the CAPE tool.

2   Process Design and Deployment

Process design has been studied in a variety of closely related domains, in particular Business Process Change [12], Business Process Reengineering [13], and workflow management [6]. Designs of processes and workflows in essence describe a sequence of tasks or steps for which actors, roles or agents are defined and for which technology support, objects, or applications are used. In workflow management there is a large role for "flow of execution control" decisions or choices that determine when the next step in the sequence is activated [6]. The same concepts are also used in modeling languages with a process perspective such as Data Flow models, IDEF0 [14], and SADT models [15]. Process design as any other design effort has similar phases as a process for decision making, problem solving or creativity [16-21]. It consist of an analysis of the current situation, possibly involving a decision about the need for a new approach or change. Next, through decomposition an initial sequence of steps is created. Alternative solutions to change and support the process are then identified and evaluated to eventually choose a sequence of steps and supporting tools that are validated (pilot, test case) to be ultimately implemented.

To support pattern-based collaboration process design, we can use this definition to define a CAPE tool, based on the definition of a CASE tool [11]." as *"a software tool that aids in collaboration process design activities including but not limited to situation analysis, process decomposition, process design, process visualization, selection, storage and addition of process design patterns, process validation, process specification, process documentation, process implementation and project management."* A CAPE tool supports the user in following the process design approach and simplifies the choices that need to be made during the design effort. It does not render a process design or implementation based on a set of requirements.

When using a pattern language, designers do not have to find new solutions but rather can select a design pattern based on known properties. Furthermore, design patterns need to be instantiated in the specific context of the process design. Thus collaboration process design with the support of design patterns offers collaboration process engineers valuable information to create and instantiate a collaboration process design. A tool to support such efforts should offer functionality to: store design patterns, add new design patterns, add variations to design patterns, Enable a community of users to discuss the design patterns, support the analysis of the situation, support the decomposition of the collaboration process, support the selection and combination of design patterns, Support visualization of the collaboration process flow, support specification of the design patterns, support implement the design patters in a process manual and in technology support and support project management.

3 Requirements in Collaboration Engineering

Collaboration Engineering is an approach to designing collaborative work practices for high-value recurring tasks, and deploying those designs for practitioners to execute for themselves without ongoing support from professional facilitators [22]. For Collaboration Engineering it is critical that the design of the collaborative work practice creates predictable outcomes, that it is reusable in different instance of the task, that it is efficacious to the collaborative goal, that it is acceptable for the participating stakeholders, and that it is transferable to practitioners. For this purpose, thinkLets are developed. ThinkLets are named, scripted, reusable, and transferable collaborative activities that give rise to specific known patterns of collaboration among people working together toward a goal with predictable results [22]. ThinkLets are design patterns for collaboration.

The design of a collaboration process for Collaboration Engineering has the following steps; eliciting requirements, creating a first sequence of activities, selecting a thinkLet for each activity and accommodating other activities such as breaks, presentations and introductions. Once all activities are specified, the collaboration process design can be validated based on a number of criteria. After validation, a process manual for the practitioner should be created containing a process model, the script for each activity, a summary of the analysis, and the cue cards [23]. Furthermore, the execution of the collaboration process can be supported with tools such as Group Support Systems, for which the information of the activity scripts needs to be instantiated as well. In summary, we propose that a CACE tool, a specific type of CAPE tool, a tool to support collaboration process design following the Collaboration Engineering approach, should offer functionality to:

- Store thinkLets, including relevant information for both the collaboration engineer and the practitioner.
- Add new thinkLets and to add variations to thinkLets.
- Enable a community of collaboration engineers, facilitators, and practitioners to discuss thinkLets.
- Support the analysis of the collaborative task to be supported.
- Support the decomposition of the collaboration process.
- Support the selection and combination of thinkLets.
- Support the specification of thinkLets.
- Support the visualization of the collaboration process flow.
- Support the validation of the collaboration process design.
- Support the creation of different types of output documents such as an agenda, a process manual, cue cards, and collaboration technology configuration settings, based on the thinkLets used in the collaboration process design.
- Support for project management.

While a CACE tool is primarily targeted for collaboration engineers, facilitators who support ad hoc thinkLets-based workshops could also use it. However, they would not need a manual for each collaboration process. Only an agenda for the process would suffice. An agenda is also a useful output for Collaboration Engineers to pilot their process designs and to validate them by sharing them with colleagues.

4 The CACE Tool

Over the past five years, the Collaboration Engineering research community has developed a number of 'paper-based' tools to support the Collaboration Engineering efforts. First the design approach as described above, has been developed and evaluated based on feedback from facilitators and students using the design approach [24, 25]. The thinkLet pattern concept has been introduced by Briggs and de Vreede [26-28], and has been further developed into its current form [9, 10, 23, 29-32]. To support the analysis of collaborative work practices, we asked facilitators about the information required to design a collaboration process [24]. For the selection and combination of thinkLets we performed a pattern analysis to derive frequently occurring thinkLet combinations, i.e. we identified patterns in thinkLet sequences (Kolfschoten et al. 2004a) and we performed in-depth interviews with facilitators to elicit the criteria they use to choose among thinkLets [29, 33, 34]. The insights on choice criteria also helped us to develop a validation framework. Finally, the facilitation process model to visualize thinkLets-based collaboration process designs has been introduced [35], and a first design support prototype tool has been developed [36]. Based on the insights from the above studies and the requirements discussed in the previous section, we created a conceptual model of the CACE tool

To store design patterns a 'master' thinkLet should be developed. A master thinkLet describes all the attributes of the thinkLet that need to be stored in the database. See [9, 10, 32] for a class diagram of the detailed content of the thinkLet concept.

To keep the pattern language coherent, relations between thinkLets such as alternatives and combinations should be captured. This represents a complex aspect of the thinkLet pattern database: when a thinkLet is added not only the new thinkLet must be adjusted, but also the other thinkLets must be updated, as (potential) combinations with the new thinkLet must be evaluated. For this purpose it would be useful to include a wizard that supports the user though the process of adding a thinkLet. An additional challenge is the support of multiple languages. Collaboration Engineers and facilitators that use the pattern language and the CACE tool should be able to comment thinkLet. It should be possible to customize the thinkLets in a design, but the master thinkLet can only be edited by an expert. The system should also enable storage of complete process designs, which can be shared with other designers/facilitators and with practitioners.

Each Collaboration Engineering project will be stored in a separate file. For this a CE project record with the participants and their rights can be specified. To support analysis a checklist that helps the Collaboration Engineer to gather all information required to design the collaboration process should be available. It might be useful to be able to gather some of the information for the analysis through (dedicated) surveys.

Based on the information in the Analysis support part of the CACE tool, a first set of constraints to the process design should be available: for example, the time frame and a lunch break etc. could already be scheduled. The next step is to label the activities in the collaboration process such as "brainstorm ideas", "select key ideas", etc. After such a sequence of activities is created the collaboration engineer can start choosing and importing thinkLets using a choice tool. A collaboration engineer should be able to import thinkLets into the process sequence supported by the following structures; an alphabetical list, classifications of the patterns of collaboration or the results, a list of known good combinations, or a list of alternatives.

During the selection process, detailed information on the thinkLets should be available to the collaboration engineer. We could think of these selection methods as topics in a topic map, where the classification term is the topic, and the relations between thinkLets are the associations, and the patterns in the library are the occurrences [37]. Finally, thinkLets can be modified to create small changes in the patterns of collaboration they create or in the result they create. Such modifications might also support the collaboration engineer in selecting a thinkLet. Therefore, the sequence builder and the choice tool should allow the collaboration engineer to select modifiers.

Besides a fit to the task and the existing thinkLet sequence, the choice of a thinkLet should also be aligned with the available resources, the group, and the practitioner. To further verify the choice of a thinkLet, the CACE tool could compare information in the project description with information in the thinkLet. When the thinkLet does not fit the group size or the complexity it can handle, timeframe, or when it does not fit the breadth of the scope, when it does not work without certain resources available or when it is too complex for the practitioners involved, it should alert the designer. When the sequence of steps is ready, information needs to be instantiated, such as the topic's questions, criteria, roles involved and tools used. This should be supported with a wizard. Furthermore, it should be possible to edit the resulting script to adjust it to the organization culture.

The thinkLet sequence should be visible for the collaboration engineer during the design effort as a Facilitation Process Model [23, 25, 35] or as an agenda. Besides the model and the design description there are several other output documents that could be created. These may include the script for the practitioner, the slides for the introduction of the collaboration process, an agenda or invitation for the participants, a project offer or account, and an export document that can be imported into a Group Support System to instantiate the capabilities required for the process. After the design is documented it can be validated.

Besides the validation with respect to the design requirements, that can partly be automated, for each thinkLet a list of challenges is specified which indicates what might go wrong or what might be difficult. This set can be used to assess the design, in combination with a framework based on the dimensions of a high quality collaboration process design. The collaboration engineer can validate the process by himself or send the design out for review among experts or users. Last, it would be useful to monitor the performance of the practitioners and to collect feedback from participants in the process. For example, each practitioner could enter his experiences for each time he executed the process, and participants of the process could offer feedback through a questionnaire. These sources can be combined to gain insight in the success of the deployment of the collaboration process.

5   Conclusions

This paper presents an overview of a CACE tool, a tool to support pattern-based design of collaboration processes following the Collaboration Engineering approach. The design of the tool is grounded in the requirements of a general computer-assisted process design tool. Initial prototypes of selected elements of the tool have been developed and tested (see e.g. Kolfschoten and Veen 2005), while others are currently in progress. Our future research efforts will focus on further elaborating on the CACE tool's functional requirements through experiences with the prototype and designing an overall architecture for the tool.

References

1. Briggs, R.O.: The Value Frequency Model: Towards a Theoretical Understanding of Organizational Change. In: Seifert, S., Weinhardt, C. (eds.) International Conference on Group Decision and Negotiation, Universtatsverlag Karlsruhe, Karlsruhe (2006)
2. Alexander, C.: The Timeless Way of Building. Oxford University Press, New York (1979)
3. Gamma, E., Helm, R., Johnson, R., Vlissides, J.: Elements of Reusable Object-Oriented Software. Addison-Wesley Publishing Company, Reading (1995)
4. Lukosch, S., Schümmer, T.: Groupware Development Support with Technology Patterns. International Journal of Human Computer Systems 64 (2006)
5. Rising, L.: Design Patterns in Communication Software. Cambridge University Press, Cambridge (2001)
6. van der Aalst, W.M.P., ter Hofstede, A.H.M., Kiepuszewski, B.: Workflow Patterns. Distributed and Parallel Databases 14, 5–51 (2003)

7. Niegemann, H.M., Domagk, S.: ELEN Project Evaluation Report (2005), http://www2tisip.no/E-LEN
8. Khazanchi, D., Zigurs, I.: An Assessment Framework for Discovering and Using Patterns in Virtual Project Management. In: Sprague, R.H. (ed.) Hawaii International Conference on System Science, IEEE Computer Society Press, Waikoloa (2007)
9. Kolfschoten, G.L., Briggs, R.O., de Vreede, G.J., Jacobs, P.H.M., Appelman, J.H.: Conceptual Foundation of the ThinkLet Concept for Collaboration Engineering. International Journal of Human Computer Science 64, 611–621 (2006)
10. de Vreede, G.J., Briggs, R.O., Kolfschoten, G.L.: ThinkLets: A Pattern Language for Facilitated and Practitioner-Guided Collaboration Processes. International Journal of Computer Applications in Technology 25, 140–154 (2006)
11. IEEE Std 1348: IEEE Recommended Practice for the Adoption of Computer-Aided Software Engineering (CASE) Tools (1995)
12. Grover, V., Kettinger, W.J.: Business Process Change; Reengineering Concepts, Methods and Technologies. Idea group Publishing, Harrisburg (1995)
13. O'Neill, P., Sohal, A.S.: Business Process Reengineering, A Review of Recent Literature. Technovation 19, 571–581 (1999)
14. Mayer, R.: IDEF0 Functional Modelling. Knowledge Based Systems, Inc, College Station, TX (1990)
15. Marca, D.A., McGowan, C.L.: Structured Analysis and Design Technique. McGraw Hill, Inc., New York, NY (1987)
16. Couger, J.D.: Creative Problem Solving And Opportunity Finding. Boyd And Fraser, Mass (1995)
17. Ackoff, R.L.: The Art of Problem Solving. John Wiley & Sons, Chichester (1978)
18. Mitroff, I.I., Betz, F., Pondly, L.R., Sagasty, F.: On Managing Science In The Systems Age: Two Schemas For The Study Of Science As A Whole Systems Phenomenon. TIMS Interfaces 4, 46–58 (1974)
19. Simon, H.A.: The Structure Of Ill Structured Problems. Artificial Intelligence 4, 181–201 (1973)
20. Checkland, P.B.: Systems Thinking, Systems Practice. John Wiley & Sons, Chichester (1981)
21. Sol, H.G.: Simulation in information systems development. Rijksuniversiteit Groningen, Groningen, the Netherlands (1982)
22. Briggs, R.O., Kolfschoten, G.L., de Vreede, G.J., Dean, D.L.: Defining Key Concepts for Collaboration Engineering. In: Americas Conference on Information Systems, AIS, Acapulco, Mexico, vol. 12 (2006)
23. Kolfschoten, G.L., van der Hulst, S.: Collaboration Process Design Transition to Practitioners: Requirements from a Cognitive Load Perspective. In: Seifert, S., Weinhardt, C. (eds.) International Conference on Group Decision and Negotiation, Universtatsverlag Karlsruhe, Karlsruhe (2006)
24. Kolfschoten, G.L., den Hengst, M., de Vreede, G.J.: Issues in the Design of Facilitated Collaboration Processes. In: Group Decision and Negotiation (in press)
25. Kolfschoten, G.L., de Vreede, G.J., Chakrapani, A., Koneri, P.: A Design Approach for Collaboration Engineering. In: Briggs, R.O., Nunamaker, Jr., J.F. (eds.) First HICSS Symposium on Case and Field Studies of Collaboration, Kauai (2006) (in press)
26. Briggs, R.O., de Vreede, G.J., Nunamaker, Jr., J.F.: Collaboration Engineering with ThinkLets to Pursue Sustained Success with Group Support Systems. Journal of Management Information Systems 19, 31–63 (2003)

27. Briggs, R.O., de Vreede, G.J., Nunamaker, Jr., J.F., David, T.H.: ThinkLets: Achieving Predictable, Repeatable Patterns of Group Interaction with Group Support Systems. In: Hawaii International Conference on System Sciences, IEEE Computer Society Press, Los Alamitos (2001)
28. Vreede, G.J., de Briggs, R.O.: ThinkLets: Five Examples Of Creating Patterns Of Group Interaction. In: Ackermann, F., Vreede, G.J.d (eds.) Group Decision & Negotiation, pp. 199–208. La Rochelle, France (2001)
29. Kolfschoten, G.L., Appelman, J.H., Briggs, R.O., de Vreede, G.J.: Recurring Patterns of Facilitation Interventions in GSS Sessions. In: Hawaii International Conference On System Sciences, IEEE Computer Society Press, Los Alamitos (2004)
30. Kolfschoten, G.L., Briggs, R.O., Appelman, J.H., de Vreede, G.J.: ThinkLets as Building Blocks for Collaboration Processes: A Further Conceptualization. In: de Vreede, G.-J., Guerrero, L.A., Raventós, G.M. (eds.) CRIWG 2004. LNCS, vol. 3198, pp. 137–152. Springer, Heidelberg (2004)
31. Kolfschoten, G.L., Santanen, E.L.: Reconceptualizing Generate ThinkLets: the Role of the Modifier. Hawaii International Conference on System Science. IEEE Computer Society Press, Waikoloa (2007)
32. Kolfschoten, G.L., van Houten, S.P.A.: Predictable Patterns in Group Settings through the use of Rule Based Facilitation Interventions. In: Kersten, G.E., Rios, J. (eds.) Group Decision and Negotiation conference, Concordia University, Mt Tremblant (2007)
33. Kolfschoten, G.L., Rouwette, E.: Choice Criteria for Facilitation Techniques. In: Briggs, R.O., Nunamaker, Jr., J.F. (eds.) First HICSS Symposium on Case and Field Studies of Collaboration, Kauai (2006)
34. Kolfschoten, G.L., Rouwette, E.: Choice Criteria for Facilitation Techniques: A Preliminary Classification. In: Seifert, S., Weinhardt, C. (eds.) International Conference on Group Decision and Negotiation, Universtatsverlag Karlsruhe, Karlsruhe (2006)
35. de Vreede, G.J., Briggs, R.O.: Collaboration Engineering: Designing Repeatable Processes for High-Value Collaborative Tasks. Hawaii International Conference on System Science. IEEE Computer Society Press, Los Alamitos (2005)
36. Kolfschoten, G.L., Veen, W.: Tool Support for GSS Session Design. Hawaii International Conference on System Sciences. IEEE Computer Society Press, Los Alamitos (2005)
37. Techquila (2007), http://www.techquila.com/topicmaps.html

Designing Mobile Shared Workspaces for Loosely Coupled Workgroups

Andrés Neyem, Sergio F. Ochoa, and José A. Pino

Department of Computer Science, Universidad de Chile.
Blanco Encalada 2120, Santiago, Chile
{aneyem,sochoa,jpino}@dcc.uchile.cl

Abstract. Recent advances in mobile computing devices and wireless communication have brought the opportunity to transport the shared workspace metaphor to mobile work scenarios. Unfortunately, there are few guidelines to support the design of these mobile shared workspaces. This paper proposes a design process and several guidelines to support the modeling of these groupware systems. Particularly, workspaces that support loosely coupled workgroups. The process and guidelines are based on a literature review and authors' experience in the development of mobile shared workspaces.

Keywords: Mobile shared workspaces, groupware design guidelines, loosely coupled work.

1 Introduction

Shared workspaces aim at supporting cooperative tasks. They provide users with a virtual space in which information can be shared and exchanged. Usually, these tools are focused on information sharing in the sense of cooperative authoring, commenting, and annotating shared documents as a group activity [35]. Besides, shared workspaces allow users to perform specific tasks and to interact with other users.

Shared workspaces are intended to increase the users' joint productivity. A number of studies and projects have shown that workspaces are also valuable for distributed collaboration [12], [35]. Typically, these groupware applications consider distributed users communicated by a wired network.

Advances in mobile computing devices and wireless communication have allowed transporting the shared workspace metaphor to mobile work scenarios. In such a scenario, a group of mobile workers are on the move to carry out the assigned activities. Workers in these groups are weakly dependent on each other and they can function autonomously; often they do so without the need for immediate clarification or negotiation with other workers. Examples of this work setting include health care [19], [30], construction management [32], m-Learning [36] and disaster relief [7], [26].

Since physical location is a changing dimension in mobile work, it is difficult for mobile workers to stay aware of others' locations and availabilities in order to communicate and coordinate work [28]. In addition, the frequent disconnections of

J.M. Haake, S.F. Ochoa, and A. Cechich (Eds.): CRIWG 2007, LNCS 4715, pp. 173–190, 2007.

wireless networks make difficult to use centralized resources and ensure the users reachability [23]. These features make the solutions designed for shared workspaces in fixed settings unsuitable for mobile work scenarios [18]. This new collaboration setting brings interesting design and implementation challenges to groupware developers [18], [23], [28].

This paper presents a process and a set of guidelines to support the design of mobile shared workspaces (MSW). Particularly, the proposals deal with supporting loosely coupled work by a mobile group of people. The process and guidelines are based on a literature review and authors' experience in the development of MSW and frameworks for mobile groupware.

Next section deals with the loosely coupled work and the requirements involved in the design of shared workspaces for such a setting. Section 3 presents the related work. Section 4 describes the design process, the major activities and the guidelines to cope with the software requirements and constraints. Section 5 provides recommendations to implement the design aspects of a MSW. Finally, section 6 presents the conclusions and further work.

2 Loosely Coupled Work

Loose coupling often occurs when it is difficult for workers to communicate directly, and a common reason for this is the physical distribution of workers across a wide distance [29]. Gutwin et al. [12] describe coupling as "the amount of work that one person can do before they require discussion, instruction, action, information, or consultation with another". Pinelle et al. [29] state that loosely coupled work is work in which people need to be aware of others' activities and decisions, but without the need for immediate clarification or negotiation. The work can proceed in parallel. Loose coupling then is a style of collaboration that occurs in groups, and implies that workers can function in a somewhat autonomous fashion without reliance on ongoing interaction with others. In order to illustrate the main requirements involved in this kind of workgroups, two work scenarios adhering to similar settings are briefly described below.

- *Healthcare Services:* Recently, home care has become an important part of healthcare organizations since it is cost-effective and it is preferred by patients over hospital and nursing home stays [6], [30]. In home care, healthcare workers deliver services to patients in their homes. Each patient is typically treated by a team of people, including therapists, nurses, social workers, and home health aides. Workers are mobile and work out of different locations. They spend most of the day in the community and may only spend minimal time in the office, so informal communication is rare, and formal communication may be difficult to arrange due to schedule variability within the team. When communication does occur, it is often limited to a small subset of the treatment team, even though all team members might benefit from involvement. This fragmentation in communication can lead to difficulties in coordinating care plans and in planning shared outcomes. Shared mobile workspaces running on tablet PCs or PDAs can be used by healthcare team members to supervise and update the status of a patient's health treatment or his/her medical record. Furthermore, the shared workspace status can be replicated in the mobile computing devices of the people in charge of taking care of such patients. Doctors meeting to analyze a complex case need to access all the patient's health information and also information of similar cases in order to make the best decisions. The decisions and their consequences should also be recorded in the MSW of the healthcare team in order to keep track of the patient's treatment or to be used as a guideline in future similar cases.

- *Building and Construction:* Typically each construction site has a main contractor, which outsources several parts of the construction project, e.g. electrical facilities, gas/water/communication networks, painting and architecture. Some of these sub-contracted companies work during the same time period and they need to know the advances of each other in order to plan the execution of pending work. In addition, periodically all these companies should report the advances to the main contractor, which is in charge to coordinate the efforts of the sub-contracted companies. For example, electrical engineers (mobile workers) belonging to a company need to be on the move in order to inspect and record the status of the electrical facilities being developed by the company employees at a construction site. During the inspection, each engineer revises various parts of the physical infrastructure and records the advances on a MSW, running on the tablet PC. After the inspection and before leaving the construction site, the engineers synchronize the used workspaces in order to get a whole view of the work status for such site (or project). If they detect incomplete or contradictory information, some of them can inspect the facilities again in order to solve such case. Before leaving the construction site, an electrical engineer shares the updated information with a main contractor's employee, who is in charge of keeping track of the construction project updates. Typically no wireless communication support is available at the construction site; however it should not be a limitation for collaboration.

In both scenarios, mobile team members do not know the set of work environments that will be involved and their features. Since these work settings must support collaboration, we have to assume the worst case. Typically, this worst case considers a work environment where no communication support is available; therefore the mobile groupware solution has to provide it. Team members have to do loosely coupled work in such work setting. Pinelle and Gutwin [28] identified four characteristics of loosely-coupled work that allow workers to cope with many of the uncertainties of wide area mobile networks, and that make workers resilient to the difficulties these uncertainties introduce in mobile groupware design:

1) Workers are autonomous and partition work so that the need for ongoing coordination and planning is minimized.
2) Artifacts and data are, in most cases, clearly owned by specific workers, so the need for negotiation and coordination of access is minimal.
3) Workers are rarely synchronous, so they rely on asynchronous means for gathering awareness information, which allows them to tolerate delays.
4) Workers carry out most of their explicit communication asynchronously, and are able to tolerate the delays inherent in these exchanges.

Although the lack of communication support is usually the main reason to adopt loosely coupled work, there are several factors that also contribute to this [28], [29]: uncertainty in the work environment that requires rapid adaptation by work units, unpredictable tasks that are difficult for managers to monitor and evaluate, employees that are professionals or that have a high level of knowledge specialization, and barriers that interfere with routine collaboration (e.g. physical distribution, mobility, and schedule variability). Next section describes the requirements that need to be addressed by groupware applications in order to support loosely coupled work.

2.1 Requirements to Support Loosely Coupled Work

The loosely coupled work supported by mobile computing devices represents a new trend in CSCW, therefore few studies are available. This section presents the requirements that should be considered when designing a MSW to support loosely coupled work, based on such studies and the authors' experience. These requirements are just those derived from the type of work to support and the features of the work and activity contexts [1]:

Discretionary Collaboration. The autonomy of the mobile workers seen in loosely coupled mobility means that collaboration with others is (in most cases) not strictly required; instead, workers engage in collaboration when they decide that it is valuable to do so. Since the collaboration processes are sporadic, the team members carry out individual work most of the time [28].

Autonomy. Given the team members' dynamic local work context and the high probability of network disconnections, mobile workers need to be autonomous (at least) in term of the software services and information required to do the assigned work [23], [28].

On-demand information sharing. Workers need to share and synchronize information on-demand [26], [29]. When information maintained by a worker is shared with the rest of the team, the sharing should be at the worker's discretion so that they can selectively protect information.

On-demand information synchronization. Since several mobile workers perform the activities autonomously and in parallel, they need instances for information synchronization. Typically this synchronization process is on-demand, and it could be attended or unattended [26], [28].

Low coordination cost. Tasks are often strongly partitioned among workers and this partitioning minimizes coordination demands and it allows workers to work autonomously and in parallel [28]. Ideally, the coordination process should be unattended [26].

Context-aware. Mobile workers are able of adapting themselves to the work context they encounter locally [6]. Synchronous and asynchronous awareness mechanisms are required to support coordination processes and collaborative work. The synchronous mechanisms are required to indicate the availability for interactions of team members. On the other hand, since workers have few direct interactions with each other, awareness information is not usually as readily available as it is in synchronous work situations. Instead, workers attempt to maintain an awareness of others not by observing them directly, but by collecting evidence of others' past activities [28], [29]. This means that delays are inherent in retrieving awareness information; however, workers are still able to function with these limitations.

2.2 Requirements for Mobile Shared Workspaces

Mobile shared workspaces allow mobile workers to interact with other people or systems in an ad-hoc way (like a plug & play mechanism), adapting themselves depending on the context information [33]. Each MSW represents the portion of the office (information and services) which is available to a mobile worker through a mobile computing device. It allows people to work almost any-time and any-place, and it is expected to have a positive impact on productivity and quality of work.

Mobile collaboration supported by these workspaces is highly diverse and there is a large variety of work scenarios where the main feature of interaction among workers is loose coupled. We can identify two types of mobile collaboration related to this kind of interaction: *foreseen* and *unforeseen*. The first type occurs when workers follow an anticipated collaboration process: a process that has been considered during the workspace design. For example, this collaboration type is present in the construction management scenario described above, when engineers meet after an inspection to integrate annotations and detect inconsistencies. In this foreseen case, the users' collaboration needs are considered in the design of the common workspace.

On the other hand, unforeseen collaboration can be done by a structural engineer belonging to the company A when s/he shares information about the inspection process with personnel from the main contractor or with electrical engineers belonging to company B. These persons are not able to use a different workspace to interact with employees of the various companies working at the construction site. Therefore, the mobile shared workspaces need to provide mechanisms to support this unforeseen collaboration. In addition to the requirements presented in the previous section, we can state the following requirements for MSW design derived from computer-supported mobile collaborative work:

Lightweight. The definition of the type of computing device running the shared workspace depends on the type of workers' mobility. For the case of high mobility (e.g., traveling salesmen, nurses in a hospital, engineers inside a construction site or children in an outdoors educational environment), issues such as device weight and size may acquire high relevance [1], [11]. The workers' mobility is inversely related to the size and computing capability of the mobile devices required to support the loosely coupled work. It has a direct influence on the usability of the solution.

Deployment ease. An important factor is the speed of having the device ready to operate. A quick boot-up time will let workers productively use death times. Applications – in particular, these workspaces – should also self-configure automatically after boot-up [26].

Self-configurability. Mobile workers do not need to be aware of most work context changes, particularly, communication issues [1], [6], [26]. The workspaces have to be automatically self-configured in order to allow a mobile worker to interact with reachable partners no matter the network setting issues. It is particularly required when unforeseen collaboration needs to be supported.

Interoperability in terms of information and services. This requirement is relevant if the shared workspace must support unforeseen collaboration. Since mobile workers from various organizations may need to do casual or opportunistic interactions, data and services formats should be standardized to ensure interoperability [23], [26]. Thus, receivers will be able to understand the information or services they get.

Sessions management support. The sessions (also called collaborative sessions, work sessions, work groups, or conferences) maintain information about the users who interact by using a MSW. Session management is necessary to deal with the work of team members, assign roles and support coordination processes [10], [25].

Users management support. The collaborators are the members of one or more sessions. Every user maintains personal information (such as username, password, full name, etc.) and s/he can have specific access rights over the shared resources according to her/his role [10], [25]. Users have an identifier that allows workspaces to make effective the users' rights.

Roles support. Not all users have the same rights to access shared resources (e.g. shared information, message delivery channels). The rights are related to the role each user has for each session s/he is working on [10], [25]. Typically these rights are related to the user capability to carry out certain operations (e.g. erase, view, modify and recover information) or processes on the shared resources (e.g. backup, message delivery).

Environments support. The environments organize and eventually coordinate multiple working sessions or user groups [25]. They can also provide general functionality for a shared workspace, such as: file transfer, message delivery, peer detection and user/sessions awareness.

Private and shared repositories. Users produce information as a result of the individual and collaborative work [23], [26]. It can be shared to other users or kept private, depending on its type. The private (or local) repository stores the private information and the shared repository stores the information the user wants to share. The rights to access the shared repository depend on the assigned role.

Asynchronous communication. The mobility and autonomy of workers and the frequent network disconnections make it difficult to achieve synchronization, so synchronous communication is not a good option to support coordination/collaboration in these settings [23], [28]. Typically when synchrony is required, it can be by short time periods and it has to be simulated using asynchronous communication.

Synchronous/asynchronous interaction support. Workers show a preference for asynchronous interaction techniques since it allows them to deal with schedule and location variability. Most user interaction is asynchronous [26], [28]. However, there are a few interactions needing information synchronization or peer detection process.

It is possible to group the requirements defined in section 2.1 and 2.2 in the three typical categories of requirements for software systems: functional, quality and constraint. Functional requirements indicate what the software has to do. Quality requirements indicate the criteria to accomplish by the software functionality. Constraint requirements establish the present constraints when the software is running. Next table summarizes and categorizes these requirements.

Table 1. Requirements for mobile shared workspaces

Functional Requirements	Quality Requirements	Constraint Requirements
Discretionary collaboration	Autonomous	Low coordination cost
On-demand information sharing	Context-aware	Lightweight
On-demand information synchronization	Easy to deploy	Asynchronous communication
Session/Users management	Self-configurable	
Roles support	Interoperable	
Environment support		
Private and shared repositories		
Synchronous/asynch. interaction support		

This set of general requirements imposes design challenges to developers of MSW. There are several other issues to consider in the design of these workspaces, such as, social aspects related to the users, readiness to use technology and specific requirements of the activity to be supported by the workspace. These additional requirements have not been considered in this stage, in order to keep the problem complexity manageable. We plan to work on them in the future.

3 Related Work

Although there is a large number of documented experiences on the design, use and impact of workspaces for fixed scenarios [4], [12], [13], [35], there are no in-depth studies about the design, use and impact of mobile shared workspaces [3], [32]. Most known studies are focused on identifying work scenarios where mobile technology can add value [11], [21], [27], [32].

There is an interesting initiative to improve the groupware design process for loosely coupled groups for the healthcare sector [29], [30]. The authors describe a contextual model for this workplace, and they provide some general guidelines for developing groupware applications that support loosely coupled work practices, such as managing clinical documentation, planning treatments, and scheduling visits with patients. These guidelines are focused on creation of asynchronous groupware systems that use a client-server architecture; therefore they provide a limited support for fully-distributed work environments. Nonetheless, the requirements identified in these two works are highly relevant in the design of MSW.

On the other hand, there are several experiences reporting the use of collaborative mobile applications [2], [14], [33], [34], [36]. Although some of these applications are fully-distributed, they do not describe or analyze the strategies used to deal with the requirements identified in section 2. Therefore, the potential design solutions cannot be evaluated, formalized through design patterns or reused in future application developments.

One of the most related works was done by Jørstad et al., who studied the feasibility of developing generic coordination services in a distributed (but stable) work scenario [17]. They concluded generic coordination services definition is feasible and they developed a model that was mapped to a Service Oriented Architecture. The generic coordination services they defined included Locking, Presentation Control, User Presence Management, Organization Management and Communication Control. These services were put together into a coordination service layer and made available to the collaborative applications. Unfortunately, this proposal does not consider changes in the local work context and people's mobility.

There is a large list of reusable designs applicable to the coordination services design of groupware applications for fixed networks [5], [10], [16], [25]. However, the contextual variables influencing the collaboration scenario (e.g. communication instability and low feasibility to use servers) and the mobile work (e.g. use of context-aware services and support for ad-hoc coordination processes) make such solutions unsuitable.

On the other hand, there are several platforms and frameworks to share information work in a wireless scenario. Most of them are not able to be dynamically adapted using contextual information or to support a fully distributed work scenario. Examples of these evolutions are the tuple-based distributed system derived from LINDA [9], such as: FT-LINDA, PLinda, TSpaces, Lime, JavaSpaces, and TOTA [31]. These initiatives are able to support mobile collaboration; therefore, they could be used to implement MSW, but not in highly dynamic scenarios. This is because they use centralized components to provide binding among components of the distributed system. Other platforms to share resources in Mobile Ad-Hoc NETworks (MANETs) are iClouds [15], Proem [18] and XMIDDLE [20]. Nevertheless, these platforms are just focused on data sharing and they do not support the autonomy and interoperability capabilities required by mobile workers.

Alarcon et al. presents a method to analyze several contexts involved in a specific loosely coupled work in order to provide some guides to design a particular mobile collaborative solution [1]. These guidelines are focused on the selection of appropriate computing devices, networking support and the paradigm for HCI.

In terms of functionality provided by a mobile shared workspace, the related works are mainly the authors' previous research in the area of mobile groupware applications for disaster relief. However, these works do not report the details of the design solutions used to deal with the requirements identified in section 2.

4   Designing Mobile Shared Workspaces

Mobile shared workspaces are used in various work scenarios to support several activities carried out by mobile workers. Thus, the design of these tools must consider different contexts involved in loosely coupled work in order to get contextualized systems. Contextualized applications are easy to adopt by the users; unfortunately the design of contextualized tools is not obvious [1]. Although diverse contexts need to be considered in the design of a MSW, this section proposes a stepwise design process that is fed just for the work and activity contexts (Figure 1). It must be emphasized that we are not proposing a new software development process, since we assume a typical process is being used, i.e., a software development process including at least the conception, analysis and design phases. Therefore, this process can be considered as a guidance tool to strengthen some development activities of mobile shared workspaces and it can be embedded in a typical software life cycle.

This process is focused on the features of the system required to support collaboration in loosely coupled work scenarios; therefore, it needs to be complemented with a traditional software design (i.e. single-user systems). The proposed process will focus on the design of groupware capabilities (e.g. sessions/users management), and the traditional design process will deal with the design of ad-hoc functionality (e.g. user interfaces).

Usually, the contexts considered in the proposed design process are the most restrictive and they provide key general requirements to take into account in a workspace design. The analysis of these contexts (first step of the process) allows developers to identify the key requirements (presented in Table 1) that are present in the design of a particular workspace.

Sometimes these requirements are contradictory or unable to be satisfied with the available resources. In such a case, the requirements should be redefined in order get a viable alternative for the development process (second step). Once the requirements have been adjusted, they need to be specified because they represent a formal entry for the design process. This activity is also part of the second step.

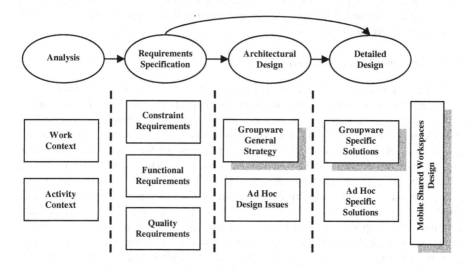

Fig. 1. Mobile Shared Workspaces Design Process

The third and fourth steps involve the architectural and detailed design based on the requirements, and both of them are part of the MSW design. The ad-hoc system design issues are also part of the MSW design. These issues represent the typical design aspects of a single-user application (e.g. ad-hoc functionality and user interfaces), which are present in every software development process. The design of these aspects will not be discussed in this paper because they are not related to groupware and they depend on any particular MSW. Next sections describe the phases of the stepwise process, emphasizing the third and fourth steps.

4.1 Analysis Phase

The analysis phase deals with understanding the problem domain. Thus, the work and activity contexts are analyzed in order to determine which requirements could be involved in the development of a particular MSW. Typically, the *work context* considers the physical conditions and technological infrastructure surrounding each collaborator while s/he is carrying out the activity. The physical space, environmental conditions and communication support are the main variables to take into account in the work context analysis [1]. Since workers are on the move when performing the activity, the work context could change from one location to another.

Typically, loosely coupled work carried out by these mobile collaborators can be split into several activities. Each activity could have its own context. The variables to consider during the analysis of the *activities context* are the type of interactions required by the group members, the communication and coordination requirements to perform the activity, and the activity criticality and duration [1]. Analyzing these variables it is possible to establish which functional requirements (presented in table 1) will be applicable to the MSW. Analyzing the variables of the work context it is possible to identify the quality and constraint requirements. Finally, the analysis of both contexts will provide useful background information to choose the best mobile devices to support the activity [11].

4.2 Requirements Specification

The list of requirements obtained in the previous phase could include contradictory or highly risky requirements, e.g. the MSW has to support some periods of synchronous work among users that are on the move in a physical space without communication infrastructure. Since it is almost impossible to satisfy such requirements combination, they need to be adjusted in order to get a sound basis for the design process. Every requirements refinement should be validated with the work and activity contexts in order to see that no contradictory assumptions are included.

A preliminary design of the mobile workers' collaboration process must be done based on the requirements definition. In addition, the technological and communication support required to perform the activity have to be defined. These design decisions influence the defined requirements and vice versa. For instance, the workers' high mobility could ask for the use of handheld devices, these devices impose restrictions on the actions that can be done by a mobile worker. Therefore, a second process to adjust the requirements should be done in order to ensure the feasibility of designing a MSW that supports the activity in the specified work contexts, considering the available technological infrastructure.

4.3 Architectural Design

It is difficult to design a one-size-fits-all system that works well under all potential usage situations. MSW designers often end up making significant assumptions about the environment and certain design aspects. Usually these MSW must be redesigned to be effectively used if the assumptions no longer hold. The guidelines associated to the design aspects for traditional collaborative systems are inappropriate for highly dynamic mobile scenarios because these solutions were design for fixed networks.

Architectures supporting mobility have to deal with several limitations which are not present in traditional groupware systems, such as: bandwidth constraints, unreliable connections, dynamic work context and computing devices with scarce resources. Next, some key guidelines to design MSW architectures are presented and Figure 2 show the architecture.

Layered. Services in a groupware system are clearly delimited: communication, coordination and collaboration [24]. Therefore, a layered MSW architecture is recommended in order to separate the concerns. Each layer groups the functions related with the same concern, thus providing flexibility and maintainability of the solution.

Fully distributed. Since the mobile workers need to be autonomous, the MSW have to be fully distributed [18], [23]. This distribution includes the communication, data and groupware services. No centralized components have to be used as part of the architecture, because they become a potential failure point. Failure probability of centralized components is unacceptably high due to the high disconnection rate in wireless networks, and particularly in Mobile Ad-hoc Networks (MANETs).

Service-oriented. The service-oriented approach lets mobile groupware systems to be extensible, flexible and interoperable in term of services discovery, consumption and provision [17], [23]. Service-oriented architectures helps decouple concerns about network availability and connectivity. It usually implies simplifications in the software, which are highly relevant when running on a handheld device. If a standard format of services is used to implement the functionality, the developer can assume such services will be interoperable, even in a heterogeneous scenario. Thus, mobile shared workspaces developed under this approach have the potential to offer and consume services on many levels of abstraction.

Asynchronous communication. The high disconnection rate allows mainly asynchronous communication [23], [28]. Therefore it is recommended the architecture adopts a message-oriented approach. Since each remote service invocation needs to ensure the channel between service consumer and provider is maintained for a significant period, unblocking remote invocations should be considered to support the interactions between mobile workers.

Low bandwidth consumption. Typically the effective data transfer rate in a wireless network is low, and it decreases with larger distance or when there are obstacles between sender and receiver. This situation is emphasized when the loosely coupled work is supported by mobile ad-hoc networks. Data synchronization capabilities and a high rate of data replication will help reduce the bandwidth consumption [20], [28].

Platform neutral. The work scenario could be heterogeneous in term of hardware, data and services involved in the loosely coupled work [26], [28]. Thus, the architectural design must emphasize the data and services interoperability, i.e. using standardized formats and interfaces. This is important when unforeseen collaboration should be supported.

Ad-hoc communication. It should be assumed no pre-existing communication infrastructure will be available to support the activity; therefore mobile ad-hoc networks will be required to collaborate [18], [23]. Even if the work scenario provides infrastructure-based wireless communication there will be many times in which mobile workers will get isolated. This is a consequence of the instability of such communication service and its limited threshold. If the architecture assumes that mobile ad-hoc communication will be required, the system capability to support collaboration among mobile workers is increased.

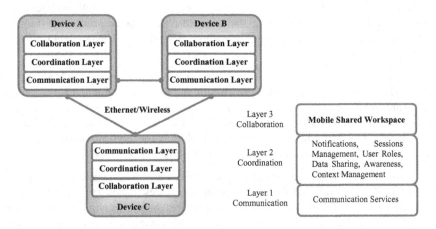

Fig. 2. Mobile Shared Workspaces Architecture

4.4   Detailed Design

This section presents the strategies to share data, and manage users, roles, sessions and context information as a way to deal with most functional requirements specified in the table 1. These design solutions are aligned with the guidelines given for the architectural design.

4.4.1   Sessions, Users and Roles Management
Mobile shared workspaces must allow multiple work sessions involving users playing several roles. Sessions, users and roles management should be fully-distributed since the MSW should be autonomous. Moreover, the loosely coupled work requires on-demand collaboration, information sharing and data synchronization; thus, explicit session management [8] should be used in the MSW design. In explicit sessions, participants must intentionally connect a client to other clients to interchange information or carry out opportunistic collaboration.

Any user in the MANET may participate in more than one session. They access a session sending a request or by invitation. Once a user gets in a session s/he becomes visible and s/he can access the shared resources of such a session. At that moment, the user's local shared resources become visible to the rest of the session members. When a user leaves a session, the local private and shared resources are kept available for him/herself, by allowing the user work asynchronously. Figure 3 shows this process.

Every user must have a local private and a shared repository for each session s/he belongs. It allows her/him to share resources on-demand. A work session is created when the first user is registered as member of it and it is deleted when the last user is unregistered. A session is potentially alive even if no users are currently connected, but there are registered users. The type of explicit work sessions matching loosely coupled work are the following ones: ad-hoc, public-subscribe and private-subscribe. The ad-hoc session is an open public resource that can be accessed by any user connected to the wireless network. The public-subscribe session involves a simple subscription process. Typically, users request a session subscription and automatically obtain the right to access it. Finally, private-subscribe sessions require a subscription process carried out by invitation. Each invitation has associated a user role. If the mobile worker accepts the invitation, then s/he will play such role in that session.

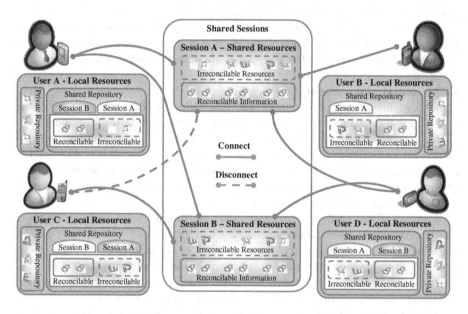

Fig. 3. General strategy for session management

4.4.2 Shared and Private Resources Management

Workspaces supporting loosely coupled work include shared information and services. Since mobile workers have to be autonomous, the resources required by a user during an activity should be reachable (locally stored). High levels of users' autonomy are obtained with high data and services replication. However, this replication adds inconsistency to shared resources and the reconciliation process increases its complexity.

Mobile workers connected to a session use a local (private) repository to store the private resources and a shared (public) repository to store the resources they want to share with the session members (Figure 3). The shared repository contains two types of information resources: *reconcilable* and *irreconcilable*. A reconcilable resource is a piece of information which is able to be synchronized with other copies of such resource (from other mobile workers) in order to obtain a consistent representation of it. These resources are shared through data reconciliation (or synchronization) processes. This process could be on-demand; therefore each user decides when to synchronize and whom to synchronize with. A user can synchronize or get (via file transfer) shared resources only if the users involved in the process are all connected to the same session at the same time. It is worth noting that the reconciliation protocol must use a mechanism to control possible conflicts between different replicas. In other words, it can be performed in an application-specific way. This strategy is fundamental for a large class of applications [22]. Therefore, programmers can easily develop complex mobile shared workspaces that need data sharing, without considering the problems related to disconnections and possible data inconsistencies. This sharing approach maximizes the opportunity for distributed asynchronous work and enables mobile workers to modify shared data without restrictions.

On the other hand, the irreconcilable resources are those pieces of information that cannot be synchronized. Typically, these are files that the system has no information about their internal structure. These resources are shared through file transfer.

4.4.3 Context Management

Context means for us everything that can influence the behavior of shared workspaces; this includes resources internal to a computing device (e.g. memory or screen size) and external resources (e.g. bandwidth, quality of the network connection, and mobile hosts' location and proximity) [6]. Context is highly dynamic in mobile scenarios. Mobile hosts may rapidly connect and leave the network. The lookup service is more complex in the mobile scenario, and broadcasting is the usual way of implementing service advertisement.

Every MSW that needs to be context-aware has to implement a context manager. This manager has to store, update and monitor current status of the context in order to adapt the MSW functionality to changes in the work scenario (e.g. a mobile worker gets isolated or networking support is not available anymore). The context manager can also be used to adapt the system functionality to heterogeneous mobile computer devices and communication scenarios. Furthermore, context information can be used to optimize application behaviors depending on the computing resources availability. Some contextual variables useful in mobile collaboration are: location, relative location, computing devices characteristics and networking support.

The context manager has to be carefully engineered in order to reduce the use of limited resources, such as battery, CPU, memory or network bandwidth. This manager must provide only a minimal set of functionalities and then it is the MSW which is in charge of monitoring and adapting its behavior according to its own needs. A service-oriented approach can be useful to design and implement this component, because it deals with the heterogeneity and shortage of resources.

4.4.4 Guidelines Summary

Table 2 presents a summary of the requirement that usually are present in the design of a MSW and the design guidelines that can be used to address them. Although these guidelines help MSW developers, they do not represent a complete and accurate strategy to deal with such requirements.

Table 2. Matching between requirements and guidelines

Requirement \ Guideline	Ad-hoc communication	Asynchronous communication	Context-aware solution	Data synchronization	Distributed sessions management	Explicit work sessions	Fully distributed	Layered	Platform neutral	Private-subscribe sessions	Reconcilable information	Selection of appropriate mobile computing device	Service-oriented architecture	Private repository	Shared repository
Discretionary collaboration	●	●							●				●	●	●
On-demand information sharing	●	●											●	●	●
On-demand information synchronization	●	●	●								●				
Session/Users management	●	●	●		●	●					●		●		●
Roles support					●		●				●	●			
Environment support	●	●		●					●				●		
Local and shared repositories			●								●		●	●	●
Synchronous/asynch. interaction support	●	●							●				●		
Autonomous							●							●	●
Context-aware	●	●					●								●
Easy to deploy				●								●			
Self-configurable				●											
Interoperable					●				●		●		●	●	●
Low coordination cost	●	●					●						●		
Lightweight													●		
Asynchronous communication	●	●						●							

5   Technologies to Implement the Guidelines

This section presents several key technologies that can be used to implement the design guidelines presented above. Some of the most relevant are the following ones:

Web services technology (WS). It provides interesting chances of getting lightweight, interoperable and loosely couple solutions. In order to show the WS capabilities, Neyem et al. have recently proposed a μWebServer that runs on several mobile computing devices and uses these technologies to expose and consume Web services [23]. WS technology also includes standards specifications for secure messaging, dynamic discovery, description, event support, and file transmission on resource-constrained mobile devices.

IEEE 802.11a/b/g (Wi-Fi). These networks allow implementing a MANET with a low effort. MANETs may be reconfigured on the fly through a protocol running on each node belonging to the network. These networks have a limited threshold (about 200 meters in open areas and 20 meters in built areas) that could be enlarged if routing capabilities are implemented on them. This limitation could be overcome when Wi-Max Mobile (IEEE 802.16e) is available.

HTTP Protocol. This protocol provides the capability of exposing Web services and executing requests to/from limited mobile devices. HTTP supports the processing of HTML, GIF and JPEG Web requests and GET and POST through SOAP components. This protocol uses a communication port (by default) that is available in any communication scenario. This ensures to MSW that changes in the work context features do not interfere with the designed interaction mechanisms. This is particularly relevant when unforeseen collaboration needs to be supported.

SOAP Messaging. Since communication between services is message-oriented, the messaging framework that supports the communication process must be standardized; therefore every service will use the same message format and transport protocol. In addition, the SOAP messaging framework provides some important message (delivery) patterns for asynchronous communication, such as: unicast one-way, multicast one-way, unicast request/response, and multicast request/unicast response. This functionality provides most of the messaging services that developers need to implement in order to support communication in a MSW.

XML (eXtensible Markup Language). This data format is a widely accepted standard, it provides flexibility and it is easy to use. Information represented with XML is potentially interoperable and reconcilable. XML Schemas can be linked to XML files in order to add semantics to such information. It ensures this information will be understandable by any MSW that access it. Furthermore, the synchronization mechanisms of XML information can help to reduce the bandwidth consumption.

6   Conclusions and Further Work

Mobile shared workspaces try to transport the shared workspace metaphor to mobile work scenarios. They seem to be useful to increase the mobile workers productivity when they carry out loosely coupled work. Reports of the MSW usage include areas such as health care [19], [30], construction management [32], m-Learning [36] and disaster relief [7], [26]. Unfortunately, there are few guidelines to support the design of these groupware systems.

This paper presents a design process and several guidelines to model MSW that support collaboration in loosely coupled scenarios. These guidelines are mainly focused on the groupware capabilities of the system, and they are based on common functional, quality and constraint requirements. The presented guidelines are mainly related to architectural and detailed design. The first ones are focused on addressing the MSW quality and constraint requirements, and the guidelines for detailed design deal with the functional requirements. These guidelines consider both foreseen and unforeseen collaboration.

Developers can use these design recommendations to model and implement contextualized MSW. For that reason, the MSW requirements involved in a groupware project can be identified by analyzing the work and activity contexts. Other contexts can also be considered in the MSW design (e.g. social and organizational contexts); however they have low influence on the design of groupware supporting mechanisms of the solution (e.g. data sharing, sessions and users management, and context awareness).

Designers must carefully consider these requirements and the impact the technological support will have on the flexibility, autonomy and interoperability of the MSW. The weight of the solution in terms of memory and CPU consumption should also be considered. Typically users with a high degree of mobility (e.g., traveling salesmen, nurses in a hospital, children in an outdoors educational environment, or engineers at a construction site) require smaller mobile computing devices in order to reduce the transportation effort. However, these devices impose limitations to the design of MSW that runs on them. The service-oriented approach may help groupware designers to conceive lightweight solutions.

The guidelines presented in this paper provide a basic foundation for the development of mobile shared workspaces for loosely coupled work scenarios. It intends to increase the technical feasibility of the solutions in the area and to reduce the development effort of MSW. Future work includes the creation and evaluation of a formal framework to guide the design of these workspaces.

Acknowledgments. This work was partially supported by Fondecyt (Chile), grants Nº: 11060467 and 1040952 and by MECESUP (Chile) Project Nº:UCH0109.

References

1. Alarcón, R., Guerrero, L., Ochoa, S., Pino, J.: Analysis and Design of Mobile Collaborative Applications using Contextual Elements. Journal of Computing and Informatics 25(6), 469–496 (2006)
2. André, P., Antunes, P.: SaGISC: A Geo-Collaborative System. In: de Vreede, G.-J., Guerrero, L.A., Marín Raventós, G. (eds.) CRIWG 2004. LNCS, vol. 3198, pp. 175–191. Springer, Heidelberg (2004)
3. Andriessen, J.H.E., Vartiainen, M. (eds.): Mobile virtual work: A new paradigm? Springer, Heidelberg (2006)
4. Appelt, W., Hinrichs, E.: Tailorability in the BSCW shared workspace system. In: Proc. WACC'99, USA, pp. 59–68 (1999)
5. Arvola, M.: Interaction Design Patterns for Computers in Sociable Use. International Journal of Computer Applications in Technology 25(2/3), 28–139 (2006)
6. Bottazzi, D., Corradi, A., Montanari, R.: Context-Aware Middleware Solutions for Anytime and Anywhere Emergency Assistance to Elderly People. IEEE Communications Magazine 44(4), 82–90 (2006)
7. Canos, J., Borges, M., Alonso, G.: An IT View of Emergency Management, IEEE Computer, vol. 38(12), 27 (2005)
8. Edwards, K.: Session Management for Collaborative Applications, ACM CSCW, 323–330 (1994)
9. Gelernter, D.: Generative Communication in Linda. ACM Transactions on Programming Languages and Systems 7(1), 80–112 (1985)
10. Guerrero, L., Fuller, D.: A pattern system for the development of collaborative applications. Journal of Information and Software Technology 43(7), 457–467 (2001)
11. Guerrero, L., Ochoa, S., Pino, J., Collazos, C.: Selecting Computing Devices to Support Mobile Collaboration. Group Decision and Negotiation 15(3), 243–271 (2006)
12. Gutwin, C., Greenberg, S.: A Descriptive Framework of Workspace Awareness for Real-Time Groupware. Computer Supported Cooperative Work 11(3), 411–446 (2002)
13. Haake, J., Haake, A., Schümmer, T., Bourimi, M., Landgraf, B.: End-User Controlled Group Formation and Access Rights Management in a Shared Workspace System. In: Proc. CSCW'04, USA, pp. 554–563 (2004)
14. Häkkilä, J., Mäntyjärvi, J.: Collaboration in Context-Aware Mobile Phone Applications. In: Proc. HICSS'05, USA, p. 33.a (2005)
15. Heinemann, A., Kangasharju, J., Lyardet, F., Mühlhäuser, M.: iClouds: Peer-to-Peer Information Sharing in Mobile Environments. In: Kosch, H., Böszörményi, L., Hellwagner, H. (eds.) Euro-Par 2003. LNCS, vol. 2790, pp. 1038–1045. Springer, Heidelberg (2003)
16. Herrmann, T., Hoffmann, M., Jahnke, I., Kiele, A., Kunau, G., Loser, K., Menold, N.: Concepts for Usable Patterns of Groupware Applications. In: ACM SIGGROUP Conference on Supporting Group Work, USA, pp. 349–358 (2003)

17. Jørstad, I., Dustdar, S., Van Thanh, D.: Service Oriented Architecture Framework for collaborative services. In: Proc. WETICE'05, Sweden, pp. 121–125 (2005)
18. Kortuem, G., Schneider, J., Preuitt, D., Thompson, T.G.C., Fickas, S., Segall, Z.: When peer-to-peer comes face-to-face: collaborative peer-to-peer computing in mobile ad-hoc networks. In: Proc. P2P'01, Sweden, pp. 75–91 (2001)
19. Markarian, A., Favela, J., Tentori, M., Castro, L.: Seamless Interaction Among Heterogeneous Devices in Support for Co-located Collaboration. In: Dimitriadis, Y.A., Zigurs, I., Gómez-Sánchez, E. (eds.) CRIWG 2006. LNCS, vol. 4154, pp. 389–404. Springer, Heidelberg (2006)
20. Mascolo, C., Capra, L., Zachariadis, S., Emmerich, W.: XMIDDLE: A Data-Sharing Middle-ware for Mobile Computing. Journal on Personal and Wireless Communications 21(1), 77–103 (2002)
21. Nah, F., Sheng, H.: The Value of Mobile Applications: A Utility Company Study. Communications of the ACM 48(2), 85–90 (2005)
22. Neyem, A., Ochoa, S., Pino, J.: A Strategy to Share Documents in MANETs using Mobile Devices. In: Proc. ICACT'06, Korea, pp. 1400–1404 (2006)
23. Neyem, A., Ochoa, S., Pino, J.: Supporting Mobile Collaboration with Service-Oriented Mobile Units. In: Dimitriadis, Y.A., Zigurs, I., Gómez-Sánchez, E. (eds.) CRIWG 2006. LNCS, vol. 4154, pp. 228–245. Springer, Heidelberg (2006)
24. Ochoa, S.F., Guerrero, L.A., Fuller, D., Herrera, O.: Designing the Communication Infrastructures of Groupware Systems. In: Haake, J.M., Pino, J.A. (eds.) CRIWG 2002. LNCS, vol. 2440, pp. 413–433. Springer, Heidelberg (2002)
25. Ochoa, S.F., Guerrero, L.A., Pino, J.A., Collazos, C.: Reusing Software Components. In: de Vreede, G.-J., Guerrero, L.A., Marín Raventós, G. (eds.) CRIWG 2004. LNCS, vol. 3198, pp. 262–270. Springer, Heidelberg (2004)
26. Ochoa, S., Neyem, A., Pino, J., Borges, M.: Supporting Group Decision Making and Coordination in Urban Disasters Relief Efforts. International Journal of Decision Syst. (2007) (in Press)
27. Perry, M., O'hara, K., Sellen, A., Brown, B., Harper, R.: Dealing with mobility: understanding access anytime, anywhere. ACM Transactions on Computer-Human Interaction 8(4), 323–347 (2001)
28. Pinelle, D., Dyck, J., Gutwin, C.: Aligning Work Practices and Mobile Technologies: Groupware Design for Loosely Coupled Mobile Groups. In: Chittaro, L. (ed.) Mobile HCI 2003. LNCS, vol. 2795, pp. 177–192. Springer, Heidelberg (2003)
29. Pinelle, D., Gutwin, C.: A Groupware Design Framework for Loosely-Coupled Workgroups. In: Proc. ECSCW'05, France, pp. 65–82 (2005)
30. Pinelle, D., Gutwin, C.: Loose coupling and healthcare organizations: adoption issues for groupware deployments. Computer Supported Cooperative Work 15(5-6), 537–572 (2006)
31. Russello, G., Chaudron, M., van Steen, M.: An experimental evaluation of self-managing availability in shared data spaces. Science of Computer Programming 64(2), 246–262 (2007)
32. Schaffers, H., Brodt, T., Pallot, M., Prinz, W. (eds.): The Future Workplace - Perspectives on Mobile and Collaborative Working, Telematica Instituut, The Netherlands (2006)
33. Tarasewich, P.: Designing Mobile Commerce Applications. Communications of the ACM 46(12), 57–60 (2003)
34. Wang, Y., van de Kar, E., Meijer, G.: Designing mobile solutions for mobile workers: lessons learned from a case study. In: Kishino, F., Kitamura, Y., Kato, H., Nagata, N. (eds.) ICEC 2005. LNCS, vol. 3711, pp. 582–589. Springer, Heidelberg (2005)
35. Whittaker, S., Geelhoed, E., Robinson, E.: Shared Workspaces: How Do They Work and When Are They Useful? Journal of Man-Machine Studies 39(5), 813–842 (1993)
36. Zurita, G., Nussbaum, M.: MCSCL: Mobile Computer Supported Collaborative Learning. Journal of Computers & Education 42(3), 289–314 (2004)

A Decentralized Middleware for Groupware Applications

Pablo Gotthelf[1,2], Alejandro Zunino[1,2], and Marcelo Campo[1,2]

[1] ISISTAN Research Institute. UNICEN University. Campus Universitario, Tandil
(B7001BBO), Buenos Aires, Argentina. Tel.: +54 (2293) 439682
[2] Consejo Nacional de Investigaciones Científicas y Técnicas Conicet
{pgott,azunino,mcampo}@exa.unicen.edu.ar

Abstract. Many advances have been done to allow groups of people to work together and collaborate in the Internet. Most of these advances rely on a single server or other centralized communication topologies. However, pure decentralized approaches can bring many benefits to groupware applications, such as scalability, robustness, availability and easy deployment. In this paper, a decentralized middleware for groupware applications is presented, which enables people to join and cooperate in groups in a robust and easy deployable way, without relying on a central server or requiring any other special infrastructure. Two applications, one for synchronous groupware and other for asynchronous collaboration are shown as examples of successful experiences. This groupware middleware is based on a binary tree as overlay structure, which implements all groupware communication functionality, including membership management and packet forwarding, at application level, making it suitable for the Internet. Comparisons with other approaches in aspects such as throughput, protocol overhead, resource utilization and group bandwidth, shows that this middleware is a scalable and robust communication scheme to synchronous or asynchronous groups in the Internet.

1 Introduction

Many advances have been done to allow groups of people to work together in the Internet [1,2]. Collaborative systems can be categorized by the way their participants are interconnected and how messages are transmitted [3,4]. In a centralized topology, messages pass through a group server. Conversely, in a decentralized topology, every peer is able to directly connect to the other peers without any central intermediation.

In centralized architectures, organizations or enterprises provide the means for supporting group interaction. This is useful when members of an organization work together in a specific task, and guidance or event tracking of the group activity is desirable. However, this schema is not always suitable. In some cases, for example, no entity is or should be in charge of the group administration, thus, having a centralized server often makes participants feel like they relinquish their control or privacy over their actions. Moreover, solutions based on a central server may compromise availability, as a central server could be seen as a single point of failure. Furthermore, for some cases, it is merely not possible for a group to afford or to have a central server available timely, for instance in emergency situations [5].

J.M. Haake, S.F. Ochoa, and A. Cechich (Eds.): CRIWG 2007, LNCS 4715, pp. 191–206, 2007.

An alternative for group communications that do not require special dedicated servers are overlay networks [6,7,8]. An overlay network is a computer network which is built on top of another network. Overlay networks provide communication services with user-level applications, relying only on unicast communications as the subjacent service. In this way, neither special routers nor extra ISP involvement is required, making this approach suitable for the Internet.

Some overlay networks, including P2P solutions, have shown to be useful to share files and resources in the Internet [9,10,11]. Nevertheless, the interaction schemes required for groupware applications demand special communication premises. As a consequence, in this paper, a middleware for groupware applications is presented. It is based on a binary tree as overlay structure [12], where each node of the tree corresponds to a host in a group and the links between them are unicast connections. This overlay network enables groups to collaborate in a decentralized way, providing scalability, robustness and easy deployment.

The whole system is intended to provide groupware communication services considering the following groupware application characteristics and requirements:

- *No data streaming:* Group members transmit for short periods of time (i.e. there is no video or audio streaming).
- *Solidarity among group members:* Every group members is interested in other members receiving group messages, even those not sent by themselves.
- *Homogeneous groups:* Group members have similar characteristics and behavior, therefore connection resources and communication demands do not differ too much from one another.
- *Unknown Topology:* In contrast with other kinds of networks, it is very difficult to determine or take advantage of the Internet topology.
- *Connection restricted clients:* Hosts behind Network Address Translators (NATs) or firewalls should not be excluded, though they may receive a degraded service.

The rest of this paper is structured as follows. The next section describes the most relevant related work. The communication middleware based on GMAC is described in Sect. 3. Two applications of the middleware, a synchronous and an asynchronous example, are shown in Sect. 4. Experimental results and comparisons with other approaches are reported in Sect. 5. Finally, concluding remarks are presented in Sect. 6.

2   Related Work

Several alternatives have been proposed in order to provide decentralized group communication services on the Internet. Overcast [13] and Scattercast [14] provide support for data streaming, such as video and audio broadcast by disseminating servers strategically across the Internet, aiming to maximize the throughput for single sender groups. REUNITE [8] uses recursive unicast trees to implement multicast services. REUNITE can be incrementally deployed, as it works even if only a subset of the routers implement it. One drawback of REUNITE is that relies on special routers thus it is very difficult and expensive to deploy. These alternatives have been created for providing data broadcast services, such as audio and video streaming. As a consequence, they are best suited for communications with a single sender and multiple receivers. Moreover, they depend on specific routers spread across the Internet leading to deployability problems.

ALMI [15] creates a MST (Minimum Spanning Tree) as an overlay structure among the hosts of a group. In order to build the MST, latency measures between hosts are taken. The main drawback of this approach is that it depends of a centralized component to generate and maintain such structure, and it is restricted to small groups, since the protocol overhead required for generating the MST increases exponentially with the size of the group. NARADA [6] implements a protocol improving ALMI by achieving decentralization, though it is still restricted to small groups. NICE [16] and LARK [17] reduce NARADA protocol overhead in order to achieve scalability, but still focus on data streaming and suffers from failure recovery delays.

Nowadays the notion of peer to peer (P2P) overlay networks [8,10,9] is attracting the attention of the Internet community due to its desirable scalability, robustness and self-organization features. Unstructured P2P approaches such as GNUTELLA [9] use for communication the TTL[1] flooding method, spreading inefficiently a large number messages through the group, or random walk techniques for enhancing efficiency, though at the cost of not reaching all participants in the group [18].

To avoid using these unstructured approaches, distributed hash tables are used to build overlay networks in structured topologies [19][20], therefore the shareable contents are indexed so they can be rapidly found. This strategy is sound for sharing files or data that is easily indexable. However, groupware applications require more general or complex lookups, rendering these alternatives not suitable.

Nevertheless, some cooperative applications based on P2P technologies such as Groove [21], COMTELLA [22] and Edutella [23], have been developed. Groove is a P2P groupware tool that provides extensive support for collaboration, including discussion boards, chat, calendar and whiteboards. Resource sharing is supported by *workspaces*, where data, documents and messages can be stored. This mechanism enables users to work offline and automatically synchronize changes upon reconnection. However these *workspaces* are based on special relay servers, acting as a single point of failure and constraining the original P2P design. COMTELLA is a P2P collaborative application based on GNUTELLA [9] that enables students to share and search for relevant articles, summarize and rate them. Edutella, also based on GNUTELLA, is an open source P2P application for searching shared resources by their semantic web metadata expressed in the resource description format.

In general, P2P systems are mostly based on loose cooperation, thus they do not require complex models of collaboration. Users share resources in an asynchronous way, and P2P systems only provide the infrastructure, search and match-making mechanisms. Therefore, present P2P collaborative systems are usually enhanced file sharing applications, adding metadata or other kinds of extended search capabilities.

In this work, as currently decentralized solutions do not address groupware communication requirements, a new approach is presented, aiming to provide the communication mechanisms necessary to build more sophisticated collaborative applications, in a scalable, decentralized, and easy deployable manner.

---

[1] Time To Live: A message only traverses a limited number of hops before it is removed from the network.

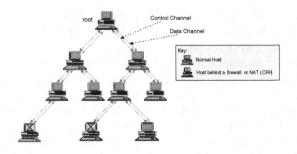

Fig. 1. GMAC tree

3   The GMAC Model

The GMAC Model is based on a binary tree formed by group members as nodes. As Fig. 1 shows, nodes are connected by two unicast links, a *control link*: through which control messages, related to the overlay building and maintenance, are transmitted and a *data link*: through which data messages are sent and retransmitted. When a data message arrives, it is immediately retransmitted to other neighbors and sent to the application layer for processing. Having a tree with a higher degree would either reduce the overall group throughput or require special metrics/heuristics, adding complexity and increasing the protocol overhead substantially.

The whole functionality of GMAC is implemented in each node in a collaborative and decentralized manner, as the responsibilities for message delivery, tree building and recovery are distributed among the group members.

GMAC also supports connectivity-restricted hosts (CRHs). This kind of hosts, as are behind Network Address Translators (NATs) or firewalls, are not able to accept incoming connections, thus they are not able to communicate to each other. GMAC only supports CRHs as leaves of the binary tree, limiting them to at most $\lfloor n/2 \rfloor + 1$, where n is the total number of group members.

There is also another component common to all groups called GMAC registry. The GMAC works as a "meeting place" for hosts wishing to join a group and it provides them with the information needed to join any specific group.

3.1   GMAC Message Types

The overlay provide four different type of messages: multicast messages, control messages, summarizing messages, and welcome messages. These messages, along with the self-organizing overlay, provide the functionality required to communicate and organize groups when developing groupware applications.

Multicast Messages. These messages are used to make announcements to the whole group. In order to provide this functionality, each host in a group sends data only to their neighbors. These, in turn, retransmit the received data in the same manner, relieving the transmitting host.

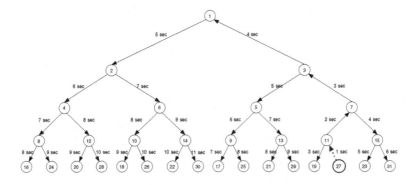

Fig. 2. GMAC message propagation example

Some properties of GMAC can be appreciated by comparing it with sequential unicast, where each group member has to send a copy of the message to all the other group members. Fig. 2 depicts an example where in a group of 31 members node labeled 27 sends a multicast message, assuming that every message transmission takes one second. The total time required to send a group message with the sequential unicast approach would be $n - 1$ seconds, being n the total number of members. On the other hand, the time required by GMAC behaves in a logarithmic way with regard to the number of group members. The best case would happen when the root sends a group message, requiring $2\left(\lceil \log_2 n \rceil\right)$ seconds to reach all nodes. The worst case arises when a message is sent by a leaf, requiring $3\left(\lceil \log_2 n \rceil - 1\right) - 1$ seconds.

Control Messages. Control message flow is ascending. This type of message is used by the overlay structure to let a node know the related control information downward the tree. Each host receives control messages from its children, updates its control state, and retransmits them upward to its own parent.

Summarizing Messages. Groupware applications often require information summarizing data that is spread over the whole group. Each group member owns parts of this information, which might encompass look-up for averages, census, minimum or maximum values for some attribute, or any summarizing calculation required, as long as it follows the incremental solving scheme described next.

For example, a member might be interested in getting the average age of the other members, based on the values given by other group members. Fig. 3 shows how this is done with the summarizing message mechanism. First a member request the average of certain attribute X to the group with a summarizing message (Fig. 3(a)). A node that receives this message propagates it to their neighbors and waits for their response. The response comes in the form of a tuple with the partial average and a coefficient representing the number of nodes involved in the average partial result. If a node has no neighbors it answers immediately with its age and number "1" as coefficient. As Fig. 3(b) shows, once a node receives the response, it calculates a new partial result, including its rating value, and propagates it to its neighbor. Fig. 3(d) shows how the final result reaches the initial requesting node. This strategy greatly reduces the number

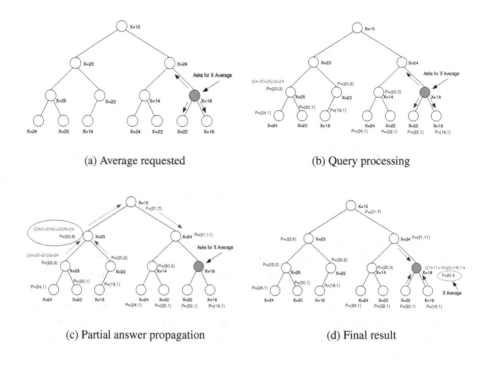

(a) Average requested

(b) Query processing

(c) Partial answer propagation

(d) Final result

Fig. 3. Summarizing message example

of messages, taking $2 * n$ messages. In contrast, the multicast message scheme would require n^2 messages. Besides the whole computation is distributed in the group.

Welcome Messages. This message is the information a member receives when joining the group. This may be suitable for telling the new member information it should know about the already established group, such as things defined by the group in its absence, member status, policies, etc. In GMAC, the parent node is responsible of transmitting this kind of messages as soon as the connection with a new member is established.

3.2 Joining a Group

When a node receives a join request it incorporates the requesting node as a child. If there is no room at that node (i.e. it already has two children) it will delegate the join request to its least weighted child (i.e. the one with the smallest subtree), to keep the tree balanced. Therefore, a host wishing to join a group will descend the tree until it is inserted as a leaf. As the overlay structure is a binary tree, a host joining a group will have to traverse at most $\log_2 n$ nodes, being n the total number of nodes. A more complex join heuristic is used in GMAC implementation to reduce the number of connections and allow, through rotations, connection-restricted hosts as leaves of the tree.

3.3 GMAC Registry

The main requirement of the GMAC registry is that it has to be globally accessible in the Internet, working as the starting place or bootstrap for hosts wishing to join a group. The GMAC registry publishes the roots of the groups by sending the root address and incoming port to a host intending to join it, provided that the correct group name and password are given. The GMAC registry works as a kind of DNS service for the active groups. Future members would be unable to find the roots if the registry is missing, but the groups would be completely functional. Nonetheless, this component has been materialized as a Web application and implemented as a cluster of redundant servers.

3.4 Failure Recovery

When a node fails or leaves a group, the tree must be restructured in order to continue providing multicast support to the rest of the group. This reorganization is done by the remaining members in a decentralized way, as follows:

- The parent node, which had the failing node as a child, just closes the connections to it, updates its state information and sends it to its own parent.
- Children nodes, which had the failing node as its parent, must reconnect to the tree by sending a connection request to the root.

For the non-adjacent nodes downward the one that failed, reorganization is transparent, as they will be reconnected along with the orphan nodes. In this way, a node failure is handled by reconnecting its children, which is done in a decentralized manner.

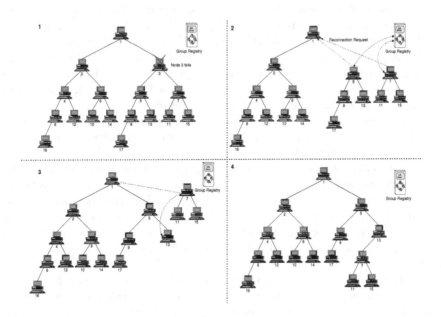

Fig. 4. Failure recovery

Fig. 4 depicts the failure recovery mechanism. Suppose node 3 leaves the group. Node 1, which had node 3 as a child, just releases the connection. Both "orphan" nodes 5 and 7 will reconnect to the root keeping their current children, thus actually a subtree is being reconnected. First, the root handles node's 5 request incorporating it as its right child. Next, the root will delegate node 7 join request to node 13.

A special case arises when the node that leaves the group is the root itself, as orphan nodes will fail when attempting to reconnect to it. Therefore, these nodes will attempt to become the root themselves, and one will succeed in asking the group registry to replace the missing root.

Failure recovery in GMAC is fast and simple, and neither extra control links nor extra control state information needs to be maintained for failure resilience purposes. As a consequence, GMAC detects and reconnects disconnected nodes immediately, rather than avoiding nodes disconnection by adding redundancy or complex heuristics.

4   Collaborative Applications Based on GMAC

Two collaborative applications where developed in order to see how GMAC handles synchronous and asynchronous communication requirements.

4.1   Chatero

Chatero is a synchronous collaborative application that allows people to join in a chat group, vote for actions, and draw over fixed background images. In most cases, groups are formed by well-known members that work together within the scope of an organization, where practices such as organization guidance and tracking are desirable. Conversely, Chatero is a discussion/brainstorming application, useful for people who join together in an ad-lib way to solve a specific task. These cases may also involve certain urgency as well, thus relying on centralized approaches would be inappropriate or even impossible. For example, collaborative systems for disaster management [5] often require easy deployment, decentralization and dynamism.

In order to join a group in Chatero, participants must provide a group name and password. Participants are identified by nicknames, and once joined, they can immediately start chatting or drawing in the whiteboard.

Fig. 5 shows how Chatero may be used to fight forest fires. A fireman can join the group to discuss and organize the way to extinguish the fire. It is also possible for the participants to vote, for a proposal, a course of action, or anything they wish. For the voting system a user must declare the voting topic and a set of possible answers to select. Afterwards a voting panel is displayed, and options are shown, as depicted in Fig. 5 (b). After a specified period of time, the panel expires and the participant losses the voting opportunity.

Chatero was implemented using GMAC multicast messages, keeping the propagation delay logarithmic. When a new user joins the group, he sends a multicast message to announce himself. A "welcome message" lets the new user know who is currently connected and the last chat messages transmitted. Summarizing messages are used to propagate the voting results. In each host, the answer is stored until the remaining

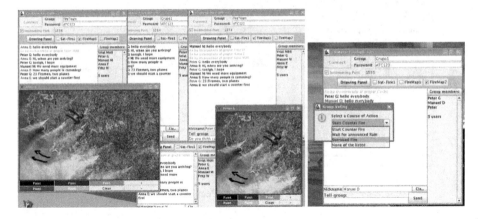

(a) Chat and whiteboard   (b) Voting

Fig. 5. Chatero, a synchronous groupware example

neighbors transmit their answers; then the joint results are transmitted. Once the whole answer is assembled in the voting requester, the results are shown to the whole group. It is important to note that when developing this application, the voting mechanism was kept transparent to the users. Thus, they do not really know whether their answer is transmitted immediately or waiting for other partial results, the same happens with the voting requester, as the final results are shown to the group without its intervention.

4.2 Science-Peer

Science-Peer, is a groupware application for asynchronous cooperation. It enables researchers to share their experiences and knowledge. Besides to the document sharing capability, Science-Peers is intended to find researchers with similar interests.

This application is built as a multi-agent system. Each user has a dedicated agent that interacts with other agents. For example, to find researchers with similar interests, vectors are generated with the articles each researcher shares and a numeric value representing the rating of each article. When an agent wants to find researchers with similar interests, the set of vectors of a researcher is transmitted with the summarizing message method (Sect. 3.1). A special function called *nearest-neighbor* was developed for this specific case. It compares the set of articles shared by researchers and their respective ratings, and gives, for each set, a proximity and an accuracy value, working as a sort of incremental K-nearest-neighbor [24] approach. For this case, the three sets with minimum distance are selected, provided they have a minimum accuracy threshold. Then, the agent stores the researchers information, so as to allow direct communications and future actions, for example to subscribe to future articles well rated by that researcher.

As Fig. 6 shows, Science-Peer is able to recommend articles other researchers share. Even though Science-Peer is still under development, it is possible to notice how the middleware satisfies this type of groupware communication requirements.

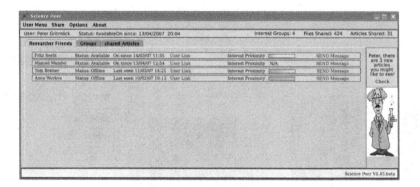

Fig. 6. Science Peer

In P2P collaboration environments there is a risk of "free-riding" [25,26], a term used to describe users that get benefits without sharing resources. Science-Peer inherently encourages users to share their resources and give feedback, as it would mean more accuracy in look-up results. Furthermore, a researcher must share and rate a minimum number of articles to be able to use the peer-searching feature.

5   Experimental Results

Several simulations were made in order to evaluate GMAC. It was compared with sequential unicast and two MSTs (Minimum Spanning Trees) variants, one maximizing bandwidth and the other minimizing latency. This could be seen as the approaches adopted by NARADA and ALMI, respectively. It is important to note that such MSTs are used as theoretical boundaries for the metrics they optimize as no other overlay tree can achieve better results. Building these MSTs would be very difficult in real conditions, since it would be necessary to know the network topology and its metrics in advance and to assume they are static, something not likely to happen in the Internet.

In order to generate the simulations, hosts were placed at random in a bi-dimensional space. Each host was assigned a bandwidth between 15 and 70 KB/s, while latency varied from 100 to 665 ms between any pair of them. It was assumed that these magnitudes were symmetrical (A→B = B ←A). Furthermore, it was considered that any host could transmit data messages with equal probability. It is important to notice that knowing the topology in advance, which, besides is static, favors the MST alternatives. Therefore this scenario is rather unfair to GMAC.

5.1   End-to-End Group Propagation Delay

Figures 7(a) and (b) show the time required by a random node to send 100KB to all the group. The MST latency approach has poor performance, as it does not take into account bandwidth metrics. The MST Bandwidth was built optimizing a 100KB message transmission, thus this is the best that can be achieved in an overlay tree. GMAC scales well, approximating the boundaries imposed by the MST Bandwidth.

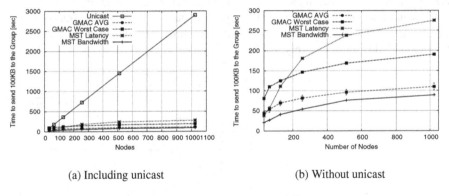

(a) Including unicast   (b) Without unicast

Fig. 7. Time (in seconds) to send a 100KB message

5.2 Throughput

Fig. 8 shows the group throughput that can be achieved with the different approaches. In distribution trees, less capable nodes act as bottlenecks, limiting the overall group to their bandwidth. In GMAC, bottleneck nodes may have to retransmit messages, thus the overall throughput is restricted to half of the less capable host bandwidth.

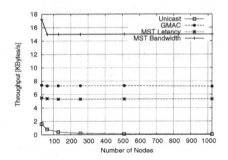

Fig. 8. Maximum group throughput

5.3 Protocol Overhead

This metric considers network traffic that does not represent useful application data. In GMAC the information required to build and maintain the tree is minimal, since this information is transmitted only when a node joins or leaves the group.

Figs. 9 (a) and (b) shows that NARADA exponential protocol overhead prevents it from scaling [17,27]. While NICE and LARK reduce NARADA exponential protocol overhead, in GMAC, as no optimization is made, the protocol overhead is minimal, and it is only affected by the overall joining or departure rate. In order to evaluate GMAC the failure rates proposed by the alternatives where used. Therefore 12.5% of the nodes from a group fail within 100 seconds. The failure rates in groupware applications are usually much lower, either in the synchronous approach, where the group is supposed to be stable until the task is complete, or the asynchronous approach, where users connects for long periods of time. In addition, the protocol overhead presented in the alternatives does not include failure recovery overheads.

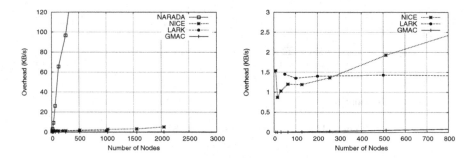

Fig. 9. Protocol overhead comparison

5.4 Group Latency

One important metric is group latency, which is the longest end-to-end delay between any pair of nodes. Fig. 10 (a) and (b) show the logarithmic behavior for GMAC end-to-end group delay simulation results for data and control messages respectively. The delay was measured for two message cases, *multicast messages latency,* representing the time required to reach the farthest node from any other node in the binary tree, and *control message latency,* representing the time for a control message to reach the root, since control messages flow bottom-up in GMAC.

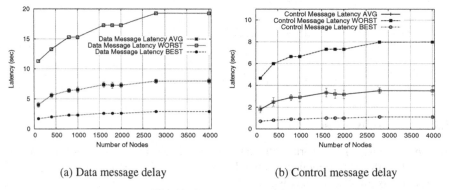

(a) Data message delay   (b) Control message delay

Fig. 10. Group messages delay

5.5 Resource Utilization

Fig. 11 shows the results related to resource utilization. The MST latency is the one with better resource. ALMI relies on this metric to build its overlay tree. NARADA, in contrast, suggests that this may not be the best choice, since the shortest path is not always the fastest one [6]. Furthermore, the assumption that on the Internet latency represents distance is not necessarily true. As a consequence, it is very difficult to achieve good network resource utilization in overlay approaches, and GMAC is no exception.

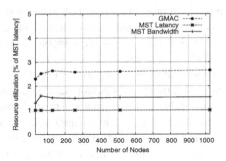

Fig. 11. Resource utilization

5.6 Failure Recovery

Fig. 12 shows the time required to recover from simultaneous failing hosts in a group with 100 nodes. As explained in Sect. 3.4, GMAC quickly recovers from node failures by reincorporating the orphan nodes along with their subtrees in a decentralized way. In addition to the fact that the tree is not affected when a leaf fails, which corresponds to half of the group nodes, thus reducing the activation of the failure recovery mechanism to half the failure probability. However, recovery in optimized overlay structures, such as ALMI, is more expensive because a host failure may trigger the reoptimization of the whole structure, producing additional protocol overhead.

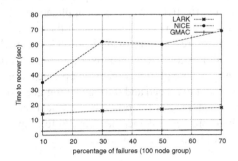

Fig. 12. Failure recovery on a 100-node group

6 Conclusions

This paper presented a decentralized middleware for groupware applications based on an overlay network named GMAC. The entire functionality of GMAC is implemented in each host at the application level in a decentralized and collaborative way, thus responsibilities for message delivery, tree building and recovery are distributed among the group members. Besides, GMAC only assumes unicast as the subjacent service, allowing any host in the Internet to use it, even those with connectivity restrictions.

Groupware collaboration can be done in a synchronous or an asynchronous way, for the latter, as it does not has a high interaction rate, P2P systems seems to be intuitively suitable. Conversely for synchronous collaboration, latency and high interaction rates are crucial, thus decentralized solutions might seem inconceivable. However the logarithmic delivery rate of GMAC have shown to be good enough to support this type of collaboration. Here the notion of awareness plays an important role, as it determines how much information from other users a participant must handle, and hence, how much information must be transmitted. For example, in a 250 member group, undoubtedly all members will not be simultaneously painting in a whiteboard. This is because in a collaborating group there is an implicit relation between the number of participants, their actions and the awareness required. This relation reduces transmission requirements, rendering synchronous collaboration possible in the GMAC model, as it allows large groups to collaborate (250 members means just an 8 level tree), where surely some participants will be actively interacting (drawing), and others observing.

GMAC works in a fully decentralized way, using a binary tree as overlay network. Once the tree is established, it behaves as a mesh, where internal nodes forward incoming messages to their neighbors. This approach is possible since the recursive nature of the binary tree allows the ascending control message heuristic. Hence a parent node receives only one control message from each child, summarizing the control state information of that entire branch, so that the upward nodes are not overloaded by control messages. In contrast, most scalable self-organizing P2P approaches [10,9,28,11,29] do not have a defined overlay network structure that could instrument a similar scheme.

Experimental results show that GMAC is a good and simple choice to provide decentralized groupware communication services. In GMAC, the complexity of generating its structure is not affected by the size of the group, protocol overhead is minimal and failure recovery is fast and effective. GMAC is an application level solution, thus network resource utilization is rather poor. This is one of the main drawbacks of GMAC, however this problem is also present in most application level overlay approaches.

GMAC main contribution is to provide groupware communication services in a decentralized and robust way, where group members cooperate among each other in a fair way, minimizing the protocol overhead and thus achieving great scalability.

GMAC proposes a new approach for providing application-level groupware communication services, therefore new enhancements and future investigation possibilities arise, such as security, optimizations, group policies, etc.

References

1. Ellis, C.A., Gibbs, S.J., Rein, G.: Groupware: some issues and experiences. Commun. ACM 34(1), 39–58 (1991)
2. Wheeler, B.C., Dennis, A.R., Press, L.I.: Groupware comes to the internet: charting a new world. SIGMIS Database 30(3-4), 8–21 (1999)

3. Ma, J., Shizuka, M., Lee, J., Huang, R.: A p2p groupware system with decentralized topology for supporting synchronous collaborations. In: Proc. of the International Conference on Cyberworlds, Washington, DC, USA, p. 54. IEEE Computer Society Press, Los Alamitos (2003)
4. Ehrlich, S.F., Bikson, T., Mackay, W., Tang, J.C.: Tools for supporting cooperative work near and far: highlights from the cscw conference. In: Proc. of the ACM Human Factors in Computing Systems Conference, pp. 353–356. ACM Press, New York (1989)
5. Scalem, M., Bandyopadhyay, S., Sircar, A.K.: An Approach Towards a Decentralised Disaster Management Information Network (2004)
6. Chu, Y.-H., Rao, S.G., Zhang, H.: A case for end system multicast. IEEE J. Sel. Areas Commun. (2002)
7. Eriksson, H.: MBONE: the multicast backbone. Commun. ACM 37(8), 54–60 (1994)
8. Stoica, I., Ng, T.S.E., Zhang, H.: REUNITE: A Recursive Unicast Approach to Multicast. In: Proc. of INFOCOM00, pp. 1644–1653. IEEE Computer Society Press, Los Alamitos (2000)
9. Ripeanu, M., Iamnitchi, A., Foster, I.: Mapping the gnutella network. IEEE Internet Computing 6(1), 50–57 (2002)
10. Rowstron, A., Druschel, P.: Pastry: Scalable, decentralized object location and routing for large-scale peer-to-peer systems. In: Guerraoui, R. (ed.) Middleware 2001. LNCS, vol. 2218, pp. 329–350. Springer, Heidelberg (2001)
11. Stoica, I., Morris, R., Liben-Nowell, D., Karger, D.R., Kaashoek, M.F., Dabek, F., Balakrishnan, H.: Chord: A scalable peer-to-peer lookup service for internet applications. IEEE/ACM Transactions on Networking 11(1), 17–32 (2003)
12. Gotthelf, P., Mendoza, M., Zunino, A., Mateos, C.: GMAC: An Overlay Multicast Network for Mobile Agents. In: Proc. of the VI Argentine Symposium on Computing Technology (AST 2005 - 34 JAIIO) (2005)
13. Jannotti, J., Gifford, D.K., Johnson, K.L., Kaashoek, M.F., O'Toole, Jr., J.W.: Overcast: Reliable Multicasting with an Overlay Network. In: Proc. of the 4th USENIX symposium on Operating Systems Design and Implementation, Berkeley, CA, USA USENIX (2000)
14. Chawathe, Y.: Scattercast: an adaptable broadcast distribution framework. Multimedia Systems 9(1), 104–118 (2003)
15. Pendarakis, D., Shi, S., Verma, D., Waldvogel, M.: ALMI: An application level multicast infrastructure. In: Proc. of the 3rd USENIX Symposium on Internet Technologies and Systems, USENIX (2001)
16. Banerjee, S., Bhattacharjee, B., Kommareddy, C.: Scalable application layer multicast. In: SIGCOMM '02: Proc. of the 2002 conference on Applications, technologies, architectures, and protocols for computer communications, pp. 205–217. ACM Press, New York (2002)
17. Kandula, S., Lee, J.K., Hou, J.C.: Lark: a light-weight, resilient application-level multicast protocol. In: IEEE 18 Annual Workshop on computer Communications, IEEE Computer Society Press, Los Alamitos (2003)
18. Gkantsidis, C., Mihail, M., Saberi, A.: Random walks in peer-to-peer networks. In: INFOCOM (2004)
19. Dabek, F., Kaashoek, M.F., Karger, D.R., Morris, R., Stoica, I.: Wide-area cooperative storage with CFS. In: SOSP, pp. 202–215 (2001)
20. Kubiatowicz, J., Bindel, D., Chen, Y., Czerwinski, S.E., Eaton, P.R., Geels, D., Gummadi, R., Rhea, S.C., Weatherspoon, H., Weimer, W., Wells, C., Zhao, B.Y.: Oceanstore: An architecture for global-scale persistent storage. In: ASPLOS, pp. 190–201 (2000)
21. Eikemeier, C., Lechner, U.: Peer-to-peer and group collaboration - do they always match? In: Proc. of the 13th WETICE, pp. 101–106 (2004)
22. Vassileva, J.: Harnessing p2p power in the classroom. In: Proc. of Intelligent Tutoring Systems, pp. 305–314 (2004)

23. Nejdl, W., Wolf, B., Qu, C., Decker, S., Sintek, M., Naeve, A., Nilsson, M., Palm&233;r, M., Risch, T.: Edutella: a p2p networking infrastructure based on rdf. In: Proc. of the 11th international conference on WWW, Honolulu, Hawaii, USA, pp. 604–615. ACM Press, New York (2002)
24. Mitchell, T.: Machine Learning. McGraw-Hill, New York (1997)
25. Feldman, M., Chuang, J.: Overcoming free-riding behavior in peer-to-peer systems. SIGecom Exch. 5(4), 41–50 (2005)
26. Adar, E., Huberman, B.A.: Free riding on gnutella. First Monday (2000)
27. Jin, S., Bestavros, A.: Small-World Internet Topologies: Possible Causes and Implications on Scalability of End-System Multicast. Computer Networks 50(6), 648–666 (2006)
28. Castro, M., Druschel, P., Kermarrec, A.-M., Rowstron, A.I.T.: Scribe: A large-scale and decentralized application-level multicast infrastructure. IEEE J. Sel. Areas Commun. 20(8), 1489–1499 (2002)
29. Zhao, B.Y., Huang, L., Stribling, J., Rhea, S.C., Joseph, A.D., Kubiatowicz, J.D.: Tapestry: A resilient global-scale overlay for service deployment. IEEE J. Sel. Areas Commun. 22(1), 41–53 (2004)

Modelling Shared Knowledge and Shared Knowledge Awareness in CSCL Scenarios Through Automated Argumentation Systems

María Paula González[1,2], Carlos Iván Chesñevar[1,2], Cesar A. Collazos[3], and Guillermo R. Simari[2]

[1] National Council of Scientific and Technical Research (CONICET), Argentina
[2] Department of Computer Science and Engineering – Universidad Nacional del Sur
Av Alem 1253 – 8000 Bahía Blanca, Argentina
{mpg,cic,grs}@cs.uns.edu.ar
[3] Department of Systems - Universidad del Cauca
FIET-Sector Tulcan, Popayán, Colombia
ccollazo@unicauca.edu.co

Abstract. Over the last few years, argumentation systems have been gaining increasing importance in several areas of Artificial Intelligence, mainly as a vehicle for facilitating rationally justifiable decision making when handling incomplete and potentially inconsistent information. Argumentation provides a sound model for dialectical reasoning, which underlies discussions among students when solving tasks collaboratively in a CSCL environment. In this setting, we identify the problem of constructing Shared Knowledge and its related Shared Knowledge Awareness. While Shared Knowledge refers to the common knowledge students acquire when they work in a collaborative activity, Shared Knowledge Awareness is associated with the consciousness on the Shared Knowledge that a particular student has. This paper presents a novel approach to model Shared Knowledge construction and the associated Shared Knowledge Awareness through an automated argumentation system.

1 Introduction

Shared Knowledge (SK) concerns the common knowledge constructed by a student group when carrying out a collaborative learning activity in a CSCL environment. In this setting, *Shared Knowledge Awareness* (SKA) has been defined as the consciousness on the SK that this student group has when performing a specific collaborative task in a restricted moment of time [1]. Indeed, the construction of SK is strongly related to the acquisition of an appropriate level of SKA, as being aware of any knowledge (in particular SK) implies learning something about it.

Students' acquisition of SKA in CSCL scenarios is not a simple task, and a number of questions that should be considered to reach it have been proposed [1]. However, it is difficult to ascertain how to provide mechanisms to model the construction of SKA in a real CSCL system. Indeed, this problem is related to different features, in particular with characterizing the students' dialectical reasoning underlying negotiation

J.M. Haake, S.F. Ochoa, and A. Cechich (Eds.): CRIWG 2007, LNCS 4715, pp. 207–222, 2007.
© Springer-Verlag Berlin Heidelberg 2007

processes when looking for an agreement or consensus about a given claim. In this context, automated *argumentation systems* [2] provide an interesting formalization tool, as they have matured in the last decade to become a sound setting to formalize commonsense, dialectical reasoning. Indeed, defeasible argumentation has been successfully used in legal reasoning, multiagent platforms and decision making systems among others [2, 3, 4].

This paper presents a novel approach for integrating automated argumentation systems as a support tool for characterizing SK and SKA in CSCL scenarios. Taking as a starting point the individual knowledge constructed by each student when performing a collaborative task, our goal is to provide an argument-based mechanism through which part of the SK can be constructed semi-automatically, expliciting as well its related SKA. For achieving this, the individual knowledge coming from every student will be collected in a common knowledge base K in which part of the knowledge is tentative (or *defeasible*). On the basis of K, different arguments (possibly in conflict) will be automatically obtained, providing additional support for the dialectical discussion performed by the students. Moreover, conflicts among arguments will be automatically detected by means of an automated argumentation system. The system will also determine which arguments ultimately prevail in a discussion, which will be called *warranted arguments*. In our proposal, such warranted arguments will provide a part of the SK among students, whereas visualization and explanation facilities provided by the argumentation system will help to make explicit the associated SKA.

The rest of this paper is structured as follows: Section 2 briefly describes the concepts of SK and SKA. Section 3 provides an overview of the fundamentals of argumentation systems. Section 4 describes our proposal for modelling SK and SKA construction in CSCL by means of an automated argumentation system. Section 5 discusses the feasibility aspects of our proposal and presents a case study. Section 6 discusses related work. Finally, Section 7 concludes and discusses future work.

2 Shared Knowledge and Shared Knowledge Awareness

Shared Knowledge (SK) concerns the common knowledge constructed by a group of students when carrying out a collaborative learning activity in a CSCL environment. It refers to the understanding that any student of the group has about several aspects of the collaborative work, including coordination, strategy communications, monitoring, and shared comprehension of the problem [1]. In this context, *Shared Knowledge Awareness* (SKA) has been defined as the consciousness on the shared knowledge that a particular student group has when carrying out a specific collaborative learning activity in a CSCL environment in a restricted moment of time [1].

Students' acquisition of SKA in CSCL scenarios is not a simple task, and it is difficult to ascertain how to provide mechanisms to model the construction of SKA in a real CSCL system. In that respect, a number of questions that should be considered to reach it have been proposed [1]. In addition, some guidelines were outlined to ensure the existence of appropriate reinforcement elements in a CSCL interface related to SKA [5]. However, those proposals focus on modelling the individual perception of the collaborative task, as it is the student who has to answer the questions mentioned before, or who will perceive a particular CSCL interface. Even when the construction of the SKA relies on individual introspective activities carried out by each student, the outcome of discussions performed within the group is crucial to detect the SK and to understand the group dynamics, i.e. to construct SKA.

In the above scenario, a *dialectical discussion* is normally performed among students when solving a collaborative task to be aware of the SK they have. This discussion includes the exchange of objective information or facts, as well as incomplete (and sometimes contradictory) perceptions of the reality related to the task to be solved, as most human activities have to deal with uncertainty and lack of complete information in the real world. In such discussion the participants may be biased in their opinions (given their own preferences, beliefs, etc.), so that a careful analysis of arguments and counterarguments advanced during the discussion is required to determine whether some particular belief is actually accepted by the group.

Modelling dialectical discussions in CSCL scenarios and their relationship with SK and SKA construction is a challenging issue nowadays. It implies moving the focus from the analysis of the isolated student perception to the study of the exchanged information within the group and its dynamics. In that respect, different alternatives have been recently proposed for identifying common aspects of dialogues in CSCL, such as the study of the students' focus of attention [6], the visualization of discussion and agreement during online discussions [7], or the analysis of the text-based communication in a web-based CSCW system [8,9]. However, to the best of our knowledge, none of those existing approaches incorporate automated argumentation systems for providing support to model conflicting situations in the dialectical communication in CSCL. Besides, most of such approaches make use of a slightly cryptic concept of SKA which is not *explicitly* presented to students. Argumentation systems are advantageous in this context, as they can be used to explore automatically *all* possible arguments associated with a given claim on the basis of the students' knowledge, helping them to clearly identify why their claims hold (or do not hold), minimizing thus the bias present in the learning process. As we will see next, automated argumentation systems can also provide a rich formal framework for computing *explicit* SKA, thus characterizing a crucial part of the SK construction in CSCL scenarios.

3   Argumentation Systems: A Brief Overview

Argumentation is an important aspect of human decision making. In many situations of every day's life, people when faced with new information need to ponder its consequences, in particular when attempting to understand problems and come to a decision. *Argumentation systems* [2] are increasingly being considered for applications in developing software engineering tools, constituting an important component of multi-agent systems for negotiation, problem solving, and for the fusion of data and knowledge. Such systems implement a dialectical reasoning process by determining whether a proposition follows from certain assumptions, analyzing whether some of those assumptions can be disproved by other assumptions in our premises. In this way, an argumentation system provides valuable help to analyze which assumptions from our knowledge base were really giving rise the inconsistency and which assumptions were harmless. Argumentation systems typically refer to two kinds of knowledge: *strict* and *defeasible* knowledge. Strict knowledge (K_S) corresponds to the knowledge which is certain; typical elements in K_S are statements or undisputable *facts* about the world, or mathematical truths (e.g. implications of the form $(\forall x)P(x) \rightarrow Q(x)$. The strict knowledge is *consistent*, i.e. no contradictory conclusions can be derived from it. On the other hand, defeasible knowledge (K_D) corresponds to that knowledge which is *tentative*, modelled through "rules with exceptions" (*defeasible* rules) of the form "if P then usually Q" (e.g., "if something is a bird, it usually flies"). Such rules model our incomplete knowledge about the world, as they can have exceptions (e.g., a penguin, a dead bird, etc.). Syntactically, a special symbol ($\Rightarrow$) is used to distinguish "defeasible" rules from logical implications.

Argumentation systems allow the user to define a knowledge base $K = K_S \cup K_D$ involving strict and defeasible knowledge. An *argument A* for a claim *c* is basically some "tentative proof" (formally, a ground instance of a subset of K_D) for concluding *c* from $A \cup K_S$ [10]. Arguments must additionally satisfy the requirement of *consistency* (an argument cannot include contradictory propositions) and *minimality* (by not including repeated or unnecessary information). Conflicting arguments may emerge from *K*; intuitively, an argument *A attacks* another argument *B* whenever both of them cannot be accepted at the same time, as that would lead to contradictory conclusions. Let us consider an illustrative example:

Example 1: Consider some basic commonsense knowledge about spiders and dangerous insects, and a particular situation a kid may be facing when reasoning about what he/she has learnt from experience. The situation will be modelled in terms of facts, and commonsense knowledge will be modelled using defeasible rules.

Situation (Facts – Strict Knowledge)

[a] The black widow is a spider. A black widow (let us call it "bw") was found on the floor.
[b] The black widow "bw" looks dead.
[c] The black widow "bw" moves its legs when touched with a stick
Defeasible rules (Commonsense knowledge)
[d] If X is a spider, then X is dangerous.
[e] If X is a spider and it is dead, then I can assume that X is not dangerous.
[f] If X looks dead, then this is a tentative reason to believe that X is dead.
[g] If X looks dead but moves by itself when touched, then usually X is not dead.

From this knowledge base K={[a],[b],[c],[d],[e],[f],[g]} different arguments may arise, some of them conflicting with each other. Let us consider some cases.

ArgA = {[a], [d]} is an argument for concluding that the black widow "bw" found on the floor is dangerous, as it is a spider [a] and spiders are usually dangerous [d].

ArgB = {[a], [b], [e], [f]} is an argument for concluding that the black widow "bw" is not dangerous, as it is a spider [a] which looks dead [b], and if something looks dead, this usually means that it is actually dead [f]. And if the spider "bw" is dead, then we can believe that it is not dangerous [e].

Clearly, arguments ArgA and ArgB are in conflict. They contradict each other as they lead to opposite conclusions. Note that another argument can be considered, which attacks Arg:

ArgC = {[b], [c], [g]} is an argument for concluding that the black widow "bw" is not dead, as "bw" looks dead [b]   but moves by itself when touched [c], and this usually means that it is not dead [g]. So we can conclude that "bw" is not dead.

Arguments ArgB and ArgC are also in conflict, but do not have opposite conclusions. Instead, the conclusion of ArgC ("bw is not dead") is contradicting an inner element in ArgB ("bw is dead").

The previous example illustrates two kinds of possible "attacks" between arguments in argumentation systems: *symmetric attack* (arguments with opposite conclusions) and *undercutting attack* (an argument attacks some "subargument" in another argument). The notion of *defeat* comes then into play to decide *which argument should be preferred*. An argument A defeats an argument B whenever A attacks B, and besides, A is preferred over the attacked part in B (with respect to some preference criterion). The criterion for defeat can be defined in many ways, being a partial order ≤ among arguments. Thus, for example, arguments can be preferred according to the source (e.g. when having arguments about weather, the argument of a meteorologist should be stronger than the argument of a layman). As a generic criterion, it is also common to prefer those arguments which are *more direct* or *more informed*. This is known as the *specificity principle* (see [10]). For example, if the arguments *ArgA* and *ArgB* from *Example 1* are considered, both arguments are in conflict, and attack each other. However, argument *ArgB* is *strictly more specific* than argument *ArgA*. Therefore, *ArgB* is preferred over *ArgA*. In the second case, argument *ArgC* is *as specific as* argument *ArgB,* as the attacker and the attacked part are equally specific.

Fig. 1(a) illustrates the notions of knowledge base, argument and conflict between arguments associated with Example 1.[1] Note that arguments are usually abstracted away as triangles with the conclusion on top, and inside the defeasible rules used to reach the conclusion. Note that the notion of defeat among arguments may lead to complex "cascade" situations: an argument A may be defeated by an argument B, which in turn may be defeated by an argument C, and so on. Besides, every argument involved may have on its turn more than one defeater. Argumentation systems allow us to determine when a given argument is considered as *ultimately acceptable* with respect to the knowledge we have available by means of a *dialectical analysis*, which takes the form of a tree-like structure called *dialectical tree*. The root of the tree is a given argument A supporting some claim, and children nodes for the root are those defeaters B_1, B_2, .. B_k for A. The process is repeated recursively on every defeater B_i, until all possible arguments have been considered. Leaves are arguments without defeaters. Some additional restrictions apply (e.g., the same argument cannot be used twice in a path, as that would be fallacious and would lead to infinite paths).

A marking procedure can be then performed for "marking" the nodes in the tree. Leaves will be "undefeated" nodes (or "U" nodes, for short), as they have no defeaters. Then we can propagate the marking from the leaves upward to the root as follows: an inner argument A_i in the tree will be marked as a "defeated" node ("D" node) if it has *at least* one "undefeated" child. Otherwise, if every child of A_i is a "D" node, then A_i will be marked as "U" node. If the root of a dialectical tree (the argument *Arg*) turns out to be marked as "U" node, then it is ultimately undefeated (given the

---

[1] The symbol "~" stands for negation [13]. Thus, ~p accounts for the negation of p.

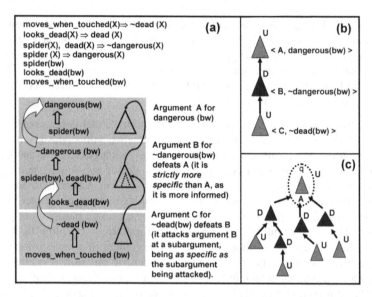

Fig. 1. Overview of the main elements in argumentation systems: (a) Commonsense knowledge, arguments and conflicts among arguments (Ex. 1); (b) Dialectical analysis for "bw is dangerous" (Ex. 1); (c) Graphical representation of a dialectical tree involving many arguments

knowledge available), so that the argument *Arg* (and its conclusion) is said to be *warranted* (i.e. ultimately accepted). Fig. 1(b) illustrates the dialectical analysis rooted in argument *ArgA* with respect to Example 1. In this particular example the dialectical tree involves just one branch, as *ArgA* has one defeater *ArgB*, which in turn is defeated by *ArgC*. Note that the marking procedure makes *ArgC* to be considered a "U" node (undefeated), as it has no defeaters. *ArgB* is then a "D" node (defeated), as it has at least one undefeated child (*ArgC*). The root of the tree (*ArgA*) is a "U" node, as every of its children (i.e., the argument *ArgB*) is marked as a "D" node. Consequently, *ArgA* and its conclusion *"bw is dangerous"* are warranted. Clearly, in complex situations the dialectical tree can actually involve many branches, each of them with several arguments, as shown in Fig. 1(c).[2]

Implemented argumentation systems provide valuable help for users who want to reason with incomplete and potentially inconsistent information stored in a knowledge base. Given a knowledge base K, such systems *automatically* compute the dialectical tree associated with any particular claim (provided by the user as an input). In this context, Defeasible Logic Programming (DeLP)[3] is a general-purpose argumentation system which has been particularly successful in real-world applications (e.g. recommender systems [11] and decision support systems [12]), providing an integrated environment for defining a knowledge base and solving user queries (claims) interactively. For any claim the DeLP engine automatically computes and visualizes the emerging dialectical tree, which acts as an explanation facility for the user,

---

[2] For an in-depth treatment of defeasible argumentation (in particular the process for computing warranted arguments) see [2,13].

[3] See http://lidia.cs.uns.edu.ar/delp_client

helping him to understand why the given claim is warranted or not. As we have seen in this Section, warranted arguments support *beliefs that are accepted beyond dispute* on the basis of the knowledge available. This notion can be applied in different contexts. In particular, in *multiple-party reasoning*, where a group of several people participate on the basis of some common knowledge (e.g. students in a CSCL scenario), warranted arguments can be seen as supporting beliefs which are part of the *shared knowledge* of the group. In the next section we will analyze how this idea can be integrated in a CSCL framework to characterize part of the emerging SK and its associated SKA by making use of a general-purpose argumentation system like DeLP as a support tool.

4   A Framework for Modelling SK and SKA Through Argumentation as a Support Tool

In what follows we will present a generic framework for integrating an automated argumentation system like DeLP as a support tool for dialectical discussions in a CSCL framework. Our framework will allow to model dialectical analyses carried out by participants in CSCL scenarios, helping them to identify the emerging SK and the explicit specification of its associated SKA. As a starting point we will consider the individual knowledge constructed by different students when performing a collaborative task (probably expressed in natural language and stored in a generic CSCL platform). We depart from the assumption that the knowledge required for solving the collaborative task is complex, so that students should be able to integrate different perspectives and conflicting opinions about the task to be solved.

Our goal is that participating students can make use of the reasoning and visualization capabilities provided by the argumentation system in order to support part of their SK construction as well as making explicit its associated SKA. Since knowledge is normally constructed iteratively by using several alternative tools (e.g. concept maps, virtual blackboards, etc.), in some cases the SK construction derived from our proposal can be later extended by means of these tools.

Fig. 2 shows a schematic view of the framework that characterizes the proposed model. For the sake of simplicity, in Fig. 2 we restrict ourselves to a particular group of only two students S1 and S2, although the proposal can be generalized to more participants. Our proposal is based on extending a conventional CSCL framework by adding the following elements:

- A *knowledge base K* which stores the individual knowledge (characterized in terms of facts and defeasible rules) constructed by each student at the beginning of the collaborative learning process.
- An automated *argumentation system* (as described in Section 3) capable of solving students' queries associated with potential claims, providing as well visualization facilities for analyzing results (e.g. visualizing the dialectical tree).
- A *Knowledge Engineer* (KE) with a solid understanding of argumentation in general and of the deployed argumentation system in particular. In many cases, with the appropriate training and support, the teacher involved in the CSCL learning process will be able to assume this role.

At the beginning, every student in the group has to exchange messages with the KE about what he/she has learnt.[4] Note that the KE is not necessarily an expert in the task to be solved collaboratively. Instead, his role will be translating different pieces of knowledge provided by each student Si (in natural language) into a set Ki of facts (strict knowledge) and defeasible rules (representing defeasible knowledge the student has learnt). This set Ki is then included as part of the knowledge base K. This exchange involves an active participation of both the student and the KE, until the student is satisfied with what the KE has written. Note that by doing this, each student has to perform a metacognition activity (construction of the *Individual Knowledge* and the *Individual Knowledge Awareness*) on the basis of the disagreements he/she has had with the KE. Indeed, the student can go back and forth in the learning process to complete, reinforce or enhance his/her individual knowledge until he/she is satisfied with the representation adopted by the KE. It must be remarked that the KE is only in charge of translating the student statements into facts or defeasible rules without judging them (i.e. whether they are true or false). In addition, the KE is not contrasting the student's contribution against the information already stored in K (coming from other participants). This way, possibly inconsistent, incomplete and contradictory rules will be added to K, which will store the sum of the individual knowledge coming from every student in the group.

When the students meet again (oval "Group" in Fig. 2) to solve the original task T, they are allowed to see everyone's contribution in K, so that their SK about how to solve the task T is in principle the sum of the knowledge of all participants involved (expressed in terms of facts and rules). Note that the visualization of K itself provides an explicit element which models part of the current SKA of the group (elements explicitating SKA are depicted in grey in Fig. 2). As usual in every CSCL learning process, students will have now to agree about their SK as a necessary step for solving T. In order to do this a dialectical discussion is performed among students, complemented by other activities (dotted lines in Fig. 2, as e.g. the joint drawing of concept maps). This dialectical discussion is aimed to achieve a consensus about the SK and tends naturally to be biased (given each student's previous knowledge and profile). For minimizing this bias and providing additional support for modelling the students' dialogues, our proposal incorporates the automatic computation of arguments.

Indeed, students will be able to analyze different claims by posing queries using the front-end from an argumentation system environment (as the one provided by DeLP). Based on K and by means of the provided argument-based engine, queries will allow to automatically find *warranted arguments* supporting a given claim. This way, potential disagreements among students can be analyzed, discussed and solved on the basis of a formal, objective approach which only relies on the available information stored in K, which stands for the sum of individual knowledge of all participants involved. As a result from this process, students will be able to identify what we call *Argument-Based Shared Knowledge* (ArgSK). As depicted in Fig. 2, this ArgSK will be formed by the sum of all individual facts in K (contributed by each student), as well as by all those warranted arguments derived from students' queries (as they are

---

[4] It must be remarked that, if neccesary, the professor in charge of the group together with the KE can provide a minimal knoweldge base K to help students to start the learning process.

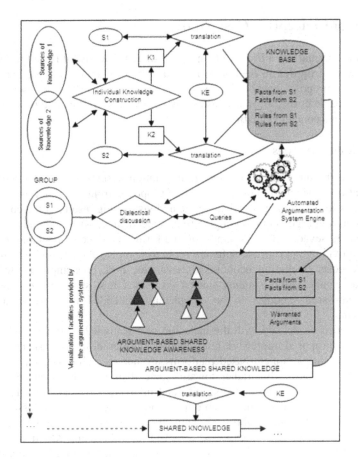

Fig. 2. Outline of the Framework. S1 and S2 represent two students, K1 and K2 represent the students' knowledge, and KE stands for Knowledge Engineer support.

ultimately accepted on the basis of the sum of the students' individual knowledge). Besides, the visualization of the dialectical tree associated with every warranted argument provides an additional, explicit element that characterizes what we call *Argument-Based Shared Knowledge Awareness* (ArgSKA): students are aware of how different conflicting pieces of knowledge are related to each other, why some of such pieces should be deemed as warranted (and some others should not), and how their own individual knowledge may be in conflict with other participants' knowledge. At the end of the construction of SK and SKA, ArgSK can be translated again to natural language sentences with the help of the KE, if necessary. This translation will help students to provide an adequate solution to the original task *T* to be collaboratively solved. Finally, the translated ArgSK and the corresponding ArgSKA evidence (visualization of dialectical trees) can be added to the global SK of the group, which will use these new rationally justified (and consequently unbiased) knowledge to solve *T* by carrying out the next steps of the CSCL process.

5 Proof of Concept: A Case Study

This section summarizes a Proof of Concept to show the workability and feasibility of the framework proposed in Section 4. First, a feasibility analysis is presented to ensure that our proposal can be deployed in CSCL frameworks in a useful manner within reasonable costs. Second, a case study is presented to illustrate how the framework works in a concrete situation.

5.1 Feasibility Analysis

Our proposal requires an automated argumentation system to be integrated in the CSCL platform, which should include an appropriate front-end for posing queries, and facilities for defining a knowledge base and visualizing results of the computation of the underlying argumentation engine (e.g. dialectical trees). As already mentioned in Section 3, several of such kinds of platforms are freely available nowadays [13, 14], providing appropriate software tools to compute ArgSK and ArgSKA with reasonable costs (including economical resources, time consumption, etc.). Thus, automated argumentation systems can be seen as a first step on the construction of argument-based modules to be completely embedded in a particular CSCL environment.

Clearly, costs associated with the inclusion of a Knowledge Engineer (KE) along the use of the proposed framework must be also considered. In that respect, it must be noted that existing argument-based platforms are not specially oriented towards experts on argumentation, but rather towards general users with a conceptual understanding about the meaning of facts, rules and inference by means of rule chaining. Such concepts are intuitive and suitable for students to learn and use (assuming they have basic abstract thinking abilities). Thus, the coordinator of the CSCL proposal (e.g. the teacher) can be also expected to act in the role of the KE, translating sentences from natural language into defeasible rules and facts (required to construct the knowledge base) while keeping an active dialogue and participation from the students. The existence of graphical front-ends included in some argumentation platforms [14] minimizes the complexity of text input for rules and facts as well as the interpretation of obtained results. Finally, from the CSCL viewpoint, it must be remarked that the integration of Artificial Intelligence techniques and CSCL has proven to be fruitful, resulting in systems such as I-MINDS [15] or SCALE [16].

5.2 A Case Study

Consider the following case study: Computer Science students from three different universities U_1, U_2 and U_3 (located in different cities) have to solve an activity collaboratively in a CSCL scenario. The activity is structured using the *JIGSAW* technique [17] and includes the task T of *detecting good and bad features in different configurations of a personal computer model called "pcu" (acronym for "PC for universities")*, which is the computer model available in the computer labs of the three universities (e.g. the three labs have pcu's with the same configuration, devices, etc). The students are divided into small groups of three people, each of them belonging to a different university. Following the JIGSAW technique, each member of the group will be responsible for analyzing a different piece of knowledge when constructing his/her Individual Knowledge. Let us focus on one jigsaw group G formed by three students, namely S_1, S_2 and S_3. As stated before, we will assume that S_1, S_2 and S_3 are using a particular CSCL system to solve T, as they are located in different cities. For the sake of example the students must learn about different topics related to pcu's as follows: 1) S_1 is assigned the topic "input/output devices"; 2) S_2 is assigned the topic "memory devices"; and 3) S_3 is assigned the topic "processors". Let us assume that students have already constructed their Individual Knowledge and they are coming back to the group G to solve T. At this moment, S_1, S_2 and S_3 have to present a well-organized report to the others members of G about the topic each of them has studied. The immediate goal is to construct SK and SKA in order to solve T. As a part of their SK and SKA, students are offered to construct their ArgSK and ArgSKA. Following our proposal, an automated argumentation platform is integrated with the CSCL scenario. It includes a knowledge base K (empty at the beginning), an inference engine for computing arguments and a suitable front-end for posing queries and visualizing results. Besides, a Knowledge Engineer *(KE)* will help S_1, S_2 and S_3 to translate their individual knowledge into facts and defeasible rules.

First, each student S_i exchanges (separately) messages with the KE about what he/she knows, and the KE writes down this in terms of rules and facts. Following our example, suppose that student S_1 has acquired knowledge about printers (as they are I/O devices). He/she has learnt the following:[5] *hp1020 and hp1018 are usually abbreviations of laser printers. Laser printers work ok if the computer has a good RAM memory. Inkjet printers work usually ok with any kind of computers.* Besides, S_1 has checked the computer model "pcu" (the object of study) and has seen that there was a printer connected, namely the hp1020. In the same way, S_2 has studied memory devices. He/she has learnt that *a RAM memory of 256 Mb or more is usually good enough for a computer, unless you want to use it with a laser printer, since in such a case a RAM of 256 KB has slow access, which is usually not a good feature.* In addition, S_2 has checked the computer model "pcu" and has seen that the computer had 256Mb of RAM memory (note that S_2 doesn't know anything about processors or printers, he just knows that they appeared as related concepts when learning about memory devices). Concerning S_3, he/she has individual knowledge about processors. He/she has learnt that *if a computer has a processor double-core, then the processor is usually fast. Pentium processors result in slow access time for RAM memory. An exception are Pentiums with the special swap technology, which do not have this problem.* He/she has checked the computer model "pcu" and has seen that it has a Pentium processor with "swap technology". At the end of all the dialogues between S_1, S_2 and S_3 with the KE, the knowledge base K stores the sum of the three students' individual knowledge, which could have been written down by the KE as follows:

Facts about the Object of Study under Analysis (Strict Knowledge)
% Facts about the computer in the lab

-    *printer(pcu, hp1020)*   *% fact from student S1*
-    *has_ram (pcu,256)*   *% fact from student S2*
-    *processor (pcu,pentium)*   *% fact from student S3*

---

[5] Names and values used here are fictitious. They are just considered for the sake of the example and not necessarily according to a real-world situation.

Defeasible rules (Commonsense knowledge) %C stands for an arbitrary computer
% Knowledge about printers coming from S₁
- *printer(C, hp1020) ⇒ printer(C, laser)*
- *printer(C, hp1018) ⇒ printer(C, laser)*
- *ram_memory(C,good) and printer(C, laser) ⇒ printer_ok(C)*
- *printer(C, inkjet) ⇒ printer_ok(C).*
% Knowledge about RAM memories coming from S₂
- *has_ram (C,X), X>=256 ⇒ ram_memory (C, good)*
- *has_ram (C,X), X=256, printer(X,laser) ⇒ ram_slow_access(C)*
- *ram_slow_access (C) ⇒ ~ram_memory (C,good)*
% Knowledge about processors coming from S₃
- *processor(C,double_core) ⇒ processor(C, fast)*
- *processor(C,pentium) ⇒ ram_slow_access (C)*
- *processor(C,pentium), has_processor(pentium,swap_tech) ⇒ ~ram_slow_ access (C)*

Now, consider that as part of task T to solve (detecting good and bad features in different configurations of a "pcu"), S_1, S_2 and S_3 are discussing about the piece of knowledge "*printer_ok(pc)*", which stands for the claim "*is it ok to have a printer connected to the computer pcu?*". By analyzing the individual knowledge provided by each S_i separately, the members of G cannot infer anything (except from the facts provided). However, if they jointly consider all the information stored in K (which accounts for part of their SK) they can rely on the automated argumentation system to automatically compute a dialectical tree rooted in the above claim, which will include all possible combinations of arguments and defeaters related to the claim. This way, they can guarantee that those pieces of knowledge subject to dialectical discussions will be part of the SK only they are warranted on the basis of the joint knowledge of the group, thus avoiding dialectical discussion based on incomplete and biased perceptions of reality. Hence, if the claim results to be supported by a warranted argument, then the above piece of knowledge can be added to the ArgSK of G on the basis of rational and justified information.

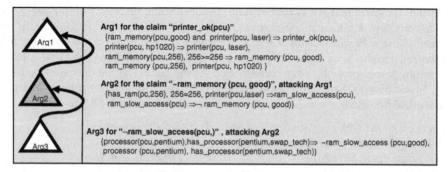

Fig. 3. Outline of the dialectical tree obtained for the claim "*is it ok to have a printer connected to the computer pcu?*". **Left:** Dialectical tree (white triangles represent warranted arguments, and grey triangle represent defeated arguments). **Right:** the argument contents provided by the argumentation engine.

In this particular example, S_1, S_2 and S_3 will obtain a warranted argument supporting the claim *"printer_ok(pcu)"* (as the warranted argument *Arg1* supports it), and
they will add the claim to their ArgSK. Note that the claim is deemed as warranted by
the underlying argumentation system, based on the dialectical tree shown in Fig. 3.
Besides, S_1, S_2 and S_3 will visualize the dialectical tree shown in Fig. 3 (left), which
explicitates a rational justification of the obtained results. Indeed, it can be seen that
there exist an argument *Arg1* supporting *"printer_ok(pcu)"*, which can be obtained by
combining knowledge from S_1 and S_2. The argument is based on knowing that "pcu"
has enough RAM memory to support hp1020, the laser printer connected to it. However, *Arg1* is defeated by *Arg2*, which supports the claim *"~ram_memory (pcu,
good)"* (the student who studied memory devices provided a defeasible rule which
states that 256 Mb usually do not suffice for a laser printer to run ok). But this argument *Arg2* is on its turn defeated by *Arg3* standing for *"~ram_slow_access(pcu)"* (the
student who studied processors provided a defeasible rule which states that computers
with Pentium processors with swap technology, as it is the case here, do not have
problems with RAM of 256 Mb). This way, the visualization of the tree will be linked
to the ArgSKA associated with the claim under consideration, helping S_1, S_2 and S_3 to
be aware of their own SK. Later on, S_1, S_2 and S_3 will be able to use the piece of
warranted knowledge (the fact that the printer connected will work ok) when going
further on the resolution of T.

6 Related Work

SK and SKA are key concepts when characterizing knowledge in CSCL scenarios.
Indeed, different proposals have been presented to model knowledge acquisition in
collaborative learning. For example, Kollar et al. introduced some methods to explicit
knowledge acquisition in CSCL by scripting [18]. Another example is shown in [19],
where a Knowledge-Building Environment (a software platform intended to support
collaborative learning) is proposed. Indeed, the process model of knowledge-building
presented in [19] provides a conceptual framework for the design, use and assessment
of collaborative systems. However, to the best of our knowledge, there are no other
approaches to extend a generic CSCL platform by incorporating automatic computation of SK as presented in this paper.

Concerning knowledge awareness, Collazos et al. have defined the notion of SKA
[1]. In addition, Ogata and Yano have proposed a mechanism to model it based on the
activities performed by the students [20]. Indeed, in [20] an information filtering
process is performed, referring to both finding desired information (filtering in) and
eliminating that which is undesirable (filtering out). Another relevant contribution is
shown in [21], where graphical representations are suggested to foster externalized
cognition and enhance the cognitive processes of managing knowledge and information in resource-based learning and problem solving environments. In this case,
knowledge and information visualizations have been shown to be effective for
enhancing the cognitive processes of learning [22]. Particularly, digital concept maps
seem to have a potential as cognitive tools to enhance individual and group-related
cognitive processes in resource-based learning and problem solving [22]. However, to
the best of our knowledge, there are no other proposals for automated construction of
explicit SKA as presented here.

Finally, it must be remarked that recent research has led to some interesting results to model dialectical discussions and negotiation in CSCL scenarios. For example, [23] discusses the understanding and participation in scientific discourses. Gervasi et al. [24] have proposed a mechanism to manage dialectical discussions when a group of people want to collaboratively define requirements in natural language. However, their proposal is based on constraint satisfaction techniques, and does not consider the use of argumentation. [25] and [26] have considered the use of argumentation and analytic reasoning on CSCL systems. However, these approaches are focused on argumentation as a meta-cognitive activity, not taking into account the automatization of argumentation nor aiming at the explicit construction of SKA, as proposed in this paper. A very interesting research work with some similarities to our approach is presented in [27], where the notion of negotiating about shared knowledge in CSCL is defined. A quantification of shared knowledge (called "degreement") is provided. Students can negotiate their beliefs about facts with the teacher, characterizing their own "perspective" as a result of this process. Interestingly, [27] mention also "argument exchange" as part of the SKA process. However, their approach does not rely on the use of a formal argumentation system, as in our case.

7 Conclusions Future Work

Shared Knowledge (SK) and its related Shared Knowledge Awareness (SKA) are key concepts to ensure an appropriate performance when solving activities collaboratively in a CSCL scenario. In this paper we have presented a novel approach for integrating automated argumentation systems as a support tool for characterizing SK and SKA in CSCL scenarios. Taking as starting point dialectical discussion of students performed in natural language when constructing SK and SKA, we have shown how argumentation systems can be used to model SK in terms of a general knowledge base which includes the individual knowledge of every participant.

The notion of warranted argument and its automated computation and visualization by means of dialectical trees provides a way of characterizing what we have called ArgSK and ArgSKA. The generic framework presented here has been tested in a prototypical version under different situations (all of them involving the resolution of a given task by collaboration), using DeLP as underlying argumentation system. At the current stage of research the obtained results account for a proof of concept of our proposal, and a full-fledged implementation (integrating CSCL and argumentation) is under development for evaluating more complex situations.

As the notions of SK and SKA are not defined using a logical formalization (as is the case for argumentation), part of our future work will be focused on establishing the scope of this proposal in real CSCL scenarios. In particular, we are interested in those cases involving a considerable volume of information or a large number of students, where the efficiency of the process required to construct the arguments is a critical problem to be solved. Research in this direction is currently being pursued.

Acknowledgment. We thank the reviewers for their comments which helped to improve the final version of this paper. This research was partially supported by projects 24/ZN10 (Secretaría de Ciencia y Tecnología, UNS, Argentina), PICT 13096, PICT

15043 and PAV076 (ANPCyT, Argentina); ADACO TIN2004-08000-C03-03 (Spain); IEA TIN2006-15662-C02-01 (Spain); Colciencias 4128-14-18008 (Colombia) and Colcencias 030-2005 (Colombia).

References

[1] Collazos, C., Guerrero, L., Pino, J., Ochoa, S.: Introducing Knowledge-Shared Awareness. In: Procs. of IASTED'02, USA, pp. 13–18 (2002)

[2] Chesñevar, I., Maguitman, A., Loui, R.: Logical Models of Argument. ACM Computing Surveys 32(4), 337–383 (2000)

[3] Kirschner, P., Buckingham, S., Carr, C. (eds.): Visualizing Argumentation: Software Tools for Collaborative and Educational Sense-Making. Springer, London (2003)

[4] Parsons, S., Maudet, N., Moraitis, P., Rahwan, I. (eds.): ArgMAS 2005. LNCS (LNAI), vol. 4049. Springer, Heidelberg (2006)

[5] González, M.P., Collazos, C.A., Granollers, T.: Guidelines and usability principles to design and test Shared-Knowledge Awareness for a CSCL interface. In: Dimitriadis, Y.A., Zigurs, I., Gómez-Sánchez, E. (eds.) CRIWG 2006. LNCS, vol. 4154, pp. 102–117. Springer, Heidelberg (2006)

[6] Maisonnasse, O., Brdiczka, N., Gourier, P.R.: Attentional Model for Perceiving Social Context in Intelligent Environments. In: 3rd IFIP Conference on Artificial Intelligence Applications and Innovations (AIAI), pp. 171–178. Springer, Heidelberg (2006)

[7] Janssen, J., Gijsbert, E., Kanselaar, G.: Visualization of agreement and discussion processes during computer-supported collaborative learning. Comput. Hum. Behav. 23(3), 1105–1125 (2007)

[8] Cadiz, J., Gupta, A., Grudin, J.: Using Web annotations for asynchronous collaboration around documents. In: Proc. of the ACM CSCW'2000 Conf. on Computer-Supported Cooperative Work, pp. 309–318. ACM Press, New York (2000)

[9] Eklundh, K.S., Rodriguez, H.: Coherence and Interactivity in Text-Based Group Discussions around Web Documents. In: Proc. 37th Int. Conf. on System Sciences (HICSS'04), IEEE Computer Society, pp. 1530–1605. IEEE Computer Society Press, Los Alamitos (2004)

[10] Simari, G., Loui, R.A: Mathematical Treatment of Defeasible Reasoning and its Implementation. Artificial Intelligence 53, 125–157 (1992)

[11] Chesñevar, C., Maguitman, A., Simari, G.: Argument-Based Critics and Recommenders: A Qualitative Perspective on User Support Systems. Data & Knowledge Engineering 59(2), 293–319 (2006)

[12] Brena, R., Aguirre, J., Chesñevar, C., Ramirez, E., Garrido, L.: Knowledge and Information Distribution Leveraged by Intelligent Agents. In: Knowledge and Information Systems (KAIS), Springer, Heidelberg (in press, 2007)

[13] García, A., Simari, G.: Defeasible Logic Programming: An Argumentative Approach. Theory and Practice of Logic Programming 4(1), 95–138 (2004)

[14] Reed, C., Rowe, G.: Araucaria: Software for Argument Analysis, Diagramming and Representation. Int. J. on Artificial Intelligence Tools 13(4), 961–979 (2004)

[15] Liu, X., Zhang, X., Soh, L-K., Al-Jaroodi, J., Jiang, H.: A Distributed, Multiagent Infrastructure for Real-Time, Virtual Classrooms. In: Proc. ICCE'2003, pp. 640–647 (2003)

[16] Soller, A., Guizzardi, R., Molani, A., Perini, A.: SCALE: supporting community awareness, learning, and evolvement in an organizational learning environment. In: Proc. of the 6th international conference on Learning sciences, pp. 489–496 (2004)

[17] Aronson, E., Blaney, N., Stephin, C., Sikes, J., Snapp, M.: The jigsaw classroom. Sage Publishing, Beverly Hills, CA (1978)

[18] Kollar, I., Fischer, F., Slotta, J.D.: Internal and external collaboration scripts in webbased science learning at schools. In: Koschmann, T., Suthers, D., Chan, T.-W. (eds.) CSCL 2005: The Next 10 Years, pp. 331–340. Lawrence Erlbaum, Mahwah (2005)

[19] Stahl, G.: A Model of Collaborative Knowledge-Building. In: Fishman, B., O'Connor, S. (eds.) 4th Int. Conf. of the Learning Sciences, pp. 70–77. Erlbaum, Mahwah (2000)

[20] Ogata, H., Yano, Y.: Combining knowledge awareness and information filtering in an open-ended collaborative learning environment. Int. Journal of Artificial Intelligence in Education 11, 33–46 (2000)

[21] Cox, R.: Representation construction, externalised cognition and individual differences. Learning and Instruction 9, 343–363 (1999)

[22] Tergan, S.-O., Keller, T. (eds.): Knowledge and Information Visualization. LNCS, vol. 3426. Springer, Heidelberg (2005)

[23] Driver, R., Newton, P., Osborne, J.: Establishing the norms of scientific argumentation in classrooms. Science Education 84(3), 287–313 (2000)

[24] Gervasi, V., Zowghi, D.: Reasoning about inconsistencies in natural language requirements. ACM Trans. Softw. Eng. Methodol. 14(3), 277–330 (2005)

[25] Yeung, D., Lowrance, J.: Computer-Mediated Collaborative Reasoning and Intelligence Analysis. In: Mehrotra, S., Zeng, D.D., Chen, H., Thuraisingham, B., Wang, F.-Y. (eds.) ISI 2006. LNCS, vol. 3975, pp. 1–13. Springer, Heidelberg (2006)

[26] Weinberger, A., Fischer, F.: A framework to analyze argumentative knowledge construction in computer-supported collaborative learning. Computers & Educ. 46, 71–95 (2006)

[27] Pfister, H., Wessner, M., Holmer, T., Steinmetz, R.: Negotiating about Shared Knowledge in a Cooperative Learning Environment. In: Proc. of the CSCL Conf., USA, pp. 454–457 (1999)

Deployment of Ontologies for an Effective Design of Collaborative Learning Scenarios

Seiji Isotani and Riichiro Mizoguchi

The Institute of Scientific and Industrial Research, Osaka University,
8-1 Mihogaoka, Ibaraki, Osaka, 565-0047, Japan
isotani@acm.org, miz@ei.sanken.osaka-u.ac.jp

Abstract. Two of the most important research subjects during the development of intelligent authoring systems (IAS) for education are the modeling of knowledge and the extraction of knowledge flows from theory to practice. It bridges the gap between theoretical understanding about learning and the practical foundations of design the knowledge of intelligent systems that support the learning process. Developing an IAS for collaborative learning is especially challenging in view of knowledge representation because it is based on various learning theories and given the context of group learning where the synergy among the learner's interactions affect the learning processes and hence, the learning outcome. The main objective of this work is to introduce an ontological infrastructure on which we can build a model that describes learning theories and to show how we can use it to develop programs that provide intelligent guidance to support group activities based on well-grounded theoretical knowledge.

Keywords: Collaborative learning design, ontological engineering, knowledge representation, intelligent authoring system, learning theory.

1 Introduction

In recent years, with the increasing use of technology, Artificial Intelligence has been gradually and successfully introduced into Education. However, major challenges still remain. Among these, we are interested in how to represent the knowledge of **intelligent authoring systems (IAS)** and then how to use this knowledge efficiently, especially within the context of collaborative learning.

Usual approaches to such issues provide their systems with a kind of expertise using a set of heuristics and domain theories built in the procedures (programming languages). This means that the programmers, not the systems, have an understanding of the knowledge being used. As a result, these systems cannot share or build new knowledge, they ignore the existence of theories on which the knowledge is based, and finally cannot justify their recommendations systematically and scientifically [2; 15].

To develop IAS to support **collaborative learning (CL)** is especially challenging in view of knowledge representation. Current knowledge concerning CL is based on various learning theories, which are always expressed in natural language and are

J.M. Haake, S.F. Ochoa, and A. Cechich (Eds.): CRIWG 2007, LNCS 4715, pp. 223–238, 2007.

particularly complex given the context of group learning where the synergy among learner's interactions affect the learning processes and hence learning outcome. It is in fact currently difficult for both humans and computers to clearly understand and differentiate between the various learning theories; however without their explicit representation, it is difficult to support the design of group activities based on well-grounded theoretical knowledge.

Our approach calls upon techniques of ontological engineering to, at first, establish a common understanding of what a learning theory is by representing it in terms of its explicitness, formalism, concepts and vocabulary. This makes theories understandable both by computers and humans. We then propose techniques of reasoning on these theories which contribute to dynamic guiding and instructional planning. And finally, we present the **CHOCOLATO** - a *Concrete Helpful Ontology-aware COllaborative Learning Authoring TOol* focusing on a sub-system that represents theories graphically to facilitate the design of effective CL activities with theoretical justifications.

2 Collaborative Learning and Learning Theories

Collaborative learning has become a popular method used by teachers in classrooms and in e-learning environments. In spite of that, designing effective CL sessions or analyzing the interaction processes among learners to capture what really happens in each session have been a very complex job due to a lack of comprehensible models for representing what is going on [10]. According to Dillenbourg [7], the key to understanding collaborative learning is to gain an understanding of the interactions among the individuals.

Many learning theories contribute to in-depth understanding and the support of collaborative learning (for instance, peer tutoring, anchored instructions, etc). However, it is not common to find models that allow explicit representation of these theories. One of the reasons is the difficulty to understand the theories due to its complexity and ambiguity. According to [9] different theories can describe the same situation using different terminologies. Moreover, each theory has its own point of view, learning focus, structure, besides many other aspects that need to be considered.

Therefore, to provide systems with theoretical knowledge for collaborative learning we must: a) to establish a common conceptual infrastructure on which we can build a model that describes what a learning theory is and what a collaborative learning is; b) to clarify how learning theories can help the design of group activities and enhance learning outcomes; and c) to propose models and structures that enable the sharing of findings and the use of computers to support the analysis and design of effective CL sessions in compliance with theories.

To deal with the problems presented above we provide a model based on an ontological structure to describe learning theories for collaborative learning and techniques to use it rationally. With that we aim to establish the initial foundations for the development of ontology-aware authoring systems for CL.

3   Graphical Representation of Learning Theories

The use of ontological engineering and ontologies for knowledge systematization have shown significant results to bridge the deep conceptual gap between how to represent the knowledge of authoring systems, considering educational theories, and how to use it adequately [6; 9; 15]. In practical terms ontological engineering helps to achieve the following [5; 16]: (a) a common vocabulary and highly structured definition of concepts; (b) semantic interoperability and high expressiveness; (c) coherence and systematization of knowledge; and (d) meta-models and foundations for solving different problems in a variety of contexts.

In CSCL (Computer Supported Collaborative Learning) research, ontologies have been successfully applied to solve problems such as: group formation [20], CL representation [12], interaction analysis and patterns [10] and modeling of learner's development [11]. With these achievements it is possible to some extent to successfully identify which kind of collaboration occurs in a CL session, to partially understand the essence of the group's interactions, and to estimate the expected educational benefits for each learner. Nevertheless, there are some limitations: (a) there is no explicit relation among interaction patterns and learner's development model; (b) it is not easy to determine what learning theory is appropriate for explaining the learner's development through a set of events; and (c) it is difficult to propose activities in compliant with the theories to enhance interactions among learners and lead them to achieve desired goals.

To overcome these limitations in previous work we clarify the relationships among interactions and learners development to understand how learning strategies provided by learning theories can help learners to acquire desired goals [13]. To allow such understanding we analyze each interaction inspired by learning theories proposed in [10] and using a structure called influential I_L event we divided the interaction process in two events: instructional event and learning event. Every instructional event has a reciprocity relationship with the learning events. In other words, during the teaching-learning process, when a person speaks, the other listens; when someone asks a question, the other answers; and so on. Each event has a related action (or actions) and its correspondent educational benefits (*I-goal*) to the initiator of the action. These actions and educational benefits are directly associated with the context (learning theory), the strategies (*Y<= I-goal*) and the roles that learners use to collaborate with other learners (Figure 1).

Based on such understanding of interactions and considering the previous achievements we propose an ontological structure to describe an excerpt of learning theories as shown in Figure 2. This structure consists of two main parts: the Learning Strategy and the Teaching-Learning Process. The Learning Strategy, composed by the members of a group and the goals of one leaner (I-role), specifies how (*Y<= I-goal*) the learner (*I-role*) should interact with other member of the group (*You-role*) to achieve his objectives (*I-goal*). For instance, in Cognitive Apprenticeship a learner interacts with other learners to guide them during the resolution of a problem. In this case the learning strategy (*Y<= I-goal*) used by this learner is "*learn by guiding*", his role (*I-role*) is known as a "*master role*", the role of the learner who receives the guidance (*You-role*) is known as an "*apprentice role*", and the goals of the learner who guide (*I-goal*) are to acquire cognitive skills (and meta-cognitive skills) at an autonomous level. Previous works of Inaba et al. [12] show the strategies (*Y<= I-goal*), learner's roles (*I-role* and *You-role*) and individual goals (*I-goal*) of several learning theories.

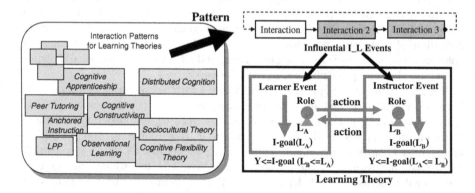

Fig. 1. Analysis of interaction patterns – relationship among interaction, strategies and roles

The Teaching-Learning Process specifies the interaction pattern of a learning theory represented by the necessary and desired interaction activities (processes) among two member of a group (for instance, master and apprentice). As mentioned before, we can describe interactions using influential I_L event for explicitly representing the interaction and its benefits from both points of view: for those who do the action and for those who receive the action. Each Influential I_L event (instructional or learning event) is composed by an actor of an action, the action, and the benefits of the player of this action.

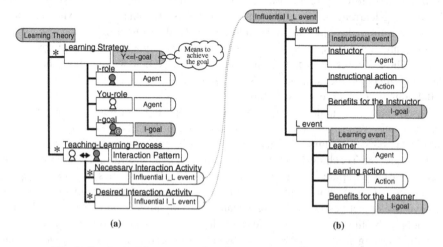

Fig. 2. Ontological Structure to describe an excerpt of Learning Theories

Then, we re-analyzed seven different learning theories frequently used to support CSCL activities: Cognitive Apprenticeship [3], Anchored Instruction [4], Peer Tutoring [8], Cognitive Flexibility [19], LPP [14], Socio-Cultural Theory [21] and Distributed Cognition [18]. And Finally, we proposed the **Growth Model Improved by Interaction Patterns (GMIP)** [13] to unify and to improve the benefits of two successful previous models that offer (a) an explicit representation of typical interactions based on learning theories [10]; and (b) a simplified way to represent the learner's growth (knowledge acquisition and skill development) [11]. With the GMIP we clarified how learning strategies prescribed by learning theories can help learners to acquire desired goals and explicitly identify the relationships among interactions, learning strategies and learning goals.

The GMIP is a graph model based on an ontological structure to describe an excerpt of learning theory [13]. It represents, in a simplified way, the learner's knowledge acquisition process in compliance with Rumelhart and Norman's work [17], and skill development process in compliance with Anderson's work [1]. It explains more precisely the relationships between learning strategies, educational benefits and interactions used to achieve these benefits. To introduce the GMIP, we have to explain more about two processes: knowledge acquisition and development of skill.

The process of acquiring specific knowledge includes three qualitatively different kinds of learning: **accretion**, **tuning** and **restructuring** [17]. *Accretion* is to add and to interpret new information in terms of pre-existent knowledge. *Tuning* is to understand knowledge through application of this knowledge in a specific situation. *Restructuring* is to consider the relationships in acquired knowledge and thus to rebuild the existent knowledge structure.

Considering the development of skills, there are also three phases of learning: the **cognitive stage** (rough and explanatory), the **associative stage** and the **autonomous stage** [1]. The cognitive stage involves an initial encoding of a target skill that allows the learner to present the desired behavior or, at least, some crude approximation. The associative stage is the improvement of the desired skill through practice. In this stage, mistakes presented initially are gradually detected and eliminated. The autonomous stage is one of gradual continued improvement in the performance of the skill.

Using these concepts, the GMIP graph has twenty nodes (Figure 3), which represent the levels of the learner's development at a certain moment of learning. Each node is composed by two triangles. The upper-right triangle represents the stage of knowledge acquisition, while the lower-left triangle represents the stage of skill development. The nodes are linked with arrows that show possible transitions between nodes in compliance with [1] and [17]. $s(x,y)$ is the simplified form of representing these nodes in our model: x represents the current stage of skill development and y represents the current stage of knowledge acquisition. For instance, $s(0,0)$ represents the node where the stage of skill development and knowledge acquisition is *nothing*; and $s(0,1)$ represents that the stage of skill development is *nothing* and the stage of knowledge acquisition is *accretion*.

Using the GMIP graph, we show the benefits of learning strategies by highlighting its path on the graph and associating each arrow with the interactions. In Figure 1 we show an example of the GMIP graph for the learning strategy *"learning by apprenticeship*" used by the learning theory "**Cognitive Apprenticeship**". Bold arrows represent the transition from one stage to the other, which is facilitated through this learning strategy using the labeled interactions. There are two kinds of interactions: the necessary interactions, represented by a black circle, and the complementary interactions, represented by a white circle. The interactions are linked by ellipses. The dashed ellipse represents a directed link between two interactions and the full ellipse represents a cyclical link between two interactions.

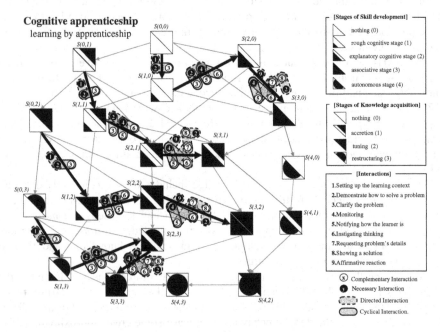

Fig. 3. Example of GMIP for learning by apprenticeship used by Cognitive Apprenticeship

The GMIP clarifies, more precisely, how interactions can affect learner's development, facilitating the learning design based on events. Thus, it becomes a powerful tool helping designers to select events (interactions) and roles for each learner considering interaction patterns and learning strategies appropriate for desired learning goals and sub-goals (and vice versa). Furthermore, we believe this model is the first step to explain what a learning theory is, making tacit characteristics explicit: for instance, clarifying expected benefits, use restrictions, guidelines for leading/performing activities, in addition to other important aspects of the teaching-learning process.

Another intriguing feature of GMIP that deserve some attention is the possibility of blending learning strategies. Because each strategy is intrinsically represented as paths on the GMIP graph, we can find common points (stages) between strategies, and thus, provide guidelines to blend learning theories by "*linking*" two or more strategies from different theories to achieve a desired goal. Considering such possibility during the design process a user could choose one strategy to lead learners to obtain some benefits and after change to another strategy to obtain other benefits that the first strategy could not offer. Note that we are not trying to say that it is possible to blend any strategy and any theory, what we want to point out is: *if we deeply understand the theories providing formal methods to represent them explicitly, it is possible to identify common points among theories and then propose techniques to blend them rationally.* To blend learning theories for CL is a challenging task and will be addressed more carefully and deeply in future research.

In summary, the main contributions of GMIP for CL design are (a) to allow the graphical visualization of theories and their characteristics. Thus, users can quickly interpret the theories, their benefits and propose sequence of activities in compliance with them; and (b) to provide a formal structure based on ontologies which allows systems to reasoning about the theories and the features (actions, roles, strategies, etc.) prescribed by them. Thus, it is possible to offer new alternatives for intelligent guidance (as shown in section 4) providing **suggestions of CL activities** for users during the design process.

4   Towards a Complete Ontology-Aware Authoring Tool for CL

As we mentioned before to propose a group formation there are many learning theories such as Anchored Instruction, Peer Tutoring, Cognitive Apprenticeship, etc. Then, to assign roles and strategies for members of a group we can select appropriate set of learning theories considering the necessary pre-conditions of learners and the educational benefits we expect to be improved for each learner in the end of a CL session. This flexibility of choosing different learning theories can therefore provide us with many ways to design and conduct learning processes. However, it also suggests the difficulty of selecting the appropriate set of learning theories during the instructional design to ensure learners' benefits and the consistency of learning processes. Therefore, to help users (instructors, teachers, designers, etc) to design effective group activities we need an elaborated authoring system that considers different learning theories to support the design in compliance with them.

According to [15] there is a deep conceptual gap between knowledge of authoring systems. Because of that these systems cannot share or accumulate new knowledge, usually are based on only one theory that is built in the procedures (programming code) to support the design of learning activities, and do not justify their recommend-dations systematically and scientifically.

Through a survey and an analysis of existing educational authoring systems (especially for intelligent tutoring) Bourdeau and Mizoguchi [2] verified that: *"few environments combine authoring tools and knowledge representation of instructional theories and principles, and that none of them possesses desired functionalities of an intelligent authoring system such as Retrieve appropriate theories for selecting instructional methods or Provide principles for structuring a learning environment"*.

To solve these problems we have been developing a theory-aware authoring system for CL, called *CHOCOLATO – a Concrete and Helpful Ontology-aware Collaborative Learning Authoring Tool*. It is based on our model GMIP and the ontological structure to describe learning theories, besides previous achievements presented in section 3. Through the use of ontologies, the theories and their features are declaratively and formally represented which (a) prevent unexpected interpre-tations of the theories; (b) provide a common vocabulary to describe them; (c) enable us to share and accumulate the knowledge; and (d) provide enough information for computational semantics to provide assistance for users based on theories. Furthermore, through the use of GMIP the system offers graphical and textual support for users providing "intelligent" guidance with theoretical justifications during the authoring process.

The architecture of CHOCOLATO is shown in Figure 4. The system is sub-divided in different sub-systems that aim to support different levels of guidance during (a) group formation that maximize the educational benefit considering the individual and group goals; (b) designing of CL activities; (c) recommendation of learning materials; (d) analysis of individual and group outcomes minimizing the difficulties during this process; and (e) proposing group re-formation and a new CL session based on learner's pre-conditions, desires and requirements. All sub-systems of CHOCOLATO are able to use three different ontologies (Learning Theory Ontology, Learning Process Ontology and CL Ontology) to support their reasoning. The connection among the sub-systems and the ontologies is made using the HOZO API (*http://www.hozo.jp*). The CL design manager controls the use of each sub-system during the design process through the authoring interface.

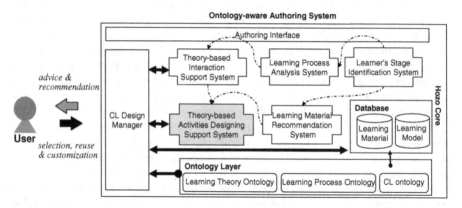

Fig. 4. Architecture of CHOCOLATO: Concrete Helpful Collaborative Learning Authoring Tool

This system assists both novice and expert users. For example, during the design process, for novice users, the design manager of CHOCOLATO provides a structured guidance considering different learning theories. Through an authoring interface using the GMIP it allows users to set initial conditions and goals for a learner or the group and the system automatically recommends theories, strategies, roles and activities to be performed by learners to achieve the desired goals. Furthermore, users can customize the recommendations in order to satisfy requirements depending on particular situations. For expert users, it offers a common language and guidelines to formally express CL activities, the interactions' flows learner's roles, strategies and benefits for learners. Thus, it is possible to describe new strategies and roles for learners, reuse and share them, and finally combine sequence of interactions to fit in different scenarios.

Considering the interaction analysis, it is difficult to know when learners acquire the desired benefit because we need to capture what roles the learners played and what kind of interactions occurred in the session. To help such process, the analysis system of CHOCOLATO identify when a CL session proceeds conform the initial scenario designed by the user. Thus, we can predict whether the learners interacted as expected and whether the CL session was successful or not. It is worth to point out that if the initial scenario of a CL session is not established previously it is much more difficult to expect concrete benefits and to analyze (quantitatively and qualitatively) how much benefits were attained by learners.

In this work we are focusing on design process in order to produce effective CL sessions. Thus, we would like to present a sub-system of CHOCOLATO (shaded block in figure 4) used to support the design of CL activities. This sub-system is called **MARI** – *Main Adaptive Representation Interface*. It is an ontology-aware system that uses ontologies developed in Hozo ontology editor to provide its theoretical knowledge and represent them on the screen using the GMIP. Through the use of ontologies MARI allows high expressiveness and interoperability among theories and their features. Nowadays MARI has 6 theories and 12 strategies, besides other information in its database.

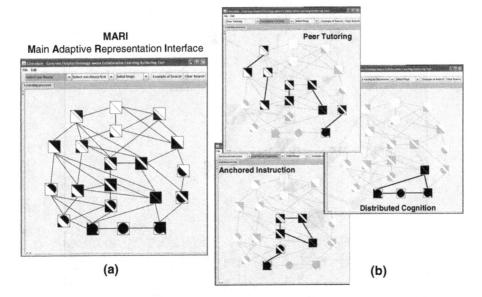

Fig. 5. Graphical visualization of different learning theories using different strategies

MARI starts with a neutral network (Figure 5a) that can represent any theory we analyzed by selecting theories/strategies through MARI's interface. MARI reasons on the ontologies to provide a graphical visualization of them using the GMIP. For example, in Figure 5b we show the theories: Peer Tutoring (using the strategy learning by teaching), Distributed Cognition (using the strategy learning by discussion) and Anchored Instruction (using the strategy learning by diagnosing). As you can observe, each of these theories has different pre-conditions to be performed and also different goals to be achieved. In the case of Peer Tutoring, a learner who follows the strategy learning by teaching (and plays the role of tutor) needs, as a precondition, the knowledge about a specific content in accretion stage, but does not necessary need skills about how to use it. In such situation, the main goal of the tutor is to acquire knowledge in tuning stage.

Each theory has strong and weak points, in our example, because the main focus of the theory Peer Tutoring is to help the tutor to obtain his benefits, it gives less attention to benefits for the learner who plays the role of tutee. On the other hand, in the case of Anchored Instructor using the strategy learning by diagnosing the learner who plays the role of instructor must have knowledge about the specific content and skills to use it to help other learners who have problems. Thus the learner-instructor can diagnose the problems of other students and solve them. The Anchored Instruction theory is interested in solving learner's problems (called anchors), thus the learner-instructor receive less attention in such situation.

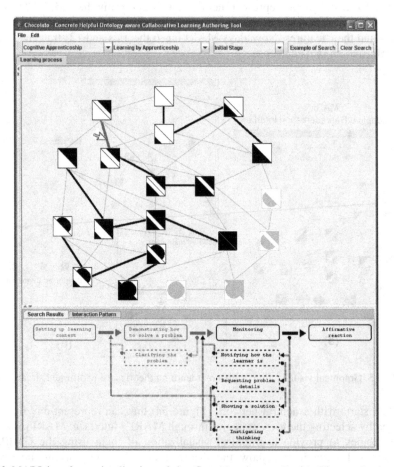

Fig. 6. MARI interface: visualization of the *Cognitive Apprenticeship* Theory. In the top it shows the learning path of the strategy *learning by apprenticeship* and in the bottom its related interactions pattern.

MARI has all these information in its database and can give recommendations for users offering an easy and quick interpretation of necessary pre-conditions and educational benefits for learners. Furthermore, by clicking in the bold arrows the system can suggest CL activities (interactions) prescribed by the selected theory which help learners in one stage to achieve the next stage. For example, using the theory Cognitive Apprenticeship and the strategy learning by apprenticeship presented in Figure 3, MARI shows in Figure 6 the necessary and complementary interactions as full boxes and dashed boxes, respectively (bottom of Figure 6). Finally when the user click in one bold arrow in the GMIP path (top of Figure 6), it shows which interactions are associates with this arrow (transition of stages).

Another useful function in MARI is to search theories by given a stage of learner's development. We can select an initial stage of a learner in the GMIP and the system will reason on the ontologies to search for any theory/strategy that has the selected stage in the beginning of the path. As same as before we can select a final stage and the system will search for any theory/strategy that has the selected stage in the end of the path. And finally, the system can search for any theory/strategy that has a path through the selected stage (it means any stage in the path). All these ways of search can be combined, thus, users can select, for example, an initial stage (pre-conditions) and a final stage (expected benefits) of a learner and the system will find the theories/strategies that help this learner to achieve the desired benefits. If more than one theory/strategy is found, users can select one of them and the system suggests activities in compliance with it.

In case we do not find any theory/strategy that helps a learner (or a group of learners) considering his initial conditions (initial stage) and desired goals (final stage), the idea of blended learning theories in the end of section 2.2, could be considered. In such a case a possible solution to help a learner is to use the GMIP to work with theories at the macro-level (strategies, learner's stages, etc) to select a strategy $S1$, which help learners in an stage $G1$ (initial stage) to achieve a following stage $G2$ (sub-goal), and then, to select another strategy $S2$, which help learners in an stage $G2$ to achieve a following stage $G3$ (final stage) that cannot be achieved by $S1$. After that, working with theories at the micro-level (activities, learner's roles, etc) the system is able to identify the sets of interactions of the strategies $S1$ and $S2$, combining them rationally, to finally, propose a sequence of CL activities that maintain the consistence of the learning process. These steps enable us to connect the strategies $S1$ and $S2$ and to create suitable set of interactions to help a learner in the initial condition, $G1$, to achieve his desired goals, $G3$.

To give an example of how to use the GMIP to blend strategies lets propose a problem: "*In a group, the desired goal of learner* **L**, *who does not have any content specific knowledge or skills,* **s(0,0)**, *is to attain skills in associative level and content specific knowledge in accretion level,* **s(3,1)**. *Considering that how can we design a collaborative learning session, supported by the theories, to help him?*"

To solve such problem, first, it is necessary to choose a theory and a strategy that lead the learner from $s(0,0)$ to $s(3,1)$ and after propose activities in agreement with it. To choose the theory/strategy, on Table 1 we show six learning theories, their strategies, roles for learners, and their respective paths in the GMIP graph. By using only a single theories in Table 1 it is impossible to help the learner L to achieve the desired goal $s(3,1)$.

Table 1. Relationships among learning theories, roles, strategies and expected benefits

Learning Theory	Learner's Role	Learning Strategy	Expected Benefits (I-goal) Initial stage → Following stage
Anchored Instruction	Anchor holder	Learning by being taught	$s(x,0){\rightarrow}s(x,1){\rightarrow}s(x,2)$; $x={0..4}$
	Anchored instructor	Learning by diagnosing	$s(2,1){\rightarrow}s(3,1){\rightarrow}s(3,2)$; $s(2,1){\rightarrow}s(2,2){\rightarrow}s(3,2)$; $s(2,3){\rightarrow}s(3,3)$;
Cognitive Apprenticeship	Apprenticeship	Learning by apprenticeship	$s(0,y){\rightarrow}s(1,y){\rightarrow}s(2,y){\rightarrow}s(3,y)$; $y={0..3}$
	Master	Learning by guiding	$s(3,y){\rightarrow}s(4,y)$; $y={0..3}$
Cognitive Flexibility	Audience	Learning by reflection	$s(x,2){\rightarrow}s(x,3)$; $x={0..4}$
	Panelist	Learning by self-expression	$s(2,y){\rightarrow}s(3,y)$; $y={1..3}$
Distributed Cognition	Full participant	Learning by discussion	$s(3,y){\rightarrow}s(4,y)$ and $s(x,2){\rightarrow}s(x,3)$; $x={3,4}$, $y={2,3}$
LPP	Peripheral participant	Learning by practice	$s(0,y){\rightarrow}s(1,y){\rightarrow}s(3,y)$; $y={0..3}$
	Full participant	Learning by discussion	$s(3,y){\rightarrow}s(4,y)$ and $s(x,2){\rightarrow}s(x,3)$; $x={3,4}$, $y={2,3}$
Peer Tutoring	Peer Tutee	Learning by being taught	$s(x,0){\rightarrow}s(x,1)$; $x={0..4}$
	Peer Tutor	Learning by teaching	$s(x,1){\rightarrow}s(x,2)$; $x={0..4}$

Using the GMIP and the idea of blending strategies, to achieve $s(3,1)$ from $s(0,0)$ we can combine learning strategies to develop skills and acquire some knowledge. As showed on Table 1, there are four learning strategies that initiate from $s(0,0)$: *learning by being taught* (used by Anchored Instruction and by Peer Tutoring), *learning by apprenticeship* (used by Cognitive Apprenticeship) and *learning by practice* (used by LPP). Nevertheless, none of them have a direct path to the desired goal $s(3,1)$. In such a situation, one strategy can be initially chosen and then be combined with another strategy to cover its lack. In Figure 7 we show one possible solution using the theory Anchored Instruction and the strategy learning by being taught. Thus, for this example we blended at the macro-level the strategies *learning by apprenticeship* (full arrows in Figure 7) and *learning by being taught* (dashed arrows in Figure 7) to find a path from $s(0,0)$ to $s(3,1)$. This solution provides four possible paths, labeled as A, B, C and D, to achieve the goal (bottom of Figure 7).

As a result of blending these two strategies, in compliance with the GMIP (Figure 7), on the bottom of Figure 8 we show at the micro-level the suggested sequence of interactions that intends to help the learner L to achieve $s(3,1)$ from $s(0,0)$ supported by *Cognitive Apprenticeship* and *Anchored Instruction*. The bold-dotted arrows labeled A, B, C and D in Figure 8, have their correspondent in Figure 7, and show where the set of interactions inside of the gray box AI (top of Figure 8) should be placed in the sequence of interactions of *Cognitive Apprenticeship* (bottom of Figure 8) to solve the problem. The gray box labeled AI is the set of interactions provided by *Anchored Instruction* which eventually helps the learner who plays the role of *anchored holder* to acquire some content specific knowledge in accretion stage, $s(x,1)$, using the strategy *learning by being taught*. This set of interactions supports the interactions provided by *Cognitive Apprenticeship*, which helps the learner who plays the role of *apprenticeship* to develop some skills in associative stage, $s(3,y)$, using the strategy *learning by apprenticeship*.

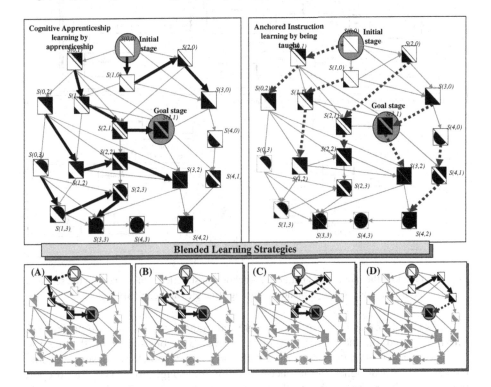

Fig. 7. In the top, two different strategies: *Learning by apprenticeship* (full arrows) and *Learning by being taught* (dashed arrows) at the macro-level to achieve the goal $s(3,1)$. In the bottom, it shows four different paths to achieve $s(3,1)$ from $s(0,0)$ done by blending the learning strategies.

Thus, the learner *L* can eventually acquire the desired benefits $s(3,1)$ during a CL session by adopting the suggested sequence of interactions as shown in the bottom of Figure 8.

It is worth to point out that to completely realize blended learning for CL it is necessary to consider the relationships among many assumptions described by theories (for instance, context, delivery methods, learning preferences, etc), besides the synergy among learners in a group. It is our intention for future research to include a more deep study demonstrating some examples and possibilities to blend learning strategies semi-automatically.

Using ontologies and the GMIP it is feasible for our system to reason on the theories at the macro and micro levels and to create a link between them. This link allows us to select appropriate learning theories and strategies at the macro-level and to suggest consistent sequence of activities for learners in a group at the micro-level.

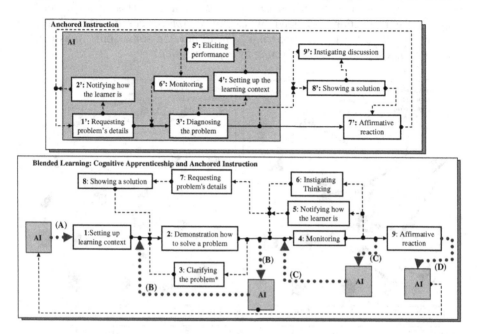

Fig. 8. On the top, the interactions pattern of Anchored instruction. On the bottom the sequence of suggested interactions based on blended learning strategies at the micro-level.

The suggestions given by our system are only guidelines for users to propose CL activities based on theories which (a) preserves the consistency of the learning process; and (b) guarantees a suitable path for learners to achieve desired benefits. However, expert designers do not need to follow the suggestions. They can propose their own path on the graph and their own sequence of activities. In such case the system also can assist these users providing different kind of information about theories, activities, strategies, learner's roles and other related information that can be useful in various situations.

5 Conclusions

The main contribution of this research is to introduce our model GMIP based on an ontological structure to describe learning theories for CL and create techniques to use it rationally. This is another step forward in the improvement of ontology-aware authoring systems that offer intelligent guidance to design CL activities supported by theoretical knowledge that solves, at least partially, the problems of knowledge representation presented in [15]. The proposed system MARI supported by our model GMIP and theories described as ontologies allow us to work with theories at the macro and micro levels and to create a link between them. This link clarifies, more precisely, how interactions can affect learner's development which helps designers to select interactions and roles for each learner with justifications based on the theories. It also allows us to reasoning on these theories semi-automatically to suggest consistent sequence of activities for learners in a group.

We also showed roughly the intriguing possibility of blending learning strategies using our model and our system as a feasible solution to deal with the problem of unreachable stages (stages that none of the analyzed theories has a path through it by itself). In such a case, during the CL design the system can suggest for users a set of activities supported by blended theories to find a suitable way to lead learners to achieve desired benefits. Our future work will deal with many open questions about blended learning theories for CL to improve our model and our system.

One delicate point we would like to emphasize is the necessity of sophisticated group formation to set strategies, roles and activities for each learner before a CL session starts. We believe that the design of CL sessions is a requisite to maximize educational benefits and to minimize the load of interaction analysis. Such approach creates favorable conditions for learners to perform CL activities and help users to estimate more easily how much benefits learners attain in the end of a session. Our approach uses theory-driven group formation with suggestions of role assignment and sequence of interactions to offer fundamental settings for an effective CL session and essential conditions to predict the impact of interactions in the learning process.

The possibility of clarifying what a CL session is and to amplify its educational benefits has been a great challenge. In this context our approach offers a declarative representation of learning theories allowing computational semantics to support the design of CL sessions in compliance with well-grounded theoretical knowledge and, because it can be explicitly demonstrated, is much more convincing and flexible than usual approaches.

References

1. Anderson, J.R.: Acquisition of Cognitive Skill, Psychological Review, 89(4), pp. 369–406 (1982)
2. Bourdeau, J., Mizoguchi, R.: Collaborative Ontological Engineering of Instructional Design Knowledge for an ITS Authoring Environment. In: Cerri, S.A., Gouardéres, G., Paraguaçu, F. (eds.) ITS 2002. LNCS, vol. 2363, pp. 399–409. Springer, Heidelberg (2002)
3. Collins, A.: Cognitive apprenticeship and instructional technology. Educational values and cognitive instruction, LEA, pp. 121–138 (1991)
4. Cognition and Technology Group at Vanderbilt: Anchored instruction in science education. Philosophy of science, cognitive psychology, and educational theory and practice, Albany, NY, SUNY Press, 244–273 (1992)
5. Devedzic, V.: Understanding Ontological Engineering. Communications of the ACM 45(4), 136–144 (2002)
6. Devedzic, V.: Web Intelligence and Artificial Intelligence in Education. Educational Technology & Society 7(4), 29–39 (2004)
7. Dillenbourg, P.: What do you mean by Collaborative Learning, Collaborative Learning and Computational Approaches, pp. 1–19. Elsevier Science, Oxford (1999)

8. Endlsey, W.R.: Peer tutorial instruction. Educational Technology, Englewood Cliffs, NJ (1980)

9. Hayashi, Y., Bourdeau, J., Mizoguchi, R.: Ontological Modeling Approach to Blending Theories for Instructional and Learning Design. In: Proceedings of the Int. Conference on Computers in Education. vol. 151, pp. 37–44 (2006)

10. Inaba, A., Ohkubo, R., Ikeda, M., Mizoguchi, R.: Models and Vocabulary to Represent Learner-to-Learner Interaction Process in Collaborative Learning. In: Proceedings of the Int. Conference on Computers in Education, pp. 1088–1096. IOS Press, Amsterdam (2003a)

11. Inaba, A., Ikeda, M., Mizoguchi, R.: What Learning Patterns are Effective for a Learner Growth? In: Proceedings of the Int. Conference on Artificial Intelligence in Education, pp. 219–226. IOS Press, Amsterdam (2003b)

12. Inaba, A., Supnithi, T., Ikeda, M., Mizoguchi, R., Toyoda, J.: How Can We Form Effective Collaborative Learning Groups? In: Gauthier, G., VanLehn, K., Frasson, C. (eds.) ITS 2000. LNCS, vol. 1839, pp. 282–291. Springer, Heidelberg (2000)

13. Isotani, S., Mizoguchi, R.: A Framework for Fine-Grained Analysis and Design of Group Learning Activities. In: Proceedings of the Int. Conference on Computers in Education. vol. 151, pp. 193–200 (2006)

14. Lave, J., Wenger, E.: Situated Learning: Legitimate peripheral participation. Cambridge University Press, New York (1991)

15. Mizoguchi, R., Bourdeau, J.: Using Ontological Engineering to Overcome AI-ED Problems. International Journal of Artificial Intelligence in Education 11(2), 107–121 (2000)

16. Mizoguchi, R.: Tutorial on Ontological Engineering - Part 1. New Generation Computing 21(4), 365–384 (2003)

17. Rumelhart, D.E., Norman, D.A.: Accretion, Tuning, and Restructuring: Modes of Learning, Semantic factors in cognition, LEA, pp. 37–53 (1978)

18. Salomon, G.: Distributed Cognitions. Cambridge University Press, New York (1993)

19. Spiro, R.J., Coulson, R.L., Feltovich, P.J., Anderson, D.K.: Cognitive flexibility theory: Advanced knowledge acquisition in ill-structured domains. In: annual conference of the cognitive science society, pp. 375–383. Lawrence Erlbaum, Mahwah (1988)

20. Supnithi, T., Inaba, A., Ikeda, M., Toyoda, J., Mizoguchi, R.: Learning Goal Ontology Supported by Learning Theories for Opportunistic Group Formation. In: Proceedings of the Int. Conference on Artificial Intelligence in Education, pp. 67–74. IOS Press, Amsterdam (1999)

21. Vygotsky, L.S.: Mind in Society: The Development of Higher Psychological Processes. Harvard University Press, Cambridge (1978)

Dynamic and Flexible Learning in Distributed and Collaborative Scenarios Using Grid Technologies

Andreas Harrer, Adam Lucarz, and Nils Malzahn

Collide Group, University Duisburg-Essen
{harrer,lucarz,malzahn}@collide.info

Abstract. This paper presents an architecture for the support of dynamic learning activities and its implementation in the GLIDE prototype. the learning courses are dynamically determined at runtime based on the available tools, devices, and situational context of a learner by using abstract descriptions of learning scenarios and the conceptual mapping of abstract activities to concrete learning support tools This is facilitated by the usage of grid service technology, e-Learning standards, and mechanisms to guarantee semantic interoperability of learning outcomes across various tools and learning activities.

1 Introduction

In recent years it can be observed that computer-supported learning moves from content-oriented and receptive courses (e.g. Hypermedia courses) to richer learner-centered scenarios, such as collaborative scenarios or scientific discovery / inquiry processes [1]. Yet, in these carefully designed learning activities there are very frequently limitations in the available technology and implementations: for example collaboration is very often limited to two children sharing the same computer [2], thus not allowing remote or asynchronous collaboration modes. Similar problems are, that usually the computer environment is closely tied to the learning scenario, which makes the re-use of the learning tools in other contexts difficult or that powerful learning tools, such as interactive simulations, exist independently of the chosen learning environment and cannot be integrated seamlessly into the learning scenario because of lack of interoperability and compatibility.

In contrast, technology-driven approaches, such as web services and the grid technology, i.e. the virtualization and distribution of computing resources, together with the proliferation of learning management systems open new perspectives for technology-supported learning. This brought up a reflection on the usefulness of web service technology for education [3] and the notion of "learning grid". This means that learning activities can be conducted by flexible assembly of distributed learning tools, content, and other resources, that might be provided by different parties. Some advances in this direction have been made in projects such as the GridCole [4] and OntoolCole [5] project. The first project combines formalized learning scenarios using the eLearning standard IMS/LD [5] with grid services for the different learning activities. In current work [5] ontological relations are used to discover concrete services at runtime to be bound to abstract service descriptions used in the LD

J.M. Haake, S.F. Ochoa, and A. Cechich (Eds.): CRIWG 2007, LNCS 4715, pp. 239–246, 2007.

document. Yet, this approach also contains some unresolved problems, such as the high effort of preparing existing tools to make them usable in this architecture. Another issue is the current lack of support of handling the transition of learning products between activities, which is required for most inquiry activities.

Based on a survey on current pedagogical and technological approaches and their potential synergies, we identified the following properties that are desirable for flexible computer-supported learning scenarios:

1. Flexible use and combination of a variety of learning tools.
2. Dynamic selection of tools based on the current learning context, e.g. learner's progress, available devices.
3. Support of learning processes by automatic sequencing and configuration of required learning environments.
4. Transferrability of learning products across different learning phases, i.e. tools have to be chosen based on semantic interoperability to use results in succeeding activities.

In this paper we present the GLIDE system (Grid-based Learning In Distributed Environments) that takes these properties into account. It aims at a flexible mix and match of learning tools realized by grid services. Based on course descriptions using IMS/LD for activities and resources, we map the activities to concrete services with well-defined interfaces with respect to transfer of data and products between the different learning activities.

2 Scenario

To illustrate the feasibility and advantages of our approach we chose the following scenario that combines individual, asynchronous and synchronous collaborative activities:

Two students – Alice and Bob – independently decide that they want to learn something about environment protection and esp. about the effect of acid rain on the rain forest. Since they know of the GLIDE system they log into system with the GLIDE client. This client offers an interface to choose one of several courses. Each one of them deals with a specific topic, e. g. a course about the "Effect of acid rain on trees". The list may be filtered concerning particular criteria such as software prerequisites or group size, i. e. if there is space left in the group for an additional member, etc. The selected course on "Effect of acid rain on trees" is divided into several parts. The first part guides Alice and Bob through several online resources (e. g. HTML-pages) individually. So the GLIDE client brings up a browser that is installed on Alice's system (e. g. Firefox) and one that is installed on Bob's machine (e. g. Safari).

In the second part of the course a system dynamics modeling tool (e. g. FreeStyler[1] with the system dynamics plugin) is needed to model the growth of a forest depending on different levels of acidness of the falling rain. Since Alice and Bob are both members of the same course instance, the GLIDE system takes care that they both

---

[1] Available from http://www.collide.info/software

have one common modeling environment installed that enables the group to collaborate if necessary. Otherwise the latecomer would have been either blocked from the course or warned that a specific tool (e. g. FreeStyler) needs to be installed (later) including a hint where to get it.

In this scenario Alice and Bob will collaborate asynchronously. This means that they both solve the modeling task and then they submit their model to the GLIDE system. When both models are ready, the GLIDE client will start the modeling environment of Alice with Bob's model and vice versa letting Alice and Bob review each other's model. Afterwards the course foresees a chat session to discuss their models. For this reason the GLIDE client opens a dialog telling Alice and Bob to meet at 12:00 in the GLIDE system. When they log into the system at the given time, the GLIDE client opens their favorite web browser again to initiate a discussion session in a web-based discussion environment.

Since every activity but the last one can be done asynchronously the users are allowed to leave the system at any time an rejoin the course later on.

3 Architecture

Taking into account the desired properties for flexible computer supported learning scenarios and the example from the previous section, we decided to use a service oriented grid architecture [7] (cf. fig. 1). This type of architecture addresses virtualized resources, service discovery, and interoperability.

As a user interface we provide a client access software to access the learning grid. It can be used on several platforms including PDAs. To generate the list of available course the client contacts the control unit through the underlying grid.

The control unit discovers and allows dynamic registration and de-registration of courses and learning resources. These learning objects are stored in course libraries and learning resource repositories (result repository, learning resource directory). A course library can be any container holding abstract learning activity descriptions. For the GLIDE project we chose the IMS LD [8] notation to define learning scenarios. The learning resources constitute the available activity services for a student. They can be divided in different types of resources: websites, local learning environments and remote learning resources. Websites are the simplest kind of resources. Local learning environments are directly available on the student's device and can vary between students and their devices. In order to integrate these local learning environments into the learning grid, the access software propagates a list of locally available applications to the grid's control unit. This information is used in the discovery process. Remote learning resources are services addressable by an URL. These can be simulations, data repositories, web applications, etc. If their learning results are meant to be shared with or propagated to the learning grid, they have to provide a container service for the communication with the access software.

Result repositories facilitate the re-use of learning products across different learning activities and learners as well as for evaluation. Given that a learning resource has an appropriate feedback channel to externalize its activity state, it is possible to save this information in those repositories.

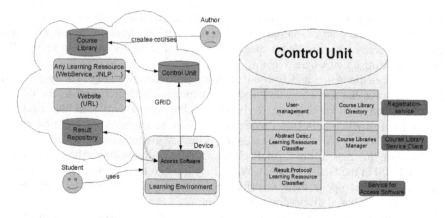

Fig. 1. GLIDE's architectural overview   **Fig. 2.** Control unit

The control unit mediates between the student and the available learning grid services. It holds the information about registered components and discovers the resources dynamically for a given learning request. In order to accomplish this task the grid needs a user management, two classifiers for learning resources, a course library directory, a course libraries manager and communication services (cf. fig. 2).

The user management handles all operations concerning the user within the grid and the user-role-assignment in the course libraries. Thus the student has to login only once at the learning grid to get access to the whole range of courses.

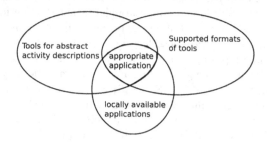

Fig. 3. Schema for application selection

Learning resources for an activity are determined (cf. fig. 3) by an intersection between the available local learning environments and the results of the two classifiers. The first classifier maps the abstract activity description to known learning resources. The second classifier looks up appropriate learning resources for an associated activity result format and/or a preselected communication protocol for synchronous, collaborative sessions, viz. the suitability of input and output formats/ protocols is checked for the current and subsequent activities.

The course library manager operates closely with the course libraries, user management and access software. It translates the user actions with the learning resources into state transitions that reflect the current state of the scenario for the involved users in the respective course library.

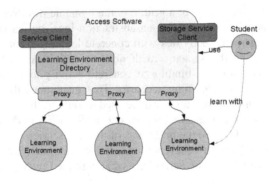

Fig. 4. Access software

The last important component of the learning grid is the student's access software. It acts as a front-end for the local learning environments. On the one hand it handles the communication with the grid and on the other hand it handles the available learning environments. To integrate existing environments into the grid, custom proxies are needed (cf. fig. 4). The proxies manage the starting and configuration of the installed learning environments. If there are artifacts to be exchanged, the access software uploads the result to the result repository.

The communication with the grid to determine the appropriate local application is done by transmitting the list of locally available environments to the control unit. This list is maintained by the learning environment directory and is used for the intersection algorithm in the control unit (s. above).

4   The Usage of e-Learning Standards

To prepare the GLIDE system for interoperability and to re-use the existing pedagogical expertise expressed by formal scenario descriptions, we considered several e-Learning standards into account in our concretization of the GLIDE system.

For the representation of the learning scenarios we chose the IMS Learning Design (IMS/LD, [8]) standard. With that the learning designer / teacher specifies the phases of a learning activity and their sequencing. Figure 5 shows an IMS/LD fragment from the system dynamics modeling phase and the associated application of the scenario from section 2.

The LD documents are collected in the course library directory (cf. previous section). The availability of the CopperCore engine[2], a component for the management and execution of LD documents, allowed us to re-use this component as one of the elements of the control unit in the GLIDE architecture.

We decided to use standardized descriptions of resources to overcome the limitation of having the learning designer to pre-define every activity tool concretely at design time. At that time he might not even be aware of new activity tools available when the course is run. To be able to determine tools to support learning activities at

---

[2] Available from http://www.coppercore.org

run-time we use the advantages of a grid, i. e. the dynamic discovery and registration of services. This is achieved by using an abstraction level on learning activities and associating these abstracted activities with concrete learning resources. The learning designer thus specifies the scenario with abstract activities, such as "draw" and "graph" (see fig. 5), while the binding to concrete activity tools to be used is done when a student enters the learning scenario. This guarantees that the most recent instrument of available grid resources can be used to support the students.

As a mechanism for this abstraction we chose the IEEE LOM (Learning Object Metadata) standard to describe the properties of the grid services (i.e. learning support tools) and their suitability for different abstracted learning activities. Figure 6 shows the XML-specification for those activities usable with the FreeStyler application.

```
<imsld:learning-activity identifier="la" isvisible="true" parameters="prop">
<imsld:title>Create System Dynamics Model</imsld:title>
    ...
<imsld:metadata>
 <imsld:schema>IMS Metadata</imsld:schema>
  <imsld:schemaversion>1.2</imsld:schemaversion>
  <lom xmlns="http://www.imsglobal.org/xsd/imsmd_v1p2" ... >
   <classification>
    <taxonpath>
    <source>
     <langstring xml:lang="en">GLIDE Taxonomy</langstring>
    </source>
    <taxon>
     <entry>
      <langstring xml:lang="en">draw</langstring>
      <langstring xml:lang="en">graph</langstring>
     </entry>
    </taxon>
   </taxonpath>
   </classification>
  </lom>
 </imsld:metadata>
</imsld:learning-activity>
```

Fig. 5. Activity description (IMS/LD) with abstract tool specification (LOM)

The LOM description in IMS/LD and the property description in fig. 6 are used to determine the availability of the FreeStyler application for the system dynamics activity in the example scenario. Here the text entities from fig. 5 (e.g. "draw", "graph") are matched with the entities (tags) in fig. 6, which results in the selection of the FreeStyler application for the modeling phase. The LOM standard is also used to specify the data formats and protocols required to make the products of learning activities and other learning materials usable across learning phases and tools.

In distributed collaborative learning settings the learners may use different applications for the same task. The simplest solution is to require the learners to use the same application. On the other hand there is no real need to use the same text editor to produce the .rtf- or .txt-files. So we decided to use metadata information about the (mime-) type of results as well as metadata about the available applications and their output formats. Using these metadata it is possible to use abstract descriptions of resulting products and thus be flexible in the respective course run.

The underlying grid technology then can be used to store the results in a result repository. The repository content is automatically annotated with information about the originating course and its creator(s) as well as "stamped" with the resource identifier needed by the LD scripts in the background. These resource identifiers allow for cross references inside of the Copper Core engine.

Besides the obvious need for some kind of result repository its contents can later be reused to build a new course or reuse the contents as a replacement for missing submissions by other group members. Especially the last use case addresses a common problem of collaborative learning scenarios. Group members may leave a course or may be absent for a longer period of time. To avoid the break down of the whole course it is good to have similar products from other sources. Of course this may not be possible completely automatically.

```xml
<?xml version="1.0" encoding="UTF-8"?>
<taxonomy>
 <draw>
  <graph>
   <environment name="freestyler" publisher="collide" version="">
    <extension name="petrinet" publisher="" version="" />
    <extension name="systemdynamics" publisher="" version="" />
   </environment>
   <environment name="internetexplorer" publisher="microsoft" version="6.1" />
  </graph>
  <freehand>
   <environment name="freestyler" publisher="collide" version="" />
   <environment name="paint" publisher="mirosoft" version="" />
  </freehand>
 </draw>
 <read>
  <environment name="acrobatreader" publisher="adobe" version="7.1" />
  <environment name="firefox" publisher="mozilla" version="1.5" />
 </read>
</taxonomy>
```

Fig. 6. Learning resource classification

5 Implementation Details

Our GLIDE prototype was developed to show the possibilities of the solution with respect to changing learning environments and diverse devices.

The chosen grid technology is Globus Toolkit 4 [7] which is a de facto standard grid toolkit. It facilitates stateful services and a notification mechanism. As mentioned before, we use the Coppercore engine [6] to realize the course library and course execution. So we profit from the built-in IMS/LD processor. The currently integrated learning resources comprise several browsers and the collaborative learning environment FreeStyler. In order to explore the technical possibilities of changing devices during or between activities we integrated some PDAs. Since the use of the globus toolkit would consume too much memory (e.g. for the jars) we decided to use an axis client[3] for the pdas, although we lose some of the advantages of grid services (viz. statefulness) it works Because of the restriction in the choice of learning environments on a PDA, we currently only support web based learning environments on them. The result repository is implemented rudimentary as a servlet, that manages the exchange of the students' products between different FreeStyler instances.

---

[3] We used Wingfoot SOAP (http://www.wingfoot.com)

6 Conclusion and Outlook

In this paper we presented a grid based collaborative learning platform combining flexible and dynamic tool selection with standardized course descriptions. The presented architecture uses grid technology advantages like flexibility, transparency and mobility. One of the main advantages of this learning grid concept is, that it is able to incorporate existing learning environments and resources by realizing a light-weight proxy-interface to communicate with the student's client software. There is no need for substantial modifications to the learning environment. This is important because there are many learning environments for particular purposes around that either cannot or should not be changed to be integrated into a uniform learning platform. Currently we are working on the integration of complex synchronous collaboration applications, i. e. joining the learners into the right collaboration sessions for such a tool set. For this another collaboration proxy has to be defined. First results are promising (cf. [9]).

Acknowledgements

We thank Marcel Pokrandt, Michael Kluz, Benjamin Tzschoppe, Stefan Barbulescu and Evgenia Nikiforova for their work implementing the GLIDE environment.

References

[1] de Jong, T., van Joolingen, W.: Discovery learning with computer simulations of conceptual domains. Review of Educational Research 68, 179–201 (1998)
[2] Kollar, I., Fischer, F., Slotta, J.D.: Internal and External Collaboration Scripts in Web-based Science Learning at Schools. In: Computer-Supported Collaborative Learning 2005, Lawrence Earlbaum Associates, Mawah (2005)
[3] Chen, W.: Web Services in Web-based Education Systems? In: Proc. of Computers and Advanced Technology in Education, ACTA Press (2003)
[4] Lorenzo, M.B., Leo, D.H., Dimitriadis, Y., Pérez, A., Sánchez, E.G., Gorgojo, G.V., González, L.V.: Towards Reusability and Tailorability in Collaborative Learning Systems Using IMS-LD and Grid Services. Advanced Technology for Learning 1(3), 129–138 (2004)
[5] Vega Gorgojo, G., Lorenzo, M.B., Sánchez, E.G., Pérez, J.A., Dimitriadis, Y., Abellán, I.J.: Ontoolcole: an Ontology for the Semantic Search of CSCL Services. In: Dimitriadis, Y.A., Zigurs, I., Gómez-Sánchez, E. (eds.) CRIWG 2006. LNCS, vol. 4154, Springer, Heidelberg (2006)
[6] The IMS Learning Design Engine [cited 2006 05.02.] (2005), available from http://www.coppercore.org
[7] Foster, I.: Globus Toolkit Version 4: Sofware for Service-Oriented Systems. In: IFIP International Conference on Network and Parallel Computing, Springer, Heidelberg (2005)
[8] IMS Global Consortium, IMS Learning Design Best Practice and Implementation, I.G. Consortium, Editor (2005)
[9] Harrer, A., Malzahn, N., Roth, B.: The remote control approach - how to apply scaffolds to existing collaborative learning environments. In: Dimitriadis, Y.A., Zigurs, I., Gómez-Sánchez, E. (eds.) CRIWG 2006. LNCS, vol. 4154, Springer, Heidelberg (2006)

Directions to Acknowledge Learners' Self-organization in CSCL Macro-scripts

Pierre Tchounikine

LIUM, Université du Maine
Avenue Laënnec, 72085 Le Mans cedex 9, France
Pierre.Tchounikine@lium.univ-lemans.fr

Abstract. In this article we present a conceptual analysis of the notion of learners' self-organization in CSCL macro-scripts. We highlight that taking into account self-organization as an emergent feature of activity requires considering issues such as conceptual and technological tools to support learners' self-organization, maintenance of coherence between the script pedagogical objective and the emergent organization and between the technological setting and the emergent activity.

Keywords: CSCL; scripts; learners' self-organization; CSCL platforms.

1 Introduction

A Computer Supported Collaborative Learning (CSCL) *script* is an activity model designed to support a group of learners engaged in a computer-supported collective[1] task. A CSCL script defines the task to be achieved, the sequence of sub-tasks, learners' individual and collective roles, the technological setting and the constraints to be respected [1, 2]. Such scripts are defined to enhance the probability that knowledge-generative interactions such as conflict resolution, explanation or mutual regulation occur during the collaboration process [1, 3]. Technology platforms designed to support CSCL scripts typically provide communication tools (chat, mail, forum or whiteboard), awareness tools and task-related tools (tools related to the tasks to achieve) within static or workflow-oriented interfaces.

Scripts can be dissociated into macro-scripts and micro-scripts [2, 4]. A *macro-script* is a kind of pedagogical method. It aims at emphasizing the orchestration of activities by setting up a given set of conditions and constraints (e.g., sequence of individual and collective tasks learners must achieve or group characteristics) in order to trigger high-order thinking activities such as elaborating on content, explaining ideas and concepts, asking thought-provoking questions, constructing arguments, resolving conceptual discrepancies or cognitive modeling. A prototypical example is the Jigsaw-script family, i.e., scripts based on making individual learners manage

---

[1] As we believe the "cooperative" / "collaborative" distinction is often a question of level of granularity, point of view and/or matter of concern, we will use "collective" as a wide concept, however using other authors' original wording when quoting specific works.

J.M. Haake, S.F. Ochoa, and A. Cechich (Eds.): CRIWG 2007, LNCS 4715, pp. 247–254, 2007.
© Springer-Verlag Berlin Heidelberg 2007

some partial knowledge and then prompting them to solve collectively a problem that necessitates knowledge from each of them. Micro-scripts are finer-grained scripts studied at a psychological level, emphasizing the activities of individual learners and providing scaffolding such as sentence starters. Examples can be found in [1, 2].

Task (the prescribed work) and *activity* (what people actually do) are two different notions. Teachers set tasks, and learners interpret the specifications of the task, their subsequent activity being a more-or-less rational response to the task [5]. A script is a task-related notion. Learners' effective activity is related to different intertwined -and for some of them dynamic- issues. In this article we study one of these issues that may, in the context of macro-scripts in particular, play a role in learners' activity emergence: *learners' self-organization.*

2 Indirect-Design in Macro-scripts

Considering CSCL scripts, 4 major dimensions can be pinpointed as artifacts that can be designed with the explicit objective of enhancing the probability that the targeted situations and interactions occur: (1) the didactic envelope [3], i.e., the set of pre-activities that allow triggering the script core mechanisms and contribute to create favorable conditions before interaction begins; (2) the script, i.e., the way groups, roles, tasks, resources, timing or constraints are defined; (3) the provided technological means; (4) the run-time regulations that aim at supporting collaboration by taking actions once the interaction has begun [6]: changing groups, relaxing constraints, modifying tasks, scaffolding, etc.

The didactic envelope, the script and the technological setting as designed by teachers set up the basic situation. The effective interaction pattern, i.e., the script as it unfolds as a set of activities and interactions taking place among the learners, is related to this basic situation (and then the regulation) but unpredictable in its details as different other dimensions from different natures may play a role: the general pedagogical and institutional context; the individual characteristics of learners; the effective motivation(s) of learners (e.g., play the game, please the teacher, solve the problem, interact with peers or gain social status) and the according effective activity/activities as related to their motivation(s); the social issues within the group such as the emergence of a leader or conflicting characters; etc. It is not possible *a priori* to exhaustively list and consider all the pedagogical parameters of a situation, the understanding of these parameters may vary (difficulty of a task, timing, balance of groups, etc.) and unpredicted events can happen (collapse of a group, pedagogical opportunity, external or technical constraint, etc.). Moreover, objects such as the script or the technological setting should not be thought of in terms of "objective" or "neutral" objects that all actors (learners, teachers) understand and consider in the same way. Learners' activity is related to the way they (as individuals, as a group) perceive and appropriate these issues for themselves, which may differ from teachers' or other students' perceptions. Technological characteristics in particular will be picked up in different ways by learners, which will appropriate them according to their purposes and in context [7]. And, things generally evolve and may vary run to run and/or during script enactment (understanding of the script, perception of the technological setting affordances, groups phenomena, motivation –e.g., using the proposed technological setting as a way to "play the game" and please the teacher but, when time runs out, focusing on completing the task satisfactorily in order to get a good mark and thus using other tools or means if more efficient).

Structuring activity is thus a challenging concept, in particular in the context of macro-scripts that leave some place for activity emergence. The script is a seed and a reference, but other dimensions play a role, and learners' activity can not be reduced and thought of just in terms of "playing the script": the way learners will perceive and enact the script can only be hypothesized. Emphasizing that designers have limited direct control over how their designs are enacted and that learning and learning environments thus can not be defined directly, [7] introduce the notion of *indirect design*. Within CSCL scripts, indirect design captures the idea that defining the script and the technological platform features and properties must be thought of as means to *influence* learners' activity, and this activity (and the impact of the designed issues) must be taken into consideration as they happen and not as they were predicted by designers. This requires taking into account the different issues that may occur in such situations. Learners' self-organization dimension is one of these issues.

3 Macro-scripts and Learners' Self-organization

A collective phase of a script can be defined as a collective *work situation*, i.e., a situation where the learners are mutually dependent in their work. Works in CSCW highlight that actors engaged in such interdependent processes must address an overhead activity, that of articulating (dividing, allocating, coordinating, scheduling, meshing, interrelating) their respective activities [8, 9]. This is a meta-level overhead activity that is not focused on producing the targeted output, but on setting the conditions of the production of this output by maintaining a more-or-less stable pattern of cooperative arrangement between people. We will refer to this as learners' self-organization, "self" highlighting that, in our context, part of the organization is set by the script and part is related to learners' enactment of the script at run-time. We thus define learners' self-organization as the meta-level activity that a group of learners engaged in a CSCL script may engage in so as to maintain, within the reference frame that is externally defined by the script, a more-or-less stable pattern of collective arrangement.

Although they both relate to the learners' collective work structure, script and learners' self-organization differ in nature. A script is a prescriptive structure defined by the teacher. Learners' self-organization is an abstract inside-group feature that emerges from the way learners collaborate and enact the script, is influenced by —but different from— the script, and may vary run to run. A script mixes in an operational way what is to be achieved and how it is to be achieved: self-organization corresponds to what learners will make from this.

In CSCL scripts, the fact learners can or have to self-develop some organization is correlated to the script granularity and flexibility, i.e., the means and latitude that learners and teachers are proposed with in order to modify some script features such as groups, detailed subtasks decomposition, timing or technological setting [4]. The need and space for organization is almost non-existent in micro-scripts. Differently, if macro-scripts core-issues such as the general sequence of subtasks or their individual/

collective nature are constrained by the script, different issues can be more-or-less left open to learners' self-organization, e.g., the precise timing, the name-by-name group composition and/or role attribution, some aspects of the tasks/subtasks decomposition (input and output, actors, roles, etc.) or the technology. As examples: in a jigsaw-script, learners can be allowed to compose the groups or modify them within the respect of the design decision stating that the group must be composed of individuals mastering different knowledge; within a setting such as grouping two learners and stating they have 3 hours to achieve a given subtask, different organizational possibilities are still open and learners can decide to spend 1 hour each on the same or on different issues and then share their thoughts, or explicitly split the 3 hours into different phases such as brainstorming, elicitation, argumentation and decision; learners may be allowed to choose the task-oriented tools, communication-tools or awareness-tools they want to use contextually, according to the emergent activity; etc. An analysis of the speech-acts detected in the mails, chats and forums used by learners while enacting a macro-script run for 6-7 weeks at University level highlighted that 20% to 50% (3 groups analyzed) were related to organizational issues such as organization proposals (e.g., "The first issue is to define the objective of this phase", "Would you agree to work on the basis of the graphic?" or "Each could be put in charge of …"), refinements, agreements or disagreements linked to these proposals, and of course organizing meetings or managing time [10]. Although this is a border-line situation (very coarse-grained and long-period script with University students) whose results are not to be generalized, it emphasizes the potential importance of learners' self-organization in script enactment.

4   Directions to Acknowledge the Self-organization Notion

4.1   Considering the Setting Potential Self-organization Issues

Focusing on organization, macro-scripts carry out a tension between different issues from which: (1) a script carries constraints that define boundaries for, and impact on, learners' eventual self-organization; (2) a script is defined by teachers; (3) a script should be easily appropriable by learners [3] (macro-scripts suppose a high commitment of learners: they create a didactical contract between the teachers and the learners and between the learners, and there is an assumption that learners will "play the game"); (4) the fact that people appropriate a structure for themselves and/or develop a shared understanding of it is generally related to how much the structure has been collectively constructed and/or refined; (5) organization is a structure that emerges, is instable and evolves during activity; (6) the technological platform may impact (constrain, allow, support) learners' activity and self-organization.

Learners' self-organization and flexibility are related issues: the flexibility that is left to learners impacts how self-organization can emerge, and under what constraints. Given the setting, taking self-organization into account can appear necessary to avoid counterproductive issues and/or be used as a means to contribute with the script in making the targeted knowledge-generative interactions appear. Leaving open to learners some organizational issues may present some interest related to learners' appropriation of the script by becoming active actors in organizing work and/or tackling unanticipated problems such as a time management problem, a learner that abandons or downloads his contribution, a bad role distribution or an inadequate technological decision. It may also be an objective *per se*, for instance as a means to make learners practice and learn how to work collectively.

Considering learners' self-organization raises questions such as: what relations can be drawn between self-organization issues and the learning targeted by the script, and/or some other high-level skills such as autonomy or collective work skills? How can one perceive and then deal with a learners' self-organization that diverges from the script pedagogical objectives? How to understand and deal with the dynamics of learners' self-organization and the central notion of breakdown [8] which can be both an opportunity for learning and/or the cause of a collapse of the learning situation? How must one deal with the fact that self-organization is an activity in itself, that can be intertwined with others but may also interfere with the flow of work? How can learners' self-organization be impacted (influenced, supported)?

As learners' self-organization is fundamentally an emergent feature, it is not to be addressed in terms of prediction and direct design but in terms of indirect design and regulation. As activity in general (cf. *supra*), self-organization is related to different complex intertwined factors which renders it difficult to predict. Some of these factors can however be impacted: the didactic envelope, the script structure and/or the technological characteristics may be used as direct or indirect means to provide seeds, opportunities and incentives. And, teachers in charge of running the process should have means to perceive the learners' activity and act if it appears that the emergent organization goes against the script pedagogical objectives.

4.2 Tools to Support Learners' Self-organization

A group facing a self-organization situation undertakes an activity (in the sense of Activity Theory [11]) that is linked to a motivation (establish a pattern of cooperative arrangement). Interestingly, it is a collective activity. As an activity, it is mediated by tools from which we can distinguish conceptual tools and technological tools.

A basic CSCL script setting implicitly carries potential conceptual tools that learners can use to conceptualize the collective work of organizing themselves and reflecting on the setting: the epistemic notions used by teachers to describe the script (e.g., "group" or "role"). The fact that self-organization is usually not considered as a specific concern is widely related to the implicit basic assumption that scripts structure learners' activity and, if any adjustment is required, learners can complement the structuring using the same conceptual notions and the available communication and awareness functionalities. This is however to be questioned: there is an issue in understanding what conceptual and technological tools can support self-organization and how, and if/how this support can be correlated with the script in order to influence activity in a way that is coherent with the pedagogical objectives. As an example, [10] reports a work where the script is presented to learners using coarse-grained notions (phases, tasks) but the technological platform provides editors allowing learners to render explicit and discuss how they intend to tackle these tasks using notions inspired from Engeström's triangle [11] (subtasks defined in terms of a subject, an object, a community and rules, tools, and division of labor), which appears to limit the risk for the script to collapse by lack of organization and commitment.

4.3 Maintaining a Coherence Script-Objectives / Emergent-Organization

Learners' self-organization and more generally learners' activity can be analyzed with respect to the script, but more interestingly with respect to the *script pedagogical objectives* as the way these objectives have been reified in the actual setting may be linked to contingent issues. As discussed previously, scripts carry a tension between structuring learners' processes and supporting knowledge-generative interactions. Learners' self-organization (among other issues) may conduct them to diverge from the teacher's *a priori* script: is this a problem?

In order to tackle this issue and allow flexibility and learners' self-organization whilst not contradicting pedagogical objectives, the conceptual dissociation between scripts *intrinsic* and *extrinsic constraints* proposed in [4] appears useful. Intrinsic constraints denote the script core mechanisms, e.g., within a jigsaw script learners must manage different knowledge. Extrinsic constraints are contingent decisions related to detailed groups composition, roles attribution, tasks/subtasks definition or technological setting. Extrinsic constraints define the space for flexibility, i.e., the space within which the structure carried by a script should be modifiable by learners and/or teachers because the related decisions result from arbitrary or practical choices. Intrinsic constraints set up the limits of flexibility, i.e., what cannot be accepted in order for the script to keep its *raison d'être* [4]. This dissociation provides a substratum to address automated and/or teacher regulation issues such as analyzing learners' self-organization with respect to the script objectives (as opposed to contingent issues), allowing and eventually supporting learners' actions that diverge from the script but remain coherent with the pedagogical objectives, acting on the setting (adapting the script, adapting the platform) or dealing with situations that go against some pedagogical objectives. The technological platform should be capable of permanently comparing the difference between the script and the actual interaction pattern (and/or helping the teacher to do so, and/or the learners) in order to check if eventual differences violate some intrinsic constraints. This requires the platform to maintain (1) a model of the script and underlying *design rationale* and (2) a model of the script enactment, updated in real time, these 2 models being interoperable [4].

4.4 Maintaining a Coherence Technological-Setting / Emergent-Activity

CSCL scripts can be associated with a generic Learning Management System (LMS) platform, i.e., a kind of generic technological platform that proposes some general-purpose tools (e.g., chat, email, shared agenda or file exchange zone). Associating scripts with platforms that are studied (designed, customized) according to the script, however, presents a list of advantages, in particular (1) the platform can be process-oriented and reify (part of) the script features (sequence of tasks, constrained access to resources, roles, etc.) and (2) the platform can propose tools that are specifically adapted to the context, the tasks to be achieved by learners and/or pedagogical objectives. Technological settings can thus be studied as a means for the two dual dimensions of a script, supporting and constraining learners' activities.

When targeting a script-related platform, the design should consider the script and the learners' activity, which may vary (in particular because of self-organization) from the script-related expectations. However, designing a platform to support activity is somewhat paradoxical as activity will emerge and is not fully predictable. An approach to this issue is to target tailorable platforms. A computer system is said to be tailorable if it proposes its users with some means to modify itself in the context of its use, as one of its functionalities [12]. In CSCL scripts, tailorability is a means to allow learners to adapt the platform to needs in context, according to how the script is enacted and the underlying emergent issues such as organizational issues if any. Introducing tailorability features in CSCL platforms however raises three major issues: (1) tailorability for learners is to be studied with respect to the scope of flexibility defined by the intrinsic/extrinsic constraints notions, and teachers' regulation [4]; (2) tailorability must be technically easy; (3) tailorability is, with respect to the learners' activity as related to the script, *another* activity; there is therefore a risk of causing a breakdown in the activity flow.

5 Conclusions

The results presented in this article are a definition of the notion of learners' self-organization, an argumentation that it is an intrinsic dimension of CSCL macro-scripts enactment that, if not acknowledged, may conduct not to reach the script pedagogical objectives, and directions to acknowledge this notion.

In section 4 we have raised different important issues to acknowledge learners' self-organization. All of these imply a detailed machine-readable modeling of the script. Different general [13] or CSCL-focused [14, 15, 16, 17] Learning Design languages allowing to model scripts have recently been proposed. From the perspective of learners' self-organization, such languages are to be considered with respect to the fact (1) they allow to model script notions that are in relation with self-organization and (2) the implementation approach allows the required flexibility. From the point of view of representation, CSCL-focused languages introduce scripting concepts (groups, roles, etc.) which facilitate making explicit organization issues (in general), and thus may facilitate learners' self-organization identification and/or representation (in settings that consider this objective). From the point of view of semantics, the issue is that of ensuring the relation between the script, its enactment and the technological platform, and the means provided to learners for flexibility. Mechanisms such as generating the platform from a graphical/formal description of the script as proposed in LAMS [17] or in [15] can allow to provide interesting run-time flexibility means for the teacher and, if extended to them, for the learners. Within such an approach, the issues are (1) the granularity of the modeling language as going into details of scripts modeling of course raises the computer-science difficulty of insuring the script/platform coherence, (2) the conditions of access to the editing (who, when, how), (3) the usability of the editor for end-users and (4) the management of the underlying coherence issues. Some of the state-of-the-art techniques thus do allow partially tackling some the issues we have raised, however not in a straightforward, articulated nor complete way.

Acknowledgement. This work has benefited from fruitful discussions within the CSCL groups of Kaleidoscope, a European Network of Excellence for Technology Enhanced Learning.

References

1. Fischer, F., Mandl, H., Haake, J., Kollar, I.: Scripting Computer-Supported Collaborative Learning – Cognitive, Computational, and Educational Perspectives. Computer-Supported Collaborative Learning Series. Springer, Heidelberg (2007)
2. Kobe, L., Weinberger, A., Dillenbourg, P., Harrer, A., Hämäläinen, R., Fischer, F.: Specifying collaboration scripts. IJCSCL (to appear)
3. Dillenbourg, P., Jermann, P.: Designing integrative scripts. In: Fischer, F., Mandl, H., Haake, J., Kollar, I. (eds.) Scripting Computer-Supported Collaborative Learning – Cognitive, Computational, and Educational Perspectives, pp. 275–301. Springer, Heidelberg (2007)
4. Dillenbourg, P., Tchounikine, P.: Flexibility in macro-scripts for CSCL. Journal of Computer Assisted Learning 23(1), 1–13 (2007)
5. Goodyear, P.: Effective networked learning in higher education: notes and guidelines, http://csalt.lancs.ac.uk/jisc/
6. Soller, A., Martinez, A., Jermann, P., Muehlenbrock, M.: From Mirroring to Guiding: A Review of State of the Art Technology for Supporting Collaborative Learning. IJAIED 15, 261–290 (2005)
7. Jones, C., Dirckinck-Holmfeld, L., Lindström, B.: A relational, indirect, meso-level approach to CSCL design in the next decade. IJCSCL 1(1), 35–56 (2006)
8. Bardram, J.: Designing for the Dynamics of Cooperative Work Activities. In: Poltrock, S., Grudin, J. (eds.) CSCW conference, Seattle, pp. 89–98 (1998)
9. Schmidt, K., Bannon, L.: Taking CSCW Seriously: Supporting Articulation Work. CSCW 1(1-2), 7–40 (1992)
10. Betbeder, M-L., Tchounikine, P.: Symba: a tailorable framework to support collective activities in a learning context. In: Favela, J., Decouchant, D. (eds.) CRIWG 2003. LNCS, vol. 2806, pp. 90–98. Springer, Heidelberg (2003)
11. Engeström, Y.: Learning by expanding. An activity-theoretical approach to developmental research. Helsinki: Orienta-Konsultit (1987)
12. Morsh, A.: Three Levels of End-user Tailoring: Customization, Integration, and Extension. In: Kyng, M., Mathiassen, L. (eds.) Computers and Design in Context, pp. 51–76. The MIT Press, Cambridge, MA (1997)
13. IMS-LD, http://www.imsglobal.org/learningdesign
14. Ferraris, C., Martel, C., Vignollet, L.: LDL for Collaborative Activities. In: Botturi, L., Stubbs, T. (eds.) Handbook of Visual Languages in Instructional Design: Theories and Practices. Hershey, PA Idea Group (in press)
15. Haake, J., Pfister, H.-R.: Flexible scripting in net-based learning groups. In: Fischer, F., Kollar, I., Mandl, H., Haake, J.M. (eds.) Scripting computer-supported cooperative learning – Cognitive, computational, and educational perspectives, Springer, Heidelberg (2007)
16. Harrer, A., Malzahn, N.: Bridging the gap – towards a graphical modeling language for learning designs and collaboration scripts of various granularities. In: Kinshuk (ed.) ICALT'2006, Kerkrade, pp. 296–300 (2006)
17. LAMS, http://www.lamsinternational.com

Supporting Informal Co-located Collaboration in Hospital Work

David A. Mejia[1], Alberto L. Morán[2], and Jesus Favela[1]

[1] Departamento de Ciencias de la Computacion, CICESE, Ensenada, Mexico
{mejiam,favela}@cicese.mx
[2] Facultad de Ciencias, UABC, Ensenada, Mexico
alberto_moran@uabc.mx

Abstract. Informal interactions, an important subject of study in CSCW, are an essential resource in hospital work; they are used as a means to collaborate and to coordinate the way in which the work is performed, as well as to locate and gather the artifacts and human resources necessary for patient care, among others. Results from an observational study of work in a public hospital show that a significant amount of informal interactions happen face to face due to opportunistic encounters. That is due to hospital work being mainly characterized by intense mobility, task fragmentation, collaboration and coordination. This encouraged us to develop an architecture and system tool aimed at supporting mobile co-located collaboration. Based on the findings of our study, this paper presents a set of design insights for developing collaborative applications that support co-located interactions in hospital work, as well as the implementation of these design insights in a collaborative tool. Additionally, we generalized the characteristic that must be fulfilled by tools that support mobile informal co-located collaboration through the design of a generic architecture that includes the characteristics of this type of tools.

Keywords: Informal interactions, mobile informal co-located collaboration, hospital work.

1 Introduction

Communication between individuals that form a work group has been the object of diverse studies and this with the purpose of understanding and optimizing the way in which it is done. The types of communication that they use are both formal and informal [8, 10, 13]. In terms of style, informal communication is often more frequent, expressive and interactive than formal communication [8]. By informal interactions we mean those that do not have a predefined schedule or place of encounter, are spontaneous, not planned and brief, and where the topic of the conversation can change during the course of the interaction. Informal interactions are often undervalued, yet, studies in office and educational environments show that these interactions play an important role in successful collaborative interactions [7, 10, 13, 14]. This kind of interaction can be triggered by people, objects, actions or

J.M. Haake, S.F. Ochoa, and A. Cechich (Eds.): CRIWG 2007, LNCS 4715, pp. 255–270, 2007.

interactions [13, 18]. Furthermore, informal interaction is grounded on awareness of the work environment such as the people, objects and activities [9].

Research on informal communication [7, 8, 10, 13, 14] argue that informal interactions are a very important mechanism to accomplish work because they allow for lightweight means to collaborate in casual ways, taking advantage of opportunities that arise opportunistically or spontaneously due to physical proximity and because they can contribute to the social as well as the production function of the group.

Further, Kraut and Streeter [14] identified and correlated physical proximity as a strong predictor of project success; and Kraut *et al.* [13] documented the negative impact on the overall results of collaboration when opportunities for casual and informal interaction are reduced or eliminated, as in remote (technology-mediated) collaboration. This way, physical proximity has been considered as the reference situation for informal interaction, and its absence has been considered problematic.

A natural consequence of these findings and assumptions was the conception and development of models and tools that provide support for informal interactions through what has been defined as "artificial proximity". Nowadays, most current tools aimed at supporting informal interactions are focused on providing *artificial proximity* in traditional office environments in which workers spend most of their time "behind their desk". In this case, informal interactions are performed through mediating technology, that is, technological tools that somehow replace the physical means that allow becoming aware of others to interact with, actually initiating and performing the interaction, and finishing it in an appropriate manner – e.g. VideoWindow and Cruiser [13], Piazza [11], Hubbub [12] and Aware Phone [2].

However, in other working environments, such as hospitals, users experience a high level of mobility that enables them to establish co-located interactions in order to collaborate and coordinate their activities with colleagues, involving the exchange and analysis of documents distributed in space or time [5]. This means that local mobility changes the rules and requirements for the provision of support for informal interaction in hospital work [1]. The main reason for this is that opportunities for face-to-face interactions in this case arise naturally while people move around to perform their work, which makes most current informal interaction tools inappropriate for this kind of work.

Nevertheless, despite the natural opportunities for collaboration that hospital work poses, this environment faces some inconveniences before and while workers are collaborating. These include waste of opportunities for collaboration -due to the lack of nearness colleagues' awareness-, interruption of interactions in order to gather information artifacts (like Electronic Health Record and X-Ray Images, among others) necessary for collaboration, and loss of information generated during collaboration. We consider that these inconveniences are mainly due to limitations on the affordances of i) the physical environment, ii) of its artifacts, and iii) of the means of communication that foster face-to-face informal collaboration and that help workers to held collaboration according to their working necessities. Examples of these limitations include i) that we cannot see through the walls, ii) that a paper-based health record can only be in one place at a time, and iii) that verbal face-to-face communication is transient, respectively.

To this date, several collaborative tools for hospitals have been developed. Two examples of these are: i) AWAREPhone [2], a mobile IM system that provides users with awareness of the context of work of others; and ii) AWAREMedia [3], a system designed to support social, spatial, and temporal awareness in a hospital enabling users to use simple, shared messaging for easy and asynchronous communication.

However, instead of requiring support to allow people having informal interactions through mediating technology, under the concept of artificial proximity, what is required is the provision of augmented support to enhance impromptu face-to-face interactions arising due to local mobility. For this reason, what we propose is to use technology to enhance and augment informal interactions that occur face-to-face, and that arise while people move to perform their work.

To achieve this, we call attention to the importance of conceptually defining an environment that integrates an ensemble of technological services that satisfy the requirements for supporting co-located collaboration while on the move. This work is organized as follows. In section 2 we present results of a field study we performed to understand informal communication in hospitals. Section 3 presents the components and characteristics of the MoCHA architecture, a generic architecture to support co-located collaboration in hospital work. In section 4 we present the development issues of a MoCHA based tool and finally, section 5 concludes this paper.

2   Understanding Informal Communication in Hospital

Due to the nature of hospital work, hospital workers have to move constantly in order to get access to places, people, resources and knowledge [1]. Most of their time, they are moving and/or working within a specific range area. This mobility (called local mobility [1,4]) allows a significant amount of co-located interactions among hospital workers. For this, in order to design a tool that provides adequate support for informal co-located interactions in hospitals, we needed to understand how they occur, which their purposes are, and how mobility is experienced by hospital workers. In this section we present the results of a field study that helped us ground our design by translating the way the work gets done into specific vignettes that capture facets of how technological support might fit into current work practices.

2.1   Methodology of the Field Study

This work is part of a workplace study conducted at a medical intern area of a mid-size public hospital, and its methodology has been described in [17]. The main contribution of this study relies in the characterization of mobile work and the information usage practices that hospital workers engage in.

Described briefly, the methodology consisted in collecting data through the non-participatory observations of ten medical workers including five physicians and five medical interns during two complete working shifts. Those roles were selected because they experiment high mobility and are responsible for patient care, the main trust of the hospital.

The activities performed by physicians during a work shift include: exchange information with colleagues related to events that arose in their absence, conduct exploratory and interrogatory evaluations of patients, update medical notes with tailored treatments and diagnoses, train and evaluate medical interns, discuss with colleagues special clinical cases and participate in surgical procedures. Likewise, the medical interns are considered physicians-in-training; they provide the most hours of patient care in the unit and are in constant movement. Interns are responsible for the care of five to six patients. One of their main responsibilities is to create clinical histories whenever a new patient arrives to the hospital. They are also responsible for providing care and following-up on patients during their staying in the hospital. Other tasks for which medical interns are responsible have a more collaborative nature, for instance, they participate in ward rounds with attending physicians and in meetings where clinical cases are discussed [17].

Later, we decided to place special emphasis on understanding how local mobility influences the interactions experienced by hospital workers. For this, we conducted a second analysis aimed at having a good sample of interactions and capture all the communication in which those workers are involved as they conduct their work, including details with respect to the nature of the actions, artifacts used, contents of conversations and physical location of individuals. The goal of this study was to: (1) consolidate a conceptual understanding of the informal collaboration among hospital workers during their everyday activities, and (2) determine design insights that could be taken into account at the development time of a tool that supports co-located informal interactions in hospital work.

2.2 Informal Interactions in Hospitals

Informal interactions can be classified based on the intentionality of the participants at the time when a conversation begins [13]. The classification is as follows: (a) conversations in which the initiator sets out specifically to visit another party (intended), (b) the ones in which the initiator had planned to talk to other participants and took advantage of a chance encounter to have a conversation (opportunistic), and (c) spontaneous interactions in which the initiator had not planned to talk to the other participant (spontaneous). Further, informal interactions can be characterized as being frequent, brief, unscheduled, often dyadic, frequently supported by shared objects, intermittent, lacking formal openings and closings, and dependant on physical proximity [8, 10, 13].

The results of our study show that on average 56% of the observed interactions in the hospital occurred due to casual encounters (i.e. are opportunistic or spontaneous), 39% of the interactions occurred because the initiator approaches the person with whom he wants to interact (i.e. are intended), and only 5% of these interactions occurred because they were pre-arranged (i.e. scheduled).

These findings suggest that physical proximity allows hospital workers to interact very frequently (as more than 55% of the interactions happen face to face due to opportunistic or spontaneous encounters) by creating opportunities for co-located collaboration, so that it could be helpful to provide them with computational support to augment or enhance their co-located interactions while on-the-move rather than just providing them with artificial proximity tools.

2.3 Main Uses of Informal Communications in Hospital Work

Informal interactions can also be classified according to their purpose or function [10]; these purposes and functions include: (a) tracking people, which involves identifying the current whereabouts, activities, and future plans of intended interactants, (b) taking or leaving messages, which refers to contacting someone via a third party, (c) making meeting arrangements, which refers to scheduling future interactions, (d) delivering documents, which refers to handing off a document with actions attached to it and, in a more complex example, involves discussions of individual actions associated with different parts of a document, (e) giving or getting help, which refers to joint problem solving for one person's benefit, and (f) reporting progress and news, which refers to updating people with relevant information.

In our study we found that hospital workers not only use informal interactions for these six purposes, but also for three additional ones: (g) delegating activities, which refers to those activities that can be performed by two or more hospital workers, but one of them asks someone else to perform all or part of these activities, (h) tracking artifacts, which involves identifying the current location or state of specific artifacts, like medical records, medical equipment, or laboratory results among others, and (i) personal conversations, which refer to social conversations concerning specific personal issues of the participants. Concerning how frequently hospital workers use informal interactions for each purpose (see Table 1), we found that the functions more often used were Reporting progress and news (about 36% on average), Giving or getting help (about 16.5%), Delegating activities (about 11%) and Document delivery (about 10.5%), standing for nearly 75% of their total interactions.

Table 1. Frequency of informal interactions by functionality in hospital work

Functions (Per total subject)	Physicians		Medical interns	
	Number of interactions	%	Number of interactions	%
Tracking people	10	2.77	20	4.81
Taking and leaving messages	6	1.66	7	1.68
Making meeting arrangements	3	0.8	4	0.96
Document delivery	40	11.09	42	10.10
Giving or getting help	69	19.11	59	14.18
Reporting progress and news	119	32.96	166	39.90
Delegating activities	60	16.62	25	6.01
Tracking physical artifacts	10	2.77	23	5.53
Personal conversations	44	12.19	70	16.83
Total	**361**	**100**	**416**	**100**

Additionally, we extend the scope of *reporting progress and news*. Our definition of this purpose involves interactions which main objective is "service synchronization" or collaborations related to patient care. In most of these interactions, the participants interacted in a co-located way and in almost 25.82% of total collaborations, they had to share or use some documents or information artifacts (e.g. patient medical records, reference articles, books, and e-libraries among others) in order to attain the objective of the interaction.

These findings suggest that the retrieval, sharing, manipulation, and management of information during informal interactions is very important, and thus it is valuable to make these operations seamlessly available in the form of pervasive e-services throughout the hospital premises.

2.4 Scenario: An Instance of Collaboration in Hospital Work

In order to better understand mobile informal co-located collaboration in hospitals, we decided to identify some of those instances that characterize this type of collaboration, as a way to frame our understanding of hospital work practices.

We next describe one of these instances:

> *A physician is in the Internal Medicine office when a medical specialist arrives and asks him about an X-Ray image he is consulting.*
>
> **[Physician]** *What do you think about this?*
>
> **[Medical Specialist]** *(Looking the X-Ray results) Mmm, I think that he has (disease's name).*
>
> **[Physician]** *Are you sure? Because he has (medical specialist explains the symptoms of patient).*
>
> **[Medical Specialist]** *Yes, I do. I had a patient with similar symptoms.*
>
> **[Physician]** *Are you sure? I think (there) could be some differences between the symptoms of these patients.*
>
> **[Medical Specialist]** *Well, let me review the health record of my patient and I will discuss with you later.*

Later, the physician and the medical specialist met opportunistically in the hallway and they restart their previous discussion.

> **[Medical Specialist]** *(showing the physician a health record) Look, these are the symptoms of the patient I mentioned. His disease has the same features as those of your patient.*
>
> **[Physician]** *Ok, you are right. But, which is the treatment for this type of disease?*
>
> **[Medical Specialist]** *(the medical specialist explains the treatment for the patient). I have a medical guide in my consulting room. Please go there later, I can lend it to you.*

We can identify some communication breakdowns in the way in which this collaboration takes place. First, hospital workers usually interrupt their interactions to gather the necessary artifacts or resources to collaborate with others. That happens because while hospital staff is moving around the hospital performing their work, information resources are usually stored in fixed specific areas or, in particular times, some of them are used or carried by other hospital workers.

Furthermore, despite that it is not explicitly described in the previous sample observation, we observed a lack of mechanism to help workers initiate impromptu meetings. In this type of interactions, collaborators usually share information artifacts by handing over or looking concurrently at the same artifact, generating with this some kind of discomfort among collaborators.

Another disadvantage of sharing information artifacts is that most of the time hospital workers can not make annotations or marks on these artifacts, resulting in the loss of valuable collaboration information that could be used both in future collaborations and in individual tasks.

Finally, we observed that despite of the physical nearness of collaborators (an opportunity for collaboration), they did not always collaborate due to lack of awareness of the location of others.

So, these findings motivate us to propose a set of design insights that help us to develop tools to adequately augment and support mobile informal co-located interactions in hospital work.

2.5 Design Insights for Tools That Support Mobile Informal Co-located Collaboration in Hospitals

As stated earlier, due to the nature of hospital settings, workers frequently interact and collaborate in hallways or bed wards due to opportunistic encounters. For this reason, we identified some characteristics that could be implemented in tools that augment or enhance co-located informal collaboration among hospital workers, including:

Prompt initiation of the interaction. An important characteristic of informal interactions is briefness. We found that 47% of all interactions lasted less than one minute. For this reason, it is necessary that systems allow workers to begin an interaction as quickly as possible. Devices must be able to identify partners and allow the use of resources available to each person, without requiring them to explicitly log in at each device they need to use.

Use of devices that allow workers getting into collaboration while on-the-move. Mobility is a predominant characteristic of hospital work. Results of a study on hospital mobility show that physicians spent almost 10% of their time in hallways [117]. They are there not only to move from one operation center to another, but also to actually have meaningful encounters and perform work while in the hallway. Moreover, in our study we found that in almost 6% of informal interactions, hospital workers had co-located collaboration in hallways involving discussions about patient care based on medical records and external medical information sources. For these reasons, we argue that it is very important that systems that intend to provide support for hospital workers must allow them to move around the hospital area and more importantly, to interact "every time - everywhere" as required by the actual situation.

Have easy access to information's sources. In hospital work, we found that in almost 26% of the total number of informal interactions, physicians and medical interns need to share or exchange information. Currently, they use physical artifacts to do this, like medical records and X-Ray images, among others. Additionally, they use external information like medical guides, medical papers, digital libraries and books among others, in order to enrich the content of their interaction. For these reasons, we argue that it is very important that systems aimed at providing support for hospital workers allow them to have easy access to digital information sources.

Use of devices and services that allow interactions based on medical evidence. Physicians and medical interns often discuss clinical cases. We observed that in 6% of the total informal interactions they used and shared information stored in physical artifacts (medical records, X-Ray images and books among others) and/or electronic devices (document stored on PCs or PDAs and digital libraries among others) in order to explain to others their opinions. All these meetings were directly related with patient's care. For these reasons, we argue for systems that allow hospital workers to use heterogeneous devices that help them to establish interactions based on medical evidence.

Reuse information generated during hospital workers' interactions. Often, while hospital workers are collaborating, important information is generated for at least one of them. In co-located interactions, the generated information is directly related with patient care and this information could be used in additional actions or interactions. For these reasons, we argue that it is very important that systems allow hospital workers to reuse information generated while they are collaborating.

Awareness of the potential for collaboration. In informal interactions there are two main elements that trigger people to initiate collaboration with others: the availability of a communication or interaction channel (e.g physical proximity) and/or the interest or need of at least one of the participants to collaborate with the other [Moran et al]. For these reasons, systems should allow hospital workers to be aware of the other's presence, identity and location, as well as of an adequate moment for starting or getting into collaboration with them.

Seamless information access and sharing. As part of their co-located interactions hospital workers usually discuss information stored in physical artifacts or electronic devices. While collaborating, information is transferred among these artifacts or devices. For these reasons, we argue that it is very important that systems allow easily sharing and exchange of information among hospital workers.

Privacy of information. Result of our qualitative analysis show that hospital workers are granted access only to the medical records of those patients that they are in charge of. For this reason, we argue that it is very important that systems should not allow users for unauthorized access to patients' medical records.

3   MoCHA Architecture: Generalizing Functionality of a Tool That Supports Mobile Informal Co-located Collaborations

Based on the design insights presented in section two, as well as on the characteristics and services of our collaborative system, we designed an architecture (see figure 1) that defines the structure of the system and integrates the functionality that must be provided by those tools aimed at providing support for mobile informal co-located collaboration in hospital work.

For this, we identified three essential elements necessary to support mobile informal co-located collaboration: people, information and services.

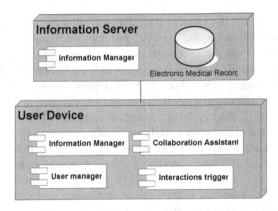

Fig. 1. MoCHA Architecture

We conceptualized *people* as the essential entity for collaboration. For this reason, we found necessary to provide people with opportunities for collaboration. Some of these opportunities are provided by the local mobility that hospital workers experience. However, we supplied people with awareness on the location of others in order to propitiate opportunistic encounters, by designing the *Interaction Trigger Component (ITC)* that is in charge of providing awareness of possible face to face opportunistic interactions. The ITC includes two main services: *location estimation and pending task manager.*

The aim of this component is to provide *awareness of the potential for collaboration* [16]. It determines a set of mobile devices in the vicinity (location estimation service) whose users have a pending topic for interaction (pending task manager service), and sends a notification to these users. The idea of the pending task manager emerges from the concept of opportunistic interactions (they happen due to opportunistic encounters and because at least one of the participants needs to collaborate with other participants) and promotes opportunistic collaboration without requiring to be aware of the others' location all the time.

Furthermore, people usually need *information* in order to augment their collaboration. Moreover, sometimes new information associated with information artifacts is generated during collaboration. This suggest the use of an information server that stores and manages patient medical records, allowing users to access clinical information every time/every where they need it.

Additionally, we designed the *Information Manager Component (IMC)* that is in charge of the negotiation and management of the patient information required for face to face interactions. In the server device, the IMC has to attend user requests and to send them only the allowed information. In contrast, in the client device, the IMC is in charge of user information requests (to the information server), the management of this information during user collaboration and saving this information at end of the collaboration if necessary. This component addresses the needs for *privacy of information and reuse of information generated in hospital worker interactions.*

Concerning *services*, these are those facilities that are provided to collaborators in order to enhance or augment the interaction. We designed the *Collaboration Assistant*

Component (CAC) that is in charge of providing a set of services that augment mobile informal co-located collaboration. The CAC provides three main services: i) seamless information transfer among heterogeneous devices [15], ii) proximity-based application sharing and iii) meeting support through the interaction of public displays and handheld computers. The idea of the seamless information transfer service consists in allowing users to transfer information to any device in the vicinity, such as a PDA, a PC or a public display, from a handheld computer [15].

Similarly, the idea of the proximity-based application sharing service consists of displaying the contents of any device in the vicinity, such as a PDA, a PC or a public display, on a handheld computer, and being able to remotely share the control of the device with its owner and/or other users [15]. Finally, the meeting support service emerged from the idea that an impromptu or unplanned co-located meeting can be supported by allowing a group of physicians to remotely control a public display with their handhelds [15].

Finally, we propose to provide support for one of the main characteristics of informal collaboration: briefness. Results of our field study show that almost 50% of total informal collaborations lasted less than 1 minute. For this, we designed the *User Manager Component (UMC)* that is in charge of providing the impromptu initiation of collaborations by associating users and devices as a unique entity (ID). In others words, the UMC sends to other users/devices the ID of each collaborator. It is helpful at the moment of ensuring privacy of information, by allowing to the IMC to send to collaborators only the information granted to them.

4   Sample Application: A MoCHA Based Tool

The design insights as well as the MoCHA architecture presented in the previous sections allowed us to address some of the questions that emerged regarding how technical support could be developed to support co-located informal collaboration in hospitals. These questions include:

1. What kind of technological setting could be used in order to allow hospital workers to get into collaboration while on-the-move?
2. What kind of technological setting could be used in order to allow hospital workers to get into collaboration based on medical evidence?
3. How current location estimation systems by themselves may enhance opportunities for impromptu co-located informal collaboration?
4. How hospital workers could access patient's information when required?
5. What kind of electronic services could be designed to augment co-located informal collaboration?

To address these questions, we extended a collaborative system designed in our laboratory [15], because it fulfills most of the proposed design insights: 1) *prompt initiation of the interaction,* 2) *use of devices that allow workers to get into collaboration while moving,* 3) *use of devices and services that allow interactions based on medical evidence,* 4) *awareness of the potential for collaboration and,* 5) *seamless information access and sharing.*

These design insight are fulfilled through four main services that the system provides: location awareness of users, seamless transfer of information among heterogeneous devices (see figure 2b), application sharing among colleagues for information visualization on their PDAs, and control of the applications that display this information (see figure 2a).

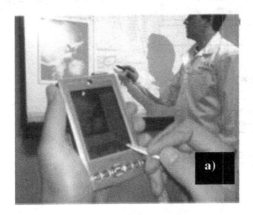

Fig. 2. a) Remote control of a large display: a physician interacts with a public display while a colleague remotely interacts with it from his PDA and, b) Selection of a file to be transferred

This functionality is provided through six agents that reside in the user devices, which are logically classified as source or target devices, depending of their role while collaborating. The *Location Estimation agent (LE-a)* determines the approximate location of users and devices within a hospital [6]. Trough this component the proximity-based functionality is provided. The *Migration component* allows the seamless transfer of information among heterogeneous devices. This component uses the *Source Proxy agent (SP-a)* and the *Information adaptation agent (IA-a)*, which resides in the client application and communicates through the broker with the *Target Proxy Agent* (TP-a); which acts as a server and must be located in the target device. Finally, the *Controller* component is used to establish the proximity-based application sharing and remote control of computing devices. This component is formed by a *Controller agent (C-a)* which resides in the source device and the *Echo server agent (ES-a)* that resides in the target device. These controllers work in pairs to provide the functionality [15]. However, as each device could be considered as source or target, physically these agents are located in the same user devices.

Even though this system allows for opportunistic collaboration among hospital workers, it must be extended in order to provide hospital workers with the resources and services required to augment co-located interactions according to the way in which hospital workers currently collaborate while performing their daily work, and as identified in our previous analysis.

We performed two extensions to this system: the addition of an information server and the development of the required services for it, and a pending task manager.

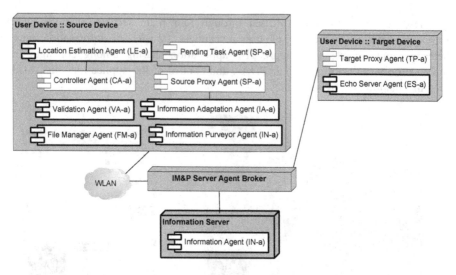

Fig. 3. Extended agent architecture of our collaborative system

The first extension consists on the use of an *information server* which stores and manages the patients' information that hospital users need to perform their work (see Figure 2). Furthermore, we introduced the *Information* agent that manages users' information requests. Moreover, to provide information privacy without sacrificing information access - sometimes it is necessary to review information that could not be viewed by others- the *Echo server agent* was modified to identify which files of the source device could be presented in the target device. Also, the information server and the *information and validation agents,* along with the modified *Echo server agent* are in charge of ensuring the privacy of patient information, in response to the insights: *having easy access to information's sources* and *ensuring privacy of information*.

Additionally, to fulfill the *reuse of information generated in hospital workers' interactions*, we developed the *File Manager agent* that identifies when a file is modified (users could add comments and/or marks) and stores the original file without modifications in the *information* server, as well as a copy of this file with the user modifications in the personal device of users.

Furthermore, in order to extend the limited *awareness of potential collaboration* that the currently *Location Estimation agent* currently provides, the second extension to the collaborative system was the introduction of a *Pending Task agent* that works in pair with the *Location Estimation agent and that has as main function to* check whether the user needs to interact with some of the nearby users.

This is done as follows (Figure 4): after the *Location estimation agent* estimates the location of the devices in the vicinity, the *Pending Task agent* must check whether the user needs to interact with some of the nearby users and if so required, it sends a notification to the users (Figure 5a). Then, the *Location Estimation agent* shows the users the map with the colleagues' location (Figure 5b).

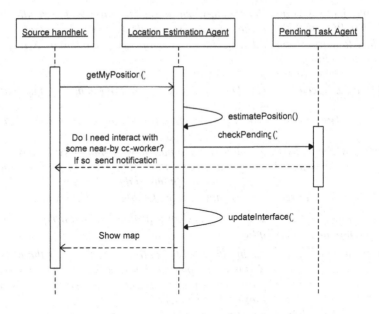

Fig. 4. Sequence Diagram of the functionality of the Interaction Trigger Component

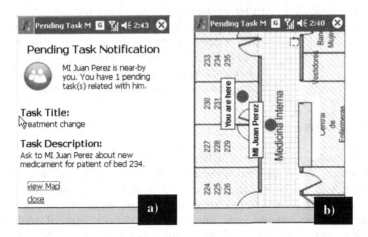

Fig. 5. Awareness of potential collaboration service: a) Notification of a near-by colleague. b) Map with location of colleague.

We performed this last modification, because sometimes hospital workers are not aware of the nearness of others colleagues, despite their being closely located to the others, because the physical structure of the hospital does not allow that users could be easily aware of the others' presence.

Finally, in order to better illustrate the features of a MoCHA based tool, we present the next scenario that shows how the instance presented in section 2.4 could be performed through the developed tool:

A physician is in a patient room when he realizes through the pending manager in her PDA that the medical specialist is walking down the corridor –which is close to her position and he decides to met him and ask about an X-Ray image he was consulting.

[Physician]   *What do you think about this?*

[Medical Specialist]   *(Looking the X-Ray results) Mmm, I think that he has (disease's name).*

[Physician]   *Are you sure? Because he has (medical specialist explains the symptoms of patient).*

[Medical Specialist]   *Yes, I do. I had a patient with similar symptoms.*

[Physician]   *Are you sure? I think (there) could be some differences between the symptoms of these patients.*

[Medical Specialist]   *Let me show you the health record of my patient.*

The medical specialist access the patient's health record through his PDA and transfers it to the public display.

[Medical Specialist]   *(Using the remote control tool, he shows the physician an X-Ray of the patient) Look, these are the symptoms of the patient I mentioned. His disease has the same features as those of your patient.*

[Physician]   *Ok, you are right. But, which is the treatment for this type of disease?*

[Medical Specialist]   *(After explaining the treatment for the patient, using the remote control tool, the medical specialist accesses his office's computer to retrieve information from a medical guide related to the medication and to the patient's condition, and transfers it to the physicians' PDA). I have this information that could be useful to you.*

5   Conclusions

In the last years, research in CSCW has highlighted the importance of informal communication in work environments. Previous studies have analyzed the characteristics of informal interactions in traditional office environments and have shown proximity as a necessary characteristic for informal interactions to occur. In consequence, these studies have motivated the development of tools aimed at providing support for this type of interactions, mainly under the form of "artificial proximity". However, in a hospital environment, proximity is usually provided by the mobility experienced by the workers (55% of total interactions in our study happen due to opportunistic encounters), due to their performing activities involved in the treatment of a patient or coordination activities and, therefore, these tools are not completely adequate in all informal interactions in hospitals.

Additionally, current collaboration in hospital work still has some breakdowns like the lack of opportunities for collaboration, loss of the information generated during impromptu collaboration, and interruption of collaboration to gather information resources, among others, and these mainly due to the way in which the work is performed and supported.

As an answer, our proposal consists in the development and integration of tools that provide support for mobile informal co-located collaboration. For it, based on the findings of a workplace study that we conducted, we propose a set of design insights that must be fulfilled in order to adequately support this type of interactions. Moreover, we generalized these design insights through MoCHA, an architecture that integrates them as a set of components that define the structure of those developed tools aimed at providing support for mobile informal co-located interactions in hospital work. It highlights the need of providing mechanisms for triggering opportunistic interactions among hospital workers, as well as providing the required resources to augment co-located collaboration in these work environments.

Based on this architecture, we extended and integrated an ensemble of collaborative services previously developed in our laboratory in order to fulfill the proposed design insights. One important addition was the interaction trigger service, which provides users with awareness of opportunistic encounters even in the absence of consciousness of nearness of possible collaborators in the vicinity.

In the same way, we provided our system with components and services that allow users to access information every-time/every-place they need, as well as mechanisms that allow users to reuse the information generated while they collaborate, such as comments or annotations on files.

These proposals help us to face the challenges that hospital work poses while workers enter into mobile informal co-located collaboration.

Acknowledgements

We thank the personnel at IMSS General Hospital who participated in the study. This work was partially financed by CONACYT under contract C03-42447, and through a scholarship provided to the first author.

References

[1] Bardram, J., Bossen, C.: Moving to get aHead: Local Mobility and Collaborative Work. In: Dourish, P., Fitzpatrick, G., Schmidt, K. (eds.) Proceedings of the Fifth European Conference on Computer Supported Cooperative Work, pp. 355–374. Kluwer Academic Publishers, Dordrecht (2003)

[2] Bardram, J., Hansen, T.: The AWARE architecture: supporting context-mediated social awareness in mobile cooperation. In: Herbsleb, Jim, Olson, Gary, M. (eds.) Proceedings of the 2004 ACM Conference on Computer Supported Cooperative Work, pp. 192–201. ACM Press, New York (2004)

[3] Bardram, J., Hansen, T., Soegaard, M.: AwareMedia – A Shared Interactive Display Supporting Social, Temporal, and Spatial Awareness in Surgery. In: Greenberg, Saul, Mark, Gloria (eds.) Proceedings of the ACM Conference on Computer Supported Cooperative Work, pp. 109–118. ACM Press, New York (2006)

[4] Belloti, V., Bly, S.: Walking Away from the Desktop Computer: Distributed Collaboration and Mobility in a Product Design Team. In: Proc. of the CSCW, pp. 209–218. ACM Press, New York (1996)

[5] Bossen, C.: The parameters of common information spaces: The heterogeneity of cooperative work at a hospital ward. In: Proc. of the CSCW, pp. 76–185. ACM Press, New York (2006)

[6] Castro, L., Favela, J.: Contiuous Tracking of User Location in WLANs Using Recurrent Neural Networks. In: Proc. of the ENC. '05, pp. 174–181. IEEE Press, Los Alamitos (2005)

[7] Contreras-Castillo, J.J., Favela, J., Perez-Fragoso, C., Santamaria-del-Angel, E.: Informal Interactions and their Implications for Online Courses. In: Computers and Education, vol. 42(2), pp. 149–168. ACM Press, New York (2004)

[8] Fish, R.S., Kraut, R.E., Root, R.W., Rice, R.E.: Video as a technology for informal communication. Communications of the ACM 36(1), 48–61 (1993)

[9] Gutwin, C., Greenberg, S., Blum, R., Dych, J.: Supporting Informal Collaboration in Shared Workspace Groupware. HCI Technical Report. Department of Computer Science, University of Saskatchewan, p. 20 (2005)

[10] Isaacs, E., Whittaker, S., Frohlich, D., O'Conaill, B.: Informal communication re-examined: New functions for video in supporting opportunistic encounters. In: Finn, K.E., Sellen, A.J., Wilbur, S.B. (eds.) the Lawrence Erlbaum book, pp. 459–485 (1997)

[11] Isaacs, E., Tang, J.C., Morris, T.: Piazza: A Desktop Environment Supporting Impromptu and Planned Interactions. In: Proc. of CSCW, pp. 315–324. ACM Press, New York (1996)

[12] Isaacs, E., Walendowski, A., Ranganathan, D.: Hubbub: A sound-enhanced mobile instant messenger that supports awareness and opportunistic interactions. In: Proceedings of the Conference Computer-Human Interaction (CHI), pp. 179–186. ACM Press, New York (2002)

[13] Kraut, R., Fish, R., Root, R., Chalfonte, B.: Informal communication in organizations: form, function and technology. In: People reactions to technology in factories, offices and aerospace. The Claremont Symposium on Applied Social Psycology, pp. 145–199. Sage Publications, Thousand Oaks (1990)

[14] Kraut, R., Streeter, L.: Co-ordination in software development. Commun. ACM 38(1), 69–81 (1995)

[15] Markarian, A., Favela, J., Tentori, M., Castro, L.A.: Seamless Interaction among Heterogeneous Devices in Support for Co-located Collaboration. In: Dimitriadis, Y.A., Zigurs, I., Gómez-Sánchez, E. (eds.) CRIWG 2006. LNCS, vol. 4154, pp. 389–404. Springer, Heidelberg (2006)

[16] Morán, A.L., Favela, J., Martínez, A.M., Decouchant, D.: On the Design of Potential Collaboration Spaces. International Journal of Computer Applications in Technology (IJCAT) 19(3/4), 184–194 (2004)

[17] Moran, E., Tentori, M., González, V.M., Martinez-Garcia, A.I., Favela, J.: Mobility in Hospital Work: Towards a Pervasive Computing Hospital Environment. International Journal of Electronic Healthcare 3(1), 72–89 (2005)

[18] Whittaker, S.: Rethinking video as a technology for interpersonal communications: theory and design implications. Int. J. Hum.-Comput. Stud. 42(5), 501–529 (1995)

Relating Interactions to Artifacts Through Content Analysis: A Practical Investigation

Adriana S. Vivacqua[1,3], Jano M. de Souza[1,2], and Jean-Paul Barthès[3]

[1] PESC/COPPE – Graduate School of Computer Science
[2] DCC/IM – Institute of Mathematics
UFRJ – Federal University of Rio de Janeiro
[3] Université de Technologie de Compiègne
{avivacqua,jano}@cos.ufrj.br, barthes@utc.fr

Abstract. Nowadays, information workers often work within networked structures, where relations between individuals become active according to the needs and workers multitask between several collaborations. One of the difficulties pointed out in these studies lies in keeping track of the many collaborations and ties to others, managing the relationships involved and the different roles and activities in each situation. Two important activities in this context are *remembering* (who one is or could be collaborating with, in what capacity, pending tasks, etc.) and *communicating* (as a means to strengthen relationships, negotiate joint work or keep others informed.) In this paper, we explore the possibility of linking relationships to activities through interaction analysis. More specifically, we explore content analysis as a means to determine collaboration themes and identify artifacts or resources that pertain to a certain social world.

Keywords: Interaction analysis, content analysis, information retrieval.

1 Introduction

Modern information workers often work within networked configurations, where relations between people become active according to the needs [18]. These workers often multitask between several collaborations, dividing their time and attention according to the urgency of the tasks at hand [12]. Organizations have been transformed by network technology into networks of interconnected individuals [4]. This is advantageous because the networked structure leads to higher adaptability and flexibility and is well suited to handle dynamic environments [2]. Computer networks have flourished and, as a result, the adoption of virtual teams (teams where individuals are remotely located and most of the time work using computer tools) by organizations has also increased [14]. These two factors lead to a configuration in which distributed individuals manage and work within their networks, forming groups to accomplish objectives.

Oftentimes, these teams are also capable of self organization [3], as members have the flexibility to reconfigure and reassign tasks according to immediate needs. Thus, work within groups and organizations happens as much as a function of individual

J.M. Haake, S.F. Ochoa, and A. Cechich (Eds.): CRIWG 2007, LNCS 4715, pp. 271–286, 2007.
© Springer-Verlag Berlin Heidelberg 2007

actions and interrelations as of group rules and organizational mandates [2]. In some situations, individuals draw upon social networks and existing relationships to accomplish part of their tasks. Add to the distance and the need for flexibility the fact that individuals often alternate between individual and joint work [14] and the problem of maintaining individuals in synch becomes more complex. To be able to adapt to new situations, workers need to have information regarding their collaborators, tasks, ongoing activities and arrangements. The group needs this information to be able to assess the situation and change configurations when necessary. Early research on awareness systems has tried to address this problem by providing information about other group members to heighten understanding of shared workspace, but has thus far not addressed the automatic constitution of these workspaces and information delivery within them.

Some of the aforementioned studies indicate that the two main problems lie in *remembering* people and activities and *communicating* with others [18]. A recurring problem is managing attention and remembering which arrangements have been made and what tasks are due in order "not to let anything fall through the cracks" [12]. Support systems for workers in engaged in multiple virtual teams must help individuals manage their multiple collaborative contexts. One way to do this is by helping them understand the social context of the work they are performing: who is involved with this project and in what capacity? What other resources are relevant? Automatic determination of collaborators and identification of collaboration themes is a step towards that goal. This social context is composed not only of a set of people, resources and tools but also of the interrelations between them, which affects ongoing work by defining how people relate, organize themselves and get work done. The group's context, informally constructed and dynamic, contains hierarchies, roles and task assignments. Discovery of these contexts is a first step towards the creation of systems to support workers enmeshed in them.

Prior work indicates that it is possible to discover collaborators through analysis of interaction patterns and social networks [7][21]. Following this reasoning, it should be possible to automatically constitute part of a worker's social contexts through interaction and content analysis. This paper looks into the applicability of content analysis to tie interactions to artifacts an individual might be working on, which could be used to define these social contexts, locating the user within a particular shared context even while working individually. Social contexts could be used by support systems to help users maintain ties to others, distribute information or locate potential collaborators and to provide added context to artifacts.

This paper is organized as follows: in the following section we present theoretical work that underlies our investigation. Then, related systems are presented in Section 3. Section 4 presents an approach to tie interactions to resources through content analysis, followed by an evaluation of this approach in Section 5. Discussion and future work are presented in Section 6.

2   Theoretical Research

This section is divided into two subsections: first, we provide a theoretical background that leads to our current investigation. We then briefly explain the information retrieval techniques involved in our study.

2.1 Networks as Organizational Forms

The network configuration, in which elements are interconnected and the intelligence is on the network itself, is now applicable to any type of activity, segment or location that can be connected electronically [4]. The network is well adapted to the growing complexity of the environment and provides added flexibility to organizations [2].

Networks exist in a global level, as enterprises connect and interact with other organizations. In this scenario, actors are highly interdependent, as organizations subcontract and collaborate to pursue their objectives and gain market penetration. Networks can also be found within organizations, as they shift from vertical bureaucracies to horizontal structures. In this new organization, administration is decentralized and work is individualized [4].

Bernoux describes the organization as a network of autonomous interacting actors, where each actor has a personal view of the organization [2]. Any association between elements is governed by contracts and rules of the pair's making, and is subject to constant negotiation and redefinition as the situation demands. Thus, the organization becomes a system of dynamic social ties, where actors may redefine the rules and the network. In this fashion, an organization functions as much as a result of actors' interactions and relations as of the organizational structure provided. Work is conducted through the establishment of cooperative work arrangements, which emerge to handle specific unforeseen requirements and dissolve when they are no longer necessary. These arrangements are organized according to specific needs and follow established patterns [26].

Autonomous workers are usually found in greater numbers in networked structures [4] (e.g., even in fairly controlled environments such as shop-floor situations, workers were observed to have a fair amount of autonomy to deal with unexpected situations [3]). Self-governing groups are groups that emerge out of a need to handle unpredictable events or contingencies, where actors have control over job allocation, day-to-day production planning and control [3]. These groups usually dissolve when they are no longer necessary, and enable an organization to quickly adapt to new demands generated by the environment, even if this means deviating from pre-established norms and rules.

Due to the underlying interdependence between tasks, workers have to articulate (i.e., divide, allocate, coordinate, etc.) their activities [26]. The organization provides a relatively stable pattern of cooperative arrangements, but new collaborative work groups emerge because actors could not accomplish certain tasks if they were to do it individually [26]. Many group decisions are the result of arrangements between peers, as is the work that finally gets done [2]. In most situations, individuals have some level of control over their work, and are capable of adjusting for errors or unusual circumstances, handling unpredictable events or contingencies.

Information is paramount for the functioning and organization of elements in the network structure. Castells [4] underlines the importance of information in the new economy, as productivity and competitiveness are strongly dependent on their capacity to efficiently generate, process and apply knowledge based information.

Information technology enables task decentralization and coordination in real time interactive communication networks, global or local. In general, the traditional forms of work are slowly being substituted for more flexible and individualized contracts

[4]. However, traditional support systems have focused on the development of effective models of the structures and processes relevant to the organization's work and adequate ways to present them, but haven't provided much in the way of supporting informal arrangements or enabling them to work more effectively [26].

2.2 Networks as Personal Resources

Over a series of studies, Wellman and his group have detected the appearance of personal communities in advanced societies: individual social networks that exist both offline and on. Communities are substituted by personal networks, where ties are specialized and diversified, as people create their own "personal portfolios" [33].

In recent studies, Nardi and colleagues [18] document the rise of personal networks in the workplace. They call these *intensional* networks and defend that the most important unit of analysis for computer supported cooperative work is not at the group level, but at the individual level in many situations. She also states that relationships outside the organization (e.g., government and press) are critical to many businesses, and that many corporations now operate in an increasingly distributed way, where workers, contractors, consultants and others work in different locations. Within organizations, constant reorganizations mean workers' responsibilities, colleagues and reporting relationships change frequently.

Intensional networks are personal social networks workers draw from to get work done. These networks are both emergent (in that they can be called into existence to accomplish particular work) and historic (in that work is based on known relationships and shared experiences, and each joint project adds to the relationship history, altering it). *NetWORKers* are individuals whose work is based on intensional networks. They spend a large amount of effort on their networks: it requires deliberate and careful work to create and maintain relationships upon which individuals can then rely for work purposes [19][27].

Different sections of intensional networks become active depending on ongoing work. When a set of contacts is live, the relations that link to them need constant renewal through communication [18]. The live substructure is a result of human interaction that happens due to ongoing group work. The subnets are the parts of a network that keep a worker most occupied, but distant contacts also need to be tended and remembered for future joint work. Working in intensional networks introduces additional complications for the participants, in remembering membership, roles and responsibilities of different individuals [18].

Information workers are typically involved in multiple collaborations at the same time, and must divide their time accordingly [12]. This means there may be several different subsections of one's intensional network active simultaneously, and the user needs to shift attention between the different *working spheres*. A working sphere groups together a set of events involving a particular group of people, a common motive and a unique set of resources [13]. One of the difficulties in this scenario is remembering the different contexts and managing transitions between them. Workers use a variety of methods to remember things, people and the current context, so they can pick up where they left off [12]. Practices include dropping in on collaborators, constantly checking email, keeping to-do lists or writing notes to oneself [12].

2.3 Organization Through Working Spheres

A working sphere contains the elements that define the social context of individual work. Some of the practices mentioned above cannot easily be executed when working in virtual teams or similar distributed work scenarios. To help individuals manage their multitasking activities and keep in step with events related to the working spheres they are inserted in, systems should keep track of the multiple working spheres and of the contacts involved in each, their roles and assignments and the shared resources involved. Discovery of working spheres involves figuring out who is involved in each group and which resources and themes these groups share. Assessing each user's individual activities and linking these to the working spheres they belong to is another important step, as it enables a system to keep track of changes happening in the working sphere. By organizing contacts and resources according to their respective working spheres, users should be able to more easily keep track of their work, of pending tasks and of shared goals. Systems could assist the user in doing so by facilitating resource organization.

Considering that working spheres are based on the individual's interrelations to others, Social Network Analysis (SNA) [28][32] appears to be an applicable technique with which to analyze and discover working spheres. SNA takes stock of relationships between individuals and their regularities to analyze individual and group behavior. Interpersonal associations are the elements through which individuals form groups and societies. They are simultaneously the means of association and of socialization between group members [29]. It is possible to study interpersonal associations because they are regular and stable, and they figure in different times and domains of social life: typical relationships, such as domination, competition, imitation or conflict can be found by studying these structures [6]. This reflects the fact that most activities are inserted in social contexts, and that the network within which they are inserted is bound by rules and practices defined by its members [28].

Interaction in distributed groups normally happens via computer-based media which usually leave traces, such as email, forum or messenger logs. Rhythms found in interactions correspond to individuals' work patterns [21], and can be used to study the evolution of an individual's interests (as he or she relates to others in different domains) or collaborative endeavors: intense message exchange usually accompanies cooperative work. Individual patterns of email exchange can also indicate hierarchy and positioning in a group [7]. Thus, an analysis of the interactions relating to each tie should yield the collaborators and themes within a working sphere.

The Locales Framework is a unifying framework for these different points of view. *Locales* are based on the notion of continually evolving *Social Worlds*. A Social World is a group of people who are committed to collective action, which forms the prime structuring mechanism for interaction [8]. Individuals are usually simultaneously involved in multiple social worlds, which means that these social worlds are interconnected and that actions in one social world may reflect in another. A *Locale* is created through the use of space and resources by a group. It describes the Social World's *sites* and *means* used to meet interaction needs. Sites are spaces (e.g. shared file systems) and means are objects contained in these spaces (e.g. the files and documents stored in this file system) [9]. Analysis of sites and means can be used to elicit details about the working sphere.

Following these lines of thought, we have been working on systems to support working spheres. These systems should take into account the fact that individuals constantly reorganize and that working spheres come and go. Collaboration support systems should help the individual connect his/her work to others, helping the individual manage the multiple working spheres and placing individual work in its social context.

3   Related Systems

Some systems have been proposed to analyzed interaction and bridge the gap between individual and group activity. Soylent [6][7] maps individual email messages as social networks, to enable the exploration and visualization of social structures. This research showed that, even from an egocentric perspective, it is possible to find structures in communication that represent, for instance, hierarchy or participation in multiple groups. It also has a module to enable users to explore historical records of interaction, to help guide future interaction. It doesn't tie interactions to resources or activities, but provides and interesting starting point. A related project, Roles [6] studied conversation patterns in usenet newsgroups. It elicited a number of different patterns in different types of groups, showing how interaction differs among distinct social contexts. Similarly, the Conversation Maps system [24] provided a social network visualization to explore usenet newsgroups. This system enabled the visualization of individual ties and also of correlation between keywords, and made it possible to explore the data and semantic relations between different words. However, it was designed as an exploratory tool, rather than a tool for inference or automated action, and had no specific way to tie individual and group work.

Social Action [22] provides researchers with a way to systematically explore and visualize social networks. In previous research Perer and Shneiderman [21] had elicited different patterns of interaction corresponding to changing interests or collaborations. This was eventually extended into EmailViz [23], which enables users to visualize statistical information about their email practices. Users found the tool could be useful for determining who was taking up their time and reflecting on their own behaviors. Again, these tools provide visualizations, but no way to tie individual work to its social contexts.

Unified Activity Management [17], proposes a generic model of activity and a framework to integrate individual, informal, work with more strict organizational workflows. It seeks to help users organize and contextualize emails within activities, and might be useful in our context as well: through an accurate classification of emails into tasks, it becomes easier to determine the activities within a social world, which should then lead us to appropriate information dissemination. Activity Explorer [10] is a project that enables this type of organization, with users bundling together resources that pertain to the same collaborative context.

Other systems construct networks of people and keywords and for discovery of people with similar interests, such as presented in [15]. This method mines email data and constructs networks of people, which can be used to determine who has knowledge on what topics. A similar approach is presented in [11], where the author uses networks to locate individuals with a certain expertise and availability through an analysis of their activities and tasks. In the aforementioned approaches, the emphasis is on finding experts, and navigating the social network to create an awareness of who knows what.

4 Constituting Working Spheres: Linking Interactions and Artifacts

Prior research has explored possibilities for automatic computation of awareness information based on the analysis of interaction patterns. The Vineyard approach [31] presents a computational method for the discovery of active working spheres, through an analysis of interaction patterns and content. For the sake of clarity, we briefly present it in this section, a fuller presentation can be found in [31].

In Vineyard, each user is assisted by a system to help identify the working spheres he or she is inserted. Additionally, the system attempts to relate current activity to these working spheres, through the artifacts being manipulated. An underlying user model reflects the user's relationships (ties) to each of his or her peers. It is represented as a graph, with the user at the center and his or her peers and their activities radiating from the center (linked by edges that represent relationships). First level edges are weighed according the level of interaction in that relationship. This model is constructed based on each user's interactions with others, and used detect ongoing collaboration.

In this network, the strength of ties between peers is measured by the frequency and intensity of email exchanges between them. This network is built taking the set of user acquaintances found in the user's email archives and adding activities (defined by the resources or artifacts involved and time and type of activity) to these interactions as leaves. The system thus performs a two stage search: (1) discovering which peers the user is collaborating with (selecting nodes at the first level); and (2) relating these collaborations to ongoing work involving information manipulation.

The first stage focuses on finding ongoing collaborators (active working spheres). It uses the values of the sender and recipient fields (From, To, CC and BCC) to build a list of potential collaborators. Messages and their replies are grouped into interactions, and individuals co-occurring in messages (e.g. multiple recipients) form the social worlds a user takes part in. Ties to each recipient are quantified by activity levels (frequency of interaction, in average and current), and, when a discrepancy is detected (more email than normal being exchanged), these alters are tagged as collaborators.

Having performed the first stage search, the system must then tie people with resources, in a first step to constitute working spheres. This involves determining what topics this interaction concerns and linking these to resources and ongoing activity. The determination of which activities are related to working spheres is performed by comparing the contents of the interactions with the contents of the documents being manipulated. In this fashion, the working sphere can be kept up-to-date and, if appropriate, the user can be notified of activities that might have an impact on ongoing work.

Documents are transformed into a representation for indexing and retrieval. Following classical information retrieval, documents are represented as statistically built keyword vectors, where words are weighed according to their relevance. To weigh the vectors, the system counts the frequency with which each word appears in the text, to determine its approximate relevance in the document. Documents undergo a special treatment to remove high frequency words (also known as stopwords) such as (e.g., "a", "the", etc.). After this step, suffixes are removed and equivalent stems are detected (a process known as stemming) to properly compute equivalent words.

Each word's relevance is calculated as a function of its frequency in the document and its frequency in all documents, using a formula known as TFiDF (Term Frequency, inverse Document Frequency) [1]: a word's relevance for a particular document equals its frequency in the document divided by its frequency in the document set. Thus, words that appear very frequently in the document set lose their distinguishing power. Keywords are used to query the corpus index and retrieve documents that contain them.

The system analyzes text from the tasks at hand and builds keyword vectors to represent these documents using the TFiDF method. Similarly, each interaction is analyzed and tagged with keywords, and the similarity between interactions and resources is calculated using the cosine measure of proximity. The Vector Model [25] represents documents as keyword vectors and calculates the cosine of two documents' vectors to compute their similarity. In this manner, each document, represented by an n-dimensional weighed vector is compared to another by calculating the correlation between them as the cosine of their angle. The closer the documents, the more similar they are (cosine = 1).

Given that most of the activities analyzed are information processing tasks that involve a high amount of textual information (word processing, website surfing and searching, chat, etc.), this approach should elicit activities that are related to previous conversations. Being established methods for information retrieval and matching, TFiDF and cosine measures have been extensively applied with good results.

5 Analysis

Initial verification of the aforementioned approach covered only analysis of interaction patterns based on interaction patterns (senders, recipients and message frequency), and content analysis was left for later studies. In this section, we present our investigations into the applicability of automatic content analysis to match interactions and activities using classic information retrieval techniques. If found to work, this could benefit not only the Vineyard approach, but a number of structural analysis systems, which could then tie themselves to resources or activity as appropriate. Our goal, then, is to verify the applicability of content analysis to tie interactions and work artifacts. To that end, we apply information retrieval techniques no measure the correlation between documents.

With that in mind, we selected a different dataset, where the language problem did not exist, and individuals didn't have as many opportunities to meet in person, which increased the likelihood that interactions would happen online. The dataset was taken from a project funded by the European Union (EU), which involves a number of teams from different countries, working together to deliver a final product. Their activities involve research and development of eGovernment solutions, and the project's initial lifespan is 4 years. Partners come from different countries, and a subset of these forms the "technical group", directly involved in the research, design and development of working prototypes. They perform requirements analysis and design for pilot regions and work towards the design of an appropriate solution to the problem. All technical partners have extensive experience in research and development of computer systems. Collaborators work from different locations and exchange information as necessary. Teams from the different organizations are often engaged in multiple tasks at a time, some related to the project and others unrelated.

Deliverables, project specifications and plans are posted to a project website. Discussion is carried out on a private threaded forum, and interaction on the forums becomes public to all partners. As it is the main tool for discussion, we extracted about two years worth of messages from the forum for analysis. It should be noted that partners have the freedom to form subgroups to address specific concerns, and they use whatever other tools they need to accomplish their goals, in addition to the forum (i.e., email, messenger, IRC, etc.). Prior to analysis, we collected 112 threads, saving individual messages in a database, extracting sender, thread titles, dates and attachments. Attachments consisted mostly of word or excel documents, so they were manually converted to pfds for ease of processing. The data set consists of 1023 messages, subdivided into 112 threads, sent over a period of roughly 24 months (the first 2 years of the project: it is an ongoing project, and these were the data available at the time of collection). There are 241 pdfs sent as attachments, to which another 42 deliverables available on the website were added. Files unrelated (96 total) to the project were added to test for false positives. A previous analysis of this data involved classifying thread types [30], but this classification was not used in this analysis. Cross referencing the results with the classification is left for another exploratory analysis. Names and affiliations have been omitted.

5.1 Analysis of Distributed Interactions

As stated before, our goal is to verify the applicability of content analysis for matching individual work to its social context. The primary measurement is the level of correlation between two distinct documents: the higher the similarity, the more correlated they will be. To that end, we devised a series of similarity matches, to verify how well different variations would work. Indexes were created for messages, threads and files. Similarity was calculated between messages, files and threads. Our results are discussed in this section. The first analysis we conducted was between individual messages and files.

An analysis of the similarity values between Messages and Resources yields poor results. Similarity ratings were low overall (see Figure 1). Almost all of the higher scores are false positives, where a message is linked to resources unrelated to its content. Most of these occurred because messages were short and contained proper names that also figured in the documents analyzed. These became the basis for the match, as there were few words in the messages. A few notable exceptions occurred: high strength correlations were found between a message that contained agenda items for a meeting, and documents with agenda items (for that meeting and other meetings). Another strong match was between a long, highly technical message about

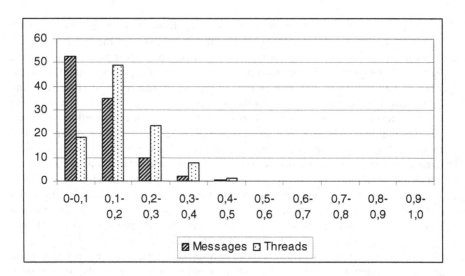

Fig. 1. Similarity rating distribution for 10 ranges of values, for messages and threads, as a percentage of total ratings

the ontologies involved in the solution and documents which discussed the lifecycle adopted for ontology construction. A third relevant match occurred between a message asking for updates on each party's contributions and a document containing task assignments.

Threads also scored higher than isolated messages in the resource match. This is understandable, as the series of messages in the thread provides extra content and establishes a discussion. As we noticed that the shorter messages yielded unreliable replies, we selected the 10 longest messages to analyze regarding precision, in our case an analysis of the relevance of the documents recalled to the message in question. The longest messages contained technical details of the project: some were specifically technical discussions, and others were documentation reviews questioning technical aspects. In all of these cases, the top three matches were relevant to the contents of the message, despite their apparently low similarity ratings (all around 0,3). A similar procedure was performed for threads, with similar results: among the top threads, similarity ratings were about 0,4, going over 0,5 in some cases. Another note, very few files unrelated to the project were brought up by these matches. For instance, there were only 25 outside files within the 1120 results for resources related to threads (about 2%). This, however, may be due to an imbalance on the document collection, which contained many more documents related to the project than not. This issue needs further investigation before a clear inference can be made. It should be noted that some of these files actually did bear some relation to ongoing discussions, as they related to ontologies, agents and semantics. Completely unrelated resources (e.g., Common LISP Reference Manual) did not figure in the results.

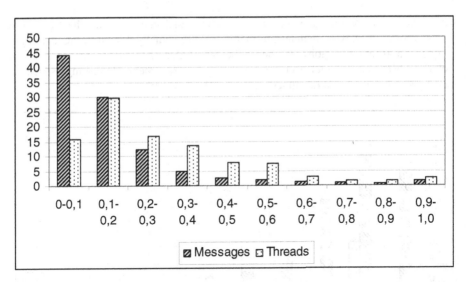

Fig. 2. Similarity rating distribution for 10 ranges of values, for messages and threads (with attachments included), as a percentage of total ratings

From our prior experience with the collocated group, we came to believe that attachments and links would provide additional content, which might be more related to the project than messages themselves. To check on this assumption, we created indexes that incorporated the contents of attachments to the body of messages, and we assume these will provide better matches than messages by themselves. Thus, our hypothesis reads: *if attachments contain more relevant content than messages, then attachments will have better similarity scores than messages by themselves.* This hypothesis is easily verified in a comparison of similarity scores between messages where the attachment content was considered and messages without the attachments. Figure 2 shows a graph of these distributions, for messages and threads. It is easy to see that similarity ratings are greater when attachments are considered than not, as attachments provide added content with which to compare documents. This corroborates our hypothesis that attachments are valuable source of project related data. In a fashion, by using links and attachments sent with messages, we are taking into account users' recommendations, as someone has already gone over these resources and judged them useful to the group.

Our last verification worked the other way around: we selected 30 files (10 attachments, 10 deliverables and 10 outside files) and attempted to match them to threads, to see is it would be possible to link an artifact with interactions that surround it. Again, we mapped these files to threads that corresponded and got fairly low similarity ratings (see Figure 3). However, there was a distinction in ratings between outside files and project-related files (whether attachments or not): outside files never rated above 0,3, while other files could go up to 0,75. With the inclusion of attachments, ratings went up considerable, further separating project files from unrelated files. This is an important point, as it can help establish a different between external and internal resources. We consider results to be good on this account. It seems that it is possible to match resources to social contexts, and the first three matches were all relevant matches, in that they were actually related to the document in question (high precision). It should be noted that the best scores came from technical discussions, which were closely related to documents describing aspects of the projects, even without the attachments for added context.

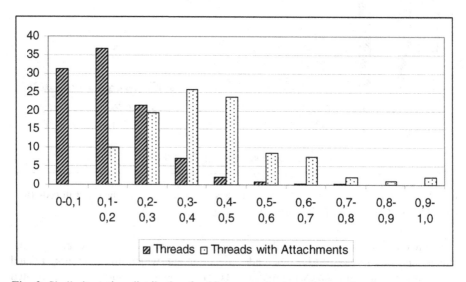

Fig. 3. Similarity rating distribution for 10 ranges of values, for matches between resources (files) and threads (with and without attachments), as a percentage of total ratings

5.2 Reflections on Results

Results were worse than we expected. One of the main problems is message length, as there were many very short messages, mainly in scheduling or meeting preparation threads (e.g., "so-and-so will be present to represent company X" or "here is company Y's contribution to the report" or "please send in the quarterly management report"). An earlier classification of messages contained in this forum (with a smaller subset), found that there were approximately 11% of messages that were strictly technical discussion, and a large part was for scheduling meetings (40%), requesting contributions (30%) or general project planning (15%) [30]. This may account for the poor results, as meeting scheduling and contribution requests usually generate only short messages that have little to do with the project themes. However, some of the contributions were sent in as attachments, in which cases they contribute to the definition of project themes.

Another surprise was the number of matches due to proper names: quite a few of the top rated matches were short messages that contained proper names (e.g., "participants A and B will be present representing company X") that were matched to for instance, activity reports that contained these people's names. While not a particularly useful match, it does bring up a possibility, of giving special treatment to proper names. These could be extracted from sender fields or signatures, and co-occurrence in messages or documents could be used to detect cooperation.

Additional treatment could also be included to take into account message sizes. Longer messages would carry more weight in defining the corpus, while short ones would have less weight. One interesting approach would be to correlate message length with thread types (organizational, technical, etc.), which would provide an indication of what types of messages one is dealing with and enable appropriate indexing.

It also seems we somewhat misjudged the group's interaction style: we expected many project discussions to happen online, but these were the minority (although when they did happen, they provided excellent content for an information based match). At one junction, two of the authors had the opportunity to participate in one of the collocated meetings, which happened roughly every 3 months. Participants took this opportunity to discuss technical details and make decisions, and tried to achieve a division of labor to minimize interaction in between meetings. Upon reflection, this is consistent with observation by Olson and Teasley [20] that distributed groups display a tendency to change the organizational structure and task distribution in order to reduce coupling of non-collocated members, thus reducing coordination needs. In fact, informal chats with group members reveled that they formed smaller subgroups that interacted more frequently, but outside the forum (via email mostly, but also IRC and on the phone when necessary). They also reported visiting each other in between group meetings when necessary, and in fact stayed on after the meeting to work together. The range of media adopted could also pose a problem, as it would be hard to cover all different interaction channels. However, this also poses new opportunities, as each channel has different affordances and will be chosen depending on specific needs and desires. From the user's choice, one could infer whether the message was urgent, for instance.

6 Applicability and Future Work

Our findings are applicable to any situation where it would be beneficial to cross reference interactions and artifacts. One such example would be ActivityExplorer [10], to automatically find relations between ongoing activities and other interactions. One possibility not explored thus far was to create indexes for ego-alter pairs, analyzing the contents of their interactions to elicit the different shared themes. This is an important step, which will be pursued in the near future, as it helps map the evolving interests between two users.

We can foresee a number of scenarios where cross referencing interactions with artifacts can be useful: for instance, as a user interacts, resources are presented that might enrich the interaction. Another possibility is to present the user with interactions that relate to the ongoing activity, so he or she will know how this impacts on others (a variation on this is to have systems automatically disseminate information to provide awareness). A resource could also be tagged with the social context it pertains to, so that it goes with it when it is sent or received to others. This would benefit, for instance, a newcomer to the project, who would better understand the multiple roles and individuals that were involved in constructing this resource.

The important part is tying individually produced artifacts with their social and collaborative contexts.

Further work should go into better analysis techniques that take into account the semantics of the interactions. One of the possibilities is the creation of an ontology, relating it to terms to elicit details about he contracts established between individuals (for instance, promises to deliver part of the work, or the expectation that something will be ready by a certain date, existing reporting structures, etc.) Another possibility is to use speech act theory, as suggested in [5], to classify messages. Cross-referencing statistical data and patterns with a classification of thread types (e.g., scheduling, technical discussion, meeting preparation) would also be interesting work, which might elicit different communication patterns for different types of threads.

As our analysis of attachments indicated that attachments are good indicators of relevant content, we are now tempted to go back to the initial group (which was partially collocated) and run a new analysis using only the attachments and links exchanged as a basis. In this fashion, it would be possible to elicit a pattern of contributions to the artifact under construction, follow changes made by different group members (with a more in depth analysis of the document itself), and possibly even design a method to calculate authorship of the document by analyzing the amount of work that went each partner put in (a naturally controversial issue, which deserves more thought).

These techniques could all benefit an effort to construct systems to support the networked, distributed work, by assisting individuals multitask between different groups and maintain their networks alive through communication. Understanding and adjusting to unforeseen work events is an everyday task, which could be better supported through automatic inference systems. This involves not only maintaining awareness of the group, but also understanding how people interact during the construction of an artifact (maintaining both a present and a historic perspective), and, conversely, what artifacts are involved in each relationship.

Acknowledgments. This research was partially supported by CAPES and CNPq, Brazilian governmental agencies for research support, tied to the Ministries of Science and Technology and Education.

References

[1] Baeza-Yates, R., Ribeiro-Neto, B.: Modern Information Retrieval. ACM Press, New York (1999)

[2] Bernoux, P.: La Sociologie des Entreprises, 2nd edn. Paris, Éditions du Seuil (1995)

[3] Carstensen, P., Schmidt, K.: Self Governing Production Groups: Towards Requirements for IT Support. In: 5th IFIP Int. Conf. on Information Technology in Manufacturing and Services (BASYS'02), Cancun, Mexico, pp. 49–60. Kluwer Academic Publishers, Dordrecht (2002)

[4] Castells, M.A: Sociedade em Rede, 8th edn. São Paulo, Paz e Terra, [portuguese translation of The Rise of the Network Society] (1996)

[5] Cohen, W.W., Carvalho, V.R., Mitchell, T.M.: Learning to Classify Email into Speech Acts. In: Proc. Conference on Empirical Methods in Natural Language Processing (2004)

[6] Fisher, D.: Understanding Communication Using Social Networks. IEEE Internet Computing (September/October 2005)

[7] Fisher, D., Dourish, P.: Social and Temporal Structures in Everyday Collaboration. In: Proceedings of the ACM Conference on Human Factors in Computing Systems CHI 2004 (Vienna, Austria), pp. 551–558 (2004)

[8] Fitzpatrick, G., Tolone, W., Kaplan, S.: Worlk, Locales and Distributed Social Worlds. In: Proc ECSCW 95, Stockholm, Sweden, pp. 1–16. Kluwer Academic Publishers, Dordrecht (1995)

[9] Fitzpatrick, G., Kaplan, S., Mansfield, T.: Applying the Locales Framework to Understanding and Designing. In: Proceedings of the 1998 Australasian Computer Human Interaction Conference (OzCHI 1998), pp. 122–129. IEEE Computer Society, Washington (1998)

[10] Geyer, W., Muller, M.J., Moore, M., Wilcox, E., Cheng, L., Brownholtz, B., Hill, C.R., Millen, D.R.: ActivityExplorer: Activity-Centric Collaboration from Research to Product. IBM Systems Journal – Special Issue on Business Collaboration (October/November 2006)

[11] Groth, K.: Using Social Networks for Knowledge Management. In: Proc ECSCW 03 Workshop on Moving From Analysis to Design: Social Networks in the CSCW Context. Helsinki, Finland (2003)

[12] Gonzalés, V.M., Mark, G.: Managing Currents of Work: Multi-tasking Among Multiple Collaborations. In: Gellersen, H., et al. (eds.) ECSCW 2005: Proceedings of the Ninth European Conference on Computer-Supported Cooperative Work, pp. 143–162. Springer, Netherlands (2005)

[13] Gonzalés, V.M., Mark, G.: Constant, constant, multi-tasking craziness: managing multiple working spheres. In: Proceedings of the SIGCHI conference on Human factors in computing systems (CHI 2004), pp. 113–120. ACM Press, Vienna Austria (2004)

[14] Gutwin, C., Greenberg, S., Blum, R., Dyck, J.: Supporting Informal Collaboration in Shared-Workspace Groupware. The Interaction Lab Technical Report HCI-TR-2005-01, University of Saskatchewan, Canada (2005)

[15] McArthur, R., Bruza, P.: Discovery of Social Networks and Knowledge in Social Networks by Analysis of Email Utterances. In: Proc ECSCW 03 Workshop on Moving From Analysis to Design: Social Networks in the CSCW Context. Helsinki, Finland (2003)

[16] Mercklé, P.: Sociologie des Réseaux Sociaux. Paris, La Découverte (2004)

[17] Moran, T.P.: Unified Activity Management: Explicitly Representing Activity in Work Support Systems. In: Proc. ECSCW 05 Workshop on Activity: From a Theoretical to a Computational Construct. Paris (2005)

[18] Nardi, B., Whittaker, S., Schwarz, H.: NetWORKers and their activity in Intensional Networks. In: Computer Supported Cooperative Work, vol. 11, pp. 205–242. Kluwer Academic Publishers, Netherlands (2002)

[19] Nardi, B., Engeström, Y.: A Web on the Wind: The Structure of Invisible Work. Computer-Supported Cooperative Work, Special issue 8(1-2), 1–8 (1999)

[20] Olson, J., Teasley, S.: Groupware in the Wild: Lessons Learned from a Year of Virtual Collocation. In: Computer Supported Cooperative Work'96, Cambridge, MA (1996)

[21] Perer, A., Shneiderman, B., Oard, D.W.: Using Rhythms of Relationships to Understand Email Archives. In: Email Archives Visualization Workshop (2004)

[22] Perer, A., Shneiderman, B.: Balancing Systematic and Flexible Exploration of Social Networks. In: IEEE Symposium on Information Visualization (Infovis 2006), IEEE Transactions on Visualization and Computer Graphics (TVCG) 12(5) (2006)

[23] Perer, A., Smith, M.: Contrasting Portraits of Email Practices: Visual approaches to reflection and analysis. In: Proceedings of AVI 2006, Venice Italy, ACM Press, New York (2006)

[24] Sack, W.: Conversation Map: An Interface for Very Large-Scale Conversations. Journal of Management Information Systems 17(3), 73–92 (2001)

[25] Salton, G.: Automatic Text Processing: the Transformation, Analysis and Retrieval of Information by Computer. Addison-Wesley Publishing, Reading (1988)

[26] Schmidt, K., Bannon, L.: Taking CSCW Seriously: Supporting Articulation Work. In: Computer Supported Cooperative Work: An International Journal, vol. 1(1), pp. 7–40. Kluwer Academic Publishers, Netherlands (1992)

[27] Schwarz, H., Nardi, B., Whittaker, S.: The Hidden Work in Virtual Work. In: Proceedings Critical Management Conference, Manchester (July 1999)

[28] Scott, J.: Social Network Analysis: A Handbook. Sage Publication, London (1991)

[29] Vandenberghe, F.: La Sociologie de Georg Simmel. Editions La Découverte, Paris (2001)

[30] Vivacqua, A.S., Barthès, J.P., Souza, J.M.: Supporting Self Governing Software Design Groups. In: Shen, W., Luo, J., Lin, Z., Bacthès, J.-P.A., Hao, Q. (eds.) CSCWD 2006. LNCS, vol. 4402, Springer, Heidelberg (2007)

[31] Vivacqua, A.S., Souza, J.M.: Using Email-Based Network Analysis to Determine Awareness Foci. In: Groupware, design, Implementation and Use: Proceedings of the International Workshop in Groupware, 2006. LNCS, Springer, Heidelberg (2006)

[32] Wasserman, S., Faust, K.: Social Network Analysis: Methods and Applications. Cambridge University Press, Cambridge, US (1994)

[33] Wellman, B., Gulia, M.: Netsurfers don't Ride Alone: Virtual Communities as Communities. In: Wellman, B. (org.) Networks in the Global Village, pp. 331–366. Westview Press, Boulder, CO. (1999)

Studying the Impact of Personality and Group Formation on Learner Performance*

Víctor Sánchez Hórreo and Rosa M. Carro

Escuela Politécnica Superior, Universidad Autónoma de Madrid
28049 Madrid, Spain
victor.sanchezh@estudiante.uam.es, rosa.carro@uam.es

Abstract. This paper presents a study being carried out at the Universidad Autónoma de Madrid to ascertain the influence of the way students are grouped to do collaborative work (regarding intelligence and personality parameters) on the results they get. Data about student's personality are analysed along with information about group composition and student performance. The results of this analysis are expected to throw light about the impact of personal traits and group formation on learning. This information can be incorporated in collaborative systems as criteria for group formation, with the aim of favouring CSCL situations in which students are prone to get better results.

1 Motivation

During the last decades, the Internet has been widely used for supporting both individual and collaborative learning. A number of Web-based systems have been developed and students are more and more used to access to this type of systems.

The students' different cognitive abilities, as well as their personality traits, determine the way each of them access to available didactic materials, processes information, solves practical work, relates to his/her mates and teachers, and, definitely, takes advantage of the teaching/learning process. This fact has been taken into account in both individual and collaborative e-learning environments, giving rise to adaptive web-based applications that guide each student during the learning process by personalizing and adapting the activities and resources to the user's needs and features [1].

Intelligence, personality and learning style are three factors that can influence student individual and collaborative learning. Obtaining conclusions regarding the effect of these parameters on the learning process would make it possible to consider them for the creation of better e-learning individual and collaborative systems. With respect to collaborative learning, we have made a study about the impact of learning styles on student grouping [2]. We think that students' personality and intelligence can also influence the way the students group themselves, the way they work together and their achievements when tackling individual and collaborative activities.

* This work is supported by the Spanish Ministry of Science and Education, TIN2004-03140. We thank teachers of *Inf. and Data Structures* from the *Dep.of Computer Science (UAM)*, as well as Prof. Manuel de Juan for his valuable help regarding the selection of the tests used.

J.M. Haake, S.F. Ochoa, and A. Cechich (Eds.): CRIWG 2007, LNCS 4715, pp. 287–294, 2007.

The ongoing work presented in this paper is devoted to study the impact of different intelligence and personality parameters on student grouping and on their achievements. The rest of the paper is organised as follows: section 2 presents a summary of related work; section 3 shows a description of the study currently being carried out; section 4 explains the results obtained so far; in section 5, the application of these results is described; and finally, section 6 includes conclusions and future work.

2 Related Work

Numerous studies dealing with the relationship between academic performance and intelligence can be found, such as [3]. Likewise, the influence of personality in the way the students get knowledge or uses it in practical applications has also been analysed [4]. Concerning the influence of personality in learning computer programming, [5] cites several works indicating that students with thinking profile tend to process information in a way that helps them to learn successfully. In [4] it is stated that conscientiousness and extraversion are clearly related to achievement, being personality the most powerful factor influencing academic performance. Most of these studies are within the framework of the traditional face-to-face educational system.

The emergence of Web-based learning platforms have given rise to a new way of learning, in which roles of teachers and students are modified, and the traditional way of transmitting knowledge has changed. Knowledge is constructed and discovered by students [6]. Individual learning is enriched through collaborative learning experiences. Collaboration tools are used in order to support communication, cooperative problem solving, and knowledge sharing and construction, among others [7].

In the e-learning framework, Younis et al. [8] analyse the influence of personality in the way of using e-learning platforms, finding no significant relation between personality and group results. This is explained as a possible lack of learning materials that favoured the exploitation of different personality traits. The impact of providing personality-aware interfaces for e-learning was studied in [9]. Statistically significant results regarding the positive effect of personality-aware interfaces over the predisposition to learn and over the results were obtained. There are also some works regarding the influence of personality in the use of CSCL systems. In [10] it is found out that personality influences the way students involve in online learning processes, including group interaction, communication and task engagement. In order to increase the effectiveness of a learning community, the potential influence of personality could be considered for group formation and for activity design in CSCL.

Concerning learning styles, in one of our previous works [2], dealing with the impact of learning styles on student grouping for collaborative learning, we found out that learning styles seem to affect the student performance when working together. In general terms, in that study it seemed that heterogeneous groups got better results.

Regarding student grouping, works about grouping in traditional classrooms and also in the field of computer supported collaborative learning are found [11]. Deibel [12] states that assigning groups (not letting the students group themselves) can be beneficial, increasing the interaction and the involvement of the students. Muehlenbrock [13] indicates that the combination of group formation based on student profiles and user context information can improve grouping quality, avoiding future drawbacks. Read et al. [14] present a framework for Intelligent Computer-Aided Language Learning that combines individual and collaborative learning and describe an adaptive group formation algorithm based on student language abilities.

In our case, we have developed a system that supports dynamic generation of collaborative workspaces as well as automatic group formation [15]. Groups are formed in two stages: i) firstly, an initial set of groups is formed according to students' features and preferences; ii) secondly, working groups are formed on the fly as soon as a task is available for several students put in the same group during the first phase.

3 The Study

A study is being currently carried out involving students from the first degree of both *Computer Science* and *Computer Science plus Mathematics* (joint studies) of the Universidad Autónoma de Madrid. They are taking the subject *Information and Data Structures* together. As explained in section 1, the main aim of this study is to investigate the influence of personality and intelligence on the way students group themselves and, more important, on the results of their work, to try to determine which combinations of persons in groups (regarding personal traits) lead to better results. In order to investigate this, it is necessary to get and analyse information about the students' personality and intelligence, as well as to collect their academic results in the exams, practical work and other activities related to this subject.

With the objective of harvesting data related to student personality and intelligence, the NEO Five Factor Inventory (NEO-FFI) test [166] and the Primary Mental Abilities (PMA) test [157] are used, respectively. Both tests were chosen because of having a proved reliability and being used worldwide. NEO-FFI gives quick, reliable and valid measures of the five domains of adult personality: extraversion, neuroticism, conscientiousness, openness to experience and agreeableness. PMA includes a test for verbal, spatial, and general reasoning abilities. The tests have been implemented as dynamic web pages. JSP and Java programs are used in order to control the time, check the answers, calculate the scores for each domain/parameter of personality, and generate the feedback page to be shown to the user. The rates given by the user for each item and the final scores calculated for each parameter are stored in XML files. The tests have been integrated within a website developed to provide the students with additional resources related to *Information and Data Structures*: detailed theoretical explanations, samples, pseudo-codes, solved exercises, exercises to be proposed to the students (with automatic feedback), etc. Links to personality and intelligence tests are included in the top frame of this website. Students log in this website with their student account, and all the interactions within the website are stored in log files.

During the semester, the students worked in pairs on four practical tasks. They were allowed to group themselves. The course also includes two exams to be taken individually, one in the middle of the semester and another at the end, composed by two parts: one related to the knowledge acquired during the lectures, and the other one related to laboratory work. The results obtained by the students when taking individual exams and also when working in pairs in laboratories are analysed to get information about the student performance.

The second semester of the academic course in Spain goes from February to May (exams take place in June). Students have been accessing to the previously described website since its publication, in March. The website is offered as an additional resource and filling the tests is not mandatory. A number of students have entered the website (110) and more than seventy have taken the tests, giving rise to the corresponding number of student profiles. Additionally, around seventy profiles more are available, coming from a different and smaller website offered to the students during the first semester. The information obtained about student personality and intelligence, group formation and individual plus group achievements is being statistically analysed with the aim of getting hints about the impact of these parameters on both group performance and individual achievements.

4 Results

The hypothesis of this study is that intelligence and personality of students working collaboratively have an effect in the results of the tasks accomplished by them and also in the learning process. Apart from the relationship between these factors and the individual academic performance, the traits of each student also condition how they group themselves, how they collaborate and the achievements of the group. This study is expected to reach conclusions regarding questions such as:

- For each parameter (personality and intelligence), whether the students follow any pattern when they group themselves (homogeneous vs. heterogeneous groups).
- Which are the groups that get better results and which the composition of these groups is. That is, which the combinations of student traits that work better are.
- Whether heterogeneous groups (from the point of view of personality, intelligence and both features together) work better than homogeneous ones.
- Whether the student improvements along the time regarding a specific subject in which they work together, are related to the way they are grouped. In the same direction, whether partners' features have an influence on the progress of individuals.
- That is, whether the students' personality and intelligence, plus the way students group regarding these parameters, have an impact on learning.

In order to test our hypothesis and reach conclusions like the ones enumerated above, the relationship between different variables is being analysed, testing whether correlations between them exist. In this paper we will focus on the analysis of data obtained from eleven pairs of students in which both the members of each pair have filled in the same tests and, specifically, on the relationships between:

- Personality (each of the five dimensions) and group formation tendency.
- Composition of groups, regarding personality, and results obtained by them.

Detailed information about group composition regarding personality parameters is shown in table 1 (with a minimum value of 5 and a maximum of 95 for each). For example, it can be seen that student 1 of pair 1 scored 50 in the scale of neuroticism.

Table 1. Personality traits of each pair

Pair	Students	Neuroticism (Ntc.)	Extraversion (Ext.)	Openness to experience (Open.)	Agreeableness (Agr.)	Conscientiousness (Cns.)
P1	St1	50	5	5	35	45
	St2	5	5	5	35	60
P2	St1	85	35	55	30	15
	St2	5	20	55	35	65
P3	St1	80	75	80	5	55
	St2	90	85	25	95	15
P4	St1	60	40	5	75	60
	St2	45	45	5	85	60
P5	St1	5	60	65	60	25
	St2	95	5	75	5	5
P6	St1	70	5	5	5	15
	St2	95	10	70	85	5
P7	St1	50	70	50	80	95
	St2	95	25	45	10	75
P8	St1	80	20	65	35	5
	St2	90	20	55	70	5
P9	St1	55	85	80	60	25
	St2	80	70	75	30	85
P10	St1	50	80	55	15	50
	St2	60	20	55	35	5
P11	St1	85	5	55	10	35
	St2	5	20	55	35	25

Table 2 shows whether each group is homogeneous/heterogeneous regarding each trait. For example, pair 1 is heterogeneous regarding neuroticism and homogeneous with respect to the rest of the dimensions. A group is considered homogeneous regarding a dimension if the difference between the values of each member in that dimension is less than the half of the maximum possible difference in the scale.

Table 2. Type of pair regarding each trait and mark obtained when working in group

	Ntc.	Ext.	Open.	Agr.	Cns.	Mark	Normalized mark
P1	Het.	Hom.	Hom.	Hom.	Hom.	8,140	1,164
P2	Het.	Hom.	Hom.	Hom.	Het.	9,500	2,067
P3	Hom.	Hom.	Het.	Het.	Hom.	9,350	2,358
P4	Hom.	Hom.	Hom.	Hom.	Hom.	7,765	2,095
P5	Het.	Het.	Hom.	Het.	Hom.	8,875	1,888
P6	Hom.	Hom.	Het.	Het.	Hom.	7,505	1,174
P7	Het.	Het.	Hom.	Het.	Hom.	7,350	1,156
P8	Hom.	Hom.	Hom.	Hom.	Hom.	9,450	1,509
P9	Hom.	Hom.	Hom.	Hom.	Het.	9,750	1,281
P10	Hom.	Het.	Hom.	Hom.	Het.	7,500	1,239
P11	Het.	Hom.	Hom.	Hom.	Hom.	9,435	1,206

Table 2 also includes data about the marks obtained by each pair of students when working collaboratively. A normalized value for these marks has been calculated too, by taking into account the marks obtained by each student separately. For example, pair 1 obtained 8,140 points out of 10, and the normalized value of this mark is 1,164.

Table 3 shows the percentages of homogeneous/heterogeneous pairs regarding each dimension, as well as the average of the normalized marks obtained by homogeneous and heterogeneous pairs (for each personality trait). Some examples about the way of interpreting the table are: i) regarding openness to experience, 81,8% of the pairs were homogeneous, while 18,2% where heterogeneous; ii) the average of the normalized marks obtained by all heterogeneous groups with respect to openness to experience is 1,77, and the average of marks obtained by heterogeneous groups regarding extroversion is 1,43.

Table 3. Percentages of homogeneous/heterogeneous pairs and average of normalized marks for each personality trait

	Ntc.	Ext.	Open.	Agr.	Cns.
% homogeneous pairs	54,5	72,7	81,8	63,6	72,7
% heterogeneous pairs	45,5	27,3	18,2	36,4	27,3
Aver. Normalized mark (hom.)	1,61	1,61	1,51	1,51	1,57
Aver. normalized mark (het.)	1,50	1,43	1,77	1,64	1,53

As it can be seen, in the case of neuroticism, no clear tendency can be observed in the way in which students group themselves (54,5% vs. 45,5%). However, students tend to group themselves in a quite homogeneous way with respect to extraversion (72,7%), openness to experience (81,8%), agreeableness (63,6%) and conscientiousness (72,7%).

Table 3 also shows that, regarding the impact of student grouping on academic performance, the most relevant differences (around 2 points) are found in extraversion and openness to experience. Homogeneous groups regarding extroversion seem to get better results than heterogeneous ones in this experiment (1,61 vs. 1,43). Regarding openness to experience, it turns out that heterogeneous groups got better results than homogeneous ones (1,77 vs. 1,51).

5 Application

The results of the complete study will give clues about the influence of personality and intelligence in collaborative learning. This information can be used with adaptation purposes in collaborative systems. One of its applications consists of establishing criteria to group students. Either when groups are dynamically formed or when they are organised by persons, knowing which combinations of students perform better will allow one to use this information as criteria for group formation. The final aim of using these criteria would be maximizing the possibility of student success during the realization of collaborative tasks and, more generally, during the learning process.

The TANGOW system constitutes an example of the application of the results of this study. It supports creation and delivery of adaptive hypermedia. It proposes the most suitable activities to be carried out by each student at each time, according to the information stored in the student model, and generates the corresponding pages dynamically. Regarding collaborative activities, it is possible to adapt, to each student: i) presence/absence of this type of activities; ii) specific activities to be proposed; iii) time in which they are proposed; iv) prerequisites for accomplishing them; v) problem statements; and vi) collaboration workspaces and tools (generated at runtime) [1].

TANGOW provides a mechanism for dynamic group formation [15]. Groups can be formed automatically according to grouping rules. The student's features and preferences, as well as their performance before the time at which they are grouped, are considered for group formation, in the way specified in those grouping rules. Since the results of this study are expected to though light about the impact of personality and intelligence on the work group, they can be incorporated as new grouping criteria (grouping rules) for automatic group formation in TANGOW.

6 Conclusions and Future Work

The goal of the work presented in this paper is to find out the impact of personality and intelligence on the way the students group themselves and also on their academic achievements. The final aim is to determine which combinations of students in groups, regarding these personal traits, lead to better results, in order to group students accordingly to favour their learning. In this paper we have presented preliminary results of the ongoing personality-based analysis. The data analysed so far indicates that students tend to group themselves in a homogeneous way regarding extraversion, openness to experience, agreeableness and conscientiousness. It seems that homogeneous groups regarding extroversion get better results than heterogeneous ones, and also that heterogeneous groups regarding openness to experience got better results than homogeneous ones. The set of data analysed was obtained from 22 students, corresponding to the first 11 pairs in which both members filled in the tests. This fact may lead to a slant. A bigger set of data is currently being analysed to check whether preliminary results are representative of what happens in other groups of students.

Currently we are also trying to find out whether there exist correlations between other variables; for example, the influence of intelligence in these results, as well as the impact of individual performance in group achievements (and the other way round). Not only can group homogeneity/heterogeneity be considered, but also discrete values obtained by the students can be taken into account in order to get conclusions about the performance of a group in which, i.e., a student is highly neurotic.

The results to be obtained after the whole analysis are expected to throw light about the influence of personality and intelligence, as well as student grouping, in collaborative learning, contributing to bring more insight about the nuances discovered so far. It must be noticed that no much contrasted information is available regarding the impact of group formation (with respect to personality and intelligence parameters) in the results obtained by the students. This study will contribute to get more information about these issues. One of its immediate applications consists of using knowledge about the combinations of students that performed better as valuable criteria for group formation. These criteria are especially useful for automatic group formation. Another application in which we plan to work consists on predicting group success/failure in order to provide the corresponding help/guidance to prevent group failure. In any case, the final aim would be maximizing the possibility of student success during the realization of collaborative tasks and, more generally, during the learning process.

References

1. Carro, R.M., Ortigosa, A., Schlichter, J.: A Rule-based formalism for describing collaborative adaptive courses. In: Palade, V., Howlett, R.J., Jain, L. (eds.) KES 2003. LNCS, vol. 2774, pp. 252–259. Springer, Heidelberg (2003)
2. Alfonseca, E., Carro, R.M., Paredes, M., Ortigosa, A., Martín, E.: The impact of learning styles on student grouping for collaborative learning: a case study. User Modeling and User-Adapted Interaction. In: Special Issue: User Modelling to Support Groups, Communities and Collaboration, vol. 16(3-4), pp. 377–401. Springer, Heidelberg (2006)
3. Rohde, T.E., Thompson, L.A.: Predicting academic achievement with cognitive ability. Intelligence 35(1), 83–92 (2007)
4. Chamorro-Premuzic, T., Furnham, A.: Personality predicts academia performance: Evidence from two longitudinal examples. Journal of Research in Personality, University College of London 37, 319–338 (2003)
5. Golding, P., Facey-Shaw, L., Tennant, V.: Effects of peer tutoring, attitude and personality on academic performance of first year introductory programming students. In: 36th ASEE/IEEE Frontiers in Education Conference. University of Technology, Jamaica (2006)
6. Johnson, D.W., Johnson, R.T., Smith, K.: Cooperative learning: Increasing college faculty instructional productivity (ASHEERIC Higher Education Report No. 4). The George Washington University, School of Education and Human Development (1991)
7. Dillenbourg, P.: Collaborative Learning: Cognitive and Computational Approaches. Elsevier, Oxford (1999)
8. Younis, N., Salman, R., Ashrafi, R.: Efficacy of present e-learning content to student personality types. International journal of information technology 1(3) (2004)
9. Abrahamian, E., Weinberg, J., Grady, M.S.: Stanton. Saint Louis University.USA: The effect of personality-aware computer-human interfaces on learning. Journal of Universal Computer Science 9(1) (2004)
10. Chen, S., Caropreso, E.: Influence of personality on online discussion. Journal of Interactive Online Learning 3(2) (2004)
11. Johnson, D.W., Johnson, F.P.: Learning together: group theory and group skills. Pearson Education (1975)
12. Deibel, K.: Team formation methods for increasing interaction during in-class group work. In: Proceedings of the 10th annual SIGCSE Conference on Innovation and Technology in Computer Science Education, Caparica, Portugal, pp. 291–295 (2005)
13. Muehlenbrock, M.: Learning group formation based on learner profile and context. Int. J. e-learning IJEL 5(1), 19–24 (2006)
14. Read, T., Barros, B., Bárcena, E., Pancorbo, J.: Coalescing individual and collaborative learning to model user linguistic competences. User Modeling and User-Adapted Interaction 16(3-4), 349–376(28) (2006)
15. Carro, R.M., Ortigosa, A., Martin, E., Schlichter, J.: Dynamic generation of adaptive web-based collaborative courses. In: Favela, J., Decouchant, D. (eds.) CRIWG 2003. LNCS, vol. 2806, pp. 191–198. Springer, Heidelberg (2003)
16. Costa, P.T., McCrae, R.R.: The NEO-PI/NEO-FFI manual supplement. Odessa, FL Psychological Assessment Resources (1989)
17. Thurstone, L.L.: Primary Mental Abilities. Chicago University Press, Chicago (1938)

Transferring a Collaborative Work Practice to Practitioners: A Field Study of the Value Frequency Model for Change-of-Practice

Robert O. Briggs[1], Alanah J. Davis[1], John D. Murphy[1], Lucas Steinhauser[1], and Thomas F. Carlisle[2]

[1] Institute for Collaboration Science, University of Nebraska at Omaha
[2] Science Applications International Corporation
{rbriggs,alanahdavis,jmurphy,lsteinhauser}@mail.unomaha.edu,
thomas.f.carlisle@saic.com

Abstract. Collaboration engineers design collaborative work practices for high-value recurring tasks and transfer them to practitioners to execute for themselves without the on-going intervention of professional facilitators. It would be useful to increase the predictability of developing self-sustaining and growing community of practice around these designed processes. This paper reports a field study that applies the Value Frequency Model (VFM) for change-of-practice to the deployment of an engineered work practice to groups in a large global organization. The results suggest that VFM provides useful insights for discovering candidate tasks for Collaboration Engineering (CE) interventions, for designing new work practices, and for designing transition interventions for creating a self-sustaining and growing community of practice.

Keywords: Collaboration engineering, organizational change, change of practice, value frequency model, acceptance, adoption, diffusion, transition.

1 Introduction

Facilitators using collaboration technology can significantly improve a group's efficiency, effectiveness, and satisfaction [1, 2]. However, the cost of facilitation services is not inconsequential which makes facilitation beyond the reach of many groups who could benefit from assistance. Collaboration Engineering (CE) is an approach to designing collaborative work practices for high-value recurring tasks and transferring them to practitioners to execute for themselves without the on-going intervention of professional facilitators [3]. CE researchers have progressed design methodology [4, 5], however, it is not yet easy to predict self-sustaining and growing communities of practitioners for a new work practice. A community of practitioners is said to be self-sustaining if a) people use the work practice without ongoing intervention of the champions who introduce the practice, b) new members are routinely trained to use the practice as the standard approach for a task, and c) when something goes wrong, the practitioners fix the problem instead of abandoning the work practice [6]. This paper reports a field study applying the Value Frequency

J.M. Haake, S.F. Ochoa, and A. Cechich (Eds.): CRIWG 2007, LNCS 4715, pp. 295–302, 2007.

Model (VFM) [7] to the transfer of engineered collaborative work practices in order to explore the research question (R1): *Are the events around the transition of new work practices in this organization consistent or inconsistent with the logic of VFM?*

2 The Value Frequency Model

VFM extends the Technology Transition Model (TTM) [6] to explain change-of-work-practice [7]. Figure 1 illustrates the propositions of VFM. It proposes change-of- practice as a multiplicative function of the *perceived-magnitude-of-value* (V) for a proposed change and *perceived-frequency-of-value* (F). Perceived-magnitude-of-value (shorted to *value* for this paper) is defined as an overall sense of the degree to which a proposed change of work practice would be good or bad for the individual.

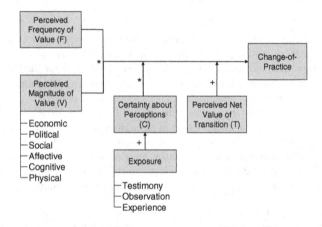

Fig. 1. Value Frequency Model for Change-of-practice

Perceived-frequency of value (or *frequency*) is defined as an overall sense of how often such value would be realized. Taken together, the multiplicative relationship between value and frequency is labeled as *the value-frequency judgment.*

VFM posits that the causal relationship between the value-frequency judgment and change-of-practice is moderated certainty-about-perceptions (C) and perceived-value-of-transition (T). *Certainty-about-perceptions* (or *certainty*) is a subconscious assessment of the likelihood that value-frequency judgments are accurate. *Perceived Net Value of Transition* (T) (or *Transition Value*) is defined as an overall sense of the positive or negative value that would derive from the change process itself.

3 The Organization

We conducted the study at the headquarters of a large global organization. The organization provides services to and receives services from its subsidiaries and cooperates regularly with external organizations on large scale projects. The organization's charter requires that it develop creative, cross-disciplinary solutions to fast-breaking opportunities and challenges in its volatile operating environment.

About 500 people conduct knowledge work at the headquarters. The competitive strength of the organization lies in the diversity of experience, skills, and knowledge held by the individuals and the speed with which it can bring this expertise to bear. *Ad-hoc* work teams form regularly with size and membership depending on the nature of the project. A given person typically leads or participates in multiple projects and managers are often leading 20+ projects at any given time. For 18 months before the research began, the most-senior leader of the organization had actively campaigned for a change of organizational culture. He argued that their old multi-layered bureaucracy was insufficiently responsive to the accelerating pace of change in their environment and he advocated for a change from a "need-to-know" culture to a "need-to-share" culture.

4 Methodology

We chose an action research approach to studying CE design transfers in the field. With action research, "...*a researcher begins with a theory and intervenes in a situation with the goal of improving both the situation and the theory*" [8]. Using the logic of VFM, we derived an interview protocol for identifying high-value recurring work practices and used the protocol to interview supervisory, managerial, and executive leaders [9]. We used the protocol to conduct 17 interviews with executives and senior managers across the major divisions of the organization. An interview typically yielded one-to-three candidate tasks. Several of the candidates were identified by multiple interviewees. When the interviews were complete, we had compiled a list of 27 tasks that varied in scope from groups of five working for an hour or two to groups of thousands working for a year.

We deemed a task to be a strong CE candidate if it had high value-frequency potential, if its practitioners found it painful to execute in some way, and if it had low barriers to change. The analysis yielded ten strong candidates including IT governance, budget planning, and competitive intelligence. VFM suggests that a new practice that delivers small value frequently would be as likely to transition as a practice that delivers large value infrequently. To maximize our opportunities to learn about the process of transferring engineered processes to practitioners we sought a widely-practiced, high-frequency task. One such task surfaced in the interviews. We designed a new collaborative work practice to improve certain aspects of its execution. We then used the logic of VFM to select potential practitioners. We conduct interventions intended to transfer the new process to practitioners to execute for themselves. We collected field notes of our interactions with the practitioners. We followed each intervention with an observation phase, during which we gathered data both about the extent to which practitioners were adopting and using the new work practice. These observations took the form of unstructured phone and face-to-face interviews, direct observations of practitioners executing the work practice, and evaluation of the content they contributed to the collaboration technology used to support the work practice. In the reflection phase we analyzed field notes, and other sources of data and reflected on the extent which a) the transfer interventions had resulted in self-sustaining use of the work practice by the group, b) the extent to which interventions had been effective, and c) the extent to which events and incidents surrounding the transfer were consistent or inconsistent with VFM. Details of the interventions appear in the following sections.

5   Critical Incidents and Events

A number of interviewees singled out the weekly staff meeting as an important yet onerous task. Hundreds of staff meetings took place in the organization every week. Many of our interviewees complained of the stultifying, painful nature of weekly staff meetings, which typically involved about 10 people and lasted about two hours. The organization had culturally ingrained practice of presenting from PowerPoint slides at these meetings. The meeting was usually the first time others saw the information in the slides. Knowledge workers briefed their managers; managers, in turned briefed executives; executives briefed senior executives up through the top levels of leadership. One senior executive said "we're in a high-pressure, time-sensitive environment and with everything that's going on, every week we have to stop the [work] to make PowerPoint slides for the boss. We all hate it. The boss hates it. But I don't think there is any way around it."

One manager observed, "people are bored out of their minds. Everybody takes 10 or 12 minutes to fill their boss in on what they've done this week, but the rest of us just aren't interested. We wait our own turn, and then we want to get out of there!"

A first line manager, Lance[1], the IT coordinator for one of the headquarters units, became our first champion for change. According to Lance, "there is so much time wasted in staff meetings and nobody but the boss gets anything out of them. It would be so much more valuable if we could use that time for creative problem solving...if we could help solve each-other's problems...if the could get help overcoming barriers...if we could work together to eliminate redundancy across our efforts...if we could find synergies that make us all more successful." However, Lance was certain that participants would not be willing to commit more time to staff meetings than they already spent and the current status updates were deemed by all stakeholders to be vital to the ongoing success of the organization.

5.1   The Process Design

Working with Lance, we designed a simple, new work practice that would convert staff meetings from narrations of recent events to discussions of how to improve team member success. Under the new approach, teams would create one shared online page for each project. Each page had four sections:

1. *Project milestones. Major events and deliverables for a project.*
2. *Accomplishments this period. Substantive progress toward milestones.*
3. *Activities next period. Proposed actions to progress toward milestones.*
4. *Issues-Risks-Barriers. Anything that would hamper achievement of activities.*

---

[1] Names have been changed to protect privacy of participants.

Team members would update these sections asynchronously throughout week. Therefore before the staff meeting participants would already know status and issues and could come prepared to discuss ways to address the issues. In the meeting project leaders would spend two-to-three minutes summarizing key accomplishments and barriers. Then the leader would ask others to pause for a moment to write down suggestions for overcoming barriers or increasing the likelihood of project success. This would be followed by oral discussion where people built on one another's ideas.

VFM suggests that to maximize the likelihood of successful transition, we had to minimize the cognitive load of both learning and executing the practice. Over the course of the first month, we simplified the process. Following VFM, this pilot implementation provided a basis for team members to give testimony on its benefits and limitations and to offer others the chance to observe the new approach in action, both of which should increase the certainty of value-frequency judgments among target practitioners. Drawing further on VFM, we chose to give the new approach a catchy name, in order to allow people to discuss it using a single word, thereby reducing cognitive load of spreading the word. One executive had expressed a sentiment reflected by others, "our processes were too slow, we can't respond fast enough to the changes in their environment." We therefore named the new work practice, *AgileStaff*, suggesting that it could improve the responsiveness of staff meetings. To reduce the time and effort required to inform people of the process, we created a one-page success story about its use. We also created an eight page practitioner's guide that provided details on how to implement the approach, a slide show that summarized the approach, and a one-hour training session practitioners.

We conducted early trials of AgileStaff on a wiki, a group support system, a shared document editor, a shared spreadsheet, and several other platforms. However, in order to minimize transition costs we sought a platform that was already in use by the organization, supported and maintained by the IT staff, and accessible to the organization at no additional cost. We wanted a platform that required no programming skills to tailor its configuration and that required no new software to be installed. The organization was already using Microsoft SharePoint for other purposes and met our constraints. We therefore offered it as an alternative when we introduced AgileStaff to a new group and it did become the unofficial standard for AgileStaff implementations within the organization. It took about 90 minutes to set up each new AgileStaff site. Once the site was created, it took users less than 30 seconds to create a new project page by adding the project name to a list. An AgileStaff site allowed users to browse to any project page by clicking the project name on a list. They could prepare weekly status reports for all projects with a single button click.

5.2 The Process Implementation

Lance observed one of the early AgileStaff sessions run by the research team for its own projects. He then invited one of his peers to observe a session and to discuss whether it should be tried in their own unit. He created a pilot site on the organization's network and showed it to people within his division. He modified the approach somewhat. We also demonstrated the approach to others in the organization highlighting the benefits for various stakeholders and describing the roles and responsibilities for the meeting leader, manager, project leaders, and team members.

Although we heavily emphasized the attention to the process rather than the technology that supported it, potential users nonetheless tended to assume that AgileStaff was a technology, rather than a process. At least two groups tried to use the technology before receiving any process briefings, but they were not able to reverse engineer the process based on the configuration of the tools. Both groups concluded that the AgileStaff approach was badly flawed and not particularly useful. We received word through informants about the dissatisfied groups and approached them to offer training, emphasizing again the importance of process over technology. Both groups initially accepted the offer. One followed through and adopted the approach once they understood how worked. The other has not yet followed through.

We sent the one-page AgileStaff success story to the head of the organization and to all our initial interviewees and asked them to distribute it to others who might be interested. We also posted the success story on the organization's internal web portal. Within a week, eight different groups in the organization called us asking for information about how to pilot test the approach. Four of the groups opted to implement trials right away. One group implemented the approach fully based only on the practitioner documentation provided by researchers, without further intervention from the research team – an early indicator that the process might take root within the organization. We collected war stories and testimonials from early adopters and incorporated them into presentations to other groups.

In the months that followed, we typically received one or two queries per week from groups at headquarters who were interested in learning more about the AgileStaff approach. To date about 10% of personnel at headquarters use the approach regularly. Contractors from two other organizations encountered the approach and adopted it for their own organizations.

Resistance to Change. After two months of low-key advocacy by Lance, key stakeholders in his division agreed to take a briefing. Attendees expressed polite interest, then positive affect as they came to understand AgileStaff. Lance's manager said, "I could use this on four projects I have right now." However, 40 minutes into the meeting, Donata, a senior manager about a month from retirement, entered the room uninvited. With raised voice and hostile tone, she declared "none of the senior leaders like the AgileStaff approach, especially Mr. Smith, the director of our division." She berated and lectured the attendees until the allotted meeting time had expired and the meeting disbanded. Three weeks later, Lance presented AgileStaff with one members of the research team to a deputy division chief who was interested in using the process. Donata learned the meeting had taken place and told Lance she was going to file charges against him for having illegally misappropriated organizational resources with respect to AgileStaff. He reported the incident to Mr. Smith, who enlisted support from senior leaders within and above the division. They assured that Donata would not interfere further.

It is not clear why Donata felt so hostile towards AgileStaff. One participant speculated that the process undermined her efforts to create a new collaborative software platform, for which she had consumed a significant portion of resources. She had received heavy criticism for the functionality of the system she championed. AgileStaff may have created strongly negative political, social, and economic values for Donata by moving people toward a different platform. Her hostile behavior created a strongly negative political, social, and affective value shift for people who had been contemplating a change to AgileStaff. All of them dropped the idea until after she left the organization. After she her departure, three different parts of the division piloted the AgileStaff approach, but none of those efforts led to an adoption.

In another unrelated case, we received word that George, the headquarters' head of knowledge management, had spoken negatively about the AgileStaff approach in a hallway conversation. We had not briefed him on the approach, so we suspected he might be responding to misinformation or misunderstandings rather than to the actual approach. VFM suggested that his testimony might dissuade others from considering the approach, so we scheduled a meeting with him to discuss it later that day. At the meeting we asked George if he declared that it had no value because it was implemented on SharePoint, which meant that one could only find its content if one already knew where to look. He questioned whether we had researched best practices, or whether we had just "made something up." We asked him if he had a best practice in his division that we might have overlooked. He described an approach that he and his deputy had implemented two months previously. His approach mapped directly to the key AgileStaff concepts – asynchronous on-line reporting of status updates. He further explained that he wanted to migrate the entire organization away from Sharepoint onto a Knowledge Portal his team had developed so that anybody in the organization could find anything they needed to know immediately. The implementation of a new process on Sharepoint constituted a negative political, social, and cognitive value with respect to his goal, giving rise to his impetus to work against its success. Once he found that AgileStaff mirrored his approach, and that it could be implemented on his preferred platform, he agreed to stop working against it.

6 Discussion: Analysis of AgileStaff Events in Light of VFM

Some practitioners found the value-frequency judgment for AgileStaff to be sufficiently high to overcome its transition cost: about an hour of training. Leaders valued the cognitive and political benefits of real-time visibility into project status and were willing to forego PowerPoint presentations. One practitioner said, "each time I update the pages it feels like a win because I know I will not have to build slide shows at the end of the week." Some participants valued the reduction of cognitive load from not building slide shows. Some felt that the approach also retained important political and social values from the old approach. Said one, "in this organization the amount of face-time you get with your superiors is an indication of your power and influence." AgileStaff offers a modest gain in productivity for the organization, in that it saves practitioners an hour or two per week, but this does not appear to have been a factor in the change decisions reported by practitioners.

The interventions to expose the approach to others and to both alert them to the potential value it may offer them increase their certainty about that value seem to have been sufficient for the early adopters. Likewise, the simple design, the practitioner's documentation, the free software platform, and the one-hour training package appear to have sufficiently reduced negative transition values so that changes-of-practice would occur.

7 Conclusions

The constructs and propositions of VFM provided a useful basis for discovering, evaluating, and selecting candidate tasks for CE interventions. It appeared to provide useful insights to inform process design efforts and transfer interventions. Incidents and events that manifested in the field with respect to changes-of-practice appeared to be consistent with an explained by the logic of VFM. Thus, this study provides evidence from the field that the theory may be useful. While the interventions described here seem to be working; only a few months have passed. It will be some months or years more before we can conclude that a self-sustaining and growing community of practice has genuinely formed around AgileStaff.

References

1. Anson, R.B., R.P., Wynne, B.E.: An Experiment Assessing Group Support System and Facilitator Effects on Meeting Outcomes. Management Science 41(2), 189–208 (1995)
2. Miranda, S.M.: Avoidance of groupthink: meeting management using group support systems. Small Group Research 25(1), 105–136 (1994)
3. Briggs, R.O.V., de G.J., Nunamaker, Jr., J.F.: Collaboration Engineering with ThinkLets to Pursue Sustained Success with Group Support Systems. Journal of Management Information Systems 19(4), 31–64 (2003)
4. Vreede, G.J.D.K., G.L., Briggs, R.O.: ThinkLets: A Collaboration Engineering Pattern Language. International Journal of Computer Applications and Technology 25(2/3), 140–154 (2006)
5. Kolfschoten, G.L.B., R.O., de Vreede, G.-J.: Appelman, J.H. Conceptual foundation of the ThinkLet concept for Collaboration Engineering. International Journal of Human-Computer Studies 64(7), 611–627 (2006)
6. Briggs, R.O., Adkins, M., Mittleman, D., Kruse, J., Miller, S., Nunamaker, Jr, J.F.: A technology transition model derived from field investigation of GSS use aboard the U.S.S. CORONADO. Journal of Management Information Systems 15(3), 151–195 (1998/1999)
7. Briggs, R.O.: The value frequency model: Toward a theoretical understanding of organizational change. In: Seifert, S., Weinhardt, C. (eds.) Group Decision and Negatiation, Karlsruhe, Germany, pp. 36–39 (2006)
8. Argyris, C., Putnam, R., McLain Smith, D.: Action science - Concepts, methods and skills for research and intervention. Jossey-Bass, San Francisco (1982)
9. Briggs, R.O., Davis, A.J., Murphy, J.D.: Discovering and evaluating collaboration engineering opportunities. In: Briggs, R.O., Nunamaker, Jr., J.F. (eds.) HICSS 2007 Workshop on Collaboration Engineering (2007)

An Agent-Based Recommender System to Support Collaborative Web Search Based on Shared User Interests

Daniela Godoy[1,2] and Analía Amandi[1,2]

[1] ISISTAN Research Institute, UNICEN University
Campus Universitario, Paraje Arroyo Seco
CP 7000, Tandil, Bs. As., Argentina
[2] CONICET, Consejo Nacional de Investigaciones Científicas y Técnicas
CP 1033, Capital Federal, Bs. As., Argentina
{dgodoy,amandi}@exa.unicen.edu.ar

Abstract. Personal information agents emerged in the last decade as an alternative to assist users to cope with the increasing volume of information available on the Web. In order to provide personalized assistance, these agents rely on user profiles modeling user information preferences, interests and habits. Inserted in communities of people with similar interests, personal agents can improve their assistance by gathering knowledge extracted from the observed common behaviors of single users. In this paper we propose an agent-based recommender system for supporting collaborative Web search in groups of users with partial similarity of interests. Empirical evaluation demonstrates that the interaction among personal agents increases the performance of the overall recommender system.

1 Introduction

The motivation of personal information agents resides in the enormous amount of information available on on-line sources, which has created a pressing need for effective personalized techniques. Built upon traditional information finding tools such as search engines, these agents help users find relevant information based on detailed models of their interests contained in user profiles. In communities of people with similar interests, collaboration among agents fosters knowledge sharing and, consequently, potentially enriches the achievable results of individual agents by taking advantage of other agent experience.

The idea of personal agents acting on behalf of users and sharing knowledge has been generally hampered by the assumption that agents begin with a predefined, common ontology instead of personalized and diverse ontologies [11]. In the context of an agent-based system, a common ontology serves as a knowledge-level specification of the ontological commitments of the participating agents. In heterogeneous environments such as the Web, however, a common ontology can hardly embrace the diverse interests users might have. Moreover, ontologies often mirror the ontology of common-sense of either a particular community or a mass of users, but they fail to capture specific concepts that might be interesting for individual users.

J.M. Haake, S.F. Ochoa, and A. Cechich (Eds.): CRIWG 2007, LNCS 4715, pp. 303–318, 2007.
© Springer-Verlag Berlin Heidelberg 2007

In this paper, we propose an agent-based recommender system for collaborative information retrieval and discovery. It diverges from the common ontology paradigm to a paradigm involving agents that can meaningfully communicate using diverse personal ontologies consisting in conceptual representations of user interests externalized by user profiles. In this approach, personal agents learn user profiles and then seek interest similarities in the profiles of other users. By locating similar semantic concepts, agents are able to overcome their lack of shared meaning and gain the ability of exchanging information.

In contrast to traditional collaborative filtering [2], which measures the similarity among users considering their entire user profiles (i.e., behavior history or opinions), we propose a novel recommendation method in which a user receives recommendations from other users with partial similarity of interests. Two users might be very similar regarding certain aspects of their preferences, yet they might have completely dissimilar interests in other aspects. In the proposed recommender system, agents focus on those interests that are common to users.

The rest of the paper is organized as follows. Section 2 reviews related research. Section 3 describes the system architecture and main components. Sections 4 and 5 are concerned with personalized and collaboration strategies for recommendation, respectively. An example of the recommender system functionality is described in Section 6. In Section 7, experimental evaluation of the system is reported. Concluding remarks are presented in Section 8.

2   Related Works

To alleviate the problem of information overload resulting from the overwhelming volume of available on-line information, collaborative information retrieval techniques have been proposed and studied in the context of computer supported cooperative work (CSCW). In [1], two general approaches have been distinguished. The first approach is concerned with situations where people use CSCW tools to support collaboration in the retrieval process. Users collaboratively search for answers to the same query, and then aggregate and unify their individual findings. In the second approach, recommender systems based on collaborative filtering techniques [2] provide users during search with information that has been useful to other users previously.

In this second line of research, an agent-based recommender system is presented in this paper for carrying out collaborative search on the Web. Based on individual user profiles as well as interests and past actions of several users with similar interests, the system recommends a set of documents or items that might be interesting to users while they are searching the Web.

Several autonomous agents and multi-agent systems have been presented in literature for helping users with information-related tasks. On the one hand, personal agents assisting users during Web search track user browsing and build user profiles in order to anticipate information needs. *FERRET* [10], for example, is a Web search agent that is able to use an explicit, a priori knowledge about a user to add context information to the user queries. Similarly, *QueryTracker* [9] learns user interests based on relevance feedback and daily resubmits user queries to a search engine, monitoring search results for changes. These autonomous agents, however, do not take advantage of the knowledge and expertise acquired by other agents acting in a user community.

Multi-agent approaches to collaborative information retrieval, on the other hand, put forward personal agents acting on behalf of their users and collaborating with one another aiming to improve browsing and/or searching experiences of their users. For example, a multi-agent Web mining system called *Collaborative Spiders*, which implies across-user collaboration in Web search, is proposed in [4]. In this system, there is an agent that performs profile matching to find information potentially interesting to users. Before searching, users have to specify the interest area, privacy or publicity of each search experience. Users then can explore similar already completed search sessions from the user community.

In [12], a multi-agent referral system in which personal agents provide users with answers to their questions is presented. From an agent point of view, other agents are classified as neighbors, which can provide answers to queries, or acquaintances, which are only reached through neighbors. This system uses pre-defined ontologies, which have to be shared by all agents, to facilitate knowledge exchanging among them. *Implicit* [3] is a multi-agent recommender system based on the concept of *Implicit Culture*, a generalization of collaborative filtering in which a new member of a community is induced to behave similarly to the other members. *Implicit* recommends specific information exploiting previous observations about the behavior of other users as asked for similar queries.

In some of these systems, users are burdened with a significant load of work that might hinder the advantages of collaboration. For instance, users are asked to specify their interest areas explicitly in order to access shared search sessions or analyze the results of numerous similar search experiences gathered from the community. Other systems are restricted to use certain pre-defined knowledge or ontologies to both describe the interests of users and compare them. In environments such as the Web, however, users not only have diverse information interests which can hardly be covered by general-purpose ontologies, but also have changing interests which can appear or disappear over time.

3   Recommender System Architecture

The agent-based recommender system presented in this paper accepts queries from a user and exploits the knowledge about this user interests and behavior patterns as well as the interests of other users in order to make personalized recommendations about Web pages. In contrast to the mentioned approaches, agents in this system acquire personalized ontologies or conceptual descriptions of individual user interests as a starting point for creating communities with common interests. Figure 1 illustrates the overall system architecture.

Individual users have their own personal agents or assistants to help them find relevant information according to their current needs. Each personal agent assisting a user in the system is mainly responsible for acquiring an accurate profile representing the user information preferences, retrieving pages from the Web upon a user query, assessing the level of correspondence of these pages with the user profile, interacting with the

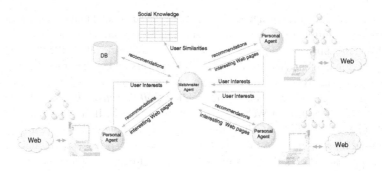

Fig. 1. Overview of the agent-based recommender system architecture

user to present recommendations and processing relevance feedback in order to adapt the user profile over time.

PersonalSearcher [6], a Web search agent that helps users to find interesting documents, plays the role of personal agent in this recommender system. In order to provide personalized assistance, this agent learns a hierarchical representation of a user interests by observing the user browsing behavior on the Web and then assists this user by filtering documents resulting from a traditional keyword-based search.

Instances of *PersonalSearcher*, each associated with a different user in the system, are integrated into a multi-agent system of cooperative agents that help users to access, manage and exchange information. The conceptual hierarchies describing individual user interests allow agents to detect partial similarities in the tastes of several users. Thus, collaboration is focused on the interests two users have in common, regardless of their dissimilarities in other concerns.

Each user group (e.g., all participants of a research project) shares one matchmaking agent which facilitates the exchanging of knowledge among the different personal agents. Matchmaker agents are designed to establish connections between users in the community exhibiting similar interests. In the recommender system, matchmaker agents are in charge of coordinating personal agents and disseminating relevant information to the interested users.

4   Personal Recommender Agents

One of the key functionalities of *PersonalSearcher* is to recommend Web documents to potentially interested users based on profile matching. In this content-based approach, recommendations are made based on the comparison of the user interest areas described in the profile and the content of Web pages. A brief overview of *PersonalSearcher*, the approach used to acquire profiles and recommend pages based on their content is given in the following subsections.

4.1   *PersonalSearcher* Overview

Each instance of *PersonalSearcher* monitors the Web activity of its associated user in order to collect documents the user is interested in. For each article read in a standard browser, *PersonalSearcher* observes a set of implicit indicators to estimate the extent of the user interest in the displayed Web page (e.g., time spent reading the page, amount of scrolling, if it was bookmarked, etc.). In this way, *PersonalSearcher* agents obtain relevant pages exemplifying information interests without distracting users from their regular activities.

Experiences of user interests identified by agents through observation are analyzed to learn a conceptual description of such interests and organized in the user profile as is explained in Section 4.2. User profiles are built starting from scratch and are constantly refined as new examples of user interests become available, using relevance feedback as a fundamental source of information. By building and adapting user profiles over time, personal agents become able to tailor the information filtering process according to the user preferences.

Users interact with their *PersonalSearcher* agents by expressing information needs through a set of keywords as in traditional search engines. In turn, agents post these queries to some of the most popular search engines, receiving documents that cover a wide portion of the Web. Incoming Web pages are evaluated by computing their relevance degree regarding the user profile to determine whether to recommend them for future reading. Once agents present some recommendations, the behavior of users is again observed to perform profile adaptations based on the acceptance/rejection of agent actions.

4.2 User Profiling Approach

To provide effective assistance, agents depend on the knowledge they have about individual users contained in user profiles, i.e. models of user interests, preferences and habits. *PersonalSearcher* employs a user profiling technique designed to support incremental learning and adaptation of user profiles in personal information agents. This technique allows the extraction of profiles consisting of a hierarchical organization of interests across different abstraction levels.

In a user profile, each experience e_i collected by a personal agent is attached with a *relevance value* denoted rel_i, i.e. the user profile consists of pairs $\langle e_i, rel_i \rangle$, where e_i is the user experience encoding mainly the Web page the user found interesting, and rel_i represents the evidence about the user interest in that experience. This relevance value is confined to the $[0,1]$ interval and is established according to the evidence collected by observation (i.e., the interest in a visited Web page estimated using implicit interest indicators).

The relevance of experiences is used for both gaining confidence in experiences which are more representative of the user interests as well as forgetting old experiences. Important experiences in the profile are those that lead to successful recommendations, so that pages which are similar to these experiences have more chances of being recommended. In contrast, irrelevant experiences that do not provide good recommendations gradually lose relevance, adapting the profile to recognize and eventually remove no longer interesting topics.

The user profiling technique is built upon a clustering algorithm, named *WebDCC* (Web Document Conceptual Clustering) [6], that allows agents to acquire profiles starting from experiences without an a priori knowledge of user interest categories, so that

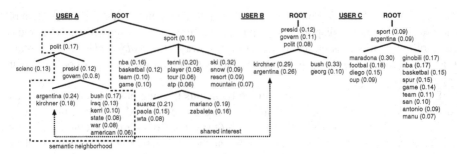

Fig. 2. Example of interest hierarchies for three users

the learning process is completely unsupervised. This algorithm belongs to the conceptual clustering paradigm, which includes clustering and characterization, i.e. the formation of intentional concept descriptions for extensionally defined clusters. In contrast to other profiling approaches, the use of conceptual clustering results in more comprehensible, semantically enhanced user profiles, which enable collaboration with other agents at a conceptual level.

Conceptual hierarchies produced by *WebDCC* algorithm are classification trees in which internal nodes represent concepts and leaf nodes represent clusters of experiences. The root of the hierarchy corresponds to the most general concept, which comprises all the experiences the algorithm has seen, whereas inner concepts become increasingly specific as they are placed lower in the hierarchy, covering only subsets of experiences by themselves. Finally, terminal concepts are those with no child concepts but clusters.

In other words, a hierarchy is conformed by an arbitrary number of concepts, denoted by $C = \{c_1, c_2, \ldots, c_n\}$, which are gradually discovered by the algorithm as new experiences become available. In order to automatically assign experiences to concepts, a text-like description given by a set of weighted terms $c_i = \langle (t_1, w_1), \ldots, (t_m, w_m) \rangle$ is associated to each concept during the process of concept formation. This description constitutes a linear classifier for the category and emerges from observing the common features of experiences in the category and those a novel experience should have in order to belong to it.

Leaves in the hierarchy correspond to clusters of experiences belonging to all the ancestor concepts. Intuitively, clusters are groups of experiences whose members are more similar to one another than to members of other clusters, so that clusters group highly similar experiences observed by the algorithm. In general terms, a set of n_i experiences belonging to a concept c_i and denoted $E_i = \{e_1, e_2, \ldots, e_{n_i}\}$, are organized into a collection of k clusters below c_i, $S_{ji} = \{s_{1i}, s_{2i}, \ldots, s_{ki}\}$, containing elements of D_i such that $s_{li} \cap s_{pi} = \emptyset$, $\forall l \neq p$.

In *WebDCC* algorithm the formation of concepts is driven by the notion of conceptual cohesiveness. Highly cohesive clusters are assumed to contain similar experiences belonging to a same category, whereas clusters exhibiting low cohesiveness are assumed to contain experiences concerning to distinctive aspects of more general categories. In the last case, concepts are extracted enabling a re-partitioning of experiences and the identification of sub-categories.

Incremental clustering outputs a hierarchical set of classifiers, each based on its own set of relevant features, as a combined result of a feature selection method for deciding on the appropriate set of terms at each node and a supervised learning algorithm for constructing a classifier for such node. Figure 2 shows three examples of hierarchical clustering solutions achieved with the algorithm to represent different profiles (actual words are not showed, but their stems).

4.3 Content-Based Recommendation

For personal agents, user profiles consist of a set of past user reading experiences organized in a conceptual hierarchy. To recommend a previously unseen Web page, an agent retrieves similar experiences from the user profile assuming that the user interest in some page will resemble the interest in similar past experiences. Hierarchical concepts or classifiers in the profile bias the search toward the most relevant experiences. This is, a page has to be classified in the different categories to select the n best matching experiences.

A confidence value in a Web page to be recommended, denoted $conf(r_i)$, is calculated by a function that aggregates the global similarity of an experience e_k with the candidate page r_i and the relevance of this experience. To assess the confidence in recommending r_i given the experience e_k, a weighted sum of the confidence value of each similar retrieved experience is calculated as follows:

$$conf(r_i) = \frac{\sum_{k=1}^{n} w_k * rel_k}{\sum_{k=1}^{n} w_k} \tag{1}$$

where n is the number of similar experiences retrieved, rel_k is the relevance of experience e_k and w_k is the contribution of each experience according to its similarity. This method is based on the well-known distance-weighted nearest neighbor algorithm [7]. Each experience has a weight w_k according to the inverse square of its distance from r_i, i.e. $w_k = \frac{1}{(1-sim(e_k,r_i))^2}$, where $sim(e_k, r_i)$ is the similarity between the item to be recommended r_i and the experience e_k which is the cosine similarity of Web page contents.

Finally, if the confidence in recommending r_j is greater than a certain *confidence threshold*, the page is recommended. Items with confidence below this threshold are considered not interesting enough to be presented to users. If the result of a recommendation is successful according to user feedback, the relevance rel_k of the corresponding experiences in the profile is increased and, possibly, new experiences are added. If the result of a recommendation is a failure, agents learn from the mistake by decreasing the relevance of the experiences that have led to the unsuccessful recommendation.

5   Collaborative Recommender Agents

Multiple personal agents assisting several users can take advantage of existing knowledge in the community they are immersed in through cooperation. Hence, individual instances of *PersonalSearcher* can improve information retrieval quality and efficiency acting not just as isolated agents, but as a part of a multi-agent system of collaborative agents.

In order to enable knowledge sharing in a multi-agent system setting, issues such as how agents determine if two users know the same semantic concepts, how knowledge is effectively exchanged between them and how collaboration affects the group performance at a given collective task have to considered. The mechanisms to handle these issues, implemented by matchmaking agents in the proposed recommender system, are described in the following subsections.

5.1   Identification of Shared Interests

Instead of committing to a common ontology, agents in the proposed recommender system based collaboration on the comparison of personal ontologies or profiles. Thus, the system provides recommendations to target users based on neighbors with partially similar long-term interests. If two agents agree on the meaning of one or more semantic concepts via the comparison of the corresponding interest hierarchies, these concepts translate to each other in the system for future information exchange.

In contrast to most methods for ontology comparison, which refer to specific tools for constructing and merging complex ontologies requiring the intervention of human experts, the Triple Matching-Model (MD3)[8] adopted to compare hierarchies learned by personal agents, allows to automatize the process of evaluating the similarity among concepts across multiple ontologies.

MD3 aims at finding quantitative values of similarity among concepts in two separated ontologies by comparing concept descriptors as well as concept interrelationships. Instead of relying on semantic concept labels, MD3 compares representations of concepts (e.g., the associated words) and defines a similarity model in terms of the common features of these representations. In turn, similarity relationships allow agents to establish anchors between two personal ontologies or profiles while keeping each of them autonomous.

In other words, this method detects which sets of terms are similar and, therefore, which concepts are good candidates for establishing links across personal ontologies. This is considered a weak form of integration between ontologies since it does not allow further inferences about concept relationships. However, it is particularly useful in dynamic user profiling in which user profiles are expected to change over time and links between ontologies have to be adapted accordingly.

MD3 matching process is defined over a single hierarchy connecting two independent concept hierarchies via an imaginary root. Using the interconnected hierarchies, the matching process is applied in successive steps to different components: (1) lexicon matching, (2) feature matching, and (3) semantic-neighborhood matching. Therefore, the global similarity value $S(a,b)$ between two concepts a and b belonging to two different profiles, p and q, is the weighted sum of the similarity of each of the mentioned components:

$$S(a^p, b^q) = w_l * S_l(a^p, b^q) + w_f * S_f(a^p, b^q) + w_n * S_n(a^p, b^q) \qquad (2)$$

where S_l, S_f and S_n denote the lexical (i.e., the similarity among names), feature and semantic neighborhood similarities, respectively, and w_l, w_f and w_n are their corresponding weights, that must add up to 1. The lexicon matching in MD3 refers to the number of common and different words in the concept labels. Hierarchies learned by personal agents, however, have not associated labels, so that only the feature and semantic neighborhood similarities are considered for hierarchy comparison (i.e., $w_l = 0$).

The feature matching $S_f(a^p, b^q)$ between two concepts a^p and b^q, where A and B are the respective term sets, is determined by the cardinality of the intersection and the difference between A and B as follows:

$$S_f(a^p, b^q) = \frac{|A \cap B|}{|A \cap B| + \alpha(a^p, b^q) * |A - B| + (1 - \alpha(a^p, b^q)) * |B - A|} \tag{3}$$

The value of α can be expressed as a function of the *depth* of concepts, which corresponds to the shortest distance from the concepts to the virtual root:

$$\alpha(a^p, b^q) = \begin{cases} \frac{depth(a^p)}{depth(a^p) + depth(b^q)} & \text{if } depth(a^p) \leq depth(b^q) \\ 1 - \frac{depth(a^p)}{depth(a^p) + depth(b^q)} & \text{if } depth(a^p) > depth(b^q) \end{cases} \tag{4}$$

MD3 also includes the semantic relationships in a hierarchy in the matching process assuming that two concepts are semantically similar if they are related to the same group of concepts. Thus, comparing relationships is transformed into a comparison of semantic neighborhoods.

The notion of semantic neighborhood, that is the set of concepts whose distance to a given concept is within a specified radius, is used to calculate neighborhood similarity. The distance between two concepts in a hierarchy is measured as the shortest path, which is formed by the smallest number of undirected arcs that connect these concepts. Since distance is a metric function that satisfies the property of minimality (i.e., the self-distance is equal to zero), the semantic neighborhood of a concept contains the concept itself. Figure 2 depicts the immediate semantic neighborhood of the concept *presidency*.

Equation 5 gives a formal definition of the semantic neighborhood N, where a^o and c_i^o are concepts in an ontology o, r is the specified radius, and $d(a^o, c_i^o)$ is the distance between the two concepts.

$$N(a^o, r) = \{c_i^o\} \text{ such that } \forall i \, d(a^o, c_i^o) \leq r \tag{5}$$

The calculus of semantic-neighborhood matching S_n is a recursive process, because comparing concepts in the semantic neighborhoods is also a similarity evaluation. This recursion stops when the specified radius is reached, at which point concepts can be compared based on feature matching. Given two concepts a^p and b^q from ontologies p and q, where $N(a^p, r)$ has n concepts and $N(b^q, r)$ has m concepts, and the intersection of the two neighborhoods is denoted by $a^p \cap b^q$, the value of the semantic-neighborhood matching $S_n(a^p, b^q, r)$ is a function of the cardinality of the semantic neighborhoods N and the approximate intersection $\cap_n$ between these semantic-neighborhoods, calculated by:

$$\frac{a^p \cap_n b^q}{a^p \cap_n b^q + \alpha(a^p, b^q) * \delta(a^p, a^p \cap_n b^q, r) + (1 - \alpha(a^p, b^q)) * \delta(b^q, a^p \cap_n b^q, r)} \tag{6}$$

with

$$\delta(a^p, a^p \cap_n b^q, r) = \begin{cases} |N(a^p, r)| - a^p \cap_n b^q & \text{if } |N(a^p, r)| > a^p \cap_n b^q \\ 0 & \text{otherwise} \end{cases} \tag{7}$$

The intersection over semantic neighborhoods is approximated by the similarity of concepts across neighborhoods:

$$a^p \cap_n b^q = \left[\sum_{i \leq n} \left(\max_{j \leq m} S(a_i^p, b_j^p) \right) \right] - \varphi * S(a^p, b^q) \qquad (8)$$

with

$$\varphi = \begin{cases} 1 & \text{if } S(a^p, b^q) = \max_{j \leq m} S(a^p, b_j^q) \\ 0 & \text{otherwise} \end{cases} \qquad (9)$$

where S is the semantic similarity of concepts and, a_i^p and b_j^q are concepts in the semantic neighborhood of a^p and b^q respectively.

Given two user profiles, a comparison algorithm [5] based on the MD3 is run to identify the concepts they have in common. Essentially, this algorithm carries out breadth-first traversals of the conceptual hierarchies. It traverses the first profile, which is considered the reference profile, taking each concept along with its neighborhood, and comparing it with all the concepts in the second profile, which is considered the target profile. The algorithm outputs one or more links denoting similarities in the profiles as the one shown in Figure 2.

5.2 Collaborative-Based Recommendation

In order to enable information exchange between users, agents have to attain knowledge about other users and find the most appropriate ones for collaboration. Each instance of *PersonalSearcher* in the recommender system is registered to one or more matchmaker agents that accomplish this goal, i.e., matchmakers are in charge of making connections between agents that request recommendations and those that are able to provide them. Thus, agents are fully connected with their peers, but only through the corresponding matchmakers.

In the communication with matchmakers, personal agents provide the knowledge about the main interests of their users (i.e., interest hierarchy, but not experiences), resources discovered about shared interests (i.e., candidate recommendations) and, optionally, user current information needs (e.g., a query or categories the user is looking information about). In this situation, the matchmaker agent determines which agents are promising candidates for a fruitful cooperation by taking advantage of the discovered links between personal ontologies.

Matchmakers determine and keep up to date the relationships or links between personal ontologies using the profile comparison method for each pair of users. If the comparison of profiles between two users A and B is successful, agents become aware of the semantic concepts each user shares with other members of the community. For instance, if A and B users are both interested in X and Y concepts, the associated agents store social knowledge registering the existence of other agents in the system which might be interested in information regarding these concepts. This social knowledge allows personal agents to notify matchmakers about the discovery of new relevant information when interesting Web pages belonging to a shared concept is found by their users.

Matchmaker agents store the knowledge gathered from the group of personal agents they are managing. In the previous example, after comparing the profiles of users A

and B the matchmaker agent stores knowledge stating that both A and B are interested in concepts X and Y with a certain degree of confidence $conf_X$ and $conf_Y$, where $conf_X = S(X^A, X^B)$ and $conf_Y = S(Y^A, Y^B)$. Hence, when the agent assisting A delivers novel information about X or Y, the agent assisting B is contacted to receive this information. The level of relevance of a candidate recommendation r_i about X for the producer user A, i.e. $conf_A(r_i)$, is multiplied by the confidence $conf_X$ in the relationship between A and B, causing an increase or decrease of the overall recommendation relevance.

Ultimately, a recommendation is deemed relevant for a given user if the page overcomes certain relevance threshold, which can be customized according to the amount of information each user is willing to receive from others. Matchmaker agents use a temporary space to store incoming recommendations, which are automatically removed if they were not delivered to users after some time. Users can choose to handle incoming recommendations of all or some particular interest categories at any time. This is, personal agents can be configured to present recommendations matching active queries during Web search or matching certain interests either upon demand or proactively.

6   Usage Scenario

To illustrate how collaboration affects the group performance in discovering information, the system functionality is exemplified using the three different users depicted in Figure 2.

User A in the example seems to be interested in two broad categories *sports* and *politics*, and several sub-categories. In *politics*, three distinctive interests are revealed in the hierarchy: *Argentinian* and *U. S. governments* and *political science*. This user is also interested in several sports, such as *basketball*, *ski* and *tennis*, and some more specialized interests, such as certain tennis players. Figure 3 shows a visualization of this profile in *PersonalSearcher* as well as a set of content-based recommendations the agent made while the user was searching using the query *'NBA ginobili'*.

The function of personal agents is to recommend novel Web pages to users as they are searching the Web, but also through collaboration with other agents. Users B and C have not interests in common, but both share one or more interests with A. User A can take advantage of the information discovered by B and C, whereas they both can be benefited by the information that A might discover related to the shared interests. Due to their orthogonal profiles, users B and C will no profit from their interaction.

From profile comparison, the matchmaker agent determines that A and C are both interested in *Emanuel Ginobili* basketball player and that users A and B are both interested in the same political subjects except for *political science*. Figure 4(behind) shows the recommendations received by user A starting from the information found by both B and C on the Web. The former provided some recommendations about *politics* belonging to the categories *Bush* and *Kirchner* presidents. The latter instead contributed with recommendations about *Emanuel Ginobili* basketball player, but did not send recommendations about *Maradona* as this is not an interest shared with A. Figure 4(front) depicts the recommendations received by user C from the other user in the system sharing the interest in *Emanuel Ginobili*, this is user A.

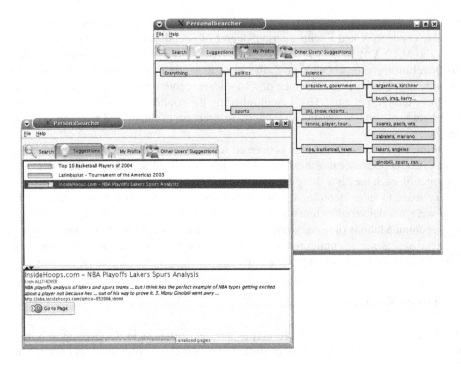

Fig. 3. Example of content-based recommendations

7   Experimental Results

Evaluation of personal agents and personalization systems in general is a difficult issue since it involves purely subjective relevance assessments. Most datasets are assembled to evaluate learning algorithms and, consequently, do not provide relevance judgments of users about documents. A specially suited dataset to evaluate recommendation is *Syskill&Webert* Web Page Ratings[1] since it contains the ratings of a single user about the interestingness of Web pages.

Syskill&Webert Web pages belong to four different categories: *Bands*, *Goats*, *Sheep* and *BioMedical*. In addition to the topical classification, a single user manually rated each page in a three point scale: *hot* or very interesting (93 pages), *medium* or quite interesting (11 pages) and *cold* or not interesting at all (223 pages). From the original collection we removed *'Not Found'* pages and those pages with not assigned rating, yielding to a total of 327 pages.

For the user who assigned rating to Web pages in the collection, regarded as the target user for experimentation, both content-based and collaborative recommendation were evaluated. To create a profile of this user we randomly selected 229 pages ($\simeq 70\%$) that were used for training, reserving for testing the remaining 98 pages ($\simeq 30\%$). This partition was made trying to keep the same proportion of examples in each class (*hot*,

---

[1] http://kdd.ics.uci.edu/databases/SyskillWebert/SyskillWebert.html

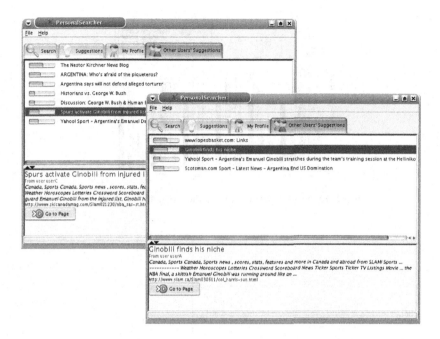

Fig. 4. Example of collaborative-based recommendations

medium and *cold*), then 72 pages ($\simeq 31\%$) of the training set belong to *hot* and *medium* classes and were added to the profile of the target user with a relevance equal to 1 and 0.5, respectively.

The assigned ratings were used as a means to measure the performance of personal agents in predicting the relevance of Web pages. Figure 6(a) shows the accuracy of recommendations as new experiences were incorporated in the profile. It can be observed in the figure that accuracy is constantly above the trivial rejector (which classifies everything as *cold* since it is the majority class), so that the profile allows recognizing some positive examples besides rejecting negative ones. In spite of the subjective judgments about the relevance of pages, which implies more than learning the topics of Web pages (i.e., classifying into *BioMedical*, *Bands*, *Goats* and *Sheep*), the profiling approach enables agents to reach good levels of accuracy in content-based recommendation.

In order to evaluate collaborative-based recommendation, we created a group of users, each interested in two of the categories of the *Syskill&Webert* dataset, according to the following steps:

1. Build a profile using a training set ($\simeq 70\%$) of randomly selected experiences in two categories of the *Syskill&Webert* dataset, setting the initial relevance of experiences in this profile randomly. Even though there will be some intersection between the training set of the target and the remaining users, the relevance assigned to the common experiences will be different, causing the profiles to focus on different aspects,

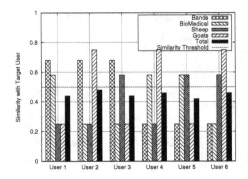

Fig. 5. Interest similarities among the target and other users

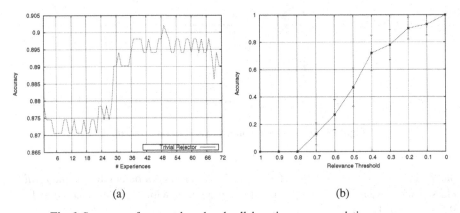

(a)   (b)

Fig. 6. Summary of content-based and collaborative recommendation accuracy

2. Obtain a testing set of Web pages matching the profile built in the previous step. For each category, select the 10 first pages resulting from a Web search using the most frequent keywords in the category and exceeding the relevance threshold regarding the profile. This procedure simulates a user searching the Web and finding novel information to share with other users,

3. Inform the matchmaker agent of the existing users in the group and the collected Web pages, so that it can perform profile comparison and generate recommendations for the target user exclusively,

4. Estimate the accuracy of recommendations received by the target user from the remaining users in the system.

Using this procedure, we created a total of six users interested in different pairs of topics, leading to interest hierarchies having at least two concepts (and some sub-concepts). Figure 5 shows the similarities between the target and other users regarding the different topics in the respective hierarchies as well as the total profile similarity. Labels were added to the figure for illustrative purpose only, but concepts are given by a set of terms (e.g., $\langle goat, milk \rangle$).

Experimental evidence showed not only that the user profiling approach was able to isolate the involved concepts to generate comprehensible descriptions of user interests, but also that the method for comparing hierarchies effectively distinguished the concepts users had in common. In fact, a similarity threshold of 0.5 allowed detecting all valuable links relating the created profiles. Note that if the global profile similarity is used, only a low similarity threshold would allow collaboration and, in that case, users would have received information about some uninteresting, non-common topics.

Figure 6(b) shows the result of collaborative-based recommendation. The average accuracy of recommendations the target user received from other users in the group and its standard deviation are reported for variations of the relevance threshold. This threshold was used in the estimation of accuracy due to the lack of real relevance judgments for pages in the testing sets to establish whether a recommendation was considered relevant for the target user. Naturally, the lower the relevance threshold the higher the accuracy since a high threshold demands Web pages to be very similar to past experiences in order to be considered interesting. In spite of being less accurate, collaborative recommendations usually entail higher novelty (not-obviousness). Indeed, pure content-based agents tend to over-specialization (i.e., users are limited to receive similar information to the pieces already seen), whereas collaborative-based recommendations imply a tradeoff between novelty and high quality.

8   Conclusions

In this paper we have described a recommender system based on personal agents assisting a group of users to find Web pages in a collaborative fashion. These agents learn conceptual hierarchies describing individual user interests through observation. In turn, the experience of multiple users with partially similar interests is exploited by means of interactions among their personal agents.

Identification of like-minded users is the basis for collaboration since it fosters social interaction. In this regard, the advantage of the proposed recommender system is twofold. First, agents acquire and maintain personalized ontologies instead of committing to a pre-defined shared ontology, which might be impractical in dynamic environments. Second, the system considers partial similarity of interests in which a user can agree with others in only certain aspects of their preferences. Thus, collaboration is focused exclusively on common interests, preventing dissimilar ones from affecting the outcome of recommendation.

Experiments carried out to evaluate the effectiveness of the system demonstrated the potential of the approach for reducing the burden of finding information on the Web. Our empirical findings indicated that the system is capable of both delivering accurate content-based recommendations and diversifying the list of resulting recommendations through collaborative information exchange among users sharing similar interests.

Acknowledgements

This research has been partially supported by ANPCyT PICT No. 34917.

References

1. Baeza-Yates, R., Pino, J.A.: A first step to formally evaluate collaborative work. In: Proceedings of the International ACM SIGGROUP Conference on Supporting Group Work: The Integration Challenge, pp. 56–60. ACM Press, New York (1997)
2. Balabanovic, M., Shoham, Y.: FAB: Combining content-based and collaborative recommendation. Communications of the ACM 40(3), 66–72 (1997)
3. Blanzieri, E., Giorgini, P., Massa, P., Recla, S.: Implicit culture for multi-agent interaction support. In: Batini, C., Giunchiglia, F., Giorgini, P., Mecella, M. (eds.) CoopIS 2001. LNCS, vol. 2172, pp. 27–39. Springer, Heidelberg (2001)
4. Chau, M., Zeng, D., Chen, H., Huang, M., Hendriawan, D.: Design and evaluation of a multi-agent collaborative Web mining system. Decision Support Systems 35(1), 167–183 (2003)
5. Giménez-Lugo, G.A., Amandi, A., Sichman, J., Godoy, D.: Enriching information agents' knowledge by ontology comparison: A case study. In: Garijo, F.J., Riquelme, J.-C., Toro, M. (eds.) IBERAMIA 2002. LNCS (LNAI), vol. 2527, pp. 546–555. Springer, Heidelberg (2002)
6. Godoy, D., Amandi, A.: User profiling for web page filtering. IEEE Internet Computing 9(4), 56–64 (2005)
7. Mitchell, T.M.: Machine Learning. McGraw-Hill, New York (1997)
8. Rodríguez, M.A., Egenhofer, M.J.: Determining semantic similarity among entity classes from different ontologies. IEEE Transactions on Knowledge and Data Engineering 15(2), 442–456 (2003)
9. Somlo, G., Howe, A.E.: QueryTracker: An agent for tracking persistent information needs. In: Proceedings of the 3rd International Joint Conference on Autonomous Agents and Multi-agent Systems (AAMAS 2004), pp. 488–495. IEEE Computer Society, Los Alamitos (2004)
10. Turner, R.M., Turner, E.H., Wagner, T.A., Wheeler, T.J., Ogle, N.E.: Using explicit, a priori contextual knowledge in an intelligent Web search agent. In: Akman, V., Bouquet, P., Thomason, R.H., Young, R.A. (eds.) CONTEXT 2001. LNCS (LNAI), vol. 2116, pp. 343–352. Springer, Heidelberg (2001)
11. Williams, A.B., Ren, Z.: Agents teaching agents to share meaning. In: Proceedings of the 5th International Conference on Autonomous Agents, Montreal, Canada, pp. 465–472. ACM Press, New York (2001)
12. Yu, B., Singh, P.: An agent-based approach to knowledge management. In: Proceedings of the 11th International Conference on Information and Knowledge Management (CIKM'02), pp. 642–644 (2002)

How to Choose Groupware Tools Considering Stakeholders' Preferences During Requirements Elicitation?

Gabriela N. Aranda[1], Aurora Vizcaíno[2], Alejandra Cechich[1], and Mario Piattini[2]

[1] GIISCo Research Group, Universidad Nacional del Comahue
Computing Sciences Department, Buenos Aires 1400 - 8300 Neuquén, Argentina
{garanda,acechich}@uncoma.edu.ar
[2] ALARCOS Research Group, Information Systems and Technologies Department
UCLM-INDRA Research and Development Institute, Escuela de Informática, Universidad de
Castilla-La Mancha, Paseo de la Universidad 4 - 13071 Ciudad Real, Spain
{aurora.vizcaíno,mario.piattini}@uclm.es

Abstract. The main challenges during global software development projects are related to the lack of face-to-face communication and the need of people feeling comfortable with the technology they use. In this paper we introduce an approach that proposes a way of choosing the most suitable technology for a given group of people, taking advantage of information about stakeholders' cognitive characteristics. As our research focuses on the importance of communication during the global requirements elicitation process, we present preliminary results of two surveys that analyze stakeholders' preferences in such environments.

1 Introduction

Communication is a common problem during requirement elicitation [5], and is even more important for Global Software Development (GSD) projects. The need of counting with the best communication channels during a collocated requirements elicitation process is aggravated when stakeholders are distributed over many distanced sites, due to the lack of face to face interaction, as well as the time difference between different sites and the cultural diversity of stakeholders [8].

One of the most common ways of classifying groupware is according to their synchronous or asynchronous characteristics (depending on if the users have to work at the same time or not) [9]. According to GSD literature, both categories are important during requirement elicitation – asynchronous collaboration allows team members to construct requirements individually and contribute to the collective activity of the group for later discussion (especially when groups are distributed across time zones), and real time collaboration and discussions are necessary components of group Requirements Elicitation (RE) sessions to give stakeholders the chance of having instant feedback [12]. However, is also true that sometimes people are keener on one kind of collaboration than the other. So, as communication among people involves aspects of human processing mechanisms that are analyzed by the

J.M. Haake, S.F. Ochoa, and A. Cechich (Eds.): CRIWG 2007, LNCS 4715, pp. 319–327, 2007.
© Springer-Verlag Berlin Heidelberg 2007

cognitive sciences, we decided to look for references into the Cognitive Informatics, an interdisciplinary research area that applies concepts from psychology and other cognitive sciences to improve processes in engineering disciplines like software engineering [17].

After analyzing varied psychological issues, we set our interest in the Learning Style Models (LSMs), which may be useful to select groupware tools and elicitation techniques according to the cognitive style of stakeholders [15]. Most of related works using LSMs in informatics concern educational purposes like [4], and only one work can be cited where cognitive styles are used as a mechanism for improving Software Engineering tasks. In [16] a controlled experiment proves that heterogeneous software inspection teams have better performance than homogeneous ones, where heterogeneity concerns the cognitive style of the participants. However, our approach differ from this one because, instead of trying to say which people seem to be more suitable to work together, our goal is choosing the best strategies to improve communication for an already given group of people.

Having this in mind, we will give an introduction to some basic concepts about cognitive informatics and learning styles models, and we will introduce a methodology, based on concepts from fuzzy logic, to select groupware tools and requirement elicitation techniques. The last sections will compare results from two different surveys we have carried out in order to get examples to validate our methodology and we will present some conclusions and guidelines for future work.

2   Cognitive Aspects of Requirement Elicitation

Cognitive Informatics relates cognitive sciences and informatics by using cognitive theories to investigate and look for solutions to software engineering problems [7]. In this sense cognitive styles are a part of cognitive psychology theories that classify people's preferences about perception, judgment and processing of information [16], and try to explain differences in human behaviour. Similarly, learning styles models (LSMs) classify people according to a set of behavioural characteristics that concern the ways people receive and process information, while their goal is improving the way people learn a given task. Considering that elicitation is about learning the needs of the users [13], and also an scenario where users and clients learn from analysts and developers [15], we can consider that during the elicitation process everybody "learns" from others. Then, even when LSMs have been discussed in the context of analyzing relationships between instructors and students, we propose taking advantage of LSMs by adapting it to virtual teams that deal with distributed elicitation processes.

After studying different LSMs, we have chosen the Felder-Silverman (F-S) Model., since according to our analysis, it covers the categories defined by the most famous LSMs (like the Myers-Briggs Indicator Type, the Kolb model, the Herrmann Brain Dominance Instrument, etc.) and, additionally, the F-S model has been widely and successfully used with educational purposes in engineering fields [11]. The F-S Model introduces four categories (Perception, Input, Processing and Understanding), each of them further decomposed into two subcategories (Sensing/Intuitive; Visual/ Verbal; Active/Reflective; Sequential/Global). For details see [10].

Classification into the different categories is obtained by filling a multiple-choice test, available on the WWW (http://www.engr.ncsu.edu/learningstyles/ilsweb.html), which returns a rank for each subcategory. Depending on the circumstances, people may fit into one category or the other; so preference for each category is measured as strong, moderate, or mild. According with their authors, people with a mild preference are balanced on the two dimensions of that scale. People with a moderated preference for one dimension are supposed to learn more easily in a teaching environment, which favours that dimension. Finally, people with a strong preference for one dimension of the scale may have difficulty learning in an environment, which does not support that preference. With the goal of making everybody feel comfortable in the virtual environment, we propose choosing groupware tools and elicitation techniques more according to their learning styles, as we explain in the next section.

3   A Systematic Process to Support Personal Preferences in Distributed Requirement Elicitation

In order to support personal preferences when selecting technologies for virtual teams, we propose a methodology that uses fuzzy logic and fuzzy sets [1] to obtain rules from a set of representative examples, in the way of patterns of behaviour.

The methodology is divided into two stages: the first one is independent of any project and comprehends phases 1 to 4, and the second one is dependent of a given project and covers phases 5 and 6, as it is shown in Figure 1.

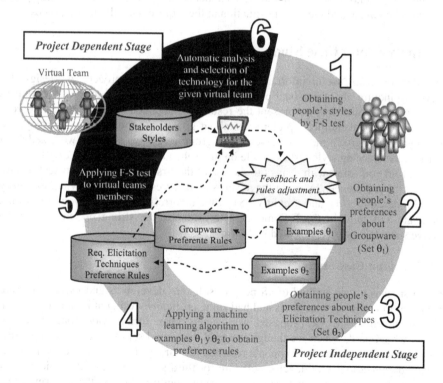

Fig. 1. Phases to define and analyze personal preferences to choose appropriate technology in Virtual Teams

Phases 1 to 3 are about looking for a set of examples, which are real data about preferences of stakeholders in their daily use of groupware tools and requirements elicitation techniques. Then, we analyse the data by using the machine learning algorithm proposed in [6], where each example is turned into an initial rule and iteratively it is found a finite set of fuzzy rules that reproduce the input-output system's behaviour (*Phase 4*). This algorithm was designed to obtain rules with a maximum degree of generality, and then it reduces the antecedent part as much as possible so as to obtain rules that can be easily understood and highly approximated to real-life examples. As we mentioned before, phases 1 to 4 constitute the *project independent* part where the example and preference rule databases can be improved along surveys and applied on different GSD projects.

The remaining phases consist of the application of our methodology to a specific GSD project during a requirement elicitation process, so that it is called the *project dependent stage*. In this stage, we obtain the personal preferences of every person who will work in a given virtual team (*Phase 5*) and stored it in a database that can be accessed every time people need to communicate to each other. The technology selection process is done by studying and confronting the personal preferences of the people that need to work together. This is done by means of an automatic tool that chooses and suggests the most appropriated technology (*Phase 6*). As we have explained in [2] such strategies must take into account other factors besides cognitive profiles of stakeholders, like time difference between sites, the degree of sharing of a common language, and the current situation at the requirement elicitation process.

4   Analysis of a Case Study

In order to obtain useful information for illustrating our approach, we designed a survey to inquire about personal preferences of stakeholders and to look for patterns of behaviour. Following we present the results we obtained in two different surveys that deal with stakeholders' preferences about groupware tools. In both surveys we asked people to give a rank to a given set of groupware tools and then we asked them to fill in the learning style test available on the web site and send us the results.

To avoid confusion with respect to the use of the first letter, in the next sections we identify the preferences by using the adverbs (and corresponding abbreviations): Very (V), Moderately (M) and Slightly (S), which correspond respectively to strong, moderate and mild in the F-S model. For example, the strong preference for the Active subcategory is represented by "VAc".

4.1   The First Case Study

The first survey was applied to 48 people; software developers and users who were accustom to use groupware tools and had some proficiency using at least two of them. The groupware tools we proposed were email, chat, forum, videoconference and shared whiteboard, which we though it would be a good set of groupware to interact among more than 2 people. 43 people returned the survey. 14 interviewees worked for private organizations that develop software for third parts; 23 were academic staff of universities that cooperate with software development projects and the rest were users of software systems at different organizations.

As the number of examples was not large enough to analyze each tool separately, we decided to analyze preferences taking into account two broader groups – asynchronous and synchronous groupware tools [9] – which are usually taken into account in literature [8, 14] to analyze their effect on GSD projects. Firstly, we analyzed the preferences of stakeholders respect to their gender and age; and we ensured that data was independent of such factors. Later we analyzed preferences of stakeholders in relation with their learning style. Then, we found out that there were no significant differences for slight or moderated preferences, but when preferences were stronger, the number of stakeholders who chose between synchronous and asynchronous tools was not similar. Especially for the Visual-Verbal category, the difference between preferences for both types of tools was about 15% for asynchronous against 85% for synchronous tools. Unfortunately, for the rest of strong preferences we did not have enough examples to obtain conclusions. For further details see [3].

4.2 The second Case Study

In order to validate the first case study we decided to run a second case study. In this case we asked 63 people to answer the questionnaires. They were also software developers and users that are accustom to use groupware tools. We changed the list of groupware tools and proposed them email, instant messaging, audio conference and videoconference. The changes obeyed to suggestions from other researchers in GSD that consider audio conference should be included because it is widely used in GSD projects. In addition, we decided to get out shared whiteboard and forums because nobody had chosen them as his or her favourite one in the first study.

This time 51 people returned the survey. 12 interviewees worked for private organizations that develop software for third parts; 25 were academic staff of universities that cooperate with software development projects and the rest were users of software systems at different organizations.

As we did previously, firstly, we analyzed the preferences of stakeholders respect to their gender and age. This time we found out a small difference between male and female answers: female percentage per synchronous tools was higher than male percentage. Also we found out (as we have supposed previously) that 40-49 people preferred asynchronous tools in a higher degree than younger people (Figure 2).

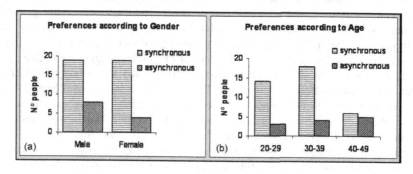

Fig. 2. Second survey results according to gender and age

When we analyzed preferences of stakeholders in relation with their learning style (which is shown in Figure 3), we found out a tendency to prefer synchronous tools over asynchronous tools in most of the subcategories, except for the SRe which represent the slightly reflexive preference (Figure 3a). This is an expected result because reflexive people prefer thinking quietly about the information they receive. The rest of the tendencies are similar in both case studies, except when the visual subcategory is strong (Figure 3c), where the difference between synchronous and asynchronous does not seem as wide as before.

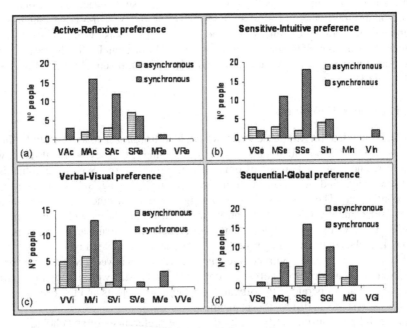

Fig. 3. Second survey results relating F-S categories to groupware type

Analyzing each F-S category regarding the tools, we can also observe something to remark. Figure 4 shows the percentages of appearance for each tool and F-S preferences. We must say that percentages must be analyzed carefully, because for some preferences we count with just one or two examples so we cannot generalize conclusions for all the preferences except for those where there are more examples.

For instance, the moderated preference for the verbal subcategory (MVe) is the one where audio conference has more adherents in proportion (Figure 4c). Also, as we expected, people with stronger preferences for the visual subcategory have chosen visual tools (videoconference, email and IM) except one single case (Figure 4c). In addition, as long as preference for active subcategory grows, people choose videoconference, which is expected because active people like having immediate feedback (Figure 4c). With respect to the Sensing-Intuitive category, when preference for sensing subcategory is stronger we notice more people prefer email over other tools and, on the contrary, very intuitive people prefer synchronous tools. This can be due to the fact that sensing people like well-organized information, which is more possible using email or other asynchronous tools, and intuitive people like acting freely, which is more compatible with synchronous tools like instant messaging and videoconference (Figure 4b). Finally, Sequential-Global category is not expected to have incidence on groupware tool preferences, and we cannot find a pattern of behaviour in the distribution of preferences (Figure 4d).

Unfortunately we do not have a wide number of examples about the strongest preferences for some subcategories. We think we need to continue looking for examples from people working on real requirements elicitation process to obtain more results about strong preferences.

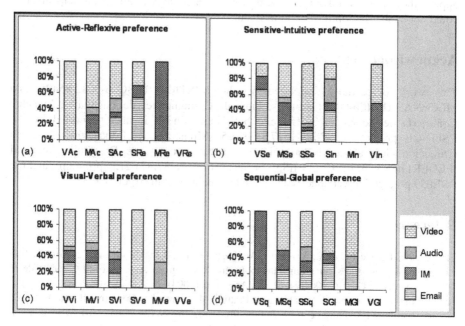

Fig. 4. Second survey results relating F-S categories to groupware tools

5   Conclusions and Future Work

Why can be important knowing the cognitive impact of human preferences? As we have explained before, when people feel uncomfortable with the technology, it is possible that their lack of motivation would lead the group to a poor collaboration. Since managers or analysts, commonly choose groupware tools, as well as elicitation techniques, in an arbitrary way, our intention is offering a strategy that takes into account information from all the stakeholders.

In a first approach to validate part of our proposal, we designed a survey whose results showed that people prefer using synchronous collaboration when their preference for the visual subcategory is stronger. In a replication of this survey we could obtain similar results for all the subcategories. However, the separated analysis of each category cannot be conclusive, and the combination of the preferences for the four categories must be taken into account. To do so we propose taking advantage of the fuzzy sets theory to find patterns of behaviour in real life projects that use groupware tools. With such an idea we have implemented a machine-learning algorithm, which is being tested, to obtain rules that combine different values for each category. We are also working on defining preferences about requirement elicitation techniques, but these results are currently under analysis, and are not shown here.

We are aware that our model faces a challenge regarding the possibility of having people in a virtual group whose preferences are the opposite, so we are currently designing strategies that take into account not just a "unique" appropriate technology, but a ranking for each style, so as when conflicts between personal preferences appear, they could be solved by looking for the technology to all the participants, that could not be the first option for all of them.

Acknowledgements

This work is partially supported by the MISTICO (PBC06-0082-8542), and MECENAS (PBI06-0024) projects, Junta de Comunidades de Castilla-La Mancha, Consejería de Educación y Ciencia, both in Spain. It is also supported by the ESFINGE project (TIN2006-15175-C05-05) Ministerio de Educación y Ciencia (Dirección General de Investigación)/ Fondos Europeos de Desarrollo Regional (FEDER) in Spain; the CompetiSoft project (506AC0287, CYTED program); and the 04/E059 project, Universidad Nacional del Comahue, from Argentina.

References

1. Aranda, G., Cechich, A., Vizcaíno, A., Castro-Schez, J.J.: Using fuzzy sets to analyse personal preferences on groupware tools. In: X Congreso Argentino de Ciencias de la Computación, CACIC 2004, San Justo, Argentina (2004)
2. Aranda, G., Vizcaíno, A., Cechich, A., Piattini, M.: Towards a Cognitive-Based Approach to Distributed Requirement Elicitation Processes. In: WER 2005, VIII Workshop on Requirements Engineering, Porto, Portugal (2005)
3. Aranda, G., Vizcaíno, A., Cechich, A., Piattini, M.: Technology Selection to Improve Global Collaboration. In: ICGSE 2006, IEEE International Conference on Global Software Engineering, Florianopolis, Brazil (2006)
4. Blank, G.D., Roy, S., Sahasrabudhe, S., Pottenger, W.M., Kessler, G.D.: Adapting Multimedia for Diverse Student Learning Styles. Journal of Computing in Small Colleges 18(3), 45–58 (2003)
5. Brooks, F.P.: No Silver Bullet: Essence and accidents of Software Engineering. IEEE Computer 20(4), 10–19 (1987)
6. Castro, J.L., Castro-Schez, J.J., Zurita, J.M.: Learning Maximal Structure Rules in Fuzzy Logic for Knowledge Acquisition in Expert Systems. Fuzzy Sets and Systems 101(3), 331–342 (1999)
7. Chiew, V., Wang, Y.: From Cognitive Psychology to Cognitive Informatics. In: Second IEEE International Conference on Cognitive Informatics, ICCI'03, London, UK (2003)
8. Damian, D., Zowghi, D.: The impact of stakeholders geographical distribution on managing requirements in a multi-site organization. In: IEEE Joint International Conference on Requirements Engineering, RE'02, Essen, Germany (2002)

9. Ellis, C.A., Gibbs, S.J., Rein, G.L.: Groupware: Some Issues and Experiences. Communications of ACM 34(1), 38–58 (1991)
10. Felder, R., Silverman, L.: Learning and Teaching Styles in Engineering Education. Engineering Education 78(7), 674–681 (1988) (and author preface written in 2002)
11. Felder, R., Spurlin, J.: Applications, Reliability and Validity of the Index of Learning Styles. International Journal of Engineering Education 21(1), 103–112 (2005)
12. Herlea, D., Greenberg, S.: Using a Groupware Space for Distributed Requirements Engineering. In: 7th IEEE Int'l. Workshop on Coordinating Distributed Software Development Projects, Stanford, California, USA (1998)
13. Hickey, A.M., Davis, A.: Elicitation Technique Selection: How do experts do it. In: International Joint Conference on Requirements Engineering (RE03), Los Alamitos, California (2003)
14. Lloyd, W., Rosson, M.B., Arthur, J.: Effectiveness of Elicitation Techniques in Distributed Requirements Engineering. In: 10th Anniversary IEEE Joint International Conference on Requirements Engineering, RE'02, Essen, Germany (2002)
15. Martín, A., Martínez, C., Martínez Carod, N., Aranda, G., Cechich, A.: Classifying Groupware Tools to Improve Communication in Geographically Distributed Elicitation. In: IX Congreso Argentino de Ciencias de la Computación, CACIC 2003, La Plata, Argentina (2003)
16. Miller, J., Yin, Z.: A Cognitive-Based Mechanism for Constructing Software Inspection Teams. IEEE Transactions on Software Engineering 30(11), 811–825 (2004)
17. Wang, Y.: On the Cognitive Informatics Foundations of Software Engineering. In: Third IEEE International Conference on Cognitive Informatics, ICCI'04, Victoria, Canada (2004)

Evaluation Methods for Groupware Systems

Valeria Herskovic[1], José A. Pino[1], Sergio F. Ochoa[1], and Pedro Antunes[2]

[1] Department of Computer Science, Universidad de Chile, Chile
{vherskov,jpino,sochoa}@dcc.uchile.cl
[2] Department of Informatics, University of Lisbon, Portugal
paa@di.fc.ul.pt

Abstract. Evaluation of collaborative systems is necessary in several situations. However, evaluation is frequently done in an ad-hoc manner or not at all. This paper presents a survey of evaluation methods for groupware systems. The analysis, comparison and classification of these methods will help developers choose the appropriate methods for their situation. Furthermore, the survey allows identification of strengths and weaknesses of existing methods, opening opportunities for research in this area. The proposed comparison criteria represent a framework to evaluate and classify new evaluation methods.

1 Introduction

The evaluation of collaborative systems is an important yet not fully solved problem in the field of Computer Supported Cooperative Work (CSCW). Despite the need for evaluation, many groupware systems are deficiently evaluated. A study of 45 articles from 8 years of the CSCW conference revealed that almost one third of the presented groupware systems were not evaluated in a formal way [12], while a study that also included the ECSCW conference and the Journal of CSCW found few articles that focused on evaluation [15]. Even when evaluations are done, many of them are ad-hoc, depending on researchers' interests or appropriateness for a specific setting [11].

The possible reasons for the lack of widespread groupware evaluation are various. First, methods for single-user systems are not always applicable to groupware, since the outcome depends on the various backgrounds of group members, organizational culture and group dynamics [5]. Second, evaluation may be expensive and the required resources may be unavailable [2]. Third, a groupware system's benefits may be long-term, so group observation should extend over long periods [5]. Finally, it is not easy for an evaluator to identify which methods to apply in a particular situation.

A survey of the evaluation methods that are currently available for groupware systems is presented. Only strategies explicitly designed for, or adapted to groupware systems are considered, since these products have particular characteristics that may render other evaluation methods inapplicable. The paper is organized as follows. Section 2 briefly describes each of the reviewed methods. Section 3 presents their comparison and categorization. It also describes a general strategy to choose the most appropriate evaluation method. Section 4 proposes a strategy to minimize the cost to evaluate a groupware system. Section 5 presents the conclusions and further work.

J.M. Haake, S.F. Ochoa, and A. Cechich (Eds.): CRIWG 2007, LNCS 4715, pp. 328–336, 2007.

2 Analysis of the Methods

This section presents a summary of the groupware evaluation methods. Each one is briefly explained to give an overview of it and the steps that must be followed to apply it. These methods can be directly used to evaluate a groupware application, or they can be part of a macro evaluation strategy. In the latter case, the global strategy may ask for iterative evaluation [8], or that it should consider several stakeholders [16]. The evaluation methods in this survey are those directly applicable to groupware systems. They are the following ones:

Groupware Heuristic Evaluation (GHE). GHE is an adaptation of the Heuristic Evaluation method, in which single-user systems are evaluated by visually inspecting the interface and judging its compliance with usability principles. GHE is based on eight groupware heuristics [4], which act as a checklist of characteristics a collaborative system should have. Evaluators who are experts in them examine the interface, recording each problem they encounter, the violated heuristic, a severity rating and optionally, a solution to the problem. The problems are then filtered, classified and consolidated into a list, which is used to improve the application.

Groupware Walkthrough (GWA). GWA is an evaluation method based on cognitive walkthrough, an inspection technique for single-user software [13]. In GWA, a scenario is a description of an activity or set of tasks, which includes the users, their knowledge, the intended outcome, and circumstances surrounding it. In order to construct scenarios, evaluators observe users and identify episodes of collaboration. Each evaluator, taking the role of all users or one in particular, walks through the tasks in a laboratory setting, recording each problem he encounters. A meeting is then conducted to analyze the results of the evaluation.

Collaboration Usability Analysis (CUA). CUA is a task analysis technique focused on the teamwork aspects of collaboration in shared tasks [14]. It provides high-level and low-level representations of the collaborative situation and task to be studied, and multiple ways to represent actors and their interactions. CUA proposes that each collaborative action can be mapped to a set of collaboration mechanisms, or fine grain representations of basic collaborative actions, which may be related to elements in the user interface. The resulting diagrams capture details about task components, a notion of the flow through them and the task distribution.

Groupware Observational User Testing (GOT). GOT is a technique based on the observational user testing method (OUT). OUT involves evaluators observing how users perform particular tasks supported by a system in a laboratory setting [6]. Evaluators either monitor users having problems with a task, or ask users to think aloud about what they are doing to gain insight on their work. GOT follows the same principle, but focuses on collaboration and analyzes users' work through predefined criteria, e.g., the mechanics of collaboration [6].

Human-Performance Models (HPM). HPM describe how a person interacts with a physical interface at a low level of detail based on a cognitive architecture, e.g., the keystroke level model (KLM) approximates the interaction of a single user with an interface. HPM adapts this model to a group of users communicating through a shared workspace [2]. In this method, evaluators first decompose the physical interface into several shared workspaces. Then, they define critical scenarios focused on the collaborative actions for the shared workspaces. Finally, evaluators compare group performance in the critical scenarios, e.g., using KLM to predict execution times.

"Quick-and-dirty" Ethnography (QDE). Ethnography refers to the qualitative description of human social phenomena to produce detailed descriptions of the work activities of actors within specific contexts. QDE [9] aims to adapt ethnography to evaluation. Here, evaluators do brief workplace studies to provide a general sense of the setting for designers. QDE accepts the impossibility of gathering a complete understanding of the setting, providing a broad understanding instead. It suggests the deficiencies of a system, supplying designers with the key issues that bear on acceptability and usability, thus allowing existing and future systems to be improved.

Performance Analysis (PAN). PAN is an evaluation method that allows formal analysis of a groupware application [3]. The application to be studied is modeled as a task to be performed by a number of people in a number of stages, and the concepts of result quality, time, and total amount of work done are defined. The evaluators must define a way to compute the quality (e.g., group recall in a collaborative retrieval task), and maximize the quality vs. work done either analytically or experimentally.

Perceived Value (PVA). PVA measures the perceived value (PV) attributed to a meetingware system by its users [1]. This method tries to measure the organizational impact and the alignment between system capabilities and developers' and users' expectations. Developers begin by identifying relevant components for system evaluation. Then, users and developers negotiate the relevant system attributes to be evaluated by users. After the users have worked with the system, they fill out an evaluation map by noting whether the components support the attributes or not. Using these ratings, a metric that represents the PV is calculated.

Scenario-Based Evaluation (SBE). SBE provides evaluators with realistic settings in which to base their evaluations. A scenario is a detailed description of an activity, which includes the task, actor, context and claims, which are statements about using the system. In a field evaluation using SBE [7], evaluators perform semi-structured interviews of the users to discover scenarios and claims about them. Then, focus groups validate these findings. The frequency and percentage of positive claims help quantify the organizational contributions of the system, and the positive and negative claims about existing and envisioned features provide information to aid in redesign.

Cooperation Scenarios (COS). The COS method aims to capture users' work and its context [17]. Scenarios (SC) are descriptions of work practices, including motivation and goals. In order to construct SC, evaluators conduct field studies, semi-structured interviews, and workplace visits. Through these activities, they identify cooperative behavior, users involved in it, their roles and the relevant context. For each role involved in the cooperative activity, evaluators analyze the new design to see how the task changes and who benefits from the new technology. Then, the prototype is presented as a SC in a workshop with users to discover design flaws.

E-MAGINE (EMA). EMA is a method based on two concepts: (1) a system should match its environment, and (2) the perception of the user is important [10]. EMA begins with a meeting between client and evaluator, in which the goals are set. Then, a quick semi-structured interview with someone familiar with the group is applied to build a profile of the group and scenario. It also guides the selection of evaluation tools, and the issues that will be evaluated, such as social cohesion and usability. Finally, the results are fed back to the group to apply the proposed changes.

Knowledge Management Approach (KMA). This method posits that knowledge is the most important asset of organizations. Evaluation using KMA measures whether the system helps users detect knowledge flows and disseminate, store and reuse knowledge [19]. The knowledge circulation process is comprised of six phases (knowledge creation, accumulation, sharing, utilization, internalization), which are also the areas to be evaluated by this approach. To perform evaluation, each area has a list of associated questions, which may be used as a checklist by evaluators.

3 Selecting Groupware Evaluation Methods

Whenever a stakeholder needs to choose a groupware evaluation method, she does it for a specific context. For instance, a project manager may want to determine how well the functionality of a groupware system under development matches the expectations of an organization. Such context allows the manager to consider some key features of each method in order to establish which ones could be appropriate.

Considering several features in the selection process will make the list of potential methods short and accurate. If the suitable methods list is empty, then an ad-hoc evaluation method should be designed. If the list contains more than one method, then the evaluator can choose one based on a prioritization of their key features. We call these key features of a method its *classification criteria*. The next sections present three classifications of groupware evaluation methods.

3.1 Classification Based on Stakeholders and Product State

Table 1 presents a classification that considers the concerned stakeholders (developpers, users and the organization) and the state of the product (under development or finished). A brief explanation of each category is included.

Evaluation methods for systems under development. While a collaborative system is under construction, the *developers* require formative and inexpensive evaluation methods that allow them to test the product, discover its flaws, and redesign it accordingly. These methods are usually done in a laboratory setting without users. The *users* of this system could be interested in ensuring that the system works as desired and allows effective and efficient collaboration. Evaluation methods must thus involve users and focus on their opinions. Finally, the *organization* as a whole requires that a collaborative system improves work, efficiency and the quality of results, allowing managers to justify investments in the technology.

Evaluation methods for finished products. Organizations acquiring a groupware system may require *developers* to adapt the product to their needs. Also, the development team may need to conduct a post-mortem analysis of a finished product. Evaluation methods should be summative and measure the matching between product functionality and the users and organizational needs, permitting developers to improve the system. The *users* of the system need to ensure the system works as desired and allows effective and efficient collaboration. Similar to the previous case, methods must involve users and focus on their opinions; however, in this case methods may be summative. Finally, an *organization* acquiring a groupware system must go through the adoption of the technology, so methods should be summative, tested in the real work setting, and measure how well a system fits in the organization.

Table 1. Method categorization based on stakeholders and product state

	Developers	Users	Organization
Products Under Development	GHE, GWA CUA, HPM, PAN	SBE, COS EMA, KMA	PVA
Finished Products		GOT, QDE	GOT, QDE PAN, PVA

It is possible to identify an initial set of relevant methods for a particular scenario considering these criteria. Stakeholders' identification and product state can be used as initial evaluation criteria because they are fast to instantiate and highly relevant.

3.2 Classification Based on Type, Scope and Duration

Table 2 classifies the evaluation methods considering the people's participation, time of application, evaluation type, place, time span and goal. This table should be used in the same way as table 1 in order to perform the selection process. The classification criteria included in table 2 are briefly described below.

People participation states who participates in the evaluation besides evaluators, usually users (U), developers (D), experts (E), or combinations of them. This criterion helps determine the viability of a method based on human resources availability.

Table 2. Classification of evaluation strategies

Evaluation Method	Who			When			Type		Loc.		Time Span			Goal		
	U	D	E	B	S	F	N	Q	W	L	H	Y	K	P	C	X
Groupware Heuristic Evaluation (GHE)			X	X	X		X			X	X			X		
Groupware Walkthrough (GWA)				X	X		X			X		X			X	
Collaboration Usability Analysis (CUA)				X	X		X		X	X	X				X	
Groupware Observ. User Testing (GOT)	X			X	X		X			X		X			X	
Human-Performance Models (HPM)				X	X	X	X			X	X				X	
Quick-and-Dirty Ethnography (QDE)	X			X			X		X			X				X
Performance Analysis (PAN)				X	X	X				X	X				X	
Perceived Value (PVA)	X	X		X	X	X	X		X		X			X		
Scenario Based Evaluation (SBE)	X			X	X		X	X				X		X	X	X
Cooperation Scenarios (COS)	X					X	X	X				X			X	X
E-MAGINE (EMA)	X			X	X		X	X				X			X	X
Knowledge Management Approach (KMA)				X	X		X	X	X	X		X			X	X

The *time to apply the method* may be: before the system is designed to test its feasibility (B); during the development process as a formative evaluation to identify redesign needs (D); or when the application is finished (F) as a summative evaluation. This criterion helps in the selection depending on the level of progress of the project.

The *evaluation type* establishes whether the collected data is quantitative (N) or qualitative (Q). Quantitative data is useful to compare the results of several evaluations, while qualitative data usually consists of human judgment and may be used for the most complex situations.

The *evaluation place* determines the location where evaluation is carried out, either a laboratory setting (L) or the users' actual workplace (W). Based on place availability, it is possible to determine whether a certain method may be used or not.

The *time span* of each method goes from hours (H) to days (Y) or weeks (K). This must be considered to establish whether there is enough time to do an evaluation.

The *evaluation goal* describes the objective of the evaluation, which can be to evaluate the product functionality (P), the collaboration process supported by the system (C), or the product functionality considering the collaboration context (X).

3.3   Classification Based on the Evaluation Cost

The *evaluation cost* is important during the selection of an evaluation method. A possible classification of evaluation methods is based on their cost, but this does not exist. We propose the evaluation cost be a function of the process duration and the effort required to conduct the evaluation, as shown in Fig. 1. The effort to do an evaluation was estimated based on the activities that must be done and the required human resources. If an evaluation method requires a high number of participants, it is considered as needing a high effort. The duration of an evaluation method may be as short as a few hours, in the case of GHE, or as long as weeks of GOT. In Fig.1, methods closest to the origin are those of lowest cost, while those in the upper right corner have the highest cost. The combination of time span and effort into a single cost measure depends on the particular situation.

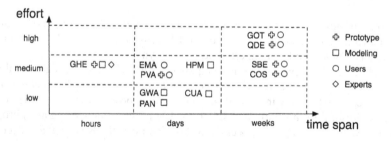

Fig. 1. Evaluation methods according to their cost

4   Evaluation Strategies

The previous section presented a strategy to find appropriate methods for a particular context. This section describes how to organize the evaluation process.

The high cost of evaluation is one of the reasons why groupware systems are not frequently evaluated. The evaluation process could require the use of several evaluation methods depending on how complete or accurate the diagnosis should be. An approach to evaluation should combine a first phase of formative lab-based methods with a second phase of field methods that involve the users and their context. If necessary, it is complemented with a third phase of qualitative studies in the real work setting. This stepwise approach is derived from Twidale et al. [18], who stress the importance of context in evaluation but also believe early evaluation in an artificial environment may remove gross errors.

Each evaluation method may be categorized according to the phase in which it is optimally applied. In the first phase, major errors should be removed, while not incurring in high costs. Therefore, ideal methods for this phase are low cost, quantitative, lab-based strategies that do not require users, e.g., KMA, HPM, CUA, GWA, PAN and GHE. In the second phase, methods that require users and context can be applied. The most suitable methods for this phase are the qualitative ones, those based on user opinion, and the ones that capture the scenario of the application to test it in the lab, such as COS, EMA, and SBE. The third phase involves summative methods that should be applied in the real work setting, such as GOT and QDE.

An expensive, time-consuming approach to evaluation may be discouraging, so the costs of a three-phase evaluation must be discussed. Focusing the most intensive evaluation efforts in the first phase should reduce the costs of subsequent evaluations, since gross errors should be discovered early on, preventing encountering errors in the final phases. The cost of training the involved actors in each method is balanced by the various perspectives gained, which provide a comprehensive view of the application. Naturally, the number of applied methods per phase depends on how much emphasis a team wants to give evaluation, but applying one evaluation strategy per phase should provide a significant outlook into the application while not substantially increasing the costs of evaluation.

5 Conclusions and Further Work

Evaluating groupware systems is necessary and yet, many of them are not evaluated. Unevaluated systems tend to be unsuccessful because they mail fail to consider the context, stakeholders and contain errors after deployment.

The classifications proposed in this paper afford visibility to each evaluation method, allowing for fast comparison according to several criteria. The categorization also provides a tool for any interested stakeholder to choose an evaluation method that is especially useful for his particular situation. The process of choosing an appropriate evaluation method is simplified, because a short list of methods is provided according to the needs of the stakeholder as well as the product state. With this reduced list, the evaluator may choose the most appropriate method by reviewing his/her available resources (equipment, time, effort, etc) and the characteristics of each method.

The categorization of evaluation methods suggests some areas that lack appropriate evaluation methods, providing opportunities for further research, such as in the case of developers who need to modify a finished product. The comparison of the twelve methods reviewed in this paper has also highlighted the fact that most evaluation methods are qualitative, and only two of them are purely quantitative. We believe the prevalence of qualitative methods is symptomatic of the complexity of groupware, as human judgment may be required to disentangle the multiple contingencies, and ultimately appreciate if a groupware application is good or not. On the other hand, the role of quantitative methods in CSCW evaluation is also important, since they permit the objective comparison of several applications, and may be automated. This suggests that new quantitative evaluation methods are needed. Further research in this area should improve the availability of methods for all stakeholders.

Using only one type of evaluation may prevent evaluators from gaining access to the complete picture in some cases. This suggests that several evaluation methods may be applied to obtain a comprehensive understanding of the system and its environment. CSCW systems are multifaceted. Conducting a thorough evaluation may provide additional perspective on how they function and how to improve them.

Acknowledgements. This work was partially supported by Fondecyt (Chile), grants N°: 11060467 and 1040952.

References

[1] Antunes, P., Costa, C.: Perceived value: A low-cost approach to evaluate meetingware. In: Favela, J., Decouchant, D. (eds.) CRIWG 2003. LNCS, vol. 2806, pp. 109–125. Springer, Heidelberg (2003)

[2] Antunes, P., Ferreira, A., Pino, J.: Analyzing shared workspaces design with human-performance models. In: Dimitriadis, Y.A., Zigurs, I., Gómez-Sánchez, E. (eds.) CRIWG 2006. LNCS, vol. 4154, pp. 62–77. Springer, Heidelberg (2006)

[3] Baeza-Yates, R., Pino, J.: Towards formal evaluation of collaborative work and its application to information retrieval. Information Research 11(4), 271 (2006)

[4] Baker, K., Greenberg, S., Gutwin, C.: Empirical development of a heuristic evaluation methodology for shared workspace groupware. In: CSCW '02, pp. 96–105 (2002)

[5] Grudin, J.: Why CSCW applications fail: problems in the design and evaluation of organization of organizational interfaces. In: CSCW '88, pp. 85–93. ACM Press, New York (1988)

[6] Gutwin, C., Greenberg, S.: The mechanics of collaboration: Developing low cost usability evaluation methods for shared workspaces. In: WETICE '00, pp. 98–103. IEEE Comp. Soc, Los Alamitos (2000)

[7] Haynes, S., Purao, S., Skattebo, A.: Situating evaluation in scenarios of use. In: CSCW '04, pp. 92–101. ACM Press, New York (2004)

[8] Huang, J.: A conceptual framework for understanding collab. systems evaluation. In: WETICE '05: 14th I. Workshop on Enabling Tech., pp. 215–220. IEEE Comp. Soc., Los Alamitos (2005)

[9] Hughes, J., King, V., Rodden, T., Andersen, H.: Moving out from the control room: Ethnography in system design. In: CSCW '94, pp. 429–439. ACM Press, New York (1994)

[10] Huis in't Veld, M., Andriessen, J., Verburg, R.: E-magine: The development of an evaluation method to assess groupware applications. In: WETICE '03, vol. 153, IEEE, Los Alamitos (2003)

[11] Inkpen, K., Mandryk, R., DiMicco, J., Scott, S.: Methodology for evaluating collaboration in co-located environments. interactions 11(6) (2004)

[12] Pinelle, D., Gutwin, C.: A review of groupware evaluations. In: WETICE '00: 9th International Workshop on Enabling Technologies, pp. 86–91. IEEE Computer Society, Los Alamitos (2000)

[13] Pinelle, D., Gutwin, C.: Groupware walkthrough: adding context to groupware usability evaluation. In: CHI '02, pp. 455–462. ACM Press, New York (2002)

[14] Pinelle, D., Gutwin, C., Greenberg, S.: Task analysis for groupware usability evaluation: Modeling shared-workspace tasks with the mechanics of collaboration. ACM Transactions on Computer-Human Interaction 10(4), 281–311 (2003)

[15] Plowman, L., Rogers, Y., Ramage, M.: What are workplace studies for? In: ECSCW '95: Fourth European Conference on Computer-Supported Cooperative Work, pp. 309–324 (1995)

[16] Ross, S., Ramage, M., Rogers, Y.: PETRA: Participatory evaluation through redesign and analysis. Interacting with Computers 7(4), 335–360 (1995)

[17] Stiemerling, O., Cremers, A.: The use of cooperation scenarios in the design and evaluation of a CSCW system. IEEE Transact. on Software Engineering 25, 140 (1999)

[18] Twidale, M., Randall, D., Bentley, R.: Situated evaluation for cooperative systems. In: CSCW '94, pp. 441–452. ACM Press, New York (1994)

[19] Vizcaíno, A., Martinez, M., Aranda, G., Piattini, M.: Evaluating collaborative applications from a knowledge management approach. In: WETICE '05, pp. 221–225. IEEE Comp. Soc, Los Alamitos (2005)

Activity-Aware Computing in Mobile Collaborative Working Environments

Monica Tentori and Jesus Favela

Department of Computer Science, CICESE Research Center, Ensenada, México
{mtentori,favela}@cicese.mx

Abstract. Highly mobile hospital workers experiment intense and ad-hoc collaboration during their everyday practices. This has motivated the introduction of collaborative applications enhanced with ubiquitous technology in hospitals. However, an environment filled with many different systems augmented with a wide range of functionality, introduces an extra burden for hospital workers in selecting the services and information that are adequate to the task at a hand. Activity-Based Computing (ABC) has emerged as a new interaction paradigm in support of these problems. In this paper, we empower the vision of ABC with a degree of consciousness about the physical changing context towards the design of activity-aware applications. Based on workplace studies conducted in a hospital, we established a set of design principles for the development of activity-aware applications. To exemplify the design principles proposed, we designed and implemented an activity-aware map that personalizes the information shown to hospital workers, enforces availability and sends collaboration warnings.

Keywords: Activity-aware computing, Collaboration, Hospital Work.

1 Introduction

In some working environments users experience a high level of mobility while requiring to collaborate and coordinate their activities with colleagues involving the exchange and analysis of documents distributed in space or time [5, 16]. Hospital workers stand out among others by the demands imposed by hospital work. This has motivated the introduction of collaborative solutions with the aim at helping hospital workers to coordinate their work and support their collaboration [4, 17]. These solutions range from simple "shared workspaces" [14] that extend the conventional single-user applications (e.g., word processors) allowing the synchronous or asynchronous collaboration across digital networks (e.g., netMeeting); to complex ubiquitous applications that allow the seamless interaction among heterogeneous devices [15], the interchange of contextual messages and the opportunistic access to relevant information while providing awareness to enrich collaboration [17].

Hence, hospital workers today are faced with many different systems and a wide range of functionality within each of these [3]. Nowadays, this problem will be accentuated with the introduction of ubicomp in hospitals. Thus, carrying out a single activity typically involves the use of several systems with different functionality and

J.M. Haake, S.F. Ochoa, and A. Cechich (Eds.): CRIWG 2007, LNCS 4715, pp. 337–353, 2007.

data presentation within each system. For example, if a physician is discussing a clinical case with an intern they might need to share the medical record, highlight areas from an X-Ray image and consult a journal article relevant to the clinical case being discussed. Both physicians must browse the documents needed to enrich the discussion, launch and login into each application and establish a session between the computational devices (i.e., PDAs) used. Since the duration of an activity in hospital work average no more than five minutes, much of this time could be spent launching the right service in their PDA and setting up the computational infrastructure (e.g., login in each application used) instead of focusing on their primary goal.

Activity-based computing (ABC), a new interaction and design paradigm has emerged in support of these problems [1, 6]. In ABC, the idea is to explore how to support the activity level directly in the computing system, by changing the basic computational unit from documents and applications (e.g., MS Word) to the activity performed by the user. In the same direction, others have proposed to reorganize collaboration to reflect the work being done rather than the technologies required. For instance the Activity Explorer by following an activity-centric collaboration allow users to define logical units of work that incorporate the tools, people and resources needed to the task at a hand [11]. Rooms, divides a user workplace in a set of 'virtual rooms' where each room contains the documents, contacts and the pending tasks [13]. Kimura, suggests to combine the virtual and physical context to drive the creation of activity representations referred as "montages" [22]. In the same direction, the mobileSJ system allows the user to manage their multiple activities and their information and contextual resources while on the move. [7], by implementing the concept of working sphere [12] and creating its computational representation: an E-sphere. However, people often have trouble labeling and delimiting new tasks and, more importantly, often forget to declare task switches. Moreover, to support users in their work activities, the computing system must understand the concept of an activity and handle it like a first class object.

One way to overcome such difficulties is to build into activity-based applications a degree of consciousness about its changing contexts and a degree of autonomy in choosing a proper adaptation strategy on-the-move, depending on what is actually happening in a specific situation. The idea is to look at how users interact with technology according to what is happening, helping designers to adapt activity-based applications for specific activities. Thus, by using the activity as the central trigger, the relevance of any contextual information will be easily discovered, informing to an application which information (i.e., resources) can be associated with the users' current activity, resulting thus, in an *activity-aware application*. Once the application has strong evidence of the users' primary activity, it could adapt itself by displaying information relevant to the task at hand, preserve privacy, filter incoming messages, launch services or notify colleagues of the user's activity.

In this paper, we introduce a set of design principles for the development of activity-aware applications that were inspired by workplace studies conducted in a hospital. We illustrate how activity-aware computing could be used in support of collaboration in mobile environments by allowing the seamless activity-based interaction among heterogeneous devices, as well as, providing activity awareness and activity-aware adaptation and personalization. To exemplify the principles proposed, we present an activity-aware map which personalizes the information shown to hospital workers, enforces hospital workers' availability and sends collaboration warnings based on the activity being executed.

The rest of this paper is organized as follows. In Section 2 we describe the results of a workplace study conducted to understand the activities executed by hospital workers. In addition, this section discusses some of the challenges identified in matching a computational activity to a human activity. In Section 3, we present two scenarios derived from the study and a set of design principles that were identified as useful for the development of activity-aware applications. Section 4 describes the implementation of an activity-aware map, used to exemplify the design principles proposed. Finally, section 5 presents the conclusions and directions for future work.

2 Understanding Human Activities: A Case Study in a Hospital

Human work activities are complex and dynamic. It is hard to *analyze activities* so as to identify the breakdowns of current practice that could be enhanced by technology. Hence, maintaining the affordances of how humans create and conduct activities generates numerous challenges for matching a human activity to a computational one.

One of these challenges is related to the definition and representation of a computational activity. The computing system must understand the concept of an activity and handle it. However, it is often unclear what information is relevant for modeling activities and how an activity can be estimated. Hence, robust approaches to estimate hospital workers activities must be developed along with the technology necessary for such estimation. These approaches must establish which information is relevant to infer an activity, how much automatic sensing is needed and which technologies are appropriate to sense the information needed for the estimation.

Although relevant work has been conducted to understand the characteristics of mobile working environments, we still have a weak understanding about the nature and dynamics of the activities performed by hospital workers. To cope with this, we decided to conduct a workplace study aimed at (1) consolidating a conceptual understanding of the activities executed by hospital workers'; (2) identified the information relevant to model activities and (3) produce a characterization of the characteristics on those activities identified. This study was conducted for nine months were five nurses, five medical interns and five physicians were shadowed for two complete working shifts and interviewed by researchers. The total time of detailed observation was about 196 hours and 46 minutes, with an average time of observation per informant of 13 hours and 7 minutes.

To understand the medical behaviors experienced by those observed, we conducted a qualitative analysis of the data collected, following the techniques to derive grounded theory [21]. For our particular case, the qualitative technique of analysis involved continuous sense making of the information collected including interview transcripts, personal notes and documents. As a result of this analysis, we developed a coding scheme that describes the activities performed by hospital workers and the characteristics of such activities identified. This information was cross analyzed by researchers and some hospital workers to validate and refine it.

2.1 Activities Performed by Hospital Staff

To clarify each activity goal discussing the artifacts used, the people involved and its location, in the following lines, we present a scenario that shows a typical working day of one of the medical interns observed. A graphical representation of all Juan's activities on that day showing the degree of fragmentation and the constant transitioning back and forth among different activities is illustrated in Figure 1.

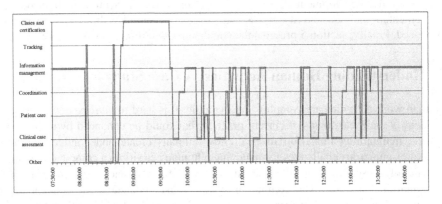

Fig. 1. A timeline of typical working day of an intern

A typical day of a medical intern
At 7:30 am at the Internal Medicine Office, Juan, a medical intern, is documenting the census of those new patients registered to the hospital. He uses a computer and he consults personal notes, medical records and nurse charts. While preparing the census, the attending physician, along with other medical interns, arrive at the office. To briefly describe the night's events and the status of some of the patients currently registered in the hospital, Juan switches of activity handing over to his peers the census just printed. After the discussion, Juan gathers the information related to the patients assigned to him and places it in each patient's bedroom. He walks down to the laboratory to gather laboratory results of his patients, and attaches them to the medical record. At 9 am, he meets at the Internal Medicine Office with the attending physician and other interns, to listen to a colleague's assessment of an interesting clinical case. While the meeting is taking place, a relative of one of the patients assigned to Juan, arrives to the office. She interrupts the meeting and asks for the prescriptions of such patient. This becomes an additional unexpected issue that Juan has to attend immediately forcing him to switch activities. Juan leaves the meeting and walks to the patient's bed to explore the patient. After a quick assessment, Juan writes the prescription. Later, Juan goes to the bed wards to participate in the ward round, along with the physician, and the other interns. During the ward round, they discuss each patient's clinical case consulting the patient's medical record and laboratory tests. During the examination of the patient in room 226, the attending physician asks Juan to insert a catheter to that patient. Juan switches activity to provide patient care. He walks to the warehouse to gather the medical equipment necessary for the insertion of the catheter. Once the catheter is inserted, Juan reports

on the medical record the diagnosis of such patient, switching activity once again. Finally, once Juan finishes the round, which occasionally lasts until 1-2 pm, he spends the rest of the shift doing paperwork in the internal medicine office.

Activity temporality
Following the descriptions of the informants and the way they conceptualize their work, we defined an activity as a particular type of hospital work that was carried out through a set of related actions which are mediated by the artifacts used and the people involved. As Figure 1 shows, we identified six activities classified with respect to how they are related to the clinical care of patients. To analyze with more detail the nature of the work in the hospital, we measured the time spent by hospital workers performing different activities. However these periods of time do not occur continuously, these periods of time are fragmented. Hence, an individual attends to an activity in small periods of time that we call *segments*. Each segment accounts for the uninterrupted engagement in a particular behavior.

We found out that informants spend segments of no more than 5 minutes on any kind of behavior. And for the total time of observation, most of the time is spent in information management (20.17%), followed by clinical case assessment (19.26%) and coordination (16.21%). An important part of the work of those observed is focused on activities that have a secondary role of caring for patients such as information management, coordination and tracking. When analyzing the information per role, we found that, the time nurses and medical interns spend in these activities surpasses the time they invest providing clinical care. In contrast, physicians spend more time evaluating clinical cases and visiting patients. Nurses and medical interns spend considerable time *"setting up"* the environment for physicians so they can focus on their main goal.

2.2 The Nature of Human Activities

Common characteristics among the activities characterized where identified. These characteristics shape the way activities are experienced and understood by hospital staff. For a clear understanding we have grouped them in two topics described next.

Activities are collaborative and multifaceted
Human beings interact with people and use a heterogeneous collection of work artifacts to carry out an activity. For example, as shown in the scenario when Juan is in the ward round, he interacts with nurses, medical interns and physicians. He consults nurse charts, medical records and laboratory studies. And he uses medical equipment for the insertion of the catheter. Hence, a community of people and a collection of artifacts mediate such activity [2]. These artifacts and people are not generally concentrated in a single place, but distributed in *space* and *time*.

This distributed nature of work demands from hospital workers to incorporate into their everyday practices strategies to maintain the collaboration and coordination required for the adequate execution of different tasks. One of those strategies emerged with the aim of guarantying that the information and artifacts will be located in the right place whenever it is needed; we call this strategy *"setting up the environment before the execution of an activity"*. For example, as shown in the scenario, before the ward round starts, Juan navigates the hospital premises gathering the information related to the patients assigned to him to later place it in each patient's room. Another strategy incorporated by hospital workers is to *"transform the function of an artifact"* by associating information to such artifact relevant or related to an activity. For example, we found that sometimes individuals transform the nature of reference artifacts by attaching to them elements that make them collaborative. For instance, we classified the patient's medical record as a reference artifact, but we observed that some times hospital workers used the record to leave notes for others, since a message might only be relevant when the next doctor is evaluating the status of a patient. Hence, in a particular place or for a certain period of time, hospital worker's use the patient's medical record to support coordination. In this case, they transformed its function because they know that the next doctor visiting the patient will consult first the patient's medical record when he is assessing the clinical case of such patient.

Table 1. Time hospital workers spend performing different activities

Interactions	Nurses			Medical interns			Attending physicians			Average total time	% of the entire day
(Time per day per informant)	Mean time of seg.	Aver. Time	%	Mean time of seg.	Aver. Time	%	Mean time of seg.	Aver. Time	%		
None	4:29:28	0:00:31	59.88	1:55:35	0:00:22	28.26	0:21:30	0:00:06	5.44	2:15:31	31.19
Verbally based	**1:04:03**	**0:00:16**	**14.23**	**1:47:35**	**0:00:22**	**26.30**	**3:13:37**	**0:00:22**	**48.95**	**2:01:45**	**29.83**
Without a phone	1:04:03	0:00:16	14.23	1:45:35	0:00:16	25.81	3:08:48	0:00:12	47.74	1:59:29	29.26
Using telephone	0:00:00	0:00:00	0.00	0:02:00	0:00:06	0.49	0:04:49	0:00:10	1.22	0:02:16	0.57
Involving artifacts	**0:16:50**	**0:00:25**	**3.74**	**2:43:20**	**0:01:25**	**39.93**	**2:11:01**	**0:00:23**	**33.13**	**1:43:44**	**25.60**
Sharing artifacts	0:16:50	0:00:25	3.74	2:03:30	0:00:49	30.20	1:24:34	0:00:16	21.38	1:14:58	18.44
Consulting information	0:00:00	0:00:00	0.00	0:26:20	0:00:23	6.44	0:30:31	0:00:04	7.72	0:18:57	4.72
Transferring artifacts	0:00:00	0:00:00	0.00	0:13:30	0:00:13	3.30	0:15:56	0:00:03	4.03	0:09:49	2.44
Observation based	**1:39:39**	**0:00:32**	**22.14**	**0:22:30**	**0:00:24**	**5.50**	**0:49:22**	**0:00:09**	**12.48**	**0:57:10**	**13.38**
Using a physical artifact	1:17:29	0:00:15	17.22	0:18:30	0:00:12	4.52	0:49:22	0:00:09	12.48	0:48:27	11.41
Without artifacts	0:22:10	0:00:17	4.93	0:04:00	0:00:12	0.98	0:00:00	0:00:00	0.00	0:08:43	1.97
All	**7:30:00**	**0:01:44**	**100**	**6:49:00**	**0:02:33**	**100**	**6:35:30**	**0:01:00**	**100**	**6:58:10**	**100**

We conducted further analysis to determine the frequency of interactions with people and artifacts. Table 2 shows the details of the interactions hold with respect to the mean times of segment observed and the total time per day spent on each activity. As table 2 illustrates 68.81% of their time, hospital staff is interacting with others to interchange information and artifacts either verbally or just by observing others. As indicated in the table, there is a very short duration of each single behavior, by spending segments of no more than 5 minutes on any kind of behavior. Considering the total time that individuals spend per day in a behavior we can see that in some of them individuals clearly spend more time. For instance, individuals spend 29.83% of their shift engaged in purely verbally based interactions. It is interesting to note that most of the time when hospital workers are using artifacts they are used to share them simultaneously (18.44%) or to transfer such artifact (2.44%).

Activities are dynamic
Hospital work is highly fragmented influenced by the mobility and temporality experienced by hospital workers during their everyday practices As table 1 shows, hospital staff average about 1.5 minutes on sustained engagement on an activity before switching tasks. We observed, that this fragmentation, normally, occurs due to an interruption or a change in the context of work (such as if a patient collapses or the arrival of a colleague); demanding from hospital workers to switch to another activity.

For instance, as illustrated in Figure 1, the ward round was conducted from 10 am to 1:30 pm. and by extracting segments of time during this period we can see level of fragmentation experienced. For example:

At 10:20 am, for 1 minite, Juan assessed the condition of a patient. During this activity, the attending physician asks to Juan to insert a catheter. Based on such interruption, he immediately switched his activity to provide specialized care (5 min). He interrupted this activity, to track medical equipment (30 sec). Later, he notified the group of some pending tasks related to the patient (3 min). And finally, he reported in the medical record the procedure conducted (2 min).

This observation corresponds, indeed, to the actions executed during the catheter insertion described in the scenario, which lasted less than 10 minutes. During the round, the activities performed presented a similar phenomenon, while the activities conducted before and after the round lasted approximately 20 min with a lower level of fragmentation. Hence, the activities performed before the round began and after the round finished, had a lower level of fragmentation than the activities conducted during the round. These results build upon the observation of previous studies that highlight the temporal patterns or "rhythms" experienced by hospital workers and often used to coordinate their activities and contribute to the regular temporal organization of work in the hospital [18]. What we observed, is that these temporal patterns can also be characterized by different levels of work fragmentation.

To analyze with more detail the fragmented nature of the work in the hospital, we measured the transitions for each activity. We found that, the activities present a recurrence phenomenon, which means, that the probability of remaining executing such activity is higher than changing to execute another one. We found that this is proportional to the location where it is executed and, to a lesser degree, to the duration of the activity. For example, classes and certification is the activity with a higher level of recurrence. As Figure 2 illustrates this activity was conducted from 1 hour (aprox) and it is executed in base locations (e.g., meeting rooms or offices). In contrast, with tracking that is conducted by navigating the hospital premises for 51 sec (on average).

In addition, during the execution of activities that have a support goal the probability of changing to conduct an activity with a main goal (activities related to the patient) is higher than the other way around. Upfront, it is clear that support activities will be followed by the execution of main activities, since the internal goal of support activities is exactly that. For example, if a nurse is preparing medicines the next thing she will do is to administer them. However, on the other hand, it is difficult to infer when a hospital worker will conduct support activities, since the choice to conduct them is based on the individual's internal goals and decisions. For example, a nurse could arrive at a patient's bed to assess his evolution. And based on such evolution a nurse might decide to notify pending tasks, to execute a medical procedure or to track the physician in charge of such patient. In this case, it is not possible to infer her internal goals until an action is executed.

These characteristics, among others, make it difficult for a computer to handle the concept of an activity, what humans are doing, their goals and intentions. Hence, an inadequate management of the dynamically characteristics of human activities could lead to the presentation of services and information disembodied from the user's current activity, creating unique challenges in designing activity-aware applications.

3 Activity-Aware Computing

The core idea of Activity-aware computing is to allow "smart environments" to respond proactively to the needs and intentions of their users. For this, we decided to empower the vision of Activity-Based Computing with a degree of consciousness about the physical changing context towards the design of activity-aware applications. Hence, if we take the activity, as the central trigger to adapt context-aware applications, we will be able to infer the contextual information that is relevant as the users' course of actions evolves. Thus, by using the activity as the central trigger, the relevance of any contextual information will be easily discovered, informing the adaptation process which contextual information can be associated with the users' current activity, resulting thus, in an *activity-aware application*.

3.1 Activity Recognition

To build activity-aware applications one of the main challenges is to estimate the activity being executed. For this, we developed an approach to estimate the activity being performed by hospital workers [9]. The approach is based on information gathered from the workplace study conducted.

Contextual information (i.e., the location of hospital staff, artifacts being used, the people with whom they collaborate and the time of the day), is used to train a back propagation neural network to estimate hospital workers activities. Thus, four neurons —location, artifacts, role and time— were used as inputs, whereas activity was used as output. The code for each contextual variable was taken from our qualitative analysis. Hence, the information gathered from the case study is transformed into inputs and outputs to the corresponding neurons. For instance, whenever an artifact or person is involved in certain activity a 1 (one) is assigned, otherwise, 0 (zero) is assigned. From the case study, we obtained a total of 2735 samples with an average, per activity, of 390 samples and a standard deviation of 338. From the total samples obtained, we formed two data sets: one for training and another for testing the network. To avoid a training influenced by the large amount of training data for some activities such as patient care, which frequency during the shift is considerable, we decided to balance the training and testing sets by taking only 150 samples (on average). Once the data sets were reduced we used 65% of the data for training and 35% for testing. We carried out several experiments using different configurations of the network as well as different size of the training set. Our results indicate that we can correctly predict hospital workers' activities 75% of the time (on average). Although, the accuracy obtained by this approach is sufficient for the development of several context-aware applications, it is not enough to support the nature of hospital work. Hence, we decided to center our efforts on improving the accuracy obtained by exploring other estimation techniques, such as Hidden Markov Models [20]. The results indicate that the user activity can be correctly estimated 92.6% of the time.

3.2 Activity-Aware Scenarios in Support of Collaboration

The findings from the study were used to inspire the creation of design scenarios that depict innovative uses of activity-aware applications in a hospital.

Providing activity-aware adaptation, personalization and coordination-awareness
While Juan, a medical intern, is in the library, the medical interns along with the physician start the ward round. Since Juan is in another building he doesn't know that he must join the group. The system aware of the activity of Juan's peers sends a collaboration-warning to Juan. By selecting the collaboration warning from his PDA, the system notifies to Juan that the ward round has begun. Juan moves to the bed wards joining the group to conduct the ward round. During the examination of the patient in bed 226, Juan inserts a catheter to that patient. For this, Juan consults the medical guide of the insertion of the catheter. He doesn't have the medical equipment to perform such procedure, thus, by consulting the activity-aware map he realizes that the closest medical equipment is down the hallway. The map, being aware of the activity being executed by Juan, highlights the relevant medical equipment and the hospital workers in charge of such patient by stumping the non-relevant information in the background. Rita, the nurse in charge of the patient in bed 226, is in the nurse pavilion preparing the medicines for such patient. Rita receives a collaboration warning in her PDA notifying her that patient care is being provided to the patient in bed 226. She decides to move to this patient bed to finish the catheter insertion in collaboration with Juan. During this activity Juan and Rita don't want to be interrupted, hence their availability is automatically set to busy.

Supporting activity-aware launching and interaction among heterogeneous devices
Dr. Diaz, a specialist, prepares the patient in room 222 in collaboration with Carmen, the nurse in charge of such patient, to conduct a medulla extraction. Carmen hands over to Dr. Diaz, a needle with the local anesthesia for the patient. Once Dr. Diaz injects the patient a medical guide of this procedure in a public display in front of the patient's bed is shown. Once the time that Dr. Diaz must wait for the anesthesia to take effect expires, the next step in the medical guide is highlighted announcing to Dr. Diaz that is time to start the medulla extraction. Based on the actions (e.g., open the patient back) executed by Dr. Diaz the medical guide stumps the actions already performed highlighting the next step in the guide for the adequate execution of the procedure. In addition, the medical equipment in the medicines tray that Carmen must hand over to Dr. Diaz, based on the step marked in the medical guide, are highlighted. Once the procedure is finished, a history of activity is displayed illustrating the

actions executed by Dr. Diaz and Carmen. Carmen selects the actions related to the medicines administered to the patient integrating this information into the nurse chart.

3.2 Desirable Features of Activity-Aware Applications in Hospitals

From scenarios such as the ones presented above we identified the following aspects to be addressed by activity-aware applications.

Activity discovery

Activities executed by hospital workers are complex and dynamic involving a set of heterogeneous resources including artifacts and people distributed in space or time. Hence, it is quite difficult for a user to identify when an activity emerges, how does it ends, how it is related to other activities and its level of fragmentation. To cope with this we propose that activity-aware applications must be able to help users to identify, create, and manage activities during their everyday practices. As shown in Scenario 1, the activity-aware map is constantly inferring the activity being executed by Juan and it is aware of his task switching allowing thus to present the information that is relevant to the task at hand. Hence, on the basis of context information regarding to location, presence of colleagues, and the artifacts being used, the infrastructure should be able to hypothesize which activities are being performed.

Activity adaptation and personalization

One of the challenges of hospital work is the management of large amounts of information, including patient records, medical guides, and scientific papers used for evidence-based medicine. This information is often associated to specific work activities. As shown in Scenario 1, when the intern is inserting the catheter he might need to gather medical equipment, consult the medical guide to find the right dose to administer and discuss with the attending physician the patient's evolution. However, he doesn't want to consult the census or a calendar, neither consult the location of the radiologist. Hence, by knowing the activity an application could adapt and personalize the presentation of information to the user. During an interview, a medical intern explained how he appreciates having his information organized based on the activity being executed: *"Sometimes I have patients in different areas of the hospital, hence it would be convenient to differentiate the person and documents by service, area or activity, it would save time. For example, it would not be useful to organize resources by room, for example the patient in room 311, rather based on what we are doing".*

Activity collaboration and coordination awareness

Hospital workers, most of their time, use the activity being executed by others to plan their tasks. For example, during the study we repeatedly observed that medical interns send SMS messages to their peers informing when the ward round has begun. Or nurses go for lunch when physicians start their ward round because they need to wait for new indications. Hence, activity awareness must be provided. As shown in Scenario 1, when Juan is in the library he doesn't know when he must join his peers to conduct the ward round. However, by receiving personalized notifications he might be able to attend his duties whenever he is needed. Since these notifications could be automatically sent by the system they reduce the time hospital workers invest in coordinating their activities, thus increasing the time they might spend in other duties (e.g. patient care). In addition, having this type of awareness promotes collaboration. For example, when Rita received the collaboration warning she decides to join Juan to finish the catheter insertion together.

Seamless Activity-aware Interaction among heterogeneous devices
Hospitals are technology-rich environments filled with heterogeneous computing devices, ranging from handheld computers to PCs and semi-public displays. **Transferring, Sharing and controlling** these devices should be seamless, so as not to interrupt the natural execution of the task at hand. However, supporting this type of interaction only for particular devices or documents could demand from hospital workers to identify the adequate information they need to transfer or share or the adequate device they need to control. Instead, the interaction must include an activity as a whole where devices and documents are already associated to the activity. During an interview, a medical intern explained how he appreciates having his information organized as a unit: *"After the ward round, we share pending tasks or documents with the medical interns that have just arrived at the ward round. However, among so many pending tasks or documents it is really common to forget to share one. Hence, it is more practical to share everything as a whole it would save you a lot of time and helps you sharing everything that might be useful, without forgetting anything"*. In addition, mobility of hospital workers must be considered in the design of such type of interactions. During an interview an intern explained: *"I like the fact that the information goes with me and I don't have to come back to retrieve the information"*. Hence, we must provide activity **roaming** by letting hospital workers resume computational activities on arbitrary devices.

Activity launching
The interactions held by hospital workers are highly fragmented due the frequent interruptions in hospital work and the constant changes in the environment. As described in section 2, hospital workers average no more than 5 minutes during any type of interaction (i.e., verbally based, involving artifacts and observational based). In addition, hospital workers spend a lot of time *"setting up the environment"* due the limited time they have to conduct an activity before a task switching. Hence, it is difficult for hospital workers to spend their time looking for, configuring, and launching the right service in their PDA in support of the interaction that it is taking place. By allowing the automatic launching of services and/or the automatic establishment of networks; hospital workers could focus only in the natural execution of an interaction, rather in selecting the adequate computational service. As shown in Scenario 2, when Dr. Diaz is conducting the medulla extraction, his attention focuses on the procedure rather in the execution of services in the display.

3.3 Limitations of Our Approach

Since the activity estimation technique proposed uses the data gathered from the workplace study, the results obtained are constrained by such data. Although, the data is exhaustive, it was collected in the internal medicine area of a mid-size hospital. However, the activities performed by hospital staff are in general the same as those in other hospitals in Mexico and other countries as reported in [5, 18], thus we believe that the general findings that we obtained are not restricted to this hospital in particular. Moreover, implementing our solution would require the deployment of technology within the hospital to infer the location of people and the artifacts being used to estimate the activity of users. However, some of these technologies are gradually being introduced in hospital environments. Once the contextual data is available, the activity estimation can be done in real time with the approach proposed. Finally, we estimate the activity by taking into account contextual information, such as location and artifacts being used, which would be estimated through other techniques or by using sensors. These methods are also prone to errors which would affect the accuracy of the estimation. However, most of the errors incurred in the estimation of the contextual variables will not have a significant impact on activity estimation. For instance, the distance between the places used as input is normally much larger than the average error of current commercially available location estimation approaches.

4 An Activity-Aware Map

Motivated by the nature of hospital work and to illustrate the capabilities provided by the activity-aware services just discussed, we implemented a system that personalizes the information of peer and document location, enforces availability and sends collaboration warnings based on the activity being executed.

4.1 Architecture

Figure 4 shows the agent-based architecture of the activity-aware map. The system includes five agents, two in the client and three in a server. The PDA's agents were implemented using mSALSA on top of Windows Mobile and the ones in the server were implemented on top of SALSA [19].

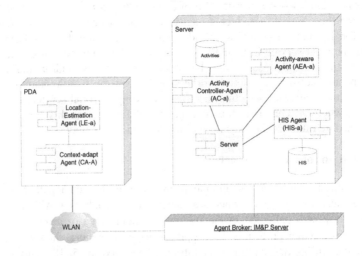

Fig. 2. The agent-based system architecture of the activity-aware map

In our architecture the *agent Broker* handles communication between agents through XML (eXtensible Markup Language) messages storing the state of agents and notifying their changes to other agents subscribed to them. The *Location Estimation agent (LE-a)* determines the approximate location of users and their proximity. Radiofrequency (RF) signals received by a mobile device carried by medical staff from at least three access points are measured to obtain their signal strength. A trained back propagation neural network is embedded within the component and is used to estimate the approximate location of the users [8]. The *HIS Agent (HIS-a)* acts as proxy to the Hospital Information System providing access to, and monitoring the state of medical information (i.e. medical records and laboratory results). The *Activity-estimation agent (AE-a)* infers the activity being executed by hospital workers. Contextual information[1], such as the location of hospital workers, artifacts being used, the people with whom they collaborate and the time of the day, is used to train a back propagation neural network to estimate hospital worker's activities [9]. The core component of the architecture is the *Activity-Controller Agent*, which is responsible to decide which action must be enforced by the *Context-Adapt agent* (CA-a). To do this, this agent uses a rule-based mechanism which maps from the inferred context (e.g., location, documents, devices) to actions (i.e., filtering resources, privacy enforcing and sending contextual messages) that must be enforced by the context-adapt client.

Thus, three main services are provided through these agents in support for mobile collaboration. In the following lines we described such services and how the agents work to support them.

4.2   Awareness for Opportunistic Interactions

To address our vision, we will have to keep in mind that the system should be able to support improvised meetings in different places, based on the status (i.e. availability) and location of artifacts and people and, based on the activity being executed by others. In this case, location and activity awareness can be a trigger for opportunistic interactions. For example, as shown in the scenario, a nurse might decide to interact with an intern when patient care is being provided to a patient under her charge. Or a physician might need to collaborate in the hallway in front of an available display.

To offer this kind of awareness we decided to provide two ways of interaction. For location awareness, a user can locate patients, other hospital staff and resources (i.e. medical equipment, PCs, printers, displays) through a floor map shown in his PDA (Figure 3b). And for activity awareness, the system will automatically send collaboration warnings to notify hospital staff the activity being executed by others whenever considered relevant. Contextual information of the user who performs the activity and the recipients, such as the user's location, the patients under the recipients' charge and recipients' role, is used to determine when the information must be sent and to whom it might be noteworthy. Collaboration warnings are formed by adding to predefined messages (e.g. is taking place in, the ward round has begun in) contextual information, such as the activity being executed and the location

---

[1] The contextual information required for activity estimation is gathered by the location estimation agent and a simulation was made that randomly generates the artifacts being used.

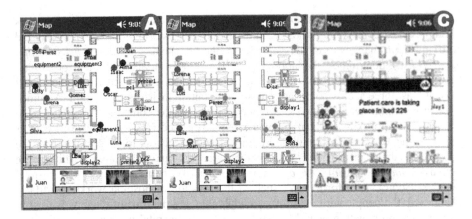

Fig. 3. The activity-aware map[2] (a) A view of the map before an adaptation (b) A view of the map adapted based on the clinical case assessment activity (c) A collaboration warning notifying a nurse that patient care is being provided to a patient under her charge

where the activity is being executed. For example, figure 3c shows a screenshot of the application showing a collaboration warning sent to a nurse. This message is sent to her to notify that patient care is being provided in front of the bed 226, to a patient under her charge. However, we need to find an adequate balance of when these messages might be useful without bothering hospital workers. Because of this, we only provide this type of awareness when the activity being executed by others is related to an essential and fundamental aspect of medical work (i.e. the clinical care of patients) and when the recipient's context is relevant.

4.3 Opportunistic Access to Relevant Information

To prevent overload in the information shown in the PDA and to provide immediate access to the information relevant to the task at a hand we personalize and adapt the information shown by the map based on the activity being executed. Figure 3a shows a view of the map before a personalization takes place. As it shows, it is quite difficult to locate an available display, the specialist in charge of a patient or a document relevant to the task at a hand. Navigating through this information can be time consuming when the users want to consult a single piece of data [17]. The users' activity can be used to identify the information relevant to the action at hand and differentiate between useful and unwanted data (with many degrees in between) and use this differentiation to meet goals, such as timely care delivery. Therefore, to identify when, depending on the activity being performed, is more relevant to consult medical information (e.g., medical record, laboratory results) than other information (e.g., the location of colleagues, journal articles), we classified the activities for which medical information is needed. For example, when hospital workers' are assessing a clinical case, caring for a patient or managing information they often consult that

---

[2] Colors are used to differentiate the roles of the hospital workers in the area. Medical interns are colored in green, attending physicians in yellow and nurses in blue.

patient's medical record. However, when they are coordinating, tracking or in classes they seldom use such information. Based on the activity being executed and the information that is considered relevant to such activity, the context aware map adapts the information (i.e., documents and location of colleagues and equipment) shown to a hospital worker. Figure 3a shows a screenshot of the map before an adaptation is made. Since, the map is not aware of the activity being executed by Juan it could not personalize the information shown. On the other hand, Figure 3b shows a screenshot of the map adapted by the activity of *clinical case assessment.* As it shows, the map aware of the activity being executed by Juan, only shows the hospital staff in charge of the patient (i.e. medical interns, the attending physician, the specialist and the nurse), stumping the non-relevant information in the background, as the scenario shows. In addition, the documents shown to Juan are the medical record and laboratory results, other documents are identified as non-relevant for this activity.

4.4 Availability Enforcement

Mobility and collaboration generate a need to contact colleagues within the hospital, either to discuss a case with a specialist or request help to transfer a patient. However, applications developed to assist in this task, are largely unaware of the social situations surrounding their usage and the impact that their actions might have. If the system is aware of the user's availability, it could use this information to negotiate interruptions at appropriate times, improving thus, human computer interaction [10].

Availability is information that can be derived from knowing the activity being performed by a person. For example, we recurrently observed that medical workers, especially interns, wait until a discussion of a clinical case finishes in order to approach a physician. In contrast, when they are engaged in other activities, such as information management or coordination, the level of their interruptibility is higher. Hence, we classified the activities identified (e.g. patient care, clinical case assessment, etc) in two main groups with respect to the level of interruptibility. The non-available activities correspond to the activities with the aim of improving the quality of patient care (i.e. clinical case assessment, patient care, classes and certification and preparation). While the others activities (i.e. information management and coordination) are the ones with a higher level of interruptibility. On the basis of the group to which that each activity belongs, availability is enforced. For example, the activity-aware map automatically enforces Juan's availability when he is evaluating a clinical case, as the scenario illustrates (Figure 2b).

5 Conclusions

We have outlined our proposal for the development of activity-aware applications in support of collaboration in mobile working environments. The core idea is to augment the vision of Activity-Based Computing (ABC) to let human activities be mirrored in computational activities associating resources and adapting the computational infrastructure based on the activity being executed. For this, we propose to automatically discover the user activity and based on such activity adapt the behavior of activity-based applications, resulting thus, in an activity-aware application. To show the feasibility of the development of activity-aware applications, we present our efforts, which include a case study and an approach to estimate hospital workers' activity, as well as, a set of design principles for the development of activity-aware applications. Finally, we describe the implementation of an activity-aware map to illustrate the design principles proposed.

We plan to refine the architecture described with the aim of building a middleware that allows dealing with the complexities associated with the development of activity-aware applications. This framework will support mobility and cooperation in human activities by managing them as a collection of tasks on a computer, as well as, integrating several activity-aware mechanisms that take advantage of the user's context to support the design principles proposed.

References

[1] Bardram, J., Christensen, H.B.: Pervasive Computing Support for Hospitals: An overview of the Activity-Based Computing Project. IEEE Pervasive computer 6(1), 44–51 (2007)

[2] Bardram, J.E.: Plans as Situated Action: An Activity Theory Approach toWorkflow Systems. In: ESCW, pp. 17–32. Kluwer Academic Publishers, Lancaster University (1997)

[3] Bardram, J.E.: The Trouble with Login – On Usability and Computer Security in Ubiquitous Computing. Personal and Ubiquitous Computing 9(6), 357–367 (2005)

[4] Bardram, J.E., Baldus, H., Favela, J.: Pervasive Computing in Hospitals. In: Bardram, J.E. (ed.) Pervasive Healthcare: Research and Applications of Pervasive Computing in Healthcare, ed. I.P.H.R.a.A.o.P.C.i. Healthcare, pp. 49–78. CRC Press, Boca Raton (2006)

[5] Bardram, J.E., Bossen, C.: Mobility Work: The Spatial Dimension of Collaboration at a Hospital. In: ECSCW, pp. 176–185. Kluwer Academic Publishers, Paris, France (2005)

[6] Bardram, J.E., Bunde-Pedersen, J., Soegaard, M.: Support for ActivityBased Computing in a Personal Computing Operating System. In: CHI. 2006, pp. 211–220. ACM Press, Montreal, Quebec, Cananda (2006)

[7] Camacho, J., Favela, J., Gonzalez, V.M.: Supporting the Management of Multiple Activities in Mobile Collaborative Working Environments. In: Dimitriadis, Y.A., Zigurs, I., Gómez-Sánchez, E. (eds.) CRIWG 2006. LNCS, vol. 4154, pp. 381–388. Springer, Heidelberg (2006)

[8] Castro, L., Favela, J.: Contiuous Tracking of User Location in WLANs Using Recurrent Neural Networks. In: ENC 2005, pp. 174–181. IEEE Press, Puebla, Mexico (2005)

[9] Favela, J., Tentori, M., Castro, L., Gonzalez, V., Moran, E., Martinez, A.I.: Estimating Hospital Workers' Activities and its use in Context-Aware Hospital Applications. In: Pervasive Healthcare, Salzburg, Austria (2006)

[10] Fogarty, J., Hudson, S.E., Atkeson, C.G., Avrahami, D., Forlizzi, J., Kiesler, S., Lee, J.C., Yang, J.: Predicting human interruptibility with sensors interruptibility with sensors. ACM Transactions on Computer-Human Interaction 12(1), 119–146 (2005)

[11] Geyer, W.: Activity explorer: activity-centric collaboration from research to product. IBM Systems Journal 45(4), 713–726 (2006)

[12] González, V., Mark, G.: Constant, Constant, Multi-tasking Craziness: Managing Multiple Working Spheres. In: CHI. 2004, pp. 113–120. ACM Press, Vienna, Austria (2004)

[13] Henderson, D.A., Card, S.K.: Rooms: The Use of Multiple Virtual Workspaces to Reduce Space Contention in a Window-Based Graphical User Interface. ACM Transactions on Graphics 5(3), 211–243 (1986)

[14] Ishii, I., Kobayashi, M., Grudin, J.: Integration of Inter-Personal Space and Shared Workspace: Clearboard Design and Experiments. In: Conference on Computer-Supported Cooperative Work, pp. 33–42. Kluwer Academic Publishers, Toronto, Canada (1992)

[15] Markarian, A., Favela, J., Tentori, M., Castro, L.A.: Seamless Interaction among Heterogeneous Devices in Support for Co-located Collaboration. In: Dimitriadis, Y.A., Zigurs, I., Gómez-Sánchez, E. (eds.) CRIWG 2006. LNCS, vol. 4154, pp. 389–404. Springer, Heidelberg (2006)

[16] Moran, E.B., Tentori, M., González, V.M., Martinez-Garcia, A.I., Favela, J.: Mobility in Hospital Work: Towards a Pervasive Computing Hospital Environment. International Journal of Electronic Healthcare 3(1), 72–89 (2006)

[17] Munoz, M., Rodriguez, M.D., Favela, J., Martinez-Garcia, A.I., Gonzalez, V.M.: Context-Aware Mobile Communication in Hospitals. IEEE Computer 36(9), 38–46 (2003)

[18] Reddy, M., Dourish, P.: A Finger on the Pulse: Temporal Rhythms and Information Seeking in Medical Work. In: CSCW 2002, pp. 344–353. ACM, New Orleans, Louisiana (2002)

[19] Rodriguez, M.D., Favela, J., Preciado, A., Vizcaino, A.: Agent-based Ambient Intelligence for Healthcare. AI Communications 18(3), 201–216 (2005)

[20] Sanchez, D., Tentori, M., Favela, J.: Hidden Markov Models for Activity Recognition in Ambient Intelligence Environments. In: ENC 2007, Morelia, Michocan (2007) (submitted)

[21] Strauss, A., Corbin, J.: Basics of Qualitative Research: Techniques and procedures for developing grounded theory. Sage, Thousand Oaks, CA (1998)

[22] Voida, S., Mynatt, E.D., MacIntyre, B., Corso, G.M.: Integrating virtual and physical context to support knowledge workers. IEEE Pervasive Computing 1(3), 73–79 (2002)

Author Index

Lecture Notes in Computer Science

Sublibrary 3: Information Systems and Application, incl. Internet/Web and HCI

For information about Vols. 1– 4244
please contact your bookseller or Springer